DEFEND THE SACRED

Water Protectors at Standing Rock, Fall 2016.
(Courtesy of Dallas Goldtooth, Mdewakantonwan Dakota)

Defend the Sacred

NATIVE AMERICAN RELIGIOUS FREEDOM
BEYOND THE FIRST AMENDMENT

MICHAEL D. MCNALLY

PRINCETON UNIVERSITY PRESS

PRINCETON & OXFORD

Published by Princeton University Press
41 William Street, Princeton, New Jersey 08540
6 Oxford Street, Woodstock, Oxfordshire OX20 1TR

press.princeton.edu

ISBN 978-0-691-19089-1
ISBN (pbk.) 978-0-691-19090-7
ISBN (e-book) 978-0-691-20151-1

Some material in the book has been taken from the author's previous publications:
"From Substantial Burden on Native American Religious Exercise to the 'Decrease
in Spiritual Fulfillment' in the San Francisco Peaks Sacred Lands Case," *Journal of
Law and Religion* 30:36–64 (February 2015); "Native American Religious Freedom as
a Collective Right," *Brigham Young University Law Review* (forthcoming); "Religion
as Peoplehood: Native American Religious Freedom and the Discourse of Indigenous
Rights in International Law," in *Brill Handbook of Indigenous Religion(s)*, eds. Greg
Johnson and Siv Ellen Kraft (Leiden: Brill, 2018); "Native American Religious
Freedom beyond the First Amendment," in *After Pluralism, Reimagining Religious
Engagement*, eds. Courtney Bender and Pamela Klassen (Columbia University Press,
2010).

British Library Cataloging-in-Publication Data is available

Editorial: Fred Appel and Jenny Tan
Production Editorial: Karen Carter
Jacket/Cover Design: Layla Mac Rory
Production: Erin Suydam
Publicity: Kate Hensley and Kathryn Stevens
Copyeditor: Dawn Hall

Jacket/Cover Credit: Standing Rock, North Dakota Water Protectors.
Courtesy of Dallas Goldtooth, Mdewakantonwan Dakota

This book has been composed in Arno

Printed on acid-free paper. ∞

Printed in the United States of America

10 9 8 7 6 5 4 3 2 1

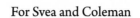
For Svea and Coleman

CONTENTS

ILLUSTRATIONS

ABBREVIATIONS

ACHP   Advisory Council for Historic Preservation (body established to oversee NHPA)

AIRFA   American Indian Religious Freedom Act (1978)

APE   Area of Potential Effect, in NHPA Review

BIA   Bureau of Indian Affairs, US Department of the Interior

BULLETIN 38   1990 National Register Bulletin that describes TCPs under NHPA

CIA   Commissioner of Indian Affairs

DAPL   Dakota Access Pipeline

EA   Environmental Assessment (lesser environmental review under NEPA)

EMRIP   UN Expert Mechanism on the Rights of Indigenous Peoples

EIS   Environmental Impact Study (fuller environmental review under NEPA)

FPIC   Free, Prior, and Informed Consent (standard affirmed in UNDRIP)

ICCPR   International Covenant on Civil and Political Rights (1966)

ICESCR International Covenant on Economic, Social, and Cultural Rights (1966)

LYNG   *Lyng v. Northwest Indian Cemetery Protective Association*, 485 U.S. 439 (1988) (logging road through Native sacred place does not violate First Amendment)

NAGPRA   Native American Graves Protection and Repatriation Act (1990)

NAVAJO NATION   *Navajo Nation v. U.S. Forest Service*, 535 F.3d 1058 (9th Cir. 2008) (en banc) (artificial snow made with wastewater on holy mountain does not violate RFRA)

NEPA   National Environmental Policy Act (1969)

NHPA   National Historic Preservation Act (1966)

NMAI   National Museum of the American Indian

OAS   Organization of American States

RFRA   Religious Freedom Restoration Act (1993)

RLUIPA   Religious Land Use and Institutionalized Persons Act (2000)

SHPO   State Historic Preservation Officer (NHPA)

SMITH   Employment Div., Dept. Human Serv., *State of Oregon v. Smith*, U.S. 872 (1990)

STANDING ROCK I   *Standing Rock Sioux Tribe v. United States Army Corps of Engineers*, 205 F. Supp. 3d. 4 (D.D.C. 2016) (does DAPL approval violate NHPA?)

STANDING ROCK II   239 F. Supp. 3d 77 (D.D.C. 2017) (does DAPL approval violate RFRA?)

STANDING ROCK III   255 F. Supp. 3d 101 (D.D.C. 2017) (does DAPL approval violate NEPA?)

STANDING ROCK IV   282 F. Supp. 3d 91 (D.D.C. 2017) (should oil flow stop pending NEPA remand?)

TCP   Traditional Cultural Property (NHPA designation of eligibility for National Register of Historic Places of places significant to living cultures)

THPO   Tribal Historic Preservation Officer (counterpart to SHPO under NHPA)

UDHR   Universal Declaration of Human Rights (1948)

UNDRIP   United Nations Declaration on the Rights of Indigenous Peoples (2007)

THIS BOOK FOLLOWS Native American peoples as they struggle to defend the sacred in and through law. Whether the sacred refers to sacred lands, practices, plants, animals, objects in museums, or ancestral remains, Native peoples have over the last fifty years increasingly sought to defend the sacred in hearing rooms, around negotiating tables, or in courts of law and public opinion. But because religious freedom law has largely failed them, Native peoples have gone through and beyond the First Amendment to defend the sacred in other fields of law—environmental law, historic preservation law, federal Indian law and treaty rights, and international human rights law. It's not only that religious freedom law has failed them, but also that *religion* as a category has failed to capture what's distinctive about Indigenous religions, local as they are to particular peoples and to living well on particular lands and waters. This book explores the varying results of these legal efforts and ultimately returns to *religion*, imagined capaciously as an Indigenous collective right keyed to the collective nation-to-nation relationship but that can carry the legal teeth of religious freedom.

Placing the Book in an Unsettling Contemporary Moment

Arguments in US courts for religious freedom appear lately to be monopolized by conservative Christians who, despite their numerical prevalence as Christians and their political power in and through their engagement with party politics, often consider their religious freedom to be under dire threat. This is ironic. The Bill of Rights guards against tyrannies of the majority, and the religious liberty provisions of the First Amendment were at the time and through most of US history engaged to protect religious (and nonreligious) minorities from becoming unduly subjected to the religious positions of majorities. The founders had their various reasons for it but viewed religious freedom as a priority and, drawing on an act in the Virginia Assembly drafted by Thomas Jefferson, settled on the following as the initial clauses of the First Amendment:

Congress shall make no law respecting an establishment of religion, or prohibiting the free exercise thereof.

Beginning in the 1940s, the Supreme Court decided that the Fourteenth Amendment applied this limitation on Congress to state and local governments as well, opening the door for courts to engage the thorny issues of American religious diversity. Courts have distinguished religious freedom case law under the headings of the amendment's two religion clauses. Establishment Clause jurisprudence has historically focused structurally on limiting government power to establish, endorse, or become excessively entangled with particular religious communities or theologies, either intentionally as discrimination or unintentionally through the workings of majoritarian democracy. Free Exercise jurisprudence has historically protected religious minorities like Jews, Jehovah's Witnesses, and others from laws and policies that effectively—even if unintentionally—prohibit the free exercise of their religion.

When I began the work that produced this book, discussions of religious freedom law were dominated by discussions of the Establishment Clause, mainly because politically powerful religious conservatives were working to undo what they saw as judicial overreach and Establishment Clause precedent that had, in their view, created a public square hostile to religion. My inquiry into how poorly the Free Exercise Clause was working for Native Americans in the courts, especially in failure after failure of sacred land claims, seemed largely impertinent given that the prevailing winds of the culture wars were then buffeting the Establishment Clause. How far would government be allowed to go in enabling the flourishing of majority religion?

In 1990, the Supreme Court dramatically withdrew the reach of Free Exercise protections for religious minorities generally in a case involving practitioners of the Native American Church, an Indigenous religion involving ceremonial Peyote ingestion. In *Employment Division v. Smith*, the Court held that it was legislatures, not courts, that should accommodate religious minorities with exemptions from neutral laws of general applicability which, like the controlled substance law in question, effectively violate religious freedom. In the wake of *Smith*, Native American free exercise claims seemed even less pertinent to larger conversations about religious freedom. In 1993, a nearly unanimous Congress restored the protections that the decision in *Smith* had taken away by enacting the Religious Freedom Restoration Act (RFRA) but failing to restore the protections for the Native Peyote religion that *Smith* criminalized. In the case of Native sacred lands cases, the courts continued to cite *Smith*-era precedent to find against Native people.

Now it is the Free Exercise Clause, and its statutory counterpart RFRA, that seem to drive the national conversation about religion, diversity, and American civic life. This is not because the public is incensed that courts are failing to protect rights of Native American and other religious minorities. It is because conservative Christians, arguing that they are beleaguered by government actions that advance a culture hostile to their faith, have turned increasingly to the Free Exercise Clause and especially RFRA for exemptions from generally applicable laws, like those protecting people with disabilities, LGBTQ people, and others from discrimination.

I type these words on the day of the seating of Justice Kavanaugh after a tumultuous confirmation process and a two vote majority confirmation that heralds another shift of the Court decidedly to the right. Under these circumstances, it seems to me particularly risky to be speaking about stepping up judicial recognition of religious freedom rights vis-à-vis other civil rights and competing goods.

At the same time, if the courts are in a process already of extending the reach of free exercise protections, I am emboldened to argue that Native American nations may find increasing traction by appealing to the discourse of religious freedom to protect what they hold sacred.

With the rightward shift in the courts, religious freedom arguments may be even more compelling, especially as those rightward shifts threaten to divest federal Indian law, civil rights law, and environmental law as robust sources of protection. What is more, jurisprudence on religious freedom appears to be embracing the notion that religious freedom is a collective, not just an individual right. There has since the 1980s been a legal studies movement to affirm religious free exercise as a matter of church autonomy, and the Supreme Court has begun to engage the logic. In *Hosanna-Tabor Evangelical Lutheran Church and School v. E.E.O.C* (2012), the Court found that a "ministerial exception" to nondiscrimination laws protected a religious school from obligations under the Americans with Disabilities Act to a teacher who was regarded, for legal purposes, as a minister. In 2014, the Supreme Court broke with its precedents under the First Amendment to recognize Hobby Lobby, a closely held private corporation consisting of tens of thousands of employees, as a person whose religious exercise was protected under RFRA from provisions of the Affordable Care Act guaranteeing access to forms of birth control that its owners said violated their Christian beliefs opposing abortion.

Why should religious freedom be extended by the courts in such circumstances as these, with such onerous consequences for the rights of those who lose in the cases, and not be extended to Native peoples who make claims to protection of sacred places and practices because of religious obligations to those places and practices that are in some cases older than Christianity itself? The rhetorical question seems simple enough.

But to argue for Native American rights via the legal argument of religious freedom, especially as a collective right of Native peoples, risks extending in other contexts the leverage of legal religious freedom arguments to evade antidiscrimination and other laws. Fuller realization of the collective rights of Native American religious freedom within religious freedom law need not entail this slippage, however, for federal Indian law has long distinguished Native peoples as legally unique. Native nations possess inherent sovereignty and treaty rights, and their citizens are distinguished by the political status of their membership in these sovereign nations, rather than by their membership in a racial or ethnic or religious group.

So the collective rights of Native American religious freedom can be said to be an inflection on US religious freedom law by means of the distinctive political status of Native American peoples, to which federal Indian law has imperfectly gestured and which, with the raised standards of Indigenous rights under international law, domestic law can deliver. I will develop further the implications of such distinctiveness within US and international law, but it will be important for the reader to bear this distinction in mind throughout.

Acknowledgments

All scholarship is in some sense collaborative. This book is unambiguously so, being in large part a work of synthesis. The work of my collaborators is accordingly summarized in the relevant chapters, but thanks to them come first. I am profoundly grateful to Suzan Shown Harjo for inspiration and consultation on the whole and particularly for the history of the American Indian Religious Freedom Act and the Native American Graves Protection and Repatriation Act. To Tisa Wenger, I am indebted for helping problematize Native religious freedom and for its nineteenth- and early twentieth-century history, with additional support from the work of Thomas Maroukis and Jennifer Graber. For insights on repatriation and the religious generativity of struggle, not to mention a wonderful friendship, I am beyond grateful to Greg Johnson. For insights into the letter and spirit of cultural resource law, I'm thankful for the learning, patience, and important voice of Thomas F. King. For generous if unwitting tutelage in international law through their publications, I'm indebted to James Anaya and Walter Echo-Hawk. For an encouraging model of engaging Native religions and cultures in the law and her leadership on these issues, I'm indebted to Kristen Carpenter. My late mentors Inés Talamantez and Larry Cloud Morgan have guided me all along.

The project germinated in the rich soil of engagement by wonderful Carleton students in several iterations of a course on the case law. The project was given better legal shape by generous law school teachers who shared their time and patience as I undertook several years of targeted legal training. Thank you Kevin Washburn, Libby Rodke Washburn, Rebecca Tsosie, David Weissbrodt, and Winnifred Fallers Sullivan. Among these, thank you also to James Boyd White, who challenged me to not simply take things apart but to suggest how courts could put things back together more justly. To that end, two more technical and constructive legal articulations of this work appear in the *Journal of Law and Religion* and in the *Brigham Young University Law Review*. Several portions were originally published in "Native American Religious Freedom beyond the First Amendment," in Courtney Bender and Pamela Klassen, eds., *After Pluralism*, copyright © 2010 Columbia University Press. Reprinted with permission of Columbia University Press.

Among those offering wisdom on drafts along the way are Courtney Bender, Pamela Klassen, Ben Berger, and other co-conspirators in the *After Pluralism* volume; Ann Braude, David Hall, Judith Weisenfeld, Katie Lofton, Sally Promey, Carla Fredericks, Steve Moore, Tiffany Hale, Dana Lloyd, Lucia Hulsether, Nicholas Shrubsole, Noah Salomon, Larry Gross, Silas Allard, Howard Vogel, Marie Failinger, Colette Routel, Manuel Anderson, Milo Anderson Jr., John Borrows, Emily Brault, Bruce White, Darlene St. Clair, Jace Weaver, Denise Reilly, Ginny Dale, John Soderberg, David Lamberth, Monica Siems McKay, Joseph Harney, Tony Manning, Stephen Young, Mark Severseike, David Hullfish Bailey; insightful colloquia of scholars of American religions at Yale and Columbia and Harvard; and audiences at the American Academy of Religion, the Native American and Indigenous Studies Association, and the University of Colorado. The Schoff Fund at Columbia supported the index. Fred Appel, Jenny Tan, Dawn Hall, Karen Carter, and anonymous reviewers for Princeton University Press have refined the book and made it better. The good ideas came from and through all these gracious people; the mistakes are mine alone.

Writing was supported by a Guggenheim Fellowship, a National Endowment for the Humanities Summer Stipend (FT-254559–17), a Carleton Faculty Development Endowment award, and steadfast support from Carleton Dean Bev Nagel and President Steven Poskanzer. Targeted legal studies training, research, and early writing were made possible by a Mellon New Directions Fellowship. Half of all proceeds from this book are directed to the Native American Rights Fund.

And finally, family: Devon Anderson brings love, depth, and encouragement to my life. Our children, Svea and Coleman, are to us the greatest gift and surest earthly hope for the future. Svea and Coleman, this book is dedicated to you.

DEFEND THE SACRED

Introduction

Cannonball, North Dakota

The three bustling camps of water protectors near the proposed Dakota Access Pipeline's crossing of the Missouri River lay along the placid banks of the Cannonball River as it joins the Missouri. The pipeline would pump nearly half a million barrels of crude daily under the river a half mile upstream from the Standing Rock Sioux Reservation. In October 2016, a friend and I set out to offer our modest support to the camps and learn more on the ground about what I had spent several weeks trying to discern in a sprawling, complex legal decision by a federal judge in faraway Washington, DC.

The judge had denied a motion by the Standing Rock Sioux Tribe to block construction, rejecting its arguments that sites of sacred, cultural, and historical significance were unlawfully endangered and specifically that the US Army Corps of Engineers, the federal agency controlling the land of the crossing and holding the power to issue the final permits to make the 1,100 mile oil pipeline a done deal, had failed to comply with the consultation procedures with the tribes under the National Historic Preservation Act.[1]

I knew that the Missouri River is vital to the seven Lakota, Nakota, and Dakota nations that make up the Oceti Sakowin, the Seven Fires of the Great Sioux Nation, not to mention the Mandan, Arikara, and Hidatsa nations of the upstream Fort Berthold Reservation. I also knew something about how utterly devastating to these nations was the flooding of their choicest bottomlands by the massive Pick-Sloan dam projects of the 1940s and 1950s, especially given the most famous treaty abrogation in US history, that of the Fort Laramie Treaties of 1851 and 1868, the incursion of gold seekers into the sacred Black Hills, and Custer's errant bravado to defend them.

FIG. 0.1. Cannonball, *inyan wakan*
A cannonball, one of the *inyan wakanagapi* or sacred stones that is the namesake of the
river along which the water protector camps lay. Although geologists explain the stones as
the product of underground water flowing through sandstone, Lakota accounts say the
rounded stones formed in the great springtime eddy at the confluence of the Cannonball
and Missouri Rivers until completion of the Oahe Dam in 1958. (Author photo)

I had time to ponder these things in the long hours of the drive across the
eastern Great Plains "out" from Minnesota to Cannonball, North Dakota. I
also pondered the name *Cannonball*; how it must have become important to
history by virtue of some US military atrocity, and how fitting it was that
what I took to be "protest" camps against the pipeline had remapped such a
place and made it a center.

I should have known better.

Even before the road arrived on the crest above the splendid camps, with
their tipis, trailers, mess tents, flags, and horse corrals, we pulled over at Cannonball's store and saw in its parking lot a monument with an olive stone orb,
the size of a large globe. This we learned, was one of the *inyan wakanagapi*,
translated into English as cannonballs by someone familiar with the US military, or perhaps that person saw a cannonball and understood it as one of the
inyan wakanagapi.

According to Lakota tradition, these sacred stones took their shape rolling
around in the powerful eddies that swirled each spring at the confluence of

the rivers.[2] Each spring, that is, until the Army Corps of Engineers built Oahe Dam in the 1950s, flooding the places where families lived, horses fed on hay, elders picked and used medicines, and ancestors were buried. The reservoir, Lake Oahe, swallowed up precious land for a staggering 250 miles upstream, the length of Lake Ontario.

It was clear on that day of our arrival that there was here a roiling confluence of sacred and profane, of the holy and of its potential desecration. But the sacred was not simply a function of the threat of desecration. As the sacred stones suggested, the sacred went deep here. The area around the confluence of these rivers was a veritable sacred district. Weeks before, construction crews clearing the way for the pipeline had bulldozed ancestral memorials and stone circles holding Indigenous sky knowledge. Visible from "Facebook Hill" above the camps, where water protectors went for cell phone reception, were the tips of Twin Buttes, two hills where the Mandan people say their ancestors descended to first walk the earth, and which a Cannonball resident told me has been known to glow at night with spirit emanations.

The three water protector camps formed at the self-same place where Sitting Bull and his Hunkpapa Lakota followers traditionally kept their winter camp. We were told Sitting Bull himself wore a small *inyan wakanagapi* around his neck as a talisman of his spiritual power. Native people of the camps spoke hopefully, not just poetically, of the return of traditional community, language, culture, and religion to this important place. The *inipi*, or sweat lodge, that a Lakota spiritual leader had created at the Rosebud Camp, where we were guests of Curly Eagle Hawk and his leadership team, was there to provide spiritual sustenance to water protectors. But the lodge also took direction, and made possible further spiritual direction, from spirits in that place. These correspondences ran deep.

So I should have known better. We had not arrived at some protest camp erected "out there" on the Plains at the arbitrary geography of a diagonal pipeline's appointed crossing of the Missouri. We had arrived at a sacred center, affirmed in the poetics of the sacred and only *re*-affirmed in the politics of the sacred. When we left, even after only a mere couple of nights at the camps, my own geography had inverted. I wasn't driving back to Minnesota from "out here"; I was leaving. Imagine how it has felt for the thousands of Indigenous water protectors who sacrificed half a year of their lives, many of whom are still paying the price.

***

This book is about such places as Cannonball, about the significance and orientation they have provided Native American communities and about the duties and obligations Native peoples have had to them for generations. I am emphatically not using the past tense, not simply to suggest that a few of these traditions are still alive; I'm using the present perfect tense in order to underscore both that Native peoples continue to practice their traditional religions and that changes made to traditions by those communities can be understood as part of what keeps traditions alive. It is also about how such places are sacred today, especially in light of threats to access, use, and integrity. It is also about the resilience and capacity of Native American peoples to tend the fires of their traditional religions in spite of centuries of concerted efforts to drown those fires by baptism, or by criminalization under American law, or by taking their oxygen through a Euro-American craving for Native *spirituality*, a craving that I will show has also undermined legal claims to Native American religious freedom.

This book is also not just about sacred places. It is also about claims to ancestral remains and sacred beings in museum and scientific collections or in the ground in places under development pressure. This book is also about claims Native American communities make, and increasingly make, to sacred practices, including ceremonial practices in highly regulated environments like prisons, but also about lifeway practices like fishing, hunting, gathering, and cultivating that are as much about living in proper spiritual relationships as they are about making a living.

This book examines how we regard the term *sacred* and its weightier corollary, *religion*, in the political and legal spaces in which these claims are made. It explores the intellectual difficulties and legal possibilities at the juncture of Native American traditions, the law, and the definition of religion. In the gaps between the urgent claims Native peoples make for places, practices, and material items that are surely religious though not plainly or solely so, and what courts, legislatures, and administrative arms of the government do with those claims, we find a space of the very making of the category of religion.

Jonathan Z. Smith argued that the concept of religion is "solely the creation of the scholar's study ... created for the scholar's analytic purposes by his imaginative acts of comparison and generalization," and having "no independent existence apart from the academy."[3] But his particular way of formulating the point so crucial to the critical turn in religious studies also bespeaks how true it is that we scholars don't get out that much. For religion is being conceptualized, and thus created, in a number of public domains beyond the scholar's study, and in a very pointed way in law. Witness stands, court opinions, statutes, and the fine print of regulatory law have formed important, if unwitting, sites in the cultural history of religion.

These definitional processes in the law have been of particular moment for Native American peoples, whose traditions have long eluded capture by the modern Western category of religion but who have of necessity appealed to the American discourse of religious freedom to assert their sacred claims. The study of this engagement can illuminate the power of that discourse to potentially include, yet often exclude, Indigenous religions.

The Presenting Problem: "No (*One*) Word for Religion"

Ojibwe people with whom I've worked the past twenty-five years hasten to point out that there is no word for "religion" in their language: religion can be found everywhere and nowhere at once in a traditional lifeway through which they seek the full integration of the sacred. It is an important point to note for the student of "religion." "If you pull on the thread of 'Native American religion,'" historian Joel Martin writes, "you end up pulling yourself into the study of Native American culture, art, history, economics, music, dance, dress, politics, and almost everything else. Talk about Hopi religion and you must talk about blue corn. One thing always leads to another and another when land, religion and life 'are one.'"[4] I turn now to the distinctive contours of Native American religious traditions.

For all their differences, Native American peoples are alike ill-served by the conventional wisdom about "religion." With over 550 federally recognized Native nations, speaking more than two hundred different languages, and practicing traditional lifeways keyed to the full range of American landscapes, diversity must be the first word. Yet there are commonalities, among them a shared reluctance to think of their having religion in the sense of a discrete aspect of life segmented off from other aspects of their traditional lifeways. Indeed, to say "we have no word for religion" can amount to a form of resistance, an assertion of intellectual sovereignty among peoples for whom the integration of religion, economy, polity, art, medicine, and agriculture can be a defining goal of life, one that stands in increasing relief in the midst of a broader society that promotes the separation of these domains as the price of entry to modernity. Following Max Weber, we might think of modernity as deeply shaped by the effort to differentiate the domains of economy and of politics from the domain of religion (difficult as it has ultimately proved to be in practice). The concept of religion as we know it today emerges reified in this process, assigned to its proper sphere apart from either economics or politics, *spiritual* concerns set off from *material* ones.

None of this has made much sense when it comes to the religious traditions of Native American peoples, for whom the spiritual and the material have been interwoven. Much of the powerful dismissal of "primitive" traditions as not fully religious has been what modern Europeans regarded as their stubborn materiality, their "savage" incapacity to rise above the natural or the fetish.[5] Think of the power of the stereotypical image of the "rain dance," mocked as a quaint, superstitious effort to control nature through magic. More recently, the problem has been one of misrecognition: lifeway practices profoundly associated with peoplehood, like harvesting wild rice, spearing walleyed pike, or netting salmon, can be economic and religious at the same time, but the deep religious elements can seem insincere or opportunistic because they can be seen to be conflated with the economic. Or with the political: "this isn't really about Native religion—these people are just making up these religious freedom claims in a last ditch effort to protest the pipeline," or the logging road, or the telescope on top of the mountain.

Native religions are diverse and dynamic. Transmitted orally rather than fixed in sacred texts, Native religions can involve considerable internal diversity in ways that confuse an outsider accustomed to seeing religions as defined by orthodox beliefs or bounded by visible institutions. There can be multiple origin or migration stories in play within one tradition. And these traditions can defy conventional wisdom about religions as cultural wholes. An Ojibwe person can participate in a Lakota leader's Sun Dance; a Navajo person can participate in the Peyote Road. More startling perhaps, many Indigenous people can see themselves as *both* committed Christians *and* observant practitioners of Ojibwe, or Lakota, or Navajo traditions.[6] Many of the traditions considered in these pages are oriented around the possibility of regular interchange with the spiritual world, of visions and ongoing revelation. In this respect religious change and religious innovations are not structurally anomalous; change—even incorporation of Christian practices—can be hardwired into the sense of the ongoing life of the religions themselves. And yet conventional wisdom that religions are mutually exclusive presents real difficulties for Native people whose practice draws on both or whose return to interrupted traditions can be regarded as discontinuous. Prison inmates may only

have one "religious preference" to check off on their intake form. To choose
Christian can block their access to Native traditions; to choose "Native American Spirituality" can defy their affiliation.

Native religions are constituted by practice more than by belief. Elsewhere I
have argued this capacity for holding multiple traditions in creative tension
has to do with the practice orientation of Native American religious traditions.[7] Beliefs matter and experiences shape lives, but Native religious traditions are often spoken of as practices, and the logic of their exercise follows
the logic of practice in ways that have frustrated those, including judges, looking for clearly defined creeds that distinguish, say, Kiowa religion from Mohawk religion from Christianity. The logic of such practices as maintaining
long hair or offering tobacco as a means of prayer or ceremonially ingesting
Peyote for healing does not always come with a singular theological reason
behind it.

Native American religions are local, not universal, and in at least three respects. First, traditional Native religions are largely coterminous with Native
collectivities: nations, tribes, villages, clans, and societies. The community,
not the individual, is the basic unit. As Vine Deloria Jr. aptly put it, "There is
no salvation in tribal religions apart from the continuance of the tribe itself."[8]
True, there are some traditions historically—the Ghost Dance, the Peyote
Road, the Shaker Church, among them—that have emerged in an intertribal
context and extend over multiple Native peoples. And there is increasingly a
practice of a self-described Native American Spirituality, but distinctive ori-
entations to community and to land can remain.

Second, Native traditions that are every bit religious typically do not make
claims that are universal in nature, or mutually exclusive from teachings of
other religions. No one is out to convert others to, say, Osage religion. Vine
Deloria Jr. has drawn on the analogy of the Jewish covenant to describe the
relationships of particular peoples with the divine. The obligations devolve
on peoples, on collectives, not simply on individuals. And the traditions have
little concern with the implications for those outside of those covenants. But
these covenants make exacting demands on Native peoples, often precise demands that belie the stereotype that for Native Americans, all nature is sacred
in some bland, nonspecific way. Obligations may be incumbent to *this* mountain, *this* spring, or *this* waterfall, and not *that* one or all others.

Third, to speak of Native religions as local is very much to acknowledge
the ways that they conform and make sense to particular lifeways tied to
particular landscapes and waters. Makah traditions focus on relations with

whales; Muscogee traditions with corn; Lakota traditions with bison. The symbolic elements of the traditions make sense in those landscapes, and religious traditions are part not just of making sense of those places but of making a living and living well on them. In these three respects, Native American traditions are often collective obligations and duties, elementally the province of communities more than that of individual belief or conscience or subjective experience.

This is part of the difficulty of fully recognizing what's at stake with Native American relationships with sacred lands. Native religions, as Vine Deloria Jr., put it in *God Is Red*, are oriented to space in contrast to the defining orientation of "Western traditions" to time. Of course, sacred space can matter in Western traditions, too, but Indigenous traditions make full sense fundamentally in relationship to traditional lands, waters, and sacred places. Native peoples can have emergence or migration stories that locate them as peoples belonging to a particular place rather than a universal genesis at the beginning of time. So it's not just that sacred places or traditional territories belong to Native peoples; it's that Native peoples belong to those places. To take one example, the Ojibwe expression for their territory, *anishinaabe akiing*, can rightly be translated as "the land of the people" or "the people of the land."

The language of religion can fall short of the range and complexity of these Indigenous commitments to lands and waters. Indigenous places can be sacred, but not necessarily in terms of a non-negotiable dichotomy between the sacred and the profane. Places may be too sacrosanct to enter, needing time to themselves, or places may be sacred at certain times or for certain purposes, but not impervious to other, less religious uses.

But sacred is not such an ill-fitting term to describe the sense of duty and obligation to such places, the sense of reciprocity with those places, and the moral standing or spiritual subjectivity of the places themselves, or the plants and animals that people them. To speak of the sacred is to invoke, properly in my view, an appreciation for the depth of these relationships, their more-than-instrumental value, and the real presence and subjectivity of spiritual others. Indeed, where many discussions on the topic hearken to what Native people may mean when they say "we have no religion," I think it useful to begin instead from Suzan Shown Harjo's way of putting the matter: "We have no *one* word for religion."[9] This is to say, Native peoples have a rich vocabulary, not to mention grammar, syntax, and idiom, for what is reductively called "religion" in the modern West. Drawing on her Muscogee and Cheyenne heritages, Harjo points to how the plethora of words for religion are subtly inflected for specific contexts, including a term for "people who go to ceremonies who don't have the *religion* to back it up."[10] Awareness of the sophistication of Indigenous dispositions to the sacred can thicken the understanding of any claim about a practice like salmon fishing or wild rice gathering, about protections of land base, or language, or manner of political deliberation and decision-making. Given the sacred thread that runs through these, it is perhaps *religion* more than keywords of the secularized vocabulary of the social sciences—*economy, ecology, law,* or even *culture*—that best gets at Indigenous peoples' lives and lifeways.

It is pretty well established by now that legal protections for religious freedom under the First Amendment or the 1993 Religious Freedom Restoration Act (RFRA) have delivered more failure than promise when it comes to Native American claims to sacred lands and Free Exercise practices. Indeed, this book follows Native peoples as they have taken their claims beyond the language of religious freedom, articulating sacred claims in the managerial discourse of cultural resource under domestic environmental and historic preservation law, the limited sovereignty discourse of federal Indian law, and, increasingly, the discourse of Indigenous rights in international human rights law, especially in light of the 2007 UN Declaration on the Rights of Indigenous Peoples.

But claims engaging these discourses have not uniformly succeeded where religious freedom claims have failed. Articulating claims to what they hold sacred in the language of culture or of peoplehood presents its own intellectual or legal limits. Indeed, if the discourse of religion has been relatively moribund for Native claims in the courts, it remains among the more rhetorically powerful ways of conveying their urgency, and of generating broad political support for such statutory protections as the American Indian Religious Freedom Act (AIRFA, 1978), AIRFA's Peyote Amendment (1994), and the Native American Graves Protection and Repatriation Act (NAGPRA, 1990).[11] The power of religious freedom discourse shown in enactments of AIRFA and NAGPRA, I argue in these pages, should make us think twice before declaring legal arguments toward religious freedom dead on arrival.

Sacred claims to religious rights protections for Native American places, practices, objects, and ancestors can be understood more properly as collective rights of Native peoples rather than as merely the private conscience rights of so many Native individuals, especially when Native nations are the litigants. This book is largely descriptive and analytical, but it is informed by a constructive argument rooted in the analysis. What I propose is an approach to Native American religious claims that aligns and conjoins such claims with elements of federal Indian law and with the emerging norms of Indigenous rights in international human rights law. Along the way, I argue that the language of religion may still have legs for Native claims in legal and political processes if Native peoples continue to insist on claiming what is distinctive about the collective structure of their religious freedom claims.[12]

This book is informed by my broader academic training in religious studies and in American religious history. It is informed and inspired by scholarship bringing humanities sensibilities to this corner of the law: work on sacred lands by Peter Nabokov, Lloyd Burton, Andrew Gulliford, and especially the generative, deeply learned and prolific work of Vine Deloria Jr.;[13] work on religious freedom generally by Robert Michaelson, Christopher Vecsey, Huston Smith, and Jace Weaver;[14] and work on repatriation by James Riding In, Kathleen Fine-Dare, and Greg Johnson.[15] The book is also informed and inspired by a growing circle of fresh scholarship on similar topics. Tisa Wenger has emerged as the go-to historian of Native religious freedom, along with Thomas Maroukis on the Peyote Road.[16] Greg Johnson has recent articles and a forthcoming book that are enormously helpful in understanding religious renewal in the crucible of legal and political struggles and bringing theoretical clarity to the task.[17] Nick Estes has powerfully placed Standing Rock's resistance to Dakota Access in a longer narrative of Indigenous resistance. Todd Morman has just published a fine book focused on the administrative public land management of sacred places.[18] Nicholas Shrubsole has published a counterpart of sorts to this book in the context of Canadian law.[19] Tiffany Hale and Dana Lloyd have just completed important dissertations (Hale on the Ghost Dance and Lloyd on the *Lyng* decision) and are in the process of bringing that work to publication.[20] The last five projects have appeared on the scene after I had written the manuscript. I can only incorporate their insights at the edges here; readers will have the benefit of engaging all views.

The analysis is particularly driven by targeted legal training that has impressed on me how little intellectual commerce there is between the fields of federal Indian law and religious liberty law. There's a tension to be sure between federal Indian law, a complex body of law based largely on treaties and the collective rights of members/citizens of Native nations, and religious liberty law, applicable in theory to all citizens equally, but under which religion has largely been interpreted to consist primarily in an individual right of conscience. Scholars of religious liberty, I've learned, are not generally conversant in the distinct political and legal framework of Indian claims, nor the elementally collective nature of those claims. This book reflects my effort to draw on both fields of law to reconsider what religion and religious freedom can mean in Native cases. For the indeterminacy of the category of religion, its capacity for reinterpretation in law and politics is a possibility, not simply a constraint.

Why Not Religion and Religious Freedom?

"Why bother?" the reader may ask. Why try to think through how better to articulate Indigenous claims in the language of the colonizer, and in particular in courts where religious freedom has so clearly been shown to be a discourse of exclusion rather than inclusion? To squeeze relationships to land, or traditional practices associated with those lands, into the category of religion is already to denature them and to concede cultural, not to mention legal, sovereignty. I cannot help but concur with such criticisms, and for at least four reasons that I must briefly identify if I am to persuade any reader of the continued relevance of religious freedom for Native claims.

Religious Freedom's Failure in Courts

First, Native claims to religious freedom have often failed in court. The two key Supreme Court decisions on Native religious practice have been flagship cases by which the Rehnquist Court restricted the reach of the First Amendment's Free Exercise clause. In its 1988 decision in *Lyng v. Northwest Indian Cemetery Protective Association*, the Supreme Court upheld Forest Service approval of a logging road through a sacred precinct of high country central to California Native nations, granting the sincerity of Yurok, Karuk, and Tolowa beliefs about the high country but reasoning that the impacts on their spiritual fulfillment did not rise to the level of an unconstitutional prohibition of religion.[21]

Two years later and building on its decision in *Lyng*, the Supreme Court found the First Amendment was not violated in the denial of unemployment benefits to two chemical dependency counselors fired for their involvement in the Native American Church, despite broad recognition of the Peyote Road as a bona fide religion and, in the respondents' case, as a keystone to their own sobriety.[22] The *Employment Division v. Smith* decision is known for restricting the reach of religious Free Exercise protections generally by excluding First Amendment challenges to "neutral laws of general applicability" even when those government actions have the effect of prohibiting religious exercise. Because Native religious exercise is effectively infringed on by any number of government actions that aren't expressly targeting it, these two decisions not only settled the particular questions at hand, but they also foreclosed countless other Native American cases that might have come before courts under the First Amendment.

What is more, when a nearly unanimous Congress acted in 1993 to restore the bedrock principle of religious freedom in the Religious Freedom Restoration Act (RFRA), specifically outmaneuvering the *Smith* decision and restoring the higher "strict scrutiny" standard of judicial review of government actions before *Smith*, Native claims have been left out in the cold. This is all the more remarkable in view of the fact that RFRA's definition of "religious exercise" was expanded in 2000 so as not to require courts to determine whether religious exercise was central or indispensable to a religion, overcoming a difficulty particularly vexing for Native claims to sacred lands. But in 2008, the Ninth Circuit Court of Appeals found no RFRA violation in government approval of a scheme to make artificial snow with treated sewage effluent for skiing on Arizona's highest mountain, a massif called San Francisco Peaks in English, but "Shining on Top" by the Navajo, a living being who is one of the holy mountains that define the Navajo world, an object of daily devotions and source of medicine and power necessary for all Navajo ceremonies.[23] For the Hopi, the massif is the home of the kachinas, ancestors who bring rain and life, a place where paradigmatic sacred events happened, and a site of pilgrimage and veneration today. The governments of four other Native nations joined the Navajo and Hopi to challenge the sewage-to-snowmaking scheme as a violation of their religious freedom under RFRA. While the court accepted all the detailed factual findings about the Indigenous claims to the sacred mountain as sincere and in force, the Ninth Circuit found as a matter of law that religious exercise was not "substantially burdened" by the treated wastewater. Since the ski area comprises only one percent of the surface of the mountain, and because there would be no limiting of access or physical destruction of plants or sites on the ski slopes, the court found that the "sole effect of the artificial snow" is on the Native Americans' "subjective spiritual experience," amounting merely to diminished spiritual fulfillment:

> That is, the presence of the artificial snow on the Peaks is offensive to the Plaintiffs' feelings about their religion and will decrease the spiritual fulfillment Plaintiffs get from practicing their religion on the mountain. Nev-

ertheless, a government action that decreases the spirituality, the fervor, or the satisfaction with which a believer practices his religion is not what Congress has labeled a "substantial burden"—a term of art chosen by Congress to be defined by reference to Supreme Court precedent—on the free exercise of religion.[24]

Here, recognized claims by tribal governments to collective duties and religious obligations—in Navajo law, the Navajo Tribal Code codifies obligations to respect and protect the six sacred mountains—are denatured into claims of subjective spiritual fulfillment that characterize romanticized misconceptions of Native American nature piety.

This approach to sacred land claims under religious freedom law prevailed in the second volley of the Dakota Access Pipeline litigation. A federal judge said the Cheyenne River Sioux Tribe's assertion that the pipeline violated their RFRA rights to religious freedom came too little and too late to support a temporary restraining order before the oil flowed. The judge found the religious freedom claims weakened for their not having been asserted legally at the outset of the court challenge and in any event unlikely to succeed on the merits of establishing a substantial burden on religious exercise, citing the failure to establish coercion against religious beliefs in the San Francisco Peaks and *Lyng* cases.[25] Again, diminished spiritual fulfillment was all the court could ultimately see.

One could rightly argue that the transmutation of religious obligation into spiritual fulfillment is precisely what is likely to happen when complex collective Native American traditions oriented to land and lifeway are conceptually assimilated into a framework of religious freedom shaped by and more accustomed to cognates of Christianity.

The Ill Fit between Native Traditions and "Religion"

Indeed, many Native peoples are understandably reluctant to speak of their traditions in the language of religion, given that their orientation to place doesn't conform to the conceptual shape of religion conventionally understood. Native peoples also have good reason to be reluctant because of frequent associations of the sacred with the secret. Where most Christians are glad to speak publicly about their beliefs and practices, for many Native peoples, to traipse out dreams, visions, or sacred knowledge belonging to a lineage or an initiatory society in public as religion is potentially to bring danger. It can also make sacred knowledge available to non-Native seekers—or academics—for uses considered unauthorized, decontextualized, or disrespectful.

What is more, to make claims in the language of religion and religious freedom can for some Native people suggest the undermining of collective self-determination. Native nations with sovereignty over internal affairs can and do regulate the religious life within their nations in ways that can provoke religious freedom claims from their own members. As Tisa Wenger shows, some of the earliest appeals to religious freedom discourse were by Christian Pueblo members challenging conscription in ceremonial dances as part of Pueblo citizenship. Other examples include past Navajo regulations against Peyote use on their reservation.[26] In part to guarantee that internal tribal sovereignty could not violate the civil rights of Native individuals on reservations, Congress passed the Indian Civil Rights Act in 1968, but there remain complex issues, some of them coming before federal courts in ways that situate religious freedom in opposition to Indigenous sovereignty.[27]

Such concerns add to the intellectual difficulty of fitting Native traditions into the category of religion. I used to think, as a student of the distinctive contours of Indigenous religions, that the issue here is fundamentally one of poetics, of translational imagination, of a search for less impoverished metaphors than "Bear Butte is our St. Patrick's Cathedral" by which jurists could better grasp the religiousness of Native religious claims.

The Masked Exclusions of Religious Freedom

But the problem of Native American religious freedom goes far deeper than one remedied by education alone. As a growing body of critical religious studies literature has shown, the reason that some religions don't fully count for religious freedom legal protection is not simply a function of their being misrecognized. The very notion of religious freedom can have baked into it a subtle but no less forceful discrimination that naturalizes and universalizes the individual, interior, subjective, chosen, belief-oriented piety characteristic of Protestant Christianity and enables such a piety to flourish at the expense of traditions characterized more by community obligations, law, and ritualized practice.

Historians have long called attention to the justification for anti-Catholic laws and policies in the nineteenth century under an assumed Catholic disregard for religious freedom. Bigotry clothed itself in sanctimony over religious freedom.[28] Seen as ineluctably oriented to Rome and committed to global dominance rather than to American democratic institutions, Catholicism was seen as antithetical to those democratic institutions. It was this rabid anti-Catholicism, argues Philip Hamburger, that was the key driver in elaborating on the language of separation between church and state.[29] Historian Daryl Sehat takes such an insight into the *Myth of American Religious Freedom*, exposing the mythmaking about religious freedom as the keystone to other American liberties and where those American liberties are exceptional in the world.[30] Although he acknowledges that the myth of religious freedom functions to help cohere an American identity around it, Sehat pursues the work of exposure of how discussions about religion in public life "trade on a series of fables about the American past."[31]

Anthropologist Talal Asad has shown how the discourses of religion and of religious freedom have served to universalize a particular, culturally specific order of things on the entire world, and thus to define Islam and Islamic nations as incommensurable with modern democracy.[32] More recently, scholars led by Winnifred Fallers Sullivan, Saba Mahmood, Peter Danchin, and Elizabeth Shakman Hurd have shown how this dark underbelly of religious freedom discourse, far from being a thing of the past, characterizes its deployment abroad as a tool of American imperialism and informs its domestic "impossibility" as a matter of US law.[33]

"Religious freedom," Hurd writes, has become a "dominant discourse" because it is "conceptually simple, enjoys a communicative monopoly, offers enormous flexibility of application, encompasses great ideological plasticity, and is serviceable for established institutional purposes."[34] The presumed universality of the discourse tidily and effectively masks the reality of the exclusions it secures; some religions count, others don't, but no one is led to believe the discourse itself is the problem.

We learn from Winnifred Fallers Sullivan's groundbreaking work that what makes all this possible is the fundamental indeterminacy of religion. "In order to enforce laws guaranteeing religious freedom," Sullivan writes, "you must first have religion."[35] And the difficulties of ascertaining, or even agreeing, on just what religion is, make its legal protection as such "theoretically incoherent and possibly unconstitutional."[36] In the book she titles *The Impossibility of Religious Freedom*, Sullivan shows how messy is the task any court faces in trying to maintain a clear boundary between religion and government, for in the doing it inevitably finds itself regulating religion. Sullivan backs up this strong position with compelling analysis of a Florida RFRA case involving competing views of what counts as properly "religious" funerary practice at a public cemetery.[37] "Courts, legislatures and other government agencies judge the actions of persons as religious or not, as protected or not, based on models of religion that often make a poor fit with religion as it is lived."[38]

Sullivan goes on to identify the very particular shape of the religion that counts in legal processes. She refers to this as "protestant" with a small *p*—private, voluntary, individual, textual, and believed—as opposed to the "public, coercive, communal, oral, and enacted religion characteristic of Catholicism and Islam but also part of the lived religion of any tradition."[39] In making determinations of what is to be legally cognizable as properly religious and what is not, Sullivan argues, courts become entangled in questions of orthodoxy and heterodoxy, of good and bad religion.

In subsequent work on publicly funded chaplaincy programs and what she views as their remarkable imperviousness to Establishment Clause challenges, Sullivan elaborates on the "naturalization" of a universally human spirituality.[40] In this later work, Sullivan chooses to use religion and spirituality interchangeably, any meaningful distinction between them being eclipsed by their similar (small *p*) protestant shape: private, voluntary, individual, textual, and believed. What's more, we learn from David Chidester that the very category of religion settles into the semantic shape by which we know it at the time of colonization in and through the regulation of Indigenous others and their untidy practices.[41] Accordingly, Native religious exclusions were fully a part of the larger capture of Native lands and people.

Tisa Wenger has recently called out just how crucial was the language of religious freedom as moral justification and call to arms for domestic colonization of Native peoples and lands and in American imperialism in the Philippines. "The dominant voice in the culture," she writes, "linked racial whiteness, Protestant Christianity, and American national identity not only to freedom in general but to this [religious] freedom in particular."[42] The civilizational assemblage of race and religion that Wenger sees coursing through US regulation of Native traditions from the 1880s to the 1930s never really seems to go away.[43] The career of the Peyote Road is instructive on this point: strategic efforts by Peyotists in the early 1900s to protect their traditions under religious freedom logic by incorporating as the Native American Church faced their challenges, to be sure, but were by and large successful until the Supreme Court, in the 1990 *Smith* decision, criminalized them as collateral damage in a broader aim of withdrawing the reach of First Amendment Free Exercise protection.

"Religion" Deployed against Native Traditions

A fourth criticism of engaging religious freedom is the legacy of the plain fact that religion has long been used against Native American peoples. The legal Doctrine of Christian Discovery gave legal authorization to conquest and theft by vesting absolute title in Christian monarchs and divesting those "without religion" of all but rights of occupancy. More pervasively still, the category of "religion" was deployed against Native peoples in the Civilization Regulations, which for more than fifty years from 1883 until 1934 criminalized Native religious practices like the Sun Dance, Potlatch, and ceremonial healing. The cumulative effect of fifty years of this policy was traumatic pushing underground the ceremonies and healing systems of traditional religions and continuing to suppress them beyond the formal disavowal of such policies in 1934. And tracing early twentieth-century efforts by Native peoples to engage religious freedom protections for what they positioned as the Native American Church were never the stable "first freedom" they were for other communities, as the 1990 *Smith* decision made resoundingly clear. So I would only underscore Tisa Wenger's caution about any sanguine engagement with religious freedom talk used so deliberately against Native people.

Why Religion? What Can Religious Freedom Mean?

But I have to say, the closer I've gotten to the stories of Native religious and cultural claim-making over the last fifty years, the less drawn I feel to the view (whether it is projected from empirical historical study or deduced more theoretically) that arguments for religious freedom are destined to be dead on arrival. A sampling of recent book titles speaks to the contemporary valuation of religious freedom talk: *Beyond Religious Freedom, The Politics of Religious Freedom, The Myth of Religious Freedom, The Production of Religious Freedom,* or *The Impossibility of Religious Freedom.*[44] As important as these projects are for their unmasking of how religious freedom discourse serves to secure and advance the power of the powerful, to exclude those at the margins of power, and to authorize discrimination—especially at this particular political moment—I think otherwise amazing work can risk contenting itself without more fully appreciating how myths and discourses work in part because even as they grease the wheels of power, they also provide the medium for resistance to power.[45]

This book takes its main cues from the claim-making of Native nations to accentuate what has become something of a footnote in much of this work:

that religion and religious freedom are not simply used to exclude those at margins; they are reworked creatively from the margins, their indeterminacy a possibility and not just a limit.

Historian Tisa Wenger stays closer to the ground in this regard, especially in her first book on the Pueblo dance controversy.[46] Wenger shows how those with relatively little power engage the discourse at the margins to create space for themselves. But in the work of others, this point amounts to an unelaborated footnote and can have the effect of reducing to pitiful dupes those who, like Native people, have shaped the discourse to their own ends—whether that be on nineteenth-century reservations or in Senate office buildings in 1989. A fair criticism from this literature is that such resistance cannot be fully effective, because it is articulated in the discursive realm already cooked up against Native peoples. But where courts can decide what religion will count for legal purposes, the discourse of religious freedom is more than just a matter of judicial outcomes. As Greg Johnson's work shows so well, the broad appeal in Hawai'i or at Standing Rock is the strategic and generative engagement with the discourse of the "sacred."[47] So even where religious freedom may fail in courts, it captures imagination in courts of public opinion precisely because of its power as a discourse.

It is this religious studies insight into the discourse of religious freedom— the exclusions encoded into its presumed universalism, the exclusions empirically felt in a series of Native American claims to religious freedom—that can embolden us to think about how that discourse can be trained in new directions. For as we've learned from any number of postmodern and postcolonial theorists, discourses don't just function as airtight expressions of colonizers' wishes; they involve contradictions, trade-offs, and in the end, consent, to continue to work. And as discourses go, I do not see that of religious freedom disappearing anytime soon—whatever the actual history of its interpretation in the courts. Given its profile in the first clauses of the Bill of Rights, "religion" will long be a term of power.

This all perhaps rings of an optimism unbecoming a religious studies scholar who is fully aware of the checkered past. I aspire to show in this book that the approach is more realistic, since the Native advocates I engage are pragmatic, not wide-eyed, when it comes to speaking their claims in the language of religion. Indeed, often as not, the legal appeals to religious freedom appear as last resorts after other, putatively more salutary, legal arguments for cultural resource protection fail.[48]

Like those advocates, I don't just ask what religious freedom means; I ask what religious freedom *can* mean. Although this book treats this question with nuance, there is an arc to my analysis toward an appreciation for the collective shape of—and the collective rights to—Native American religions. I draw on a number of sources of legal authority for this overall argument.

Where I End Up: Religion as Peoplehood

This book looks to the possibilities of eliding what's *religious* about Native claims to sacred lands, practices, ancestors, and material heritage into notions of sovereignty and peoplehood. This replaces the conceptual gymnastics required to render claims as those of Native American "religion" and relieves Native peoples of having to reveal proprietary, initiatory, or secret traditional knowledge to make a showing of "religion." Most importantly, eliding the religious honors Indigenous peoples' rights to self-determination, including the rights to determine for themselves what's sacred and how to treat it.

So this is where I end up. In chapter 7, I focus on affirmations of sovereignty and treaty rights under domestic federal Indian law, where Native nations have quite successfully protected traditional practices associated with ceremony and peoplehood—salmon fishing and whaling in the Northwest; fishing and wild rice practices in the Great Lakes—when there are treaty provisions on which to hang the argument and when courts aren't otherwise held back by federal Indian law's racist and colonizing apparatus tied to the Doctrine of Christian Discovery, congressional Plenary Power. Chapter 8 celebrates the enormous potential of rights as Indigenous peoples under the ripening norms of international law after the passage of the United Nations Declaration on the Rights of Indigenous Peoples (UNDRIP) in 2007 and its adoption with reservations by the United States in 2010.[49]

Keeping Religion in the Mix: Toward Religious Sovereignty

But as a matter of legal and political effectiveness, this book does not content itself with the elision of religion into something else. Apart from the relative weakness of international law norms in US courts, in the case of UNDRIP, religious rights are very much a species of cultural rights that make a lot of sense in the world of international law but that lack constitutional or other meaningful legal reference points in domestic US law. And the distinctive legal architecture of federal Indian law seems increasingly precarious, with increasingly conservative courts determined to decimate what they only see as "special rights" as though federal Indian law is one more instance of affirmative action.[50]

So while I end up beyond the First Amendment, beyond RFRA, I maintain there's legal and political value in keeping "religion" and "religious freedom" in the mix, toward a bundle or hybrid construal of religious freedom law in terms of the collectivist protections of federal Indian law and emerging norms of Indigenous rights in international law, for something we might call *religious sovereignty*. What I mean by religious sovereignty is less grandiose and more specific than it might seem. First, it builds on important work of Indigenous law scholar Rebecca Tsosie, who argues out from the experience of cultural appropriation, and cultural property, repatriation, and intellectual property law toward a full-throated cultural sovereignty, a complement and completion to the political sovereignty that is so often the concern in federal Indian law. Tsosie glosses cultural sovereignty not primarily in terms of sovereignty over cultural matters, though that to be sure is implied. It has more to do with "the internal construction of sovereignty by Native peoples themselves that will elicit the core meaning and significance of sovereignty for contemporary Native communities."[51] It reflects Native jurisprudential understandings of the matters that find their way to courts, and among other things an implicit rejection of forms of law, including delimited sovereignty, that "emphasize the secular nature of 'legitimate governance.'" In this, cultural sovereignty doesn't shy away from aspects of Native law that extend to what we might call the religious—spiritual relationships, responsibilities, and rights. Tsosie writes with the long-serving leader of the Comanche Nation, Wallace Coffey:

> We must create our own internal appraisal of what "sovereignty" means, what "autonomy" means, and what rights, duties, and responsibilities are entailed in our relationships between and among ourselves, our Ancestors, our future generations, and the external society.... It requires us to articulate the appropriate norms of governance and the contours of our own social order, from both a political and spiritual perspective.[52]

Coffey put the spiritual matter more directly still: "Cultural sovereignty is the heart and soul that you have, and no one has jurisdiction over that but God."[53] For as religious as such an utterance is, Coffey and Tsosie stop short of calling this *religious* sovereignty because like *political* sovereignty, religion is a decidedly non-Indigenous category. I agree. But I do think wedding notions of sovereignty and peoplehood to an indigenized inflection of religion can make pragmatic legal sense. *Religious sovereignty,* as I offer the term, is not a claim for the collective autonomy of *any religious* group but is tailored to the special legal status and nation-to-nation relationship between Native nations and the United States and also to the prerogative of Indigenous peoples themselves to determine what matters are sacred to them. But more than *cultural sovereignty,* it brings to bear a legibility that carries force in American politics and law.

Sources of Authority for the Argument

My argument rests on a lawyerly conviction that the indeterminacy of the category is a possibility, not just a limit, and draws on a number of sources of legal authority. First, where religious freedom claims have largely failed in the courts, Native leaders have had success in drawing on the rhetorical power of religious freedom to get Congress to pass Native specific legislative accommodations, especially the American Indian Religious Freedom Act of 1978 and the Native American Graves Protection and Repatriation Act of 1990. Remarkable because Congress was moved by a group with very little political power—fewer than two percent of the US population and a relatively poor two percent at that; remarkable also for the deft ways that religious freedom arguments could engender protections that conform less to the individual rights logic of religious freedom and instead conform to the collective rights implicit in the nation-to-nation relationships of federal Indian law.

Second, US courts have acknowledged the distinctly collective shape of Native religious claims, at least through the back door. On the one hand, courts have consistently upheld off-reservation treaty rights to fishing and hunting that form the basis of chapter 7. In these cases, the collective nature of the claims is explicit but their religious nature, I argue, is implicit and often overlooked from the vantage point that they are merely economic rights. As Frank Ettawageshik put it, "the true treaty right" his Odawa people have to Lake Michigan fish is not a quantifiable property right but a right to continued relationship: "Our ancestors didn't say 'those are our fish.' Rather, they reserved the right to fish. That meant they reserved a right to sing to the fish, to dance for the fish, to pray for the fish, to catch and eat the fish but to live with the fish, to have a relationship with the fish."[54]

On the other hand, courts have consistently affirmed the collective rights to Native religions in a colorful batch of case law involving possession of ceremonial eagle feathers.[55] In these cases, the religiousness of the claims is explicit but the collective nature of the claims is implicit. An exemption to the criminalization of feather possession under the Bald and Golden Eagle Protection Act for members of federally recognized tribes, administered by a permitting and distribution process under the US Fish and Wildlife Service's Eagle Repository in Denver, has been upheld against legal challenges by individual practitioners of Native religions who are not members of federally recognized tribes.[56] Several appellate courts have recently invoked the federal trust responsibility—the special government-to-government obligations to acknowledged tribes that are the progeny of treaties and the corpus of federal Indian law—in addressing Native religious freedom objections under RFRA to the federal permitting process for possession of bald eagle feathers.

Third, if working out the kinks of the Eagle Act accommodation is seen as merely an instance of judicial reasoning about Native religions as group rights sneaking in through the back door of the US legal system, I turn to the forthright front-door reasoning of international human rights law, particularly as clarified in the 2007 UN Declaration on the Rights of Indigenous Peoples, which was endorsed by the United States in 2010. The Declaration doesn't create any new human rights but clarifies that existing human rights in international law, if they're to apply meaningfully to the globe's Indigenous peoples, must apply as collective, and not just individual, rights. I agree with Walter Echo-Hawk, Robert Williams Jr., and others that recent Supreme Court cases have destabilized the already shaky foundation of federal Indian law, making claims to sovereignty based on that foundation less reliable in courts. I agree with them that federal Indian law must more fully incorporate the elaboration of the aspirational standards set out in the UN Declaration to sink those foundations deeper into the bedrock of Indigenous peoplehood.

If to have religious freedom you must first have "religion," and if religion is as problematic a moniker for urgent and sacred Native claims, it is also true that Native nations and their advocates are less interested in whether religious freedom is conceptually bankrupt or not. And too much focus on court cases can skew our sense of how claims made in the register of religion are useful in courts of public opinion, shaping the political context for positive legislative and administrative developments.

In arguing toward a religious sovereignty, toward the collective rights of Native American religious freedom sewn into to the special political and legal status of Native Americans in the United States, it is useful briefly to acknowledge the promise of parallel developments in Canada. A recent book by Nicholas Shrubsole, to which readers are heartily referred for a fuller treatment, argues that First Nations' rights to sacred places can and should rest on a hybrid of legal protections for religion freedom under Article 2 of the Canadian Charter, and the Constitution Act's Section 35(1), which provides that "the existing aboriginal and treaty rights of the aboriginal peoples of Canada are hereby recognized and affirmed." Drawing on work that elaborates Canada's First Nations peoples as "citizens plus," Shrubsole points toward a "religions plus" framework that weds the discourse of religion with the formal acknowledgment of collective aboriginal rights.[57] As Shrubsole's book was taking shape, the Supreme Court of Canada rejected arguments that the Ktunaxa First Nation, in their effort to block development of a year-round ski resort on sacred lands, enjoyed such a hybrid claim to collective religious freedom.[58] Indeed, a whole potential chapter of this book might have been dedicated to that case had the Supreme Court of Canada held otherwise, but Shrubsole's argument, especially in an era of formal Canadian commitments to and energetic public discussion of reconciliation, can commend a legal framework where Indigenous rights are unambiguously a constitutional matter.

Even without an equivalent provision to Canada's 35(1), US law has also established a constitutional grounding for recognition of the inherent sovereignty of Native nations and their special legal status. Although the chapters of this book will further develop the implications, we turn now, by way of introduction, to the political status of Native American peoples.

The Distinctive Political Status of Native American Peoples

Both US courts and Congress have recognized Native Americans—at least those who are members of federally acknowledged tribes—not simply as members of a racial or ethnic minority or protected economic class but as Americans with a distinctive political status.[59] Recognition of this status has multiple sources in US law. First and most important, it is rooted in the "inherent sovereignty" of Native nations who predate the Constitution and whose inherent sovereignty is elaborated in the nation-to-nation structure of treaties.[60] The US Constitution speaks of Native peoples in several places, and in ways that clarify their distinct status. Art. 1, Sec. 2, Clause 3 states, "Representatives and direct Taxes shall be apportioned among the several

States ... excluding Indians not taxed." The Commerce Clause allocates to Congress the power "to regulate commerce with foreign Nations, and among the several States, and with the Indian Tribes."[61] Early legislative acts and early Supreme Court decisions elaborated on this political status, ensuring that the nation-to-nation relationship would align Native nations with the federal government, not state governments. Finally, the special political status of Native Americans has been ensconced in a legal doctrine of the federal trust responsibility with Native tribes, under which courts have held the United States accountable as a trustee of Indian interests and resources with whom it has a particular responsibility.[62]

Federal Indian Law

The distinctive political status of Native peoples has given rise to a discrete body of law commonly known as federal Indian law. In part because this body of law is distinguished by the political status of Native peoples, it is not uniformly well known by jurists unless they encounter its distinctive cases on a regular basis. Even for its specialists, however, federal Indian law is characterized by core tensions, ambiguities, even contradictions, that are often identified within early Supreme Court efforts, led by Chief Justice John Marshall, to integrate into the common law and American law traditions the colonization of Indigenous peoples. Native peoples' presence on their traditional territories has raised vexing moral, intellectual, and practical legal questions for settler colonialism. At different moments in this book, I attend to the so-called Marshall trilogy of Supreme Court cases and join federal Indian law scholars trying to come to terms with the contradictions. *Johnson v. M'Intosh* (1823) introduces into American law the Doctrine of Christian Discovery, a crucial legal doctrine that secures most title to the United States atop the theological presumption rooted in early modern papal decrees and later adopted by the Protestant British Crown that the sovereigns who "discover" New World lands in the name of Christianity enjoy absolute title to those lands, reducing Native rights to rights of occupancy only. *Cherokee Nation v. Georgia* (1831) likens Native peoples to "domestic, dependent nations," dramatically limiting their recognized sovereignty to internal matters and construing them in terms of a ward/guardian relationship with the United States. *Worcester v. Georgia* (1832) explicitly affirms that the sovereignty of Native nations, limited as it may be under the circumstances, is no less an "inherent sovereignty," and that the rights reserved by Native peoples in treaties are not grants or gifts from the United States but obligations respecting Native inherent sovereignty. As a later Supreme Court decision put the matter:

> The treaty was not a grant of rights to the Indians, but a grant of rights from them—a reservation of those not granted.[63]

All three cases codify racist stereotypes of the day and reason from these outmoded views of Native peoples as savage, incapable of civilization. Astoundingly, these cases remain on the books, leading many to call for their complete rejection by courts in an age where few share the racist views on which "good law" is premised.[64] Others are left trying to reform and rewrite federal Indian law, trying to maintain what is valuable in this body of precedent, such as the distinctive political status of Native American peoples affirmed in *Worcester*, in spite of these racist views.

Shifting Winds of Federal Indian Law

With its unstable base in the Marshall trilogy, federal Indian law has proved most susceptible to rapid changes over time, caught in shifting winds of popular opinion and policy without the ballast that lends stability and coherence to other bodies of law.[65] For example, assimilation policies from 1871 until 1934 took the view that "tribalism" was a thing of the past, and so too, the solemn treaties with Native nations, and that the future was for Indians, as individuals, to assimilate to American economy, policy, society, culture, and Christian religion. The Supreme Court gave legal backing to this astounding pivot in 1903, ruling in *Lone Wolf v. Hitchcock* that forced allotment to individual Indians of collective Kiowa reservation lands (and sale of the surplus to white settlers) was lawful because the treaty securing those lands had been made with the foreknowledge that Congress could violate the terms of the treaty to effect policies it knew would be good for Indians.[66]

Like the Marshall trilogy, *Lone Wolf* remains "good law" in federal Indian law, but the prevailing winds have changed again and again. Assimilation Policy ended abruptly in 1934 when Congress passed the Indian Reorganization Act (IRA), restoring collective rights to land, language, culture, and Native self-government. Tribal governments were established initially using template constitutions from the Indian Bureau, in up/down votes by Native peoples themselves.[67] These governments are the ones formally recognized by the United States as the agencies of tribal sovereignty, but in many cases today are still called "IRA governments" in Native circles to mark their departure from Indigenous governance traditions. Efforts by Native leaders to seek re-dress for the wrongs of Assimilation Policy, and to reclaim religious and cul-tural rights, were many. Less known, because not overtly or plainly religious in appeal, were their efforts to reclaim sacred lands under the Indian Claims Commission process, begun in 1946 to settle outstanding claims once and for all with the tribal governments.[68] With the formation, also in the 1940s, of the National Congress of American Indians, came the coalescence of these tribe-specific efforts.[69]

In the 1950s, Indian policy took a pendulum swing back toward dissolving the special status of Indians. The United States sought to terminate tribes through settlements to individuals, and successfully did so to many tribes, some of which, like the Menominee Nation, later sought reinstatement. US policy also incentivized Native people to leave reservation homelands for relocation in cities to access industrial jobs in the postwar recovery. By the 1970s, fully half of the Native population of the United States lived primarily off reservations in these cities, among other things fueling an intertribal American Indian identity, reconfigured religious practices, and the burgeon-ing American Indian Movement.

The 1970s also saw the beginnings of a formal policy of Indian self-determination, a policy posture that has strengthened in decades since Native people and Native nations have played an increasing role in shaping policies affecting them. The implications of self-determination policy for statutory religious and cultural protections are detailed in chapter 5, but it behooves us to reflect here on a key facet of policies of self-determination: the federal trust responsibility.

Federal Trust Responsibility

The notion of a federal trust responsibility is paternalistic on the face of it. And to be sure, the trust relationship is rooted in the metaphor, first intro-duced in *Cherokee Nation v. Georgia*, of Indian wards to their federal guard-ians. Unsurprisingly, this has provided a source of federal power, including a source of power to intervene in tribal affairs to protect the individual rights of tribal members.[70] But the trust responsibility has also offered some impor-tant legal leverage toward Native self-determination, seen most prominently perhaps when the United States litigates on behalf of tribes. Some of the most important treaty rights cases have pitted the United States on behalf of tribes against states, as in *U.S. v. Washington*, and much of the case law considered in these pages involves the United States acting legally in its trustee role. Even when the United States is the defendant in actions brought by tribes against it, the trust responsibility can serve as a legal lever for courts to hold the United States accountable to the "highest fiduciary standards" in its trustee role. David Wilkins, Vine Deloria Jr., and others, for all their criticism of the paternalism involved, observe that the trust responsibility admits of important ambiguities; it could signal guardian and ward or it could signal a fuller "protectorate" relationship between the United States and Native nations with limited inherent sovereignty. Or it could even be imagined from an Indigenous perspective as a "trust" that the other party only do "what is diplomatically agreed or consented to."[71] For some courts, it really is like the assimilation era's view of government's paternalistic power to identify what's in Native peoples' best interest subject only to honor and "good faith." But courts have increasingly held the United States legally accountable for its conduct as a fiduciary that is legally, not just morally, obligated to preserve or enhance tribal resources.[72] In 2009, a class action challenge to federal malfeasance as trustee resulted in a $3.4 billion settlement.[73]

While the federal trust responsibility applies in fairly plain legal fashion to the fiduciary management of natural and economic resources, it has also been understood to extend to cultural resources: the languages, cultures, and religions of tribes.[74] Even beyond the legal obligations of the highest fiduciary standard, the trust responsibility can be understood to encompass a federal responsibility to provide affirmative remedies for past failures as trustee in preserving and protecting Native natural and cultural resources. But rooted in treaties and the recognition that tribal governments are the third source of sovereignty in US law (with the federal and state governments), the trust relationship also distinguishes federal relationships to federally recognized tribes from its treatment of other minority populations.

Equal protection, due process, voting rights, and other civil rights challenges to this approach to federal Indian law and policy have been many. In the late 1970s, even as it was ruling otherwise in the *Bakke* case,[75] the Supreme Court made clear that it was the political, rather than racial, character of American Indian status elaborated in federal Indian law. The Supreme Court held in *Morton v. Mancari* (1974) that the Bureau of Indian Affairs' hiring preference for Indians survived challenges that it was discriminatory,[76] and its rulings in *Santa Clara Pueblo v. Martinez* (1978),[77] *United States v. Antelope*

(1977),[78] and *Washington v. Confederated Bands and Tribes of the Yakima Indian Nation* (1979) suggested that laws that "might otherwise be constitutionally offensive" might be acceptable if they are enacted pursuant to the United States' trust relationship.[79] To underscore the nonracial basis for this decision, the Supreme Court in *Morton v. Mancari* made explicit that the focus on members of federally recognized tribes, rather than on American Indians generally, suggested the political and nonracial basis for the unique relationship.

Nonrecognized Native Peoples

Among the most problematic aspects of the distinctive political status under federal Indian law is the striking exclusion of the many Native people who, for a range of reasons, are not members of federally acknowledged tribes. A Native person might be the daughter, son, or even parent, of a member of a federally recognized tribe but fail to have sufficient heritage if a given tribe is one of the many that continue to use "blood quantum" as part of its citizenship/membership criteria. Or a Native person might be a full member of one of the hundreds of peoples that are not among those formally recognized by the United States. Or that people may be among those terminated by the United States in the 1950s. That people may have been among the many that opted out of seeking recognition in the 1930s as a tribe under the Indian Reorganization Act, convinced as many were after fifty years of forced assimilation that further incorporation into government systems would only harm them. Or perhaps that people is stuck in the slow administrative process of federal acknowledgment. Many Native people feel, and rightly so, that the terms of federal recognition are not only bureaucratic but also racist, oppressive, humiliating, and irredeemably colonizing.[80]

I tell the story in chapters 5 and 6 of Native efforts to align religious freedom matters to the government-to-government structure of federal Indian law, begging questions of who is left out. Those efforts made clear attempts to include the religious freedoms for all Native Americans, not just those who count in federal Indian law. I wrestle most with this question at the end of chapter 5, but admittedly without a fully satisfying result. Chapter 4's consideration of environmental law and historic preservation law offers another legal resource in this regard, where Native peoples lacking federal recognition are not shut out from potential protections. The final chapter's consideration of Indigenous rights in international law offers the more expansive way of rethinking the law in this regard.

The Shape of the Book and Major Findings

In the service of sustaining attention to the problem of religion and religious freedom as engaged by Native peoples, I have organized the chapters not overtly in terms of the issues involved—sacred lands, repatriation of sacred items in museum collections, religious exercise in prison, and such—but in terms of the legal languages in which Native peoples make their sacred claims. These include *religion as religion* (or *spirituality* as the case may be) in religious freedom law; *religion as cultural resource* in environmental and historic preservation law; *religion as collective right* in statutory federal Indian law; and *religion as peoplehood* in domestic treaty law and in international law. Still, I cover most bases in terms of the range of religious practices to which Native peoples make those legal claims. I discuss prison religion in chapter 2; sacred lands in chapters 3 and 4; the Peyote Road in chapter 5; repatriation and ceremonial access to eagle feathers in chapter 6; and customary lifeway practices, like whaling and fishing, in chapter 7. And although I organize the book in terms of available legal languages for Native sacred claims, I strive to ensure each chapter is not beholden to judicial renderings of the Native concerns, a trap into which much of the legal studies literature falls, rooted as it is in readings of case law opinions. Still, some parts of the book are necessarily quite technical, and readers who need less technical detail are invited to make good use of introductory and concluding sections of each chapter, and to skim sections about the detailed processes, such as those under NEPA and NHPA, in order to be fresh to other moments in the book that speak to them.

The initial chapter, "Religion as Weapon," not only offers crucial historical context; it also shows just how freighted the category of *religion* can be for Native peoples. Religion, or its absence, served as a key instrument in the legalization of the dispossession of North America, first through the legal Doctrine of Christian Discovery, which continues to inform federal Indian law, and second through the criminalization of traditional religions under the federal Indian Bureau's Civilization Regulations from 1883 to 1934. As devastating as the regulations and their assemblage of civilization with a thinly veiled Protestant Christianity were, affected Native people strategically engaged religious freedom discourse to protect those threatened practices that they increasingly argued were their "religions" and protected under religious liberty. A desire to heal from historical trauma is what brought Peyotists in the 1910s to incorporate as the Native American Church; it is also how many spoke of their no-DAPL protest/ceremony. Even as the government and missionary sought to curb Native religious practices thought to retard civilization, Euro-Americans began in earnest to fantasize about a Native spirituality that they could collect, admire, and inhabit. But while this awakened Euro-American appreciation for Native cultures served to help lift the formal confines of the Civilization Regulations in the 1930s, it has continued to beset Native efforts to protect collective traditions.

Chapters 2 and 3 form a couplet of sorts as they treat straightforward claims under religious freedom law. But arguments about distinctive Native religions are shown to be haunted by the power of Euro-American desire for Native spirituality. This manner of putative respect for Native cultures has served in important cases to erode rather than sharpen an appreciation for the religiousness of Native claims to religion, and so I have titled these chapters "Religion as Spirituality." Chapter 2 considers the relative success of court decisions accommodating certain individual Native American inmates in their religious exercise in prisons, especially the sweat lodge. These cases reveal a pattern of what officials refer to as "Native American Spirituality." Especially insofar as the cases largely involve a triad of intertribal practices: sweat lodges, pipe ceremonies, and access to medicinal tobacco, sage, cedar, and sweetgrass.

Chapter 3 traces the failure, by contrast, of efforts by Native nations to secure sacred places on public lands under the First Amendment and the Religious Freedom Restoration Act. In the tracing, I query what has been so problematic about legal definitions of religion, since courts have consistently misrecognized collective claims to sacred lands as those of individuals cultivating interior spirituality. Read as a couplet, the chapters relate the legal success in prison cases and the legal failure in the sacred lands cases by the common thread coursing through both outcomes: claims to protect Native religions as *religions* are seen by the courts through the powerful lens of spirituality. Individual, voluntary, interiorized spirituality that makes few claims on the public gain entry to legal protections for Native American religious freedom. But where religion extends beyond the self, making claims on sacred lands, and on an American project based on theft of that land, spirituality alone doesn't pass legal muster. Where the redress sought concerns of collective, obligatory, and material claims, those claims fail to pass the "substantial burden" threshold, viewed simply as diminished spiritual fulfillment.

Chapter 4 considers the protections sought for "Religion as Cultural Resource," especially under environmental and historic preservation law and the complex world of cultural resource management, and considers the fine grain of the litigation in the Standing Rock case. Recognizing the importance of procedural protections under the National Environmental Policy Act and the National Historic Preservation Act, my case studies show the legal limitations of rendering the sacred in this managerial discourse of cultural resource.[81] *Culture* proves to be as indeterminate as *religion*, frustrating efforts for legal protection, but without religion's status as a power word in the Constitution.

Chapters 5 and 6 consider what Native peoples have done with the indeterminacy of religion, how they have stretched it to argue for "Religion as Collective Right." Chapter 5 considers efforts to legislate Native American religious freedom in the American Indian Religious Freedom Act (AIRFA, 1978). If the legal force of "religious freedom" discourse has been only dimly effective for Native sacred claims in courts, this chapter is the one that most pointedly shows how Native peoples drew on the rhetorical power of the sacred and religious freedom to win significant legislative protections specific to Native peoples. Interviews with Suzan Shown Harjo show how the remarkable legislative accomplishment of AIRFA and, later, the Native American Graves Protection and Repatriation Act (1990), carry the rhetorical force of religious freedom into the legal shape of federal Indian law, with its recognition of treaty-based collective rights and the United States' nation-to-nation relationship with Native peoples.

Chapter 6 follows this inquiry in the context of repatriation law and a cluster of legal cases involving possession of ceremonial eagle feathers, where courts have consistently affirmed the collective contours of Native religions. Courts have upheld an exemption to the criminal penalties for feather possession tailored to members of federally recognized tribes against legal challenges by individual practitioners of Native religions who are not members of those tribes. These cases illustrate well the difficulties and the possibilities of *religion* as a category encompassing collective Native traditions.

Chapters 7 and 8 together explore the argument for "Religion as Peoplehood," for folding claims to what is arguably religious into broader claims of tribal sovereignty under federal Indian law and Indigenous rights under international law. Chapter 7 explores landmark court cases where treaty rights are asserted for the protection of traditional places and practices. The cases involve salmon fishing and whale hunting in the Pacific Northwest, and off-reservation fishing and gathering rights in Wisconsin and Minnesota.

Chapter 8 extends this discussion of "Religion as Peoplehood" beyond the very real limits of federal Indian law, exploring the possibilities and drawbacks of increasing appeals to Indigenous rights under international human rights law. As rich as the possibilities are of the United Nations Declaration on the Rights of Indigenous Peoples and its implementation apparatus for protecting Native religions under Indigenous rights and thus without having to define them as such, the approach is slow to grow domestic legal teeth in the United States. Its incremental development as authoritative law can, I think, be strengthened by making clearer associations with US religious freedom law.

My aim in these chapters is not to pick the proper register in which to articulate claims. The question is what is lost and what is gained by thus articulating claims in each register, in different legal and political environments? Unlike academic scholars of religious studies, jurists are pragmatically driven, even obligated, to layer arguments in different registers: religious freedom, cultural resource law, federal Indian law, treaty rights, and international law.

The book concludes with a nod in the direction of successful negotiated settlements and other agreements that grab fewer headlines and leave fewer public traces because they can avoid the courts altogether and proceed in the context of the nation-to-nation relationship. For an example, I will turn to the newly created and recently embattled Bears Ears National Monument, a collaboratively managed preserve of sacred lands, cultural landscapes, and traditional knowledge in southern Utah. Since the quiet goal for most Native people is to protect what is sacred to them without calling attention to themselves, the best outcomes for Native American religious freedom are so far beyond the First Amendment and its legal counterparts they can remain entirely off line, and so it shall be fitting to end there.

1

Religion as Weapon

THE CIVILIZATION REGULATIONS, 1883–1934

Introduction: Religion as Weapon

Religion has never been a neutral category when it comes to Native traditions, much less the legal contexts in which they happen. The category of religion, in fact, has been central in the dispossession, colonization, and regulation of Native peoples. While this book centers on more recent history and contemporary law, the roots of the discussion go deep into the nineteenth century, and so this initial chapter explores how the category of religion had been weaponized and used against Native American peoples in the dispossession of their lands, languages, and cultures. Although the story begins this way, in the end it was not simply their supposed lack of religion that authorized this dispossession; it came with an insistent *spiritualization* of Native cultural riches, an equally dehumanizing, if more insidious way of laying claim to Native goods and one that continues to haunt and undermine Indigenous claims today. Scholars have long analyzed the workings of the noble savage motif and the way the *noble* and the *savage* turn out to be two sides of the same Euro-American coin. More recently, historian Tisa Wenger has shown just how important were emerging notions of Native American religion that were, on the one hand, deployed to contain the reach of Native claims and, on the other, tweaked at the margins by Native people themselves to lay claim to their own traditions as *religion*. In this chapter, I owe a tremendous debt to the careful archival work of Wenger—as well as that of Thomas Maroukis on the history of Peyotism.[1] Here, I wish to build on Wenger's analysis, paying closer attention still to the Code of Indian Offenses (1883–1934), also known commonly as the Religious Crimes Code or the Civilization Regulations, to explore how US policy deployed religion and how, in turn, Native peoples strategically engaged the language of religion in response.

It was not the distinctive shape of Native American religions, but their complete absence, that characterized early modern understandings of Native American cultures by explorers and later colonial administrators of various European powers. As the conquest and colonization process compelled moral and legal elaboration, this lack of "true religion," like the lack of law, government, and other marks of so-called civilization, rendered Native peoples savage and properly subject to European domination and/or improvement.[2] The presumption originates with several fifteenth-century papal bulls that conferred the Church's blessing on title to Christian sovereigns based on "discovery" of non-Christian lands.[3] The Reformation obviously complicated the legal force of Vatican decrees, but British law had already incorporated the spirit. Under Henry VII, the doctrine of terra nullius gave legal justification for the English monarch's absolute title to discovered lands not already in possession of a Christian monarch even if occupied by Indians according to their own customs but not in a way recognized by European law as valid. Legally, such lands were considered *terra nullius*, vacant land.

The legal Doctrine of Discovery hardwired this theological presumption that Europeans had religion and Native Americans didn't to title and underwrote the dispossession of Native lands and livelihoods.[4] European monarchs, by dint of their being Christian, enjoyed absolute title to the lands "discovered" in their name in what to them was the New World, and that peoples native to those lands enjoyed at best aboriginal rights of occupancy because of their lack of Christianity, their lack of "religion" in the parlance of the day. The doctrine was applied by Chief Justice John Marshall in a case before the Supreme Court in 1823, but tellingly the dispute was not between Native peoples and Euro-Americans. *Johnson v. M'Intosh* involved a title dispute between two white men, each having bought the same parcel of land in the Midwest.

As he lay the cornerstone of federal Indian law, Marshall wrote with a curious detachment about the doctrine he effectively called on to resolve the title dispute. "Conquest gives a title which the courts of the conqueror cannot deny," Marshall wrote for the Court, "whatever the private and speculative opinions of individuals may be respecting the original justice of the claim which has been successfully asserted."[5] He used the term "conquest" not in reference to overt military victory but rather to the Law of Nations that had emerged to settle disputes among European states to newly "discovered" lands, assigning rights to Christian sovereigns of dominion and absolute title over non-Christian lands discovered in their name. Marshall reasoned that the British assertion of absolute title came with the "the exclusive right of extinguishing the title which occupancy gave to [Indians].... It is not for the Courts of this country to question the validity of this title, or to sustain one which is incompatible with it."[6]

If Marshall made it sound like the Court's hands were tied, he managed to argue from inherent Indian savagery that it was not entirely uncouth to turn to the theological reasoning of Christian discovery. "Although we do not mean to engage in the defense of those principles which Europeans have applied to Indian title," Marshall wrote, "they may, we think, find some excuse if not justification, in the character and habits of the people whose rights have been wrested from them."[7] Even though the Native people in question led largely settled lives oriented around agriculture, representation trumped reality: they were "fierce savages, whose occupation was war, and whose subsistence was drawn chiefly from the forest." "To leave them in possession of their country was to leave the country a wilderness; to govern them as a distinct people, was impossible, because they were as brave and as high spirited as they were fierce, and were ready to repel by arms every attempt on their independence."[8] Again, there was no one in the legal proceeding to argue the case of the Indian people whose title had just been legally gutted to that of occupancy, and who had in the stroke of a pen lost an ability even to sell rights to land to whomever they wished, guaranteeing the United States could dictate the price.[9]

The theological presumption about who has religion and who doesn't later became embedded into official US Indian policy from the 1870s through the 1930s. Assimilation Policy is most widely known for the era's boarding schools, with the forced removal of Indigenous children from their families for English-only reeducation in schools run on military discipline. Also well-known is the era's allotment, a land policy that carved up communal lands on reservations secured by treaty into individually "owned" plots and that opened up surplus reservation land to non-Native settlement, resource extraction, and speculation. Our concern will be on the third prong of Assimilation Policy, the Civilization Regulations that outright criminalized Native religions for more than a half century. While their enforcement helped produce Indigenous resistance using the language of religious freedom, the regulations were crucial to government efforts to extract what was left of Native lands and lifeways. Traditions went underground, of course, and resilient peoples kept their sacred fires kindled out of view even as they took on religious freedom arguments for traditions they'd never viewed merely as religion.

The aim of this chapter is to make plain just how thoroughgoing and ramified was the outlawing of Native religious practices and to synthesize the scholarship in order to appreciate just how fraught is the category of religion and religious freedom for Native people. Acknowledging this history helps us appreciate even more fully the resourceful wherewithal of Native peoples who engaged the discourse then and now.

The criminalization of Native religions is so stunning because, as Wenger points out, it played out at the same time that Americans increasingly extolled the power and triumph of religious freedom at home and abroad.[10] How could there be such blindness to the contradiction of this governmental treatment of Native American peoples in the land of religious freedom? Part of the answer surely emerges from an ideology: savagism is to civilization as heathenism is to Christianity as no religion is to religion.[11] But it is also a function of the practice of power, a point that requires rethinking our very categories of church and state. Paul Christopher Johnson, Pamela Klassen, and Winnifred Fallers Sullivan offer a helpful theoretical framework for considering the way that settler colonialism exerted a force at once religious and political. They coin the term *churchstateness* in an effort to get at what they see as a long-standing "twinning of church and state" in the Americas, "an ill-defined yet powerful churchstateness composed of the interpenetrating and mutually constitutive forces of religion, law, and politics."[12] Johnson draws on Foucault's attention to the capillary action of power in an analysis of colonial practices in Bahia, Brazil's "indirect techniques of unmaking a people, rendering them expendable excess and legitimately sacrificeable."[13] In the capillary-like places where the edges of state power meet Indigenous peoples, state and church are not only blurred categories, sacramental and political power flows also as one in and through the bodies of subjects. Closer to home, Klassen examines the capillary action of churchstateness in the local workings of Canada's 1876 Indian Act, which corresponds to concurrent policies of assimilation in the United States. Revisions to the 1876 act outlawed the Potlatch and the Sun Dance and other ceremonies, but in the doing denied they were actually outlawing religion; churchstateness could see to having that cake and eating it too. "Casting these ceremonies as heathenism," Klassen writes, "as threatening to both the economic and political systems of Canada, the Indian

Act sought to destroy Indigenous sovereignty in part through denial of 'religion' as an operative concept for Indigenous peoples."[14]

As David Chidester shows in the case of Africa, the definitional questions that framed the contours of the early academic study of religion—what counts as religion, what doesn't, and how—were deeply imbricated with the work of the colonization of Europe's others.[15] The study of Indigenous religions, Chidester makes clear, must account for the ramifications of dispossession and erasure enabled by the intellectual edifice of religion. At the same time, Indigenous others were no fools. In their resourceful struggles against, with, and through colonization, Native peoples have appropriated the discourse of religion as a useful means of self-assertion and of defending what they hold sacred. This chapter attends to both elements of this history.

Assimilation Policy

The period of treaty-making ended abruptly in 1871 by a unilateral act of Congress.[16] Now, Indians were no longer formally considered members of nations but individuals whose assimilation to US political, economic, cultural, and religious life was seen as an educative and regulatory duty of government. But formal policies to assimilate Indians had already begun by 1869 under President Grant's Peace Policy. In part because Christianization was seen as tantamount and necessary to the American civilization to which assimilation policies were directed; in part because policy reformers came largely from (especially Protestant) Christian churches, Grant's policy relied on the leadership, not merely the cooperation, of Christian denominations. Grant created the Board of Indian Commissioners in 1869 to oversee the Indian Office, and he appointed to it officials representing the leading denominations. Grant also empowered regional church leaders to appoint Indian agents on reservations.[17] In an effort to address widespread graft and corruption among local agents in their management of treaty annuities, Grant's Peace Policy entangled churches in the work of government in a manner that baffles the imagination in a land with constitutional religious freedom.[18]

Denominational oversight of the Indian Office and appointment of Indian agents were discontinued when they ceased to be the silver bullet reformers expected, but the underlying *churchstateness* of Assimilation Policy strengthened in the ensuing decades. Indeed, the policy ideas were consistently incubated at annual Lake Mohonk conferences, which from 1884 to 1916 brought church elites together with philanthropists and government officials at an upstate New York resort as "Friends of the Indian." Their good intentions notwithstanding, the policies that emerged, and the unholy alliance involving the churches, amounted to what has been broadly considered nothing short of cultural genocide.[19]

Assimilation Policy had three key components: allotment of communal lands, boarding school education, and the Civilization Regulations. My focus here will be on the Civilization Regulations, but it is important to note the interrelationships between these policies and their unifying churchstateness. In 1874, the commissioner of Indian Affairs spoke forthrightly of the importance of churches in accomplishing his federal agency's work:

> The Indians deepest need is that which the Government, through its political organization and operations, cannot well bestow.... No amount of appropriation and no governmental machinery can do much towards lifting an ignorant and degraded people, except as it works through the willing hands of men made strong and constant by their love for their fellow men. If therefore, it shall be possible to continue the sympathy and aid of the religious people in this work, and to rally for its prosecution the enthusiasm and zeal which belong to religion ... every year will witness a steady decrease of barbarism.[20]

Allotment and Boarding Schools

Allotment became a nationwide policy under the 1887 Dawes Act, carving up communally held reservation lands and assigning them to individuals (160 acres to male heads of household, eighty acres to single adults, forty acres to those under eighteen) as a blow to "tribalism" and under the agrarian notion that a sense of private ownership and working to "improve" a particular plot of land would promote civilization. As Jennifer Graber shows, allotment was no land policy alone. Missionaries and Lake Mohonk elites celebrated it as a breakthrough for Christianization, as many felt that private property and the plow would clear ground for the Christian faith.[21]

Not coincidentally, the division of vast reservation lands into a relatively small number parcels opened up sizeable amounts of "surplus" lands available for non-Native settlement. The theft of such lands reserved by treaties was conceived instead as educational, giving Native people on the reservation non-Native neighbors as living examples of "civilized" agrarian, patriarchal, Christian homes. Even those lands allotted to Native peoples ill-suited to agriculture or fractionated as allottees died intestate proved vulnerable to the exploits of timber and mining interests and land speculators. Many Native leaders saw this coming. Graber details the story of Kiowa resistance to allotment of their reservation, again not simply as a land policy but as an assault on treaty rights and on everything the Kiowa Nation was doing to survive. Led by Lone Wolf, the Kiowa fought allotment all the way to the Supreme Court, but lost in a 1903 decision that recognized Congress's "plenary power" over Indian affairs, and freed the allotment act from any judicial constraints citing treaty law, subject only to the United States' good faith.[22]

The results were catastrophic. By 1934, roughly two-thirds of the reservation land base had passed out of Native hands, and many nations, their legal sovereignty restored, struggle still to control a meaningful share of the lands, including sacred sites, enclosed on their reservations.[23] White Earth Ojibwe own only about 8 percent of their own thirty-mile-square reservation; some of the social factionalism that came with allotment still afflicts the community.[24]

The second major prong of Assimilation Policy, boarding school education, also served to break up the social fabric of Native communities.[25] Captain Richard Henry Pratt founded Carlisle Indian School in 1879 based on his motto, *Kill the Indian to Save the Man*, and Lake Mohonk reformers were thrilled with the model of removing children from home, family, elders, and land and educating them in residential schools drawing on military discipline, corporal punishment, and education. In 1883, the schools were uniformly made English-only and children were punished and publicly humiliated for speaking their own languages. Pratt said in his memoir *The Battlefield and the Classroom*: "In Indian civilization I am a Baptist, because I believe in immersing the Indians in our civilization and when we get them under holding them there until they are thoroughly soaked."[26]

As Pratt's alarming comment suggests, the churchstateness of the boarding schools was not simply a matter of using Christian materials in their curricula. Between 1882 and 1892, roughly half were run directly by denominations under contract with the Indian Office, funded by an average of $463,000 in taxpayer dollars—at least $12 million in 2018 dollars.[27] What brought an end to the denominational contract school model was not concern over blurring of church and state, but rather the professionalization of educational principles. Indeed, any religious freedom challenges to boarding school allocations conformed to Catholic and Protestant disputes about government giving the other party the upper hand.

Civilization

Allotment, boarding schools, and the Civilization Regulations were part of what Tisa Wenger refers to a "civilizational assemblage." Assimilation Policy enacted the faith that Christian belief and practices were of a piece with Anglo-American culture, the English language, government, agrarianism, Victorian gender roles and manners of regulating sex, marriage and family life, management of time, thrift, foodways, forms of hair length and dress, hygiene, and architecture. Like the *churchstateness* that flows in the capillary action of assimilation, the notion of a civilizational assemblage is helpful to understanding the criminalization of Native religious practices, for the Civilization Regulations were not *overtly* or manifestly targeting the wrong "religion" or even just an obstacle to Christian conversion. Indeed, for much of the period, the practices weren't recognized as even religious. Rather, the threat of those practices was in their excess, their capacity to exceed the bounds of religion proper into medicine, economy, and polity. What was seen as inimical to civilization was what transgressed the boundaries that civilization was imposing on "religion."

This helps understand why the criminalization of Native religions was seen as so crucial to the bringing of regulation and government to reservations. For even as Assimilation Policy began to regard Native peoples as individuals rather than collectives, as potential citizens of the United States rather than citizens of Native nations, reservations had become legal vacuums of sorts. "Civilization has loosened, in some places broken, the bonds which regulate and hold together Indian society in its wild state," an Episcopal missionary bishop in South Dakota pointed out in 1877, observing that civilization had "failed to give the people law and officers of justice in their place."[28]

We turn now to the system of Civilization Regulations advocated by missionaries and assimilation-minded officers of the Indian Bureau to serve this purpose. It behooves us here to concentrate on these regulations, their legality, and their enforcement because they form the legal scaffolding around religious repression and cultural trauma that recent US law and policy has decried and sought to redress.

Civilization Regulations

There is a reason that the Code of Indian Offenses, drawn up in the regulatory law of the Indian Office in 1883, came to be called the Civilization Regulations, but also eventually the Religious Crimes Code, because the practices thus criminalized we would rightly call religious in nature; they were seen to hold a power equivalent to that of religion.[29] The document commissioning the regulations came from a directive from the secretary of the interior in 1882. "I desire to call your attention to what I regard as a great hindrance to the civilization of the Indians," wrote Secretary Henry Teller to the Commissioner of Indian Affairs Hiram Price;

> Viz., the continuance of the old heathenish dances, such as the sun-dance, scalp-dance, etc. These dances, or feasts, as they are sometimes called, ought, in my judgment, to be discontinued, and if the Indians now supported by the Government are not willing to discontinue them, the agents should be instructed to compel such discontinuance.[30]

"Active measures should be taken, the secretary proclaimed, "to discourage all feasts and dances of the character I have mentioned."[31] In addition to heathenish dances, the secretary singled out for action what he regarded as disordered Native sexual and marriage practices, the practices of medicine men, and "giveaways" and potlatches that honored the dead through ritualized generosity and gift giving. On the face of it, all were targeted not because they represented false religion—though such a view drove the logic at a generative deeper level—but because they were "hindrances to civilization."[32] "The value of property as an agent of civilization ought not to be overlooked," Secretary Teller wrote of giveaways:

> One great obstacle to the acquirement of property by the Indian is the very general custom of destroying or distributing his property on the death of a member of his family. Frequently on the death of an important member of the family all the property accumulated by its head is destroyed or carried off by the "mourners," and his family left in desolation and want.[33]

"Another great hindrance to the civilization of the Indians is the influence of the medicine men," Teller continued. "The medicine men resort to various artifices and devices to keep the people under their influence, and are especially active in preventing the attendance of the children at the public schools, using their conjurers' arts to prevent the people from abandoning their heathenish rites and customs."[34]

Secretary Teller then made the policy statement that would regulate Native religions for over fifty years:

> I therefore suggest whether it is not practicable to formulate certain rules for the government of the Indians on the reservations that shall restrict and ultimately abolish the practices I have mentioned.[35]

In response, the commissioner of Indian Affairs drew up regulations approved in April 1883, not only authorizing but also directing Indian agents to "see to it that the requirements thereof are strictly enforced with the view of having the evil practices mentioned by the honorable Secretary ultimately abolished." Those rules were revised in 1892 and again in 1904, but despite decreasing anxieties about the continuation of those practices in the Commissioner of Indian Affairs Annual Reports (apart from marriage regulations) the enumerated religious crimes remained unchanged as codified until they were rescinded in 1934.[36]

Courts of Indian Offenses

The rules established Courts of Indian Offenses to be made up of three judges appointed by the local Indian agent from among the first three officers of the local Indian Police, which had been established in the late 1870s. In this they became not only police but also judges, empowered to arrest anyone they suspected of violating the crimes. The courts were not only appointed by the agent; they served entirely at his pleasure. The agent could reject their decisions. Appeals came to the agent, subject only to an appeal to the Indian Office in Washington. And on those reservations where an agent didn't find them useful, or where he couldn't recruit tribal members to serve on them, Courts of Indian Offenses were simply not empaneled, leaving the agent to hear disputes himself and to dispatch the Indian Police as he saw fit. The regulations did not require the courts to keep a written record of their proceedings, and indeed most of the work of these tribunals stayed below the radar.

Rule 3 empowered a court to offer judgment on "all such questions as maybe presented to it for consideration by the agent, or by his approval," and gave it original jurisdiction on the enumerated "Indian offenses" that constituted the religious crimes of concern here: dances, ceremonies, practices of medicine men, funerary giveaways, and customary marriage practices. The ninth and final rule gave the courts jurisdiction over misdemeanors, civil suits among Indians, and drunkenness or distributing liquor. But the core of the regulations were those on the five enumerated "Indian offenses," and they specified a range of punishments from withholding annuity payments from entitled tribal members under the treaties to fines or confiscation of property, to hard labor, to imprisonment. Detailed consideration of each shows the *churchstateness* flowing through the code; later critics justly referred to it as the Religious Crimes Code.[37]

Dances and Feasts

Rule 4 criminalized "the 'sun-dance,' the 'scalp dance,' the 'war-dance,' and all other so called feasts assimilating thereto." Offenders' rations were to be withheld for up to a month and/or they were to be jailed for up to a month. At issue was not only the bodily movements, the drum, and musical repertoires thought to hinder civilization but also the protracted time obligations of the ceremonial complexes, as indicated by the criminalization of "the feasts assimilating thereto." Secretary Teller's authorizing letter was affixed to the 1883 regulations to add further clarifications to the administrative law. These dances, the secretary wrote, are "not social gatherings for the amusement of these people" but "intended and calculated to stimulate the warlike passions of the young warriors of the tribe." He styled the dances in question as "continuations of the old heathenish dances," and the stimulated passions, read as warlike, were forms of religiosity deemed excessive, embodied, and collective and requiring regulation.[38]

This is the reason for the singling out of the Sun Dance, the preeminent ceremony of many nations of the Plains and Great Basin. Although Sun Dances were, and still are, complex multilayered ceremonies involving a range of practices bringing cosmic, social, and personal renewal, missionaries and Indian Bureau officials fixated on the sacrificial practice of Sun Dancers who pierce their chests or back and dance tethered to the central pole until their flesh tears free.[39] As concerning to officials was the very fact of Indigenous assembly occasioned by the Sun Dance, which often brought Native people together across band and reservation boundaries for protracted periods and in orbit around Indigenous religious authority.

Medicine Men

Rule 6 criminalized "usual practices of so called medicine-men," especially where the influence or practice "operates as a hindrance to the civilization of a tribe," "resorts to any artifice or device to keep the Indians under his influence," serves to "prevent the attendance of children at the agency schools," or "prevents the Indians from abandoning their heathenish rites and customs." When found guilty of these practices "or any other in the opinion of the court of an equally anti-progressive nature," courts were to detain medicine men for no less than ten days or until the court and agent were persuaded "he will forever abandon all practices."

Practices associated with medicine people varied by Native nation; they could involve herbal healing, ceremonial doctoring, divination, spiritual and ritual direction, and the charismatic authority and religious generativity of powerful visions and dreams. Along with their ability to command a following and present competition with other forms of authority, medicine people represented a violation of the boundary distinguishing religion from secularizing domains like medicine. Indian Office physicians could regard medicine people as competitors, at once cunning frauds and competent healers, especially when it came to orthopedic issues and herbal healing. "Some of their remedies are extremely efficacious," wrote J. M. Woodburn, the physician at Rosebud in 1889, adding that many cases were "very successfully managed by them, unforeseen conditions arising being met by promptness really commendable."[40] But he noted they numbered among "my most numerous patients," seeking tips and goods from his apothecary, "and should their cunning prevail and prescription given be of service, of course all credit would be ascribed to their own "tom-tom" and "noisy doings." Dr. Woodburn hastened to point out that medicine men were only as authoritative as their success would commend, "exerting influence and commanding only during the progress of a treatment, at which time they become superlatively the head of the household." In the end, Woodburn thought, his kind of medicine would prevail, the medicine man's days being "numbered."[41]

Funerary Giveaways and Potlatches

Indigenous religious excess was also seen to violate the boundary of private property. Many Native peoples have funerary tradition—giveaways or potlatches—to honor the dead and contend with grief through ritualized gift giving and even sacrificial offering of the property of the deceased. These practices were especially vexing for assimilationists professing their faith in the civilizing power of private property. Rule 7 masked the religious obligations of these funerary traditions by simply identifying the offense as the destruction or theft of property, but circled back to add "it shall not be considered a sufficient or satisfactory answer to any of the offenses set forth in this rule that the party charged was at the time a 'mourner,' and thereby justified in taking or destroying the property in accordance with the customs or rites of the tribe." Offenders were to return the property, or if it were ceremonially sacrificed/destroyed, pay back the value and in any case be imprisoned for up to thirty days.

Where the penalty is stiff, the persistence must also be. "No custom," the agent at Pine Ridge found in 1888, "is more pernicious in its effects or more difficult to break up than that of giving away and destruction of property at the death of a member of the family." "Their respect for the custom is so great," he noted, that he had used "every possible means ... to induce at least a modification of the order," but he redoubled his resolve to "make war" on the practice.[42]

Customary Practices of Marriage

Two other rules criminalized forms of customary marriage that also were seen to hinder civilization. Rule 5 on "Plural Marriage" criminalized "any plural marriage hereafter contracted or entered into" by Indians, and offenders were to pay fines of "not less than twenty dollars"—something closer to $500 today—or hard labor for twenty days. Unrepentant offenders would also forfeit all treaty rations for as long as they "continue in this unlawful relation." Conjoined to the logic of this rule was not simply the continuation of polygamous or polyandrous marriage systems but also a desire to criminalize any customary marriage or divorce that departed from Victorian norms of monogamous marriage for life. Courts could order the withholding of treaty annuities from a tribal member who "fails, without proper cause, to support his wife and children." Rule 8, styled "Immorality" in its 1892 iteration, criminalized the payment or offer to pay "any money or other valuable consideration to the friends or relatives of any Indian girl or woman, for the purpose of living or cohabiting," a way of putting the matter that made dowry-like practices, themselves forms of social regulation, seem little more than blatant prostitution.[43]

Indian Office documents throughout the period of Assimilation Policy are rife with references to the vexing nature of continuing Indigenous traditions of marriage and family. In 1901, the Indian Office released new regulations directing agents to issue marriage licenses after scrutinizing whether any current husband or wife was still living and not formally divorced, and to keep a scrupulous record of marriage transactions. The stated reason for the regulations was to keep track of heirship of allotments, but clearly the effort was also meant to step up regulation of customary marriage and divorce. In addition to these reissued regulations, the Indian Office issued the "Short Hair Order" in 1902, directing field agents to take necessary steps to discourage long hair among men and to enforce against any face painting.

The Legality of the Civilization Regulations

The criminalization of religious and customary traditional practices could be particularly effective in the difficult years of life on reservations in the late nineteenth and early twentieth centuries. Traditional economies were difficult to sustain on reduced reservations, many of them further decimated by logging or other extractive industries. Withholding rations or exacting cash fines, much less imprisoning people or conscripting forced unpaid labor, was an effective assault on traditional religious practices under these circumstances.

None of this conformed to legal standards for courts and criminal law under the Constitution, but it didn't seem to matter under the Supreme Court's broader legalization of challenged facets of Assimilation Policy.[44] The Constitution assigns powers to the legislative, not the executive, branch, to make law or to create courts, and Congress never formally delegated these powers to the Indian Office. What's more, there was precious little distinction between the empaneled courts, the Indian Police, whose officers sat on the courts, and the Indian agent who could order arrests himself. As Kevin Gover put it: "Conduct by an Indian that had not been prohibited by any legislature became a criminal offense by the word of the Secretary and subjected Indians to deprivations of liberty and property. That's an extraordinary thing in our legal system and yet it was upheld with only minimal comment by the federal courts."[45]

The legal tenuousness of Courts of Indian Offenses is tangible in the annual reports of those charged with their operation. Commissioners of Indian Affairs repeatedly called for congressional action to place the courts and the Code of Indian Offenses on a firmer basis.[46] At the same time, these commissioners argued that the appropriation of $5,000 to pay the judges constituted sufficient congressional intent to allay any legal arguments that the courts had no lawful basis. When a constitutional challenge did emerge, a federal court upheld the courts on the basis of the paternalistic, educative purposes of the reservation system. In *U.S. v. Clapox* (1888), a federal judge in Oregon rejected a challenge to the lawfulness of a Umatilla woman's imprisonment for adultery under the Civilization Regulations.[47] The judge agreed Courts of Indian Offenses "are not constitutional courts" but nonetheless viewed them as valid "educational and disciplinary instrumentalities" by which the United States is "endeavoring to improve and elevate the condition of these dependent tribes to whom it sustains the relation of guardian."[48] The court found that the Umatilla had, by signing the Treaty of 1855, agreed to submit to all laws, rules, and regulations made by the United States.[49] "In fact," the judge added, "the reservation itself is in the nature of a school, and the Indians are gathered there, under the charge of an agent, for the purposes of acquiring the habits, ideas, and aspirations which distinguish the civilized from the uncivilized man."[50]

Although the decision was made at the lowest level of the federal court system, David Wilkins draws on these narrative moves in *U.S. v. Clapox* as emblematic of the "masking of justice," where the law functions crucially to narratively mask not only the political process it legitimizes but also to impose "legal constructs which suppress the humanity of a participant in the process."[51] As Matthew Fletcher writes, the courts took the metaphor of ward and guardian that appeared ad hoc in earlier Supreme Court decisions without elaboration and made "it the law of land."[52]

Enforcement and Religious Freedom Resistance

The Civilization Regulations remained in force and largely unchanged until 1934, but the story of their enforcement is varied and complex, in part because of deference to the discretion of the local Indian agent, and in part because even as courts they were not required to keep detailed records. To fully reckon with the reach of these courts and the criminalization of Native religious and cultural practices would require its own book-length study. Here, I'll simply make several soundings into illustrative moments about their enforcement cited in Indian Office reports.

First of all, not all agents availed themselves of the courts. Some, like Pine Ridge agent H. D. Gallagher, preferred to "settle all difficulties among the Indians myself" rather than to empanel a Court of Indian Offenses, where he would have to "be involved anyway" to get at the facts.[53] Others revealed that they had too much difficulty recruiting tribal members for the work, especially with so little pay. "At some of the agencies," Commissioner John Atkins observed, "it has been found impracticable to establish these courts for the fact that good men cannot be found who are willing to serve as judges without compensation."[54] Between the lines may be found the logic: *You couldn't pay me enough to do that.*

Native peoples under reservation agents who did not empanel the courts were hardly free to practice their traditions. These agents were both authorized and directed to use their Indian Police to punish those practicing criminalized traditions. And commissioners of Indian Affairs continued to commend the model of the tribunals to their agents in the field. When he took the helm of the Indian Office, T. J. Morgan in 1889 found the courts "a tentative and somewhat crude attempt to break up superstitious practices, brutalizing dances, plural marriages, and kindred evils," but "notwithstanding their imperfections and primitive character, these so-called courts have been of great benefit to the Indians and of material assistance to the agents."[55] Morgan sought a fivefold increase in the appropriation to expand them.

Although the courts were not required to keep records, Indian agents' annual reports to the commissioner often tallied the number of cases and sometimes broke them down by offense. At the Nez Perce Reservation, for example, guilty verdicts of drunkenness and assaults were consistent over the first decade of the regulations, but so too were verdicts of adultery, with as many as six per year. Plural marriage, especially in the first four years of the regulations, appeared regularly, and seven guilty verdicts were recorded against medicine man practices in 1886 (out of a total of forty criminal cases that year).[56] But at Nez Perce as elsewhere, there appears to be underreporting of dance, medicine men, and funerary gifting.

The Standing Rock Reservation offers another illuminating example. Agent James McLaughlin made ample use of the Court of Indian Offenses, most famously in the pursuit of Sitting Bull for his involvement in the Ghost Dance in the spring of 1890, and his eventual assassination by Indian Police in the chain of events that led to the massacre at Wounded Knee soon thereafter. The Standing Rock court met every other week in a separate room at the agency police headquarters. Seated as judges through 1888 were the two officers of the Indian Police and a Sihásapa Lakota leader, Charging Bear, or John Grass. McLaughlin praised Grass as "a man of excellent judgment who spoke English, was in favor of allotments and boarding schools, wore 'citizens dress,' and 'conforms to the white man's ways.'"[57] In 1889, McLaughlin replaced the police officers with two other leaders. Gall was a leader of the Hunkpapa Lakota who spoke only Lakota and who was not in favor of allotments, but who wore "citizen's dress" and was in favor of the schools. The third was Standing Soldier of the Lower Yanktonais. All three stopped serving in March 1890, and the court returned to Indian Police control.

In his 1890 report for the previous year, McLaughlin tallied ninety-one criminal cases decided by the Standing Rock court, enumerating them as follows:

Adultery, 8; assault, 9; attempt at rape, 10; taking second wife, 3, taking second husband, 2; elopement with another man's wife, 3; desertion of wife and family by husband, 7; desertion of husband and family by wife, 3; seduction, 1; resisting arrest by police, 6; abusive language, 2; maiming cattle, 3; malicious lying, 1; evil speaking, 1; wife beating, 1; offering insult to married woman, 4; selling rations, 2; drunkenness 2; larceny, 4; family quarrels incompatibility, etc., 19.[58]

It is revealing that one-third of offenders arguably were found guilty of observing traditional Lakota customs of marriage and divorce. It is also revealing how few references there are in this year to more demonstrably religious crimes: giveaways, dances, and medicine man practices. At Standing Rock as at other reservations, these were likely prosecuted and punished more directly under the agent rather than brought before the court. They may also have been seen as unobjectionable to judges like Charging Bear, Gall, or Standing Soldier. Agents interested in efficient prosecution of the Indian Office's directive to stamp out these "hindrances to civilization" could and did undertake them on their own authority for efficiency's sake—who would need to bring witnesses to establish whether a funerary giveaway or a healing or a Sun Dance had transpired?

Tom Frosted, Medicine Man

The 1887 story of one arrested and imprisoned medicine man at Standing Rock may reveal something about these "legal" processes, especially since no mention of him appears in McLaughlin's report to the commissioner of that year, even in his discussion of the fifty-two cases heard by the Court of Indian Offenses. A striking 1888 photograph of Frosted, a Yanktonais Dakota dreamer and medicine man, tethered to a ball and chain in front of a Fort Yates prison, became something of a cause célèbre, with copies turning up in historical societies in North Dakota, Colorado, Montana, and Minnesota.

Although an obituary in a local paper identified him as a Catholic, married in the church in 1880,[59] he continued to practice traditional Dakota ceremonies of vision-seeking and healing and had earned the enmity of the priest, who viewed his "infernal incantations" as "literally raising the devil."[60] Frosted had found a meaningful practice of both traditions in these years and clearly had developed a following that led the priest to regard him with jealousy and contempt as a "devil dreamer."

According to an 1888 military report, Frosted was met with a vision that a Crow party was approaching Standing Rock to attack while the main chiefs were away. He persuaded 150 young warriors to take arms and to confront the

Frosted

FIG. 1.1. Tom Frosted Detained at Standing Rock
Yanktonais medicine man Mato Ska (Tom Frosted) was detained at Fort Yates
in 1888 in violation of the Civilization Regulations. Photograph by D. F. Barry.
(Courtesy Montana Historical Society Research Center)

envisioned Crow off the reservation before they could attack the Standing Rock camps. Leaving the reservation was an offense in itself, and the acting agent ordered the Eighth Cavalry to compel the party to return to the reservation from the lands just north of the Cannonball River (near where the no-DAPL encampment would took place). Frosted was arrested and detained in the Fort Yates prison.[61] While in the guardhouse, Frosted claimed that he had the sacred power to make the Standing Rock, the sacred stone over the Missouri River for which the reservation was named, come to him, and the acting agent scoffed that he would be set free if he could.[62]

Frosted's story suggests a way to think about enforcement of the Civilization Regulations as they pertain to traditional religious practices. What's clear is the threat that traditional visionary knowledge and those recognized with authority based on that knowledge could pose to missionary and Indian Office authorities. Tolerated to a point, if those practices raised issues of authority and governance they could attract sufficient attention and be prosecuted under the regulations. What is striking about Frosted's story is his proximity to "Christian civilization" and the urgency of policing boundaries between that civilization and the continuation of traditional practices. The widely circulated picture figures him as medicine man in ball and chain for his crimes, but subsequent pictures of Frosted and his obituary reveal that he joined the Standing Rock Indian Police two years later, rising through the ranks to become part of a delegation to Washington in 1912. He became a county constable in 1914, helped recruit Native men for service in World War I, and continued to perform naming ceremonies.[63]

Agent McLaughlin's most notorious use of the Code of Indian Offenses, however, was his order for the Indian Police to arrest the traditional resistance leader Sitting Bull for his leadership of the Ghost Dance, which swept through the reservations in the Dakotas in the late summer and fall of 1890. The Ghost Dance has its own complex history, beginning in Nevada during a solar eclipse the previous year with the visions of Wovoka, a Paiute ranch hand and holy man. In obedience to his vision, Wovoka taught a repertoire of sacred song and sacred dance that would ritually regenerate a new world for Native peoples and return the dead to life. The Ghost Dance spread like wildfire across the Great Basin and the Plains, in a story that has been told and retold, often in a tragic register.[64] Tragic, indeed, for struggles over the Ghost Dance wound up in the bloody snows of the Wounded Knee Massacre in December 1890, with its iconic photos of the frozen bodies of the slaughtered noncombatants.

McLaughlin considered Sitting Bull to be the hub of his Ghost Dance problems, the "high priest and leading apostle of this latest Indian absurdity."[65] The ceremonial dance was to McLaughlin menacing for several reasons. First, as is well known, he took the position of military authorities that the Ghost Dance was more sedition than ceremony, likely to ignite armed conflict. And Sitting Bull had consistently led the opposition to the reservation's survey and allotment. Second, the Ghost Dance movement called into question the success of the assimilation program. The "infection," as McLaughlin regarded it, "has been ... so pernicious that it now includes some of the Indians who were formerly numbered with the progressive and more intelligent, and many of the very best Indians appear dazed and undecided when talking of it, their inherent superstition having been thoroughly aroused."[66] The protracted time of the ceremony and its encampment away from the agency, and away from labor too, raised concern.

Although the path to the Wounded Knee Massacre by the Seventh Cavalry makes it sound like a military matter from the beginning, the agent was empowered to act by the Civilization Regulations. This seemed to him the very epitome of the usefulness of the criminalization of the practices. "A great many Indians," he wrote, "become silly and like men intoxicated over the excitement. The dance is demoralizing, indecent, and disgusting."[67]

In October 1890, people at Standing Rock were performing the Ghost Dance. On October 9, Sitting Bull sponsored a dance led by Kicking Bear, and having heard from agents at Pine Ridge and Rosebud, McLaughlin sent thirteen Indian Police led by two officers to arrest Kicking Bear and escort him from the reservation, "but they returned without executing the order, both officers being in a dazed condition and fearing the powers of Kicking Bear's medicine."[68] McLaughlin reported that Sitting Bull was "determined to continue the Ghost Dance as the Great Spirit had sent a direct message by Kicking Bear that to live they must do so," but he conceded that he would come to the agency to speak about the matter before continuing any dancing. But the dance had resumed by October 17, and McLaughlin asked that the military get involved and confine Sitting Bull and his entourage in a military prison "some distance from the Sioux country." Commissioner of Indian Affairs T. J. Morgan concurred, and President Benjamin Harrison dispatched the military to Pine Ridge.

At Standing Rock, under McLaughlin's direction, the Indian Police under Lieutenant Bullhead went to Sitting Bull's camp to arrest him, "with United

States troops within supporting distance." In a skirmish, the Indian Police shot Sitting Bull dead.[69] Chaos ensued and the army responded. Many Sioux, even those not involved with the Ghost Dance, fled to the Badlands and were encircled. The Cheyenne River Ghost Dancers led by Bigfoot were pursued and despite their willingness to surrender were brutally massacred, 150 men and 230 women and children, at Wounded Knee Creek on December 29, 1890. Military officers were dispatched to oversee the Sioux agencies.

For McLaughlin, the Ghost Dance was an Indian offense as much as it was a new religious movement. But dancers, like those at Pine Ridge, had considered their ceremonial obligations as a "religious dance."[70] And some of this appeal came from aligning the Ghost Dance with the Christian church. As Wenger reports, a Ghost Dance leader said in the wake of the Wounded Knee Massacre, "this dance was like religion; it was religious."

> Those who brought the dance here from the West said that to dance was the same as going to Church.... The Messiah told us to send our children to school, to work our farms all the time, and to do the best we could. We and our children could dance and go to church too; that would be like going to two churches.[71]

James Mooney, the government ethnologist who interrupted other research to spend three years researching and reporting on the Ghost Dance, framed the movement, as the title of his magisterial 1896 study suggested, as *The Ghost Dance Religion*. Mooney aligned the Ghost Dance with numerous millenarian movements within Christian history and included chapters on the many specific prophetic movements sweeping across tribal lines in Native North America, including the Shaker Church, a movement following the Indigenous prophet Smohalla and distinct from the Shakers of New England.[72] Wenger observes that Mooney's boss at the Smithsonian, John Wesley Powell, published *The Ghost Dance Religion* with reservations, cautioning readers about "comparing or contrasting religious movements among civilized peoples with such fantasies as that described in the memoir."[73]

But the question of whether and how Native American traditions—especially those formally prohibited by US administrative law—counted as religion, was by then no longer an academic question. For Native American leaders—many of them putting their boarding school educations to good use—were already engaging the language of religious freedom in order to continue to practice their traditions and getting considerable traction, in turn prompting a retrenchment of the Civilization Regulations. We turn now to two major examples of this engagement in the early twentieth century: the Peyote movement and the Pueblo dance controversies.

The Peyote Road

Following his work on the Ghost Dance, James Mooney turned his attention next to the Peyote movement. Peyote, the harvested button of a cactus native to the border region of South Texas and Northern Mexico, has a long tradition among the Huichol, whose traditional lifeway was oriented significantly around pilgrimages to the Peyote Gardens and ceremonies related to the plant.[74] Like the Ghost Dance, the Peyote Road spread rapidly on the Southern Plains, with a lineage that ran through Lipan Apache spiritual leaders but that was also directed by visionary experiences of the Comanche Quanah Parker. Almost from the beginning, Peyotism involved a range of variations of teaching and ritual practice, each fusing a range of Christian forms and ideas, but brought healing, renewal, and a tangible power to peoples beleaguered by loss and disease. Peyote ceremonies share elements of purification, protracted prayer, arrangements of sacred altars, songs and ritual gestures that are regarded as spiritual directions received through visions. With the regulated ritual structure led by a Road Man, ceremonial ingestion of Peyote, which adherents respectfully regard as Medicine, Power, Teacher, Healer, Sacrament, can bring new revelations, healing, and restored community. In difficult times of confinement to reservations and subjection to agents and policies of the United States, many early adherents found the Peyote Road offered an ethical system and a means for self-regulation and hope in the midst of disease, disruption, and trauma. Its critics, then as now, could see little to the Peyote Road except what chemists would call a hallucinogen.

The history of Peyotism's spread has been told over and again, most recently in Thomas Maroukis's detailed *The Peyote Road: Religious Freedom and the Native American Church.*[75] As Maroukis's title suggests, even more than the Ghost Dance, followers of the Peyote Road engaged the discourse of religious freedom to push back against efforts by Indian agents and missionaries and other assimilationists, including some Native people, to create space for the practice of their ceremonies.

From the time it appeared in field agent reports in 1886, the Indian Bureau regarded Peyote as a serious threat.[76] Commissioner of Indian Affairs (CIA) T. J. Morgan in 1890 identified Peyote as an intoxicant and directed agents and Courts of Indian Offenses to prosecute its use or sale.[77] Subsequent commissioners in the 1900s and 1910s singled out Peyotism as a matter of major concern, viewing it through the lens of intemperance and also through the lens of ritual excess, of what they saw as a demoralizing "enthusiasm" that distracted Native people from the work of civilization. In 1899, Indian Office pressure pushed the Oklahoma Territorial Legislature to outlaw possession, trade, and use of Peyote, sometimes called mescal beans, with fines of twenty-five to two hundred dollars.[78] But absent a federal law prohibiting Peyote, Indian agents had difficulty enforcing their concerns under the Civilization Regulations alone. Moving such legislation was among the increasing obsessions of the CIA annual reports. In the meantime, the Indian Office used all the tools at its disposal. A major crusader against Peyote was William "Pussyfoot" Johnson, whom Theodore Roosevelt had appointed to enforce regulations against alcohol on reservations.[79] "The legislation outlawing intoxicants on reservations did not mention Peyote," Maroukis notes, "but Johnson took it upon himself to interpret the law to include Peyote," and he had strong backers in the capital.[80]

These efforts met with an equally determined effort on the part of Peyote Road practitioners to represent their tradition as a religion, especially in terms of its Christian content, and to claim general protection for their Peyote within the discourse of religious freedom. When Oklahoma attained statehood, Quanah Parker appeared before a committee of its constitutional convention in order to lift the territorial legislature's ban on Peyote. "I do not think this Legislature should interfere with a man's religion," Parker argued, adding that Peyote promoted health and helped address alcoholism. These arguments carried the day, and the territorial prohibition was repealed.[81] Nevada, Colorado, and Utah passed anti-Peyote laws, but state laws did not apply to reservations.[82]

Local enforcement against Peyotists continued in varied ways. As part of his effort to restrict the supply, Pussyfoot Johnson boasted that his enforcement unit had bought and destroyed nearly 200,000 Peyote buttons.[83] Officials at the Yankton Reservation in South Dakota didn't stop with facilitating Johnson's efforts to take down the supply chain. A series of agency superintendents reported in 1911 and 1912 that they were detaining tribal members who were merely present at the ceremonies until they signed "a statement to the effect that they will quit the use of Peyote and its attendant practices."[84] The Civilization Regulations, recently revised in 1904, continued to direct enforcement against such ceremonial hindrances to civilization. But Maroukis observes that the Indian Bureau took issue with the incarceration of Peyotists. For one official, "the mere fact of holding such meetings or the use of peyote or mescal cannot be considered an offense."[85] At Yankton, the superintendent nonetheless hastened to "continue a policy of harassment and confiscation of peyote buttons until the religion was stamped out."[86]

Tensions between the field office and the Indian Office in Washington may very well have been because Peyotist leaders had taken their religious freedom arguments to Indian Office officials in Washington in an effort to change the policy. Albert Hensley, the Ho-Chunk (Winnebago) spiritual leader who developed the "Cross Fire" variant stressing that ceremonial Peyote ingestion offered privileged insight into biblical truth, told federal officials that Peyotism, like other forms of Christianity, was a wholesome factor in promoting sobriety, community, and ethical relations.[87] The Indian Office "relented slightly by allowing Peyotists to possess a small number of Peyote buttons for personal use."[88] It may have helped that Congress passed a 1912 exemption of communion wine from other Indian Country liquor laws.[89]

But as calls for prohibition stepped up, so did the resolve of the Indian Office to block the Peyote Road. In a detailed discussion of government chemists' analysis, Commissioner of Indian Affairs Leupp in 1909 stressed that any "beautiful visions" experienced, even with "great elevation of spirit and a feeling of good will toward all mankind," were about chemicals, not religion. After the "artificial paradise" wore off, he wrote, "lassitude" took over, and continued use "deprived the user of mental and physical rigor." "Apparently for the purpose of justifying the use of this narcotic," the commissioner reasoned, "a religious cult has been built up based on its use."[90] Leupp and his successor called on Congress to enact a specific prohibition on Peyote, to untie their hands at enforcement on reservations. Things came to a head in 1918, when after colorful hearings with voices for and against Peyotism, the House passed a bill that included Peyote in the liquor traffic laws. But according to Maroukis's detailed account of the proceedings, it never passed the Senate to become law because Peyotist leaders had successfully lobbied Oklahoma's senators to lead opposition to it.[91]

In response to the House vote, Peyotists' intellectual argument for religious freedom evolved to a structural one as practitioners incorporated formally as churches. Certain congregations had already incorporated as churches at a small scale, but in August 1918, Peyote leaders from across Oklahoma convened to incorporate. Counseled by James Mooney—the Smithsonian ethnologist who had attended numerous Peyote ceremonies and who had testified in the congressional hearings—they formally incorporated as the Native American Church.[92] Again, it was not Mooney's idea initially to form as churches; there had been others before, but at this August 1918, meeting, the choices were particularly strategic. Maroukis found in an oral history with a Kiowa-Apache man that it was Mooney who recommended the name "Native American Church," but it was the group that selected an organizational structure for the church and that took pains to make a "clear articulation of Peyote as a sacrament," which previous churches had not done.[93] Approved by Oklahoma in October, this charter became the model for incorporation elsewhere.

Still, Indian Bureau obsession with Peyote continued, renewed by Charles Burke, a former South Dakota congressman who took over as commissioner of Indian Affairs in 1922. Given that only 4 percent of Indians were Peyotists, Maroukis understands the obsession with Peyote to be not just its association with intoxication, but because the tradition so resolutely drew on Indigenous forms of music, spirituality, and sociality, and because the Peyote Road was disproportionately peopled with those who had attended boarding schools.[94] The faithfulness of followers of the Peyote Road, in other words, put to the test assimilationist's faith in their own project.

Burke's Circular 1665: "Indian Dancing" and the Pueblo Dance Controversy

Even as American anthropology was jettisoning notions of cultural evolution and racial determinism as old fashioned in favor of a vision of cultural relativism, Commissioner Burke was working to breathe new life into the Civilization Regulations, and Peyote was only the beginning of his concerns. In 1921, he issued Circular 1665 on Indian Dance, a memorandum directing agents in the field to step up their regulation of, and in many cases, to forcefully prohibit, dances.

The circular made clear that existing regulations were still very much in force prohibiting the Sun Dance "and so-called religious ceremonies." But Burke expanded the range of the criminalization to any dance involving

acts of self-torture, immoral relations between the sexes, the sacrificial destruction of clothing or other useful articles, the reckless giving away of property, the use of injurious drugs or intoxicants and frequent and or prolonged periods of celebration which bring the Indians together from remote points to the neglect of their crops, livestock, and home interests; in fact any disorderly or plainly excessive performances that promotes superstitious cruelty, licentiousness, idleness, danger to health, and shiftless indifference to family welfare.[95]

Circular 1665 did not prohibit all dances, cautioning that "the dance *per se* is not condemned," and not inherently uncivilized. But field agents would rightly have been confused with the mixed message. It was clear that Burke thought Indian dances of all stripes had the tendency to become uncivilized. "The dance under most primitive and pagan conditions is apt to be harmful," Burke wrote. "We should control it by educational processes as far as possible, but if necessary, by punitive measures when it's degrading tendencies persist."[96]

Burke counseled officials "to be somewhat tolerant of pleasure and relaxation sought in this way or of ritualism and traditional sentiment thus expressed," but he still advised his field force to place restrictions on dances they found did not plainly violate the regulations on the Sun Dance and its ilk as the circular clarified it. With such a nondiscursive form as dance, the instability of what counts as religious, much less what counts as "degrading," was very much in the eye of the beholder. To contain this ambiguity, two years later, the Indian Office made six recommendations for regulating dances, even ones deemed merely social. Among these were, rather astonishingly, restricting dances to daylight hours, disallowing participation by anyone under fifty, and committing to a propaganda and educational campaign against dancing.

As officials tried to negotiate such direct orders with exigencies in the field, there grew a particularly charged contrast between dances that were merely social and those seen as religious. But some dance traditions, like the complex traditions of the various Pueblo communities in New Mexico, proved particularly vexing for government regulators and practitioners alike.

The Pueblo Dance Controversy

In *We Have a Religion*, Tisa Wenger provides a nuanced book-length treatment of the 1920s controversy over Pueblo dances, as Burke's Indian Office, combined with Protestant missionaries, and even some Protestant Pueblo individuals, squared off with Pueblo governors, Catholic leaders, anthropologists, and artists, each complexly drawing on the discourse of religious freedom to advance their interests.[97]

Pueblo communities have continuously observed seasonal ceremonial dances since time immemorial, many of which became tied to the liturgical calendar of devotional Catholicism, fusing ancient Pueblo traditions with patronal feasts in complex ways. Although undeniably keyed to sacred myth, ritual knowledge, and the spiritual world, these dances, we learn from Wenger, were obligations of communal labor incumbent on Pueblo members as part of their citizenship, not unlike the maintenance of irrigation channels.

Although feasts had been entwined with devotional Catholicism for centuries, the Indian Office under Dance Circular 1665 targeted these protracted ceremonial complexes as hindrances to civilization. Efforts to regulate Pueblo dances were driven by complaints of what missionaries considered the lurid and degrading sexuality of the dances. This is ironic, given the socially conservative ethos of the Pueblos and the highly regulated structures of the dances. Maybe it is even tragic, a crusade led by assimilationists unwise to the refreshing humor of the ritual clowns who can dramatically cross (and thus articulate) polite boundaries and even single out persons in the audience for friendly ridicule.

At first, appeals to religious freedom with regard to the dances were raised between Protestants and Catholics and had nothing to do with the integrity of Pueblo "religion" itself. Presbyterian missionaries trying to convert Pueblos not only to Christianity, as was already largely the case in the Catholic Pueblos, but also to the civilizational assemblage of Anglo-Protestant culture, were concerned that their Pueblo adherents were coerced to perform in the dances in violation of their religious freedom rights. For their part, Catholic officials and some Pueblo advanced religious freedom claims with Indian agents to protect them from a tide of Protestant incursions on Pueblos, including school curricula and agent efforts to contain patronal feast dances.[98] Priests defending the dances could identify them as Pueblo custom "and sometimes even as legitimate Catholic practice—certainly not as a competing 'religion.'"[99]

But especially with the enforcement of Burke's Dance Circular, Pueblo leaders themselves began to appeal to religious freedom as a means to push back against missionary and government efforts. In this, they were joined by a relatively small but highly influential network of what Wenger identifies as cultural modernists, who were celebrating their own primitivist version of breathtaking Pueblo religion. This circle included writers like D. H. Lawrence, anthropologists like Elsie Clews Parsons, and other elites hosted at the Taos salon of Mabel Dodge Luhan. Notable was the deep involvement of

John Collier, then a staff person for an advocacy organization of women's groups, who would eventually transform Indian affairs under President Franklin D. Roosevelt.

Pueblo tribal leadership was generally "traditionalist" in its approach to negotiating tradition and change and increasingly willing to engage the modernists' counsel in defending their ceremonies as a matter of religious freedom. Led by figures like Pablo Abeita of Isleta Pueblo and Sotero Ortiz of San Juan Pueblo, they had organized as the Council of All New Mexico Pueblos in 1922 in opposition to a bill that sought to reduce their land holdings. Pueblo leadership viewed government regulation of ceremonies at the time as similarly offensive to the Pueblos' collective rights of sovereignty. For ages, ceremonial dancing had been regarded not principally as a matter of individual piety or spiritual fulfillment but as a collective duty, an obligation of membership in the Pueblo. It required time, energy, sacrifice, and work. But assimilation policies targeting the ceremonies had made it increasingly difficult to ensure the future and prompted leaders to press the issue. At Taos Pueblo in 1924, Governor Antonio Romero dutifully petitioned the Indian Bureau so that a group of boys could be excused from compulsory schooling for a season of initiatory training in the cultural knowledge necessary to lead the dance ceremonies. For these leaders, the discourse of religious freedom was of strategic use to the exercise of political and cultural sovereignty.

But they weren't the only Native people for whom religious freedom could be of strategic use. There was also a vocal and well-connected minority of self-styled "progressives," largely trained in boarding schools and desirous of reforming Pueblo traditions for what they viewed as a more secure modern future. Wenger writes of Pueblo members who challenged the obligation of ceremonial dancing as a matter of full Pueblo membership. They appealed to religious freedom to exempt them from obligatory participation in dances they thought compromised their Christianity.[100]

In 1924, officials settled the controversy through a compromise around these two usages of religious freedom discourse. Pueblo dances and the traditional ceremonial initiation would be protected from overt government regulation, and individual Pueblo members would be protected from obligatory participation. More enduringly, though, the controversy cast the mold for the ascendance of the cultural modernist position in the Indian Bureau, especially through John Collier.

Two summary points are in order. First, although the controversy shows just how pliable the language of religious freedom can be, Wenger highlights an important contrast between the competing Pueblo appeals to religious freedom. For the Protestants claiming religious freedom protections from conscription to dance against their conscience, religious freedom was very much a matter of just that: individual conscience rights protectable against their Pueblo government. For the Pueblo governors, however, the claims to religious freedom were seeking protections against US government encroachment on their collective rights to religious and cultural sovereignty.[101] In their case, Wenger makes an important point: religious freedom discourse is malleable enough for Indigenous peoples to have engaged it in defense of collective traditions while also insisting that those collective practices were not merely *religion*, not wholly coopted into the individualized terms that typically came with that term[102]

Second, the Pueblo dance controversy shows that assimilationists frustrated with the poor results of their policies increasingly turned their attention to cultural attachments like those of "dance" and "ceremony" as the reason for the failure. In effect, assimilationist officials turned up the regulatory heat on Native ceremonial traditions at the eleventh hour of their reign in Washington, DC. The embedded force of the assumptions on which their policies rested would not disappear overnight with the naming of John Collier as the head of Indian Bureau and with the emergence of vocal, boarding-school-educated Indian leaders, but the intensified support of the regulations in the 1920s frustrates a simple progressive narrative of that history.

Rescinding the Civilization Regulations

The Civilization Regulations remained law until January 1934, when Collier rescinded them as one of his initial acts in office as commissioner. But even in the years leading up to Burke's 1929 departure from that position, the regulations' enforcement had begun to wane. In 1926, Burke sought from Congress a bill outlawing traditional dances and wedding ceremonies.[103] His boss, Secretary of the Interior Hubert Work, appointed a blue ribbon advisory committee to advise the Indian Office, and the "Committee of One Hundred" prioritized other matters for policy reform apart from the Civilization Regulations, even questioning Burke's hard line on Peyote by calling for an independent study to determine whether Peyote was actually harmful.[104]

When the Meriam Report, commissioned to audit all Indian policy during the assimilation period, came out in 1928, it pointed not only to the dismal health, education, and economic statistics that spelled the failure of allotment and boarding schools; it also criticized the Civilization Regulations for having sought to abruptly stamp out Native traditions, rather than commend and build on them. "Leadership will recognize the good in the economic and social life of the Indians in their religion and ethics," the report recommended, "and will seek to develop it and build on it rather than to crush out all that is Indian."[105] The Meriam Report took aim at the Indian Office's obsession with dancing, calling it "biased with race prejudice." But the report stopped short of criticizing the policies as violations of the integrity of Native religions:

> All those interested in bringing the Indian into any degree of economic prosperity are bound to see the extremely deleterious effects of unbridled Indian dancing. On the other hand, there is no reason why we should sacrifice *in toto* their idealism, their art and the good of their ancient religion to our ideas of economic prosperity.[106]

Indeed, the Meriam Report's criticisms were fueled by a drive for bureaucratic effectiveness, not for a wholesale reversal of ideology, and only took to talk of Indian rights in cultural matters in terms of the basic rights of Indian peoples to be persuaded, rather than coerced, into their own "civilization." A concluding chapter of recommendations for missionaries made this plain:

> Each Indian tribe has had its own religion and its own code of ethics.... If the missionary is to reconstruct the life of the Indian by a new gospel he must be able to see the social edifice already there and have the power to evaluate its structural qualities.[107]

The Meriam Report did much of the policy review to enable President Franklin Roosevelt to effect the policy changes commonly termed the Indian New Deal: ending allotment policy; affirming the collective rights of Native Americans to land, language, and culture; and even acknowledging their rights to religious freedom in principle.[108]

Appointed by Roosevelt to run the Indian Bureau, John Collier made it one of his early priorities to stem the damage of the Civilization Regulations, which he came to call the Religious Crimes Code. Even before the regulations were formally rescinded, as one of his first acts of office in January 1934, Collier sent a policy letter directing agency superintendents to publicize it widely and to regard it "as an instruction superseding any prior regulation, instruction, or practice." The letter is worth quoting at length for the novelty of its formal recognition of government responsibilities with respect to Native religions:

> No interference with Indian religious life or ceremonial expression will hereafter be tolerated. The cultural liberty of Indians is in all respects to be considered equal to that of any non-Indian group. And it is desirable that Indians be bilingual: fluent and literate in the English language and fluent in their vital, beautiful, and efficient native languages.... [I]n no case shall punishments for statutory violations or for improprieties be so administered as to constitute an interference with, or to imply a censorship over, the religious or cultural life, Indian or other.
>
> The fullest constitutional liberty, in all matters affecting religion, conscience, and culture, is insisted on for all Indians. In addition, an affirmative, appreciative attitude toward Indian cultural values is desired in the Indian service.[109]

The Question of Religion

Tisa Wenger rightly observes that the 1883, 1892, and 1904 iterations of the Civilization Regulations "classified Native American traditions not as religions ... but instead as impediments to the Indians' proper exercise of freedom and to their civilizing progress more generally."[110] But in 1934, when John Collier took to nullify those regulations, he did so expressly because, as he said, they violated "American Indian religious freedom."[111] This turnaround was, as Wenger shows so compellingly, not simply because non-Natives had a change of mind, though it is true that cultural modernists like Collier, anthropologists like James Mooney, and others engaged the term strategically. More elementally, it was because Native peoples had themselves engaged the discourse of religious freedom.

They reconfigured Indigenous traditions in order to move forward, to shape meaningful lives under difficult conditions. Movements like the Peyote Road already reflected the influence of Christianity and of the larger society's concepts of religion. "Even when they did not succeed, their appeals to religious freedom require[d] further accommodations to those norms."[112]

"In the process, however," Wenger cautions, "Native people found their practices and traditions transformed. In order to meet the demands of BIA officials and lawmakers for what counted as a legitimate religion, they had little choice but to restructure their traditions to fit the model set by Christianity."[113] "At an even deeper level," Wenger continues, "their appeals had the effect of forging new distinctions between the religious and the secular in their own societies."[114] Wenger brings keen insight to the Native case from other peoples forced to reckon with the "religious freedom" of American imperialism.

Still, it is important to elaborate on wherein lies the strategic engagement with religious freedom. This is, I think, more than an interpretive quibble, since a reader can conclude from Wenger that there is something tragic in the engagement with religious freedom—an unforeseen consequence that introduces unprecedented, unanticipated, and unwanted change to Native religious traditions. The pace of that change was unprecedented to be sure, but to suggest it was something of a devil's bargain is to suggest that Native peoples are tragically disempowered by their own choices.

I think the strategic nature of the engagement with the language of religion is both overstated and underappreciated here. A nuanced treatment of the prophetic movements by Joel Martin suggests that "more than colonialism pushed, the sacred pulled Native Americans into new religious worlds."[115] In this view, colonialism does push Native peoples to new prophetic religious forms, those like the Ghost Dance that challenge the social order, and others like the Peyote Road that offer redemptive visions for living in that new social order. As I have developed elsewhere, Native traditions, with their consistent orientation toward practice, could encompass engagement with new traditions, new ceremonial complexes in part because of the logic of practice, in part because, as among the Lakota, the possibility of new revelation was deeply woven into their religious traditions. This dynamic encompassed the practice of multiple traditions at once, including for some Native people, Christianity.[116]

The prophetic movements of the nineteenth and early twentieth century were, to be sure, in response to culture change, and the lightning speed with which they spread intertribally was markedly new, as revitalization theorists have observed.[117] What is not so new, and this is an important continuity, is how Native religions—especially those shaped by visionary experiences like those of the Lakota—have, on their own terms, consistently made room for new dances, new songs, and new ceremonies. Even if leaders of movements like the Ghost Dance and the Peyote Road accentuated elements of their practice that were legibly Christian and thus legally and socially respectable, these "new" religions proceeded according to Indigenous idioms of revelation and authority.

There are also today remarkable continuities of tradition. Despite the vise grip of a half century of Civilization Regulations, Pueblo feasts, with their ceremonial dances, continue apace in their appointed season. Sacred clowns attend to their serious work of mocking any notion that tragic cultural loss has carried the day.

Native American Spirituality: A Genealogy

In the same decades that the United States criminalized Native ceremonies, dances, medicine traditions, and marriage customs, there grew a proportional American fascination and desire for collecting, having, owning, and venerating the very traditions that formal policy was eradicating. As Philip Deloria has argued, this Euro-American desire is no sideshow to the main drama of the assimilation era. The desire to play Indian and to celebrate Indian-ness signaled tectonic ambivalence about the American project, modern progress, and market capitalism.[118] But the cultural dispossession of Native peoples performed important work in cementing their material dispossession. It functioned to absolve Americans of their transgressions in stealing Native lands— to have their cake and eat it too—and to erase Native presence by proclaiming the tragic death of *real Indian* cultures and, in turn, by castigating the surviving Native people as no longer practicing real Indian things.

So a discussion of the effort to curb Native religions under Assimilation Policy is necessarily, too, a discussion of a germinating American romance with Native spirituality that I will show in subsequent chapters so consistently blurs recognition of the religiousness of Native legal claims to religious freedom. The drive to erase living Native cultures was also fueled by the craze to collect Native material culture and ancestral remains and stow them away in museums before those cultures completely vanished.

Wenger shows in the Pueblo dance controversies that Pueblo engagement with the discourse of religious freedom was in part fueled by modernists' romance with Pueblo dance traditions. Wenger's point is important, not only because the "religion" that Pueblo leaders strategically appealed to as a vehicle for claim-making changed how they saw their traditions but also because it shows how Native "religion" for those anthropologists and artists was itself caught up in this desire for a spiritualized Indian-ness that could be disaggregated from the regulation and collective obligation of Native peoples, not to mention the local specificity to stolen lands. Thus spiritualized and interiorized, Native "religion" could become a universally available experience.

Although the term used by Mooney, Collier, and others was *religion*, the Native religion they imagined worth protecting was caught up in their own desires to render Native traditions safely within the bounds of that category. Tiffany Hale has called attention to Mooney's strategy of diminishing the anticolonial dimensions of the Ghost Dance movement by reducing it to a merely *religious* movement.[119] This was, she suggested, not only strategy, it was also caught up in Mooney's own enthrallment by the spiritual riches of Native peoples he visited.

An irony of this romance with Native spirituality was the simultaneous craze to collect artifacts and ancestral remains of vanishing Native cultures while espousing the Assimilation Policy designed to erase those cultures. If there are no more Native nations, and no more "real Indians," then their material culture, like their lands, could be the rightful property of the American nation as a whole. Collectors and field anthropologists often sweet-talked and swindled their way to acquiring important ceremonial items; others just robbed graves. The effort amassed the remains of between one hundred thousand and two million deceased Native persons in museums and scientific institutions—the Smithsonian having remains of 18,500 individuals.[120] Numerous sacred items—pipes, drums, masks, medicine bundles too many to count—were bought in rip-and-run expeditions. Many of the items considered "persons," or items belonging to collectives, were bought coercively from people who didn't own them. Some were even entrusted to museum collectors for safekeeping with the understanding that they would continue to be cared for, used ceremonially.

Pueblo leaders and Peyote Road practitioners engaged the discourse of *religion*, not spirituality, to render their traditions legible to Americans law. But as Wenger shows, this had consequences for the forms of Native practice that might be seen as religious; these forms map onto the engagement with Native spirituality. In the next chapter I will argue, following Winnifred Fallers Sullivan, that spirituality is not significantly distinguishable from the kind of religion that is broadly recognized in contemporary America.[121] This is not to say that various people, including many Native people, cannot assert meaningful distinctions when they represent Native traditions as spirituality rather than religion. Indeed it is true that *religion* has been regarded by many

Native people as a colonizer's term, all but specific to Christianity. But so, too, is *spirituality* a colonizer's term, and perhaps more insidiously so.

The ongoing romance with Native spirituality emphasizes the individual over the collective: it is a matter of choice, of interior experience more than obligation to a collective. This facet makes Native spirituality extractable from Native peoples themselves and makes it available as a spiritual practice to others. Accordingly, spirituality emphasizes freedom over regulation, and this in frequent distinction from "organized religion." Spirituality stresses interior piety over outward practice, with its bodily regimens. Finally, and perhaps most importantly for our purposes, spirituality asserts the universality of Native traditions, deemphasizing their rootedness in local landscapes and their restriction to particular peoples. If it's really *religion*, so the logic goes, it must be universally applicable and available to anyone anywhere. By turns, this universality spiritualizes the traditions from their concrete, even material, embeddedness in lifeways lived on particular landscapes.

Conclusion

The Civilization Regulations have been broadly referenced as outlawing Native religions, and there is a common belief, despite Collier's rescinding them in 1934, that only with the 1978 American Indian Religious Freedom Act were Native peoples free again to practice their religions. This belief is not unwarranted, since government actions since 1934 have consistently continued to prohibit those traditions in inadvertent ways. It is especially true if one factors in the capillary action of the state's power of regulation as it had become internalized by Native people. This was grimly effective on reservations, where the local authority of the agent was twinned with that of missionaries and backed up by a system where treaty annuity payments were turned into purse strings for punishing indigeneity. Churchstateness weaponized religion.

Suzan Harjo has said it well:

It wasn't just to break Indians' backs; it was to break the Indian spirit so the Indian person would relinquish attachment one way or the other to land, to religion, to parents, to language. That's why the Indian kids were taken so far away from their parents, from the Dakotas, from Indian Territory, to Pennsylvania, to Virginia, to be anglicized and Christianized and never returned. And used as slave labor in the summers for the local gentry. That was all part of breaking the spirit of the Indian people.[122]

It is true that many ceremonial traditions went underground or became fused with approved Christianity, or became merely "social." Others went dormant, awaiting more propitious conditions to spring back to life. Each of the subsequent chapters tells of further difficulties, legal among them, facing Native peoples as they seek to fulfill their religious obligations, but those chapters also bear witness to the extraordinary survivance and renewal of Native religion in the doing.

2

Religion as Spirituality

NATIVE RELIGIONS IN PRISON

Introduction

The last chapter explored early twentieth-century strategic efforts by leaders of the Native American Church and Pueblo governments to articulate their traditions as matters of religious freedom in an effort to outmaneuver the Civilization Regulations (1883–1934). This next pair of chapters follows suit, tracking the career in the courts of sacred claims made by Native peoples in the discourse of religious freedom under the First Amendment, and subsequently under a series of religious freedom statutes passed by Congress. If it seems unremarkable that Native peoples should argue for legal freedoms of religion as religion, there is nothing straightforward about what courts have understood when they say they understand the religion of Native American religious freedom claims.

Religious freedom claims by Native peoples to this point have largely failed in the courts, especially so when they have involved claims to sacred lands and waters. Chapter 3 will examine a series of sacred land claims under the First Amendment that culminated in the devastating 1988 loss before the US Supreme Court in *Lyng v. Northwest Indian Cemetery Protective Association*, a decision that was instrumental to its *Employment Division v. Smith* decision two years later, through which the Rehnquist Court restricted the reach of the First Amendment's Free Exercise Clause protections generally. Even after Congress answered the Supreme Court by restoring and even extending Free Exercise protection in the Religious Freedom Restoration Act (1993) and the Religious Land Use and Institutionalized Persons Act (2000), Native claims to sacred lands under the statutes have generally failed, still construed through the logic of the Court's First Amendment decision in *Lyng.*

But the story of religion as religion, of Native claims in the courts to religious freedom, has not uniformly been one of failure, and this is where this chapter comes in. Where Native American religious freedom claims have had some success in the courts, they have prevailed in cases where the religion asserted has conformed to the shape of religion that religious liberty protections privilege: private, individual, believed. I don't want to suggest all such claims prevail; they don't. But taken as a whole, the cases involving Native claims to free exercise in prison stand in striking contrast to the sacred lands cases that fail. Here, those winning free exercise claims are not those of Native *peoples*, but Native *people*, Native individuals as individuals, and for their individual practices of religious expression, sacrament, prayer, or even assembly for worship that are tied to the rights of individuals to do so.

This pair of chapters emphasizes what the contrasting results in the sacred land and prison cases share: even when sacred claims to religion are made in the language of religion, Native claims are flattened to those of spirituality. To underscore this, we may justly regard this pair of chapters not in terms of the argument—religion as religion—but in terms of its reception—religion as spirituality.

The conceptual move from Native American religion to spirituality can make a lot of intellectual sense to some scholars and practitioners of Native traditions.[1] It equips one to follow the contours of Native traditions that don't comport with religion as conventionally understood. But as we shall also see, the term *spirituality* comes with its own baggage, especially when conjoined to Native traditions. The last chapter's discussion of the development of an American romance with Native spirituality laid the groundwork, but the cultural appropriation of Native American spirituality by non-Natives has greatly intensified since the 1960s and 1970s. This chapter considers how courts have come to view Native claims to religious freedom through the distorting lens of this coveted spirituality.

This imagined Native American spirituality is anything but "organized religion.'" It is personal, authentic, one with nature, yet portable enough to be freely available to all who seek it. Even when jurists don't number themselves among the seekers, romanticized notions pervade the decisions on religious freedom claims, misrecognizing some claims, like those made by tribes to sacred lands out of collective obligation, and rewarding other claims that fit with this pervasive view of Native religions.

In the prison cases, "Native American Spirituality" emerges as a term of art from corrections management, a line on the intake form for religious preference, and keyed to the language of the federal chaplaincy manual.[2] Prison chaplaincy programs use it in an effort to articulate what's often exceptional and irreducibly diverse about Native religious traditions and to articulate what makes them so difficult to pin down. Like those who profess "spiritual, not religious" to distinguish their commitments from organized religion, chaplaincy officials denominate Native spirituality in an effort to acknowledge its difference from other, more organized religions. Native spiritual leaders, for example, often are not credentialed in ways cognizable to administrators accustomed to ordination. "Native American Spirituality" is also a function of the intertribal forms so common to inmate piety: smudging with burning sage, safekeeping of medicine bags and sacred herbs, pipe ceremonies, and the sweat lodge. While nearly every tribe-specific religion can have its own variation on these forms with attendant teachings and obligations, as a bureaucratic matter it has made sense to speak of the congeries of practices as spirituality. Lastly, and crucial to our concerns, Native spirituality enables chaplains to speak fluidly of its practice not just by those who are citizens of Native nations or who have a clear tribal affiliation but by the full range of inmates, Native and non-Native alike, who list it as their preference.

Naturalization of Spirituality

This is a particular instance of what Winnifred Fallers Sullivan identifies as a much broader and broadly ramified "naturalization of spirituality."[3] In a study of chaplaincies in the secular spaces of hospitals, universities, legislatures, military bases, and prisons, Sullivan argues that the citizen is increasingly "understood to be fundamentally spiritual" as an aspect of being human.[4] Although spirituality has entered the contemporary lexicon in frequent distinction from organized religion, the semantic difference between religion and spirituality is of little consequence for Sullivan here. In a previous work on several Establishment Clause cases, Sullivan had written of "religion naturalized," but in her book on chaplaincy, she uses the terms interchangeably, favoring spirituality.[5] Her larger point is that both remain largely unproblematic for any potential improper establishment of religion, because the courts increasingly see such religion as "neither particularly threatening nor particularly in need of protection."[6] Because people are naturally spiritual, soldiers can be measured for their "spiritual fitness," Veterans Administration hospitals can require "spiritual assessment" on admission, and "spiritual care" can be required of any hospital accredited under government guidelines.[7] "Religious life is so entirely disaggregated and religious authority so thoroughly shifted to the individual," Sullivan elsewhere argues, "that both establishment and disestablishment are functionally impossible. There are no churches left to establish or to disestablish."[8] Sullivan acknowledges there "still are, and will be excluded disfavored religions under this new legal regime, of course, but the arbiter will no longer be the courts."[9]

"The spiritual religion practiced by chaplains," Sullivan writes, aspires to be "inclusive, therapeutic, and self-consciously constitutional," often serving secular purposes, and "deeply ambiguous in its metaphysical assumptions and its regulatory purposes."[10] Its legal management falls below the levels of the courts, in what Sullivan calls "spiritual governance" that fuses the religious and the secular a manner that resembles *churchstateness* (discussed in chapter 1).

The thing is that the spirituality that fails to trigger constitutional limits on government establishment of religion in Sullivan's cases also fails, in the Native sacred land cases, to trigger the protections for free exercise, as we will see in the next chapter. In the prison cases, however, Native religious claims to individual spirituality are relatively legible to the courts. To argue this is to risk sounding too sanguine about the fortunes of incarcerated Native Americans as they seek to practice their religions with dignity. There are very real inequities of access to religious services for Native inmates, and there is urgency for their access to the healing that these religions can bring. This is the conclusion of a 2014 report submitted as part of a UN review process by the Native American Rights Fund, the National Congress of American Indians, and Huy, a nongovernmental advocacy organization in the Pacific Northwest.[11]

The law accords considerable deference to prison officials, resulting in a wide range of access to Native religious practices across states and localities. Most grievances die at the institutional level, where severe power inequities can quiet legitimate arguments of discrimination. Many claims that do make it to the courts are filed pro se by inmates without benefit of professional counsel, and these cases unsurprisingly rarely go far.[12] So it is true that Native inmates do not broadly enjoy religious freedom in prison. Still, where Native American religious freedom gains any meaningful traction in the courts, inmate claims to Native religious free exercise in prisons stand out.

Native American Spirituality in Prisons

Native Americans are imprisoned at alarming rates. A 1999 Department of Justice study found that the rate of incarceration on a per capita basis was 38 percent above that of the national average.[13] A 2011 government study counted 29,700 Native American inmates, most of them in state prisons and local jails.[14] The disproportion is even more regionally pronounced. In South Dakota, Native Americans make up fully one-fourth of the prison population while only making up 9 percent of the state's population.[15] As Walter Echo-Hawk has written, the incarcerated Native population is deserving of religious liberty not only as a matter of individual right; this religious liberty is urgent to the cultural survival of Native peoples as peoples:

> When they are released, it is important to the cultural survival of Indian tribes and Native communities that returning offenders be contributing, culturally viable members, rather than further alienated and assimilated by their experience in the White Man's prisons. Therefore, virtually every Native American and Indian Tribe is directly and vitally impacted by prison policies which affect the rights, rehabilitation and well-being of these prisoners.[16]

Indeed, one can argue that the American Indian Movement had its genesis in 1963 ceremonial activities and the religious transformations of Anishinaabe activist Clyde Bellecourt and medicine man Edward Benton-Banai, Navajo activist Lenny Foster, and other inmates at the state corrections facility in Stillwater, Minnesota.[17] Bellecourt told a reporter that "things have improved" in state and federal prisons, "but there are still problems."[18]

Of course convicted offenders surrender many liberties, such as rights to assembly and movement, but rights to religious freedom are not, in principle, surrendered. Rights of conscience and belief are broadly recognized; rights to practice are balanced with competing government obligations. The challenge, from the perspective of corrections officials—even those who are inclined to support Native religious accommodations—is the balancing of safety, security, and equality of treatment. These determinations are also very much a function of scarce resources. I was told by a group of state corrections chaplaincy administrators that sweat lodge ceremonies, often requiring specific kinds of wood and stones (some stones can "explode" when superheated), antlers, and other items, are the most expensive accommodation they face.

Some accommodations pertain to individual practice, like an inmate's right to possess a medicine bag and/or sacred herbs; others pertain to group ceremonies that require staff supervision and the budget to pay for it. Increasing demand for these kinds of accommodations can run up against declining chaplaincy budgets.

Most prison chaplains are Christian, but as professionals, their job generally involves providing spiritual support to inmates of other traditions. As administrators, not just direct providers of religious services, chaplains contract out and arrange volunteers from various religious groups and serve as de facto arbiters of religious and cultural diversity.[19] Whether they are effective advocates depends on their will and capacity to advocate, and even on their budgets.[20]

If Native religious freedom challenges to restrictive prison policies have been generally successful in courts in recent years—relative to sacred land claims, that is—it has been because of the persistent, tireless advocacy of Native activists like Lenny Foster (Navajo) and Native spiritual leaders. It has also been because of advocates within the ranks of chaplains, such as Susan Van Baalen, OP, who retired as the head chaplaincy administrator for federal corrections.[21] But especially so because of the changed legal terrain after the 2000 passage of the Religious Land Use and Institutionalized Persons Act.[22]

Among other things, Van Baalen saw to the production in 2002 of the Federal Bureau of Prisons best practices manual, *Inmate Religious Beliefs and Practices*, which includes a twenty-five-page description of "Native American Spirituality" (Islam, too, gets twenty-five pages; Protestant Christianity twenty).[23] The section includes an introduction by Osage scholar George Tinker and the full text of the American Indian Religious Freedom Act (1978). Although it documents de facto practices of Native American Spirituality as they have materialized in prison contexts, the manual also plays a defining role. I would stop short of saying the manual *makes* Native American Spirituality in the doing, but it is among the shaping influences, to be sure. In its effort to guide chaplains and corrections officials, the manual does the work of demarcating the authorized contours of Native American Spirituality, contours that hover above but draw on tribe-specific religions and their teachings about the practices. It capitalizes the terms of the practices it describes, subtly reifying them as proper nouns. Most importantly, its text appears in judicial decisions that make fine-grained determinations of what accommodations count.

Salient features of Native American Spirituality include ceremonial actions —the sweat lodge, the pipe ceremony, smudging, fasting, festivals like an

This schematic provides suggested dimensions for the sweat lodge;
altar and fire pit. This is sacred space for the Native American
spiritual tradition in the Outside Worship Area.

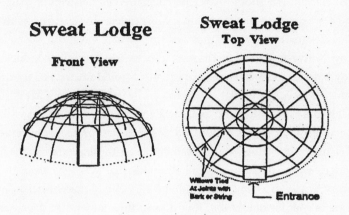

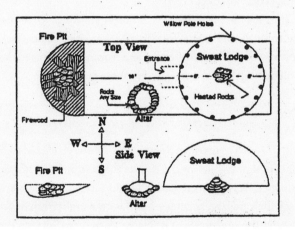

FIG. 2.1. Schematic of Sweat Lodge, Federal Bureau of Prisons Chaplaincy Manual
This schematic in the official federal prison chaplaincy manual regularizes
and reifies the sweat lodge even as it clarifies the accommodation.
Federal Bureau of Prisons *Inmate Religious Practices.*

occasional powwow, visits by Native American spiritual leaders, and listed religious items from medicine bags and drums to tobacco, sage, sweetgrass, cedar, copal, eagle feathers, and other animal parts.

The manual takes pains to properly direct officials in their response to specific situations that arise. "Native American spiritual leaders should receive the same professional courtesy and access to inmates that is afforded to ordained clergy" and should have the chaplains only visually inspect sacred items they bring with them, "avoiding x-rays unless absolutely necessary." The manual designates the sacred pipe and the sweat lodge as the "cornerstones" of most Native American traditions.[24] Sweats are "generally conducted on a weekly basis in a correctional setting" and "should not exceed four hours," and the manual clarifies that all aspects of the ceremony are sacred from the spatial layout of the lodge and its associated fire to the final rinse and disposal of the ashes. Each step is sacred and deserves staff protocols of respect, including not entering the lodge or walking across the line between the fire and the lodge. Sweats should be scheduled at times that won't involve institutional interruptions, such as "out-counts," but if a "count" should be necessary, officials are to wait for one of the "four doors," the moments in the ceremonial process when the lodge is opened to receive rounds of hot "Grandfather" stones and accompanying prayers.[25]

The manual makes plain that it is not meant to formally define the features, even if it effectively does so. It "follows a best practices guide," taking religious liberty law as well as the "corrections environment" into account and reiterates, in bold letters: "Final program decisions rest with the Warden."[26]

Universality of Native American Spirituality

Importantly, "Native American Spirituality" is not restricted to Native Americans at the level of law below the courts that Winnifred Sullivan calls "spiritual governance." It is in this regard in tension with Native American religious traditions, which are largely coterminous with membership in Native nations. As I will show, the universalism of Native American Spirituality is related to its legibility in the law as protectable *religion*, and hence, relatively successful in the courts.

A search of federal case law in the LexisNexis database generated fifty-six different cases meaningfully using the term "Native American Spirituality." All but five of those concerned religious practices in prison; none of them concerned sacred lands. The pattern of correlation illuminates how the dis-

FIG. 2.2. Sweat Lodge and Fire Pit, Donovan Corrections Facility.
A sweat lodge and fire pit erected for regular use in the recreation area of the R. J. Donovan
Corrections Facility in California, 2000. During ceremonies, the frame is covered with
blankets or tarps and red-hot stones are welcomed as Grandfathers to make medicinal
steam during songs and prayers. (Photo Angela Carone/Courtesy of KPBS San Diego)

course of spirituality shapes judicial approaches to Native cases. In several
cases concerning hair length in prison and places of employment, Native litigants themselves used "Spirituality" as a term with a broader semantic range
than religion. But in the vast majority of the cases, *spirituality* is no mere
synonym for Native American religion, religions, or religious exercise; it is
invoked as a term to distinguish spirituality from particular tribal religions.
With one minor exception, cases involving the term do not concern tribe-
specific claims to sacred sites or religious practices but rather deal with gen-
eralized claims to religious freedom in prisons and, not infrequently, with
claims asserted by *non-Native* practitioners.

The federal chaplaincy manual suggests, in its entry for "Native American
Spirituality—Membership," that Native traditions "vary greatly with tribes,"
and that "local religious authorities or tribal elders should be consulted."[27]
But for the intertribal practices like the sweat lodge that prompt its sustained
attention, the manual makes plain that participation "is not usually limited to
those of Indian ancestry alone." The recommendation is that "an understanding

of Native American traditions, as well as religious preference will be considered in authorizing participation in the Sweat Lodge."[28]

There is a lack of good data on the religious affiliation of inmate populations generally, but a Pew Research Center survey of over seven hundred prison chaplains suggested that Native American Spirituality was among the four highest growing religions, measured by religious affiliations that had been changed in prison. One-fourth of chaplain respondents said, "Native American Spirituality is growing a lot." This could be an indication of Native inmates who switch affiliation from Christian to Native American Spirituality, but it is more likely a function of non-Native inmates switching affiliations to an earth-based religion. "Paganism/Earth Based Traditions" like Wicca and Asatru Fellowship, was the third fastest growing in the estimation of the chaplains, behind Protestantism and Islam.

Perhaps because of a felt need to restrict access to the popular—and expensive and difficult to manage—accommodations for Native American Spirituality, at least one state, New York, has required a showing of Native identity for access to accommodations for Native American Spirituality. "Only inmates who have a documented Native American designation will be allowed to participate in approved Native American ceremonies," a 2015 directive provides, adding that "appropriate verification of the inmate's ancestry" by an administrator "in consultation" with the department's Native American chaplains is required.[29] Courts have struck down such policies in other prison contexts as violations of rights to equal protection.[30] Such a measure can be at the urging of Native religious leaders trying to limit ceremonies to community members.[31] But perhaps it has also to do with insincere interest in Native Spirituality. The Pew survey found a common concern among chaplains that inmates were seeking religious accommodations in an effort to game the system. New York's directive does not require participants to be members of federally recognized tribes, appearing to leave room for discrete judgments of sincere practice. And in any case, New York appears to be an outlier in its restriction to those with documented Native identity.[32]

In fact, the universality of Native American Spirituality, its availability to those non-Native inmates who simply designate it as their religious preference, has been underscored by the courts. A generative precedent has been *Morrison v. Garraghty*, a 2001 case in which the Fourth Circuit agreed with a lower court that a non-Native practitioner's equal protection rights to his "Native spirituality" were violated by a Virginia prison's policy requiring substantiation of Native American heritage for religious accommodations.[33] Even though the inmate had professed a sincere belief in "the creator, mother earth, the sacredness of all living things, that everything has a spirit and is connected," and was a member of a prisoner group called HEART—Heritage Examined Among Redman Traditions—authorities forced him to yield a number of spiritual objects and herbs, including sage, cedar, sweetgrass, and kinnickinnic. The court found the prison's policy was plain: "acquiring or maintaining existing articles of Native American faith will only be considered for those inmates who are bona fide Native Americans"—and the denial was based solely on identity, not on the basis of an inquiry into his sincerity or for any reasons of security or safety.[34] Specifically, the Fourth Circuit held that "Morrison pursues not a constitutional right to obtain the religious items, but a constitutional right to be treated the same as Native American inmates requesting the same religious articles."[35] It is clear from a host of cases that have followed, "Native American Spirituality" is a common usage in prison environments for ritual traditions like the sweat lodge and attendant paraphernalia. The paraphernalia are associated with Native American traditions but are not tribe-specific and must be open, on equal protection grounds, to participation by non-Native inmates.[36] As a term of art that signals inclusiveness, "Native American Spirituality" can also admit of skepticism, suggesting the added "hassle factor" prison officials can associate with inmate access to what they view as any number of objects, medicines, and practices associated with Native Americans, and with enough play in its semantic range to account for possible imposture. I base this observation on two consultations with a group of state chaplaincy administrators, many of whom I understood to be quite sympathetic to such claims but keenly aware of the relatively costly nature of these accommodations.[37] "Native American Spirituality" has even been associated with claims of identified prison groups like the Mexican Mafia using the moniker, as one court found, for nefarious assembly purposes.[38]

Religious Freedom Law: A Brief Historical Sketch

As with other religious free exercise claims in the courts, Native American claims to religious practices in prison have fared differently over time, and it is important to understand these claims, as well as the claims to sacred lands that we encounter in chapter 3, in the context of a brief history of religious freedom jurisprudence. It seems counterintuitive today, but federal courts only seldom heard religious freedom claims before the mid-twentieth century, when the First Amendment's Free Exercise Clause, "Congress will make no law respecting an establishment of religion or prohibiting the free exercise thereof," was legally incorporated into the Fourteenth Amendment and thus formally applied to state and local government actions, where by far more controversy takes place.[39]

The Supreme Court under chief justices Warren and Burger had given broad interpretations of the reach of Free Exercise Clause protections. The key case in Free Exercise Clause jurisprudence was *Sherbert v. Verner* (1963), in which the Supreme Court found unconstitutional the denial of unemployment benefits to a Seventh Day Adventist who had been fired for failure to work on the Adventist Sabbath when her schedule was abruptly changed.[40] The Court articulated the three-part *Sherbert* test, which instructed subsequent courts in Free Exercise Clause cases to ask (1) whether a claimant could show that a government action placed a demonstrable burden on sincere religious exercise, (2) whether a government could justify its action with a compelling interest, and (3) whether the government could show it had exhausted alternative actions that would not thus burden religious exercise. By raising the judicial standard for reviewing governmental regulation of religion from "rational basis" to "strict scrutiny" (the application of the compelling interest and least restrictive means analysis), the *Sherbert* test effectively put the burden on government to show that its interests outweighed those of religious freedom. This logic extended through a number of expansive religious freedom protections for conscientious objectors who were not plainly religious in their affiliation or belief and beyond to *Wisconsin v. Yoder*, a 1972 case in which a Wisconsin compulsory education statute was found to violate the rights of an Amish community to commend its way of life by educating young people on its own terms after eighth grade.[41]

Yoder is often cited as the high-water mark for Free Exercise Clause jurisprudence, and I think the details of the case offer an analogy for Native American religious freedom. Yoder was an Amish father who was prosecuted along with two others for refusing to enroll children in public schools after eighth grade, under Wisconsin's compulsory education law. They took the issue to the courts, claiming that Wisconsin's law violated their free exercise of religion, and ultimately won soundly in a 6–0 decision where the Court applied the *Sherbert* test: first determining that the Old Order Amish community's religion had been burdened by the generally applicable law, and second that Wisconsin had failed to prove its interest in compulsory education outweighed Yoder's free exercise right. Most religious freedom commentators gravitate toward the *Yoder* Court's now quite remarkable pronouncement: "only those interests of the highest order and those not otherwise served can overbalance legitimate claims to the free exercise of religion."[42]

Even more germane to the question of the protection of Native traditions as religion is the extensive analysis the Court undertook in its weighing of Yoder's free exercise right. Perhaps as critics have pointed out, this is rooted in a sentimental regard for the countercultural Amish, but in any case the Court held that First Amendment protections extended to the entire Amish way of life, having ascertained that this way of life was "inseparable and interdependent" with Amish religion and distinguished from merely "subjective" rejection of social values that are merely "philosophical and personal":

> The Old Order Amish religion pervades and determines virtually their entire way of life, regulating it with the detail of the Talmudic diet through the strictly enforced rules of the church community.[43]

An argument can be made that it is pointless to appeal for First Amendment protections to *Yoder* or any decision prior to *Employment Div. v. Smith*. But the *Smith* Court in 1990 didn't overturn *Yoder*; it merely found the case as not controlling. Justice Scalia's majority opinion in *Smith* took pains to distinguish *Smith* from the *Yoder* Amish case, since the Wisconsin compulsory education law in question was, like the Oregon controlled substance statute, a neutral law of general applicability.[44] Scalia reasoned that in *Yoder*, it was not religious freedom alone that tipped the scales, but religious freedom claims bundled together with other rights—parental rights in the case of *Yoder*—and Scalia saw no such bundle of rights present in the *Smith* case.[45]

In the conscientious objector cases during the Vietnam era, the Supreme Court expanded the definitional parameters of what it would consider *religion*.[46] In *U.S. v. Seeger* (1965), the Supreme Court changed course from granting previous exemptions for conscientious objectors only when the convictions were religious—not merely moral—and upheld an atheist's religious free exercise rights to conscientious objection.[47] Citing theologian Paul Tillich's consideration of God as a matter of "ultimate concern," the Court found Seeger's convictions legally "religious" even as they were unapologetically atheist.[48] In this environment, the courts appeared somewhat friendly to Native free exercise claims that pushed the envelope of what would be considered religion. In those days, the issues turned on men wearing long hear in institutional settings. Long hair had become an accentuated symbol of Indian identity and related to traditional duties of mourning—if you don't have hair to cut in a pronounced way, you cannot mourn. Not all courts regarded the

Indian claims as sufficiently religious to merit protection,[49] but when Jerry Teterud, a Cree inmate, challenged an Iowa prison's restrictions on hair length as a violation of his religious right to long hair, a federal court found the policy unconstitutional.[50] The judge drew on expert testimony and an analogy between the interrelatedness of Native religion and culture and that of the Amish communities of *Yoder*.[51] Two other hair length victories at the appellate level for Native prison inmates bolstered the *Teterud* holding in the Fourth and Sixth Circuits.[52]

But as the Rehnquist Court began to address what its conservative justices regarded as too-broad free exercise protections vis-à-vis government interests and other competing goods, Native inmates' efforts to win court backing for their religious freedom ran aground. In *O'Lone v. Shabbazz* (1987), the Supreme Court changed the approach to balancing individual free exercise rights and the compelling government interest, hewing toward considerable deference to prison officials and their "legitimate penological interests."[53] Three years later, the Supreme Court in *Smith* all but nullified any inmate claim to violation of free exercise rights, since most prison policies are "neutral laws of general applicability" that, after *Smith*, no longer require a showing of the government's compelling interest to pass constitutional muster. It didn't help any Native prisoner's case that *Smith*, and its 1988 predecessor on sacred lands, *Lyng*, were cases involving Native American religious freedom claims.

Employment Division v. Smith (1990)

Employment Division v. Smith was an unemployment compensation case involving two Oregon substance abuse counselors who had been fired because they had been found to be members of the Native American Church and had continued to ritually ingest Peyote at ceremonies as part of their own wellness and religious discipline.[54] As we know from chapter 1, the Native American Church is a religious organization that Native leaders strategically incorporated as a "church" in the 1910s to help secure First Amendment protection. Peyote practitioners had considerable success in courts winning legal protection for their tradition.[55] But the *Smith* Court reversed that trend, criminalizing overnight the religion of tens of thousands of Native people. The Court found that the state's right to enforce its controlled substance laws outweighed the free exercise rights of Peyotists but went beyond applying the *Sherbert* test to arrive at its result, an audacious move that Justice O'Connor's strongly worded concurring opinion found to be gratuitous.[56] Writing for the majority, Justice Scalia reframed the entire structure of Free Exercise Clause jurisprudence, holding as constitutional "valid and neutral laws of general applicability" that do not intentionally and expressly deny free exercise rights even if they have the effect of the same, and turning away practitioners of minority religions from the courts to legislatures for explicit protection.[57] As a matter of law, the *Smith* decision found constitutional Oregon's controlled substance law, and by extension, any other neutral, generally applicable government action even if such government actions had the effect of burdening the free exercise of religion. The *Sherbert* test would apply only in those rare cases where governments expressly act to prohibit or burden religious free exercise.[58]

Where *Sherbert* had placed the responsibility on government to justify actions that burden sincere religious exercise with a full showing of the compelling state interest behind the action and a showing that the action involved the least restrictive means to accomplish that compelling interest, *Smith* placed the burden on legislatures to generate such accommodations. But legislatures, it might be pointed out, rarely act in a majoritarian democracy in favor of the religious practices and beliefs of minority communities. This was particularly true of the 1980s, with a declared war on drugs gripping the public imagination.

Critics of the decision, and there are many, have pointed out how the *Smith* Court effectively gutted the Free Exercise Clause as it pertains to minority religions in which no clear line exists between inviolate beliefs and the practices that purportedly merely express them. They have also found *Smith* to significantly devalue the weight of the Free Exercise Clause, giving it credence only when conjoined in bundles of hybrid rights with other, nonreligious rights. Justice Scalia's view was that the strict scrutiny standard of "compelling governmental interest" as applied to religious freedom in *Sherbert v. Verner* "waters it down" and "subverts its rigor in the other fields where it is applied." In the case at hand, Scalia added, the application of the standard would be "courting anarchy":

> Precisely because "we are a cosmopolitan nation made up of people of almost every conceivable religious preference," and precisely because we value and protect that religious divergence, we cannot afford the luxury of deeming presumptively invalid, as applied to the religious objector, every regulation of conduct that does not protect an interest of the highest order.[59]

Plenty of critics, including Justice Blackmun in his strong dissent, have called this slippery slope concern into question, noting that Peyote exemptions in particular have never generated many challenges to the government enforcement of drug laws.[60] Here, my interest is in identifying why a case involving Native practices should trigger Scalia's doomsday scenario of "courting anarchy."

Read generously, *Smith* was evenhanded in its explicit reluctance to involve the courts deeper and deeper in the business of evaluating the centrality of various religious beliefs and practices to ascertain their relative weight in balancing tests like the *Sherbert* test. "What principle of law or logic can be brought to bear to contradict a believer's assertion that a particular act is 'central' to his personal faith?" Justice Scalia wrote. "Judging the centrality of different religious practices is akin to the unacceptable 'business of evaluating the relative merits of differing religious claims.' "[61] But as with *Lyng*, what results from this logic for the case at hand is "cruelly surreal": substance abuse counselors are denied free exercise protections even though they practice a religion long acknowledged to promote sobriety and to have passed so many historic layers of scrutiny as to be specifically exempted in many states. Here the burden of proof for the slippery slope argument, it would seem, would be on the outlier, Oregon.

Deep-seated myths about the vanishing Indian remain the controlling frames of understanding Native American claims. I'm convinced that Scalia's "courting anarchy" concerns are evidence of the power of the vanishing Indian trope in jurisprudence on Native religious freedom claims, especially when read in the context of Justice O'Connor's hasty application of the *Bowen v. Roy* analogy as controlling in the denial of Native free exercise rights to sacred lands in the *Lyng* decision two years earlier.[62] The logic of this drift goes something like this: "real Indians" vanished long ago, and contemporary Native religious practitioners have been degraded by a tragic history of dispossession. At best these claimants are inventing traditions and at worst making novel and thin claims to sacred places, or to beliefs like *Roy*'s claimant that a Social Security number could damage his daughter's spirit. Against this backdrop, Native peoples claiming First Amendment protections are emblematic of the far-fetched demands that wizened judges come to associate with freaks and mavericks. Perhaps this is the answer to the pressing question of why the major cases withdrawing the reach of the Free Exercise Clause are cases concerning Native American peoples rather than cases involving practitioners of less obviously established minority religions. In the end, the lesson of *Smith*, and even of *Lyng*, in that when Native peoples have sought protections for their religious and cultural traditions under the First Amendment, they have ended up being confused by the courts with what Kevin Washburn playfully referred to as "long-haired guys with bongs and microbuses" making opportunistic and arguably excessive claims about religion.[63] That Justice O'Connor in *Lyng* and Justice Scalia in *Smith* explicitly do not take issue with the sincerity of the Native American beliefs at hand is belied by the extent of their miscalculation of how centrally their decisions obstruct Native free exercise.

Congress Responds with RFRA and RLUIPA

Emboldened by an alliance of religious and civil liberties groups from across the ideological spectrum who were unified in their distaste for the Supreme Court's *Smith* decision, Congress in 1993 responded with a statutory restoration of pre-*Smith* religious freedom, the Religious Freedom Restoration Act (RFRA), which restored the compelling interest and least restrictive means prongs of the *Sherbert* test for any government action that substantially burdened a person's religious exercise.[64]

The Supreme Court responded four years later to find RFRA unconstitutional as it applied to the states, finding among other things that constitutional interpretation is the job of the courts, not Congress.[65] *Boerne v. Flores* (1997) caused a number of states to pass state-level versions of RFRA, but it also prompted Congress to respond in 2000 with a more narrowly tailored statute, the Religious Land Use and Institutionalized Persons Act (RLUIPA). RFRA would continue to apply to federal government actions, but in 2000, Congress reopened the doors to religious freedom claims of the vast majority of prisoners, those in state and local corrections. With RLUIPA, Congress didn't just reopen the door narrowly closed by *O'Lone* and shut tight by *Smith*, it opened it wider than previously available:

> No government shall impose a substantial burden on the religious exercise of a person residing in or confined to an institution, as defined in section 1997 of this title, even if the burden results from a rule of general applicability, unless the government demonstrates that imposition of the burden on that person—(1) is in furtherance of a compelling governmental interest; and (2) is the least restrictive means of furthering that compelling governmental interest.[66]

RLUIPA was expressly aimed at furthering religious freedom protections against zoning laws and regulations in government institutions like prisons. RLUIPA explicitly removed any centrality test a court might apply; religious freedom claimants only need demonstrate the sincerity of their religious exercise, not the centrality of the burdened practice in question to their religion. Congress mapped this expanded definition of protectable religion by amending RFRA in the RLUIPA statute.

The Supreme Court has twice thus far considered challenges to RLUIPA. First, in *Cutter v. Wilkinson* (2005) the Court both affirmed RLUIPA and restricted its reach: it confirmed no need for a showing of centrality in substantial burden analysis, but it also reiterated some measure of "due deference to the experience and expertise of prison and jail administrators in establishing necessary regulations and procedures to maintain ... security ... consistent with consideration of costs and limited resources."[67] In 2015, the Supreme Court expanded prisoner free exercise even further. In *Holt v. Hobbs*, the Supreme Court unanimously reversed lower court rulings and found a Muslim inmate was entitled to grow a beard for religious purposes even though it violated the regulations of an Arkansas corrections facility.[68] Where the lower courts had found the grooming policy didn't pose a substantial burden to his religion, the Supreme Court concluded the inmate had clearly shown a substantial burden to his religious exercise:

> The District Court erred by concluding that the grooming policy did not substantially burden petitioner's religious exercise because "he had been provided a prayer rug and a list of distributors of Islamic material, he was allowed to correspond with a religious advisor, and was allowed to maintain the required diet and observe religious holidays." In taking this approach, the District Court improperly imported a strand of reasoning from cases involving prisoners' First Amendment rights.[69]

The *Holt* Court found "the availability of alternative means of practicing religion" to be "a relevant consideration," but importantly the error was not tied to this particular strand of reasoning but to that used in cases involving prisoners' First Amendment rights, because "RLUIPA provides greater protection."[70] In this regard, the Court in *Holt* underscored its *Hobby Lobby* holding in the previous year that Congress intended RFRA and RLUIPA to expand religious freedom protections beyond the First Amendment, applying that logic to the substantial burden analysis in *Holt*. The Court rooted its view of the substantial burden on the inmate's religious exercise because the state of Arkansas had put to him the choice of violating his beliefs or facing disciplinary sanctions, a coercive choice that lined up with that of *Hobby Lobby*. The Court proceeded to reject Arkansas's compelling interest and least restrictive means arguments, since forty-one other states were able to accommodate religious beards.

Native Inmate Religious Freedom in the Courts

RLUIPA has hardly ensured that every religious freedom claim to Native American Spirituality prevails in courts. Many inmates in state or local corrections facilities subject to RLUIPA, especially those who are non-Native, have been unable to persuade courts of the sincerity of their religious exercise, and those who do can have difficulty persuading courts that their particular grievance outweighs corrections officials' claims to the urgency of security, safety, health, and equality of treatment in their policies, restrictive as they might be for Native spirituality. Given the Supreme Court's deference to corrections officials in *Cutter*, this has created some inconsistencies in RLUIPA decisions across different circuits.[71]

What is more, most limitations of Native religions in correctional facilities happen well below the radar of the courts, at the level of what Winnifred Fallers Sullivan calls "spiritual governance" or "law on the ground."[72] But especially since RLUIPA, Native American religious freedom claims have succeeded where they haven't with other kinds of religious claims. Five cases stand out in this regard, each decided at the federal appellate level. The cases concerned a range of religious concerns, including hair length, ceremonial food and tobacco, and sweat lodge access.

Hair Length and Ceremonial Food

In *Warsoldier v. Woodford* (2005), the Ninth Circuit held that a Cahuilla inmate in a state prison had a religious freedom right under RLUIPA not to be punished for refusing to cut his hair under the prison's grooming policy.[73] There had been a number of earlier cases in the 1970s affirming religious freedom under the First Amendment for Native inmates to maintain long hair for religious reasons, including the ability to properly mourn by cutting long hair.[74] But the prison religion jurisprudence had, in the meantime, taken a more deferential position with regard to legitimate penological interests. In *Warsoldier*, the Ninth Circuit reversed a lower court's conclusion that the inmate had no substantial burden on his religion. And the Supreme Court's ruling in *Holt v. Hobbs* affirming a Muslim inmate's religious freedom from beard length restrictions has cleared further ground for Native inmates claiming accommodations to grooming policies inconsistent with their religiously inspired hair length. There remains, though, inconsistent treatment of Native inmates' claims.[75] The Eleventh Circuit (and effectively all lower courts in that circuit) repeatedly held against a Native inmate's religious freedom challenges to Alabama regulations governing hair length in a similar case in 2013.[76] The deference to corrections professionals signaled by the Supreme Court in *Cutter* appeared to carry the day.

Not so in the Seventh Circuit, which in 2015 cited *Holt v. Hobbs* to reverse a lower court ruling and to hold that a Navajo inmate who was denied venison for an annual Ghost Feast ceremony by a Wisconsin prison had rights under RLUIPA to that food and to a headband he could wear during prayer. In *Schlemm v. Wall*, a federal district court found that the inmate had not demonstrated a substantial burden on his religious exercise in the denial of his request for ceremonial venison.[77] Even if he did, the district court conjectured, the prison had a sufficiently compelling interest to maintain food safety and costs by the least restrictive means of procuring only USDA-inspected meats. The Seventh Circuit disagreed, issuing a preliminary injunction to the restrictive policies.[78]

Although Schlemm successfully received a headband for ceremonial use, there emerged difficulties in the meantime with the food accommodation, since Schlemm's options could only involve "shelf-stable" venison from approved vendors, the cost of which he would be asked to bear. Court documents illuminate the detailed texture of the accommodations:

> Ultimately, plaintiff requested that he be permitted to order: (1) a jerky combo including venison, elk and buffalo jerky from Cabela's online website, for $65.94; (2) a beef Indian Taco from a local restaurant, Frybread Heaven, for $6.75; and (3) a venison Sloppy Joe from another local restaurant, the 1919 Kitchen and Tap, for $19.00. The jerky arrived at GBCI before the Ghost Feast, and the venison sloppy joe and Indian Taco were scheduled to be delivered on the date of the feast. The total cost for the food would have been $91.69, plus tax and additional delivery charges for the restaurant food.[79]

According to the court, Schlemm withdrew from the September 2015 feast four days prior, indicating that it "would not be a proper Ghost Feast unless it: (1) was held in October or November, not September; (2) included a Sweat Lodge, tobacco burning, and spiritual songs; and (3) included foods more traditional than those being offered."[80] But Schlemm's own story notwithstanding, the Wisconsin corrections agency revamped its policy for periodic celebratory religious meals, opening possibilities for various individuals to procure for themselves in a regulated process the shelf-stable foods that would fulfill their religious obligations.[81]

Ceremonial Tobacco

Access to ceremonial tobacco has become a major point of recent case law with stricter enforcement of tobacco free rules. Formal accommodations remain in some states, like Minnesota, for access to ceremonial tobacco, often in an admixture with red willow bark, sealed in medicine bags or tobacco ties (offerings/embodiments of prayer), and in pipe ceremonies.[82] In other states, like South Dakota, inmates have persuaded courts to compel such accommodations. Especially given the public health interests that stand behind the tobacco prohibitions, some courts' willingness stands out for their acknowledgment of the significance and necessity of tobacco for many tribal traditions of ceremony and prayer. Recall that one-fourth of South Dakota state inmates are Native, many of them Lakota/Dakota whose traditions plainly center on the pipe and offerings of tobacco. A challenge under RLUIPA to that state's total ban's extension to Native ceremonies won in federal district court, which mandated a revision of the policy and then issued its own remediation order when the parties could not agree on a policy.[83] Even though the remediated order included an even "weaker" admixture of tobacco with red willow bark, the South Dakota Department of Corrections appealed. In *Native American Council of Tribes v. Weber* (2014), the Eighth Circuit found with Native inmates Blaine Brings Plenty and Clayton Creek and rejected the state's argument, citing several other Lakota spiritual leaders, that red willow bark, not tobacco, is the real traditional substance of Lakota ceremonies.[84] Or rather, the Eighth Circuit avoided having to involve itself in such a judgment by finding a substantial burden on religious exercise as a consequence.[85] Even though the state argued any amount of tobacco in a mixture could make the substance a valuable commodity inside prisons and invite abuse, the Eighth Circuit found that the state's total tobacco ban was not the least restrictive means of accomplishing its aim of health and security and ordered the policy of allowing a ceremonial admixture to be sufficient.

Access to the Sweat Lodge

Like ceremonial tobacco, sweat lodges are a key component of Native American Spirituality in prisons, and like the policies on ceremonial tobacco, policies on inmate access to sweat lodges vary widely from state to state.[86] In these cases, too, especially since RLUIPA's enactment in 2000, courts have stepped in to protect prisoners' rights of access to sweat lodges. A Tenth Circuit decision in *Yellowbear v. Lampert* (2014) is notable for the courts' affirmation of the weight of a prisoners' right of access to the sweat lodge in relation to the government's compelling interest to limit that access in favor of safety and security, and in this case, budgetary limitations.[87] It is also notable as an opinion written by Neil Gorsuch, a Tenth Circuit judge prior to his appointment to the Supreme Court, and one of the ten cases he submitted to the Senate confirmation process as emblematic of his thinking on religious freedom. Andrew Yellowbear, a Northern Arapaho tribal member, had been denied access to a sweat lodge by a Wyoming prison because the terms of his incarceration required a lockdown to protect him, and thus, prison officials argued, he effectively would enter the lodge alone. This presented the prison with a cost it considered "unduly burdensome."[88] A district court sided with Wyoming Corrections, granting summary judgment and thus requiring no bench trial to try facts, but the Tenth Circuit vacated and remanded for trial consistent with an opinion that went out of its way to underscore the legitimacy of Yellowbear's claims. "A burden can be "substantial," Judge Gorsuch wrote, even if it does not compel or order the claimant to betray a sincerely held religious belief." He cited a Tenth Circuit decision that found sufficient coercion in a government action that forces "an illusory or Hobson's choice where the only realistically possible course of action available to the plaintiff trenches on sincere religious exercise."[89]

> It is enough that the claimant is presented with a choice in which he faces considerable pressure to abandon the religious exercise at issue. The term "substantial," after all, doesn't mean complete or total, so a "substantial burden" need not be a complete or total one.[90]

Having established the substantial burden, the opinion goes on to weigh how compelling is the government interest, and dutifully cites the deference to corrections officials on matters of security, safety, and cost in *Cutter v. Wilkinson*, but this "does not extend so far," Judge Gorsuch stated, "that prison officials may declare a compelling governmental interest by fiat," and also suggested a lockdown for religious freedom purposes could well be as necessary as one for medical purposes.[91] The court noted Yellowbear's high burden—"no access of any kind, ever"—and "the cost to the prison left undefined and thus presumably low." "In these circumstances," the court held, "we don't doubt a reasonable trier of fact could find a RLUIPA violation." Judge Gorsuch's opening makes clear that Native traditions will count, and he even refrains from using the language of spirituality:

> Andrew Yellowbear will probably spend the rest of his life in prison. Time he must serve for murdering his daughter. With that much lying behind and still before him, Mr. Yellowbear has found sustenance in his faith. No one doubts the sincerity of his religious beliefs or that they are the reason he seeks access to his prison's sweat lodge—a house of prayer and meditation the prison has supplied for those who share his Native American religious tradition. Yet the prison refuses to open the doors of that sweat lodge to Mr. Yellowbear alone, and so we have this litigation. While those convicted of crime in our society lawfully forfeit a great many civil liberties, Congress has (repeatedly) instructed that the sincere exercise of religion should not be among them—at least in the absence of a compelling reason. In this record we can find no reason like that.[92]

As made clear in a PhD dissertation by Emily Brault based on her experience as a chaplain in an Iowa prison, sweat lodges are remarkable for physical, emotional, psychological, social, and spiritual healing.[93] Sweat lodge ceremonies in the middle of prison yards offer practitioners an extraordinarily powerful space and time for tapping into realities that transcend the confines of the prison, and that offer purification, renewal, and community. Not surprisingly, perhaps, sweat lodge ceremonies are compelling to many inmates seeking healing and transcendence who are not Native American and who have encountered a sweat lodge before their time in prison, where it can shine like a beacon in the drab yard.

This is the context of a case decided in the same year as *Yellowbear* in the Sixth Circuit Court of Appeals. Three death row inmates in Kentucky, Robert Foley, Roger Eppinger, and Vincent Stopher, sought unsuccessfully to hold a sweat lodge that they offered to pay for at their own expense, to have access to ceremonial bison for an annual powwow, and to receive visits by a Native spiritual leader. Joined by Randy Haight and Gregory Wilson, who had other religious freedom complaints, the five inmates represented themselves in a challenge under RLUIPA.[94] Although the court record in *Haight v. Thompson* doesn't specify their identity, each of the five is identified racially as "white" in the Kentucky inmate information system.[95]

Initially, the five lost their case in district court, which granted summary judgment without a bench trial, and thus without the process of discovery and evidence that substantially encompasses the facts of the case. On appeal, the Sixth Circuit vacated the summary judgment and remanded the case to the district court for a bench trial informed by the appellate court's guidelines for the case. Addressing Kentucky's argument from the slippery slope that exceptions here and there will breed other unlimited exceptions, the Sixth Circuit wrote:

> Rejecting accommodation requests on the ground that an exception to a general prison policy will make life difficult for prison wardens is a fine idea in the abstract and may well be a fine idea under *Smith*. But it has no place as a stand-alone justification under RLUIPA.[96]

The decision found difficulty with Kentucky's argument that its prohibition was rooted in a compelling government interest, citing numerous examples of sweat lodge access upheld by courts in other states.[97] But the decision also cautioned that RLUIPA prison cases are highly contextual, acknowledging without challenging other circuit court decisions that upheld prison denials of sweat lodge access.[98]

Conclusion

Contextual, indeed. It is easy to overstate the strength of the inmates' hands in these cases. Even when pro se inmates win at the appellate court level, their substantive claims to religious freedom in their particular prison can go unfulfilled. Andrew Yellowbear's pro se efforts ultimately failed to produce his desired access to a sweat lodge when the district court in Wyoming took his case on remand.[99] Despite the strongly worded opinion by the Tenth Circuit, the full range of Yellowbear's grievances were dismissed in deference to the prison official's legal pleadings. And in the *Haight* case, the district court, flatly and without elaboration denied a motion for summary judgment by the Kentucky inmates, who again were acting pro se and were presumably lacking the resources or liberty to undertake a bench trial.[100] So neither did their effort to have a sweat lodge result in a court injunction.

But the victories in the appeals court phase of the *Yellowbear* and *Haight* proceedings stand tall nonetheless, shaping the legal interpretation of RLUIPA that bolsters a wide range of claims in their wake, and more importantly, promises to shape the approaches taken by prison officials. And the RLUIPA victories at the appellate court level call attention to how even for non-Native seekers/practitioners of Native American Spirituality, it is the spirituality, not the identity, of the practitioner that matters. Nothing in the court record of the three phases of *Haight v. Thompson* engages the question of the identity of the plaintiffs.

Religious preference is part of an initial intake screening for inmates in the federal system. Federal regulations provide that "by notifying the chaplain in writing, an inmate may request to change this designation at any time, and the change will be effected in a timely fashion."[101] Native American Spirituality is a religious preference, not a heritage keyed to citizens of a Native nation.

We turn now to consider the contrasting career of Native American claims to sacred lands in the courts, which have consistently failed to persuade judges that religious exercise involving sacred lands is substantially burdened. The cases to which we turn are distinguished from the prison cases by their collective nature; claimants are consistently tribal governments, not individuals. But with a few exceptions in lower courts, they have failed under the First Amendment or under RFRA. As we will see, the common thread between the inmate victories and the tribal sacred lands losses is that both are viewed in terms of the controlling image of Native American *spirituality*.

3

Religion as Spirituality

SACRED LANDS

Introduction

Where Native people in prison have been relatively successful petitioning courts to protect their religious freedom from various measures of corrections officials, Native peoples have been consistently unsuccessful in winning court recognition of religious freedom claims when it comes to sacred lands. Scholars from Vine Deloria Jr. on have identified the distinctiveness of place-based piety of Native American religions.[1] Where many religious traditions are oriented to time, Deloria argued, Native religions are oriented to land, and to living well on particular lands and in proper ritual and ethical relationships with the flora and fauna of those lands. Their distinctiveness in this regard has rendered Native American religions especially illegible in American law, but the issue for local Indigenous religions is as much a question of whether religion is to be construed as a collective matter of obligation, including to land, as it is a question of whether the law can fully encompass Native nature piety.

The consistent failures in the sacred lands cases are rooted in the same judicial disposition to regard claims to religion as claims to spirituality that produced the relative success of the prison cases. In the prison cases, since the asserted claims are those of individuals and because Native American Spirituality has become a term of art in chaplaincy and correction management, judicial recognition of spirituality has led to relatively meaningful accommodations for inmates' religious practice that courts require of corrections facilities. In the sacred land cases, though, the story is one of judicial misrecognition of religion as merely spirituality. Where Native practitioners

94

in prisons have handily demonstrated the substantial burdens of various corrections policies, with only a few exceptions at lower court levels, courts have been unwilling to recognize substantial burdens on religious exercise in the case of obstructed access to, or threats to the integrity of, sacred sites. Courts have consistently seen any such burden involving sacred places as being a matter of diminished spiritual development or fulfillment. To diminish spiritual fulfillment, these courts consistently hold, is not to substantially burden religious exercise, and thus not to trigger protections under the First Amendment or the Religious Freedom Restoration Act.

This chapter examines the failure in the courts of Native appeals to religious freedom protections for sacred lands, and it extends the previous chapter's analysis of the reception of Native claims to religion as *religion*. Where a religious claim conforms to the subjective, interior spirituality that has become naturalized in the United States, it has worked reasonably well in the courts. This is emphatically not the case where claims involve religious relationships with, uses of, and obligations to, land. My aim is to explain how courts reason their way out of taking steps to protect Native American religious freedom when sacred places are threatened, a puzzling matter in that courts consistently acknowledge the sincerity of the religious beliefs and practices associated with those sacred places. Along the way I develop a fuller sense of the workings of the discourse of Native American spirituality as it comes to control judicial comprehension of Native religious freedom claims.

A fitting conclusion of this chapter is a consideration of the second round of the Standing Rock litigation, in which Standing Rock's downstream neighbor, the Cheyenne River Sioux Tribe, argued that Army Corps approval of the pipeline's crossing of the Missouri River violated their religious freedom rights under RFRA because the river is sacred and because as the sole source of ritually pure water, a contaminated Missouri would preclude the observance of necessary ceremonies. In this respect, Cheyenne River took pains to align their case with the successful efforts by Native American prisoners to assert religious freedom rights under RLUIPA, experiencing a substantial burden on their religion because they had no other options, rather than with precedents thematically tied to the Native sacred land cases. I wish to help explain the consistency of judicial misrecognition of Native religious freedom claims to sacred lands, and to offer an explanation. This is to help understand the cases, not to foreclose on the possibility of a different judicial recognition in the future. Subsequent chapters will develop a way of regarding collective Native claims to religious freedom as peoples.

The San Francisco Peaks Case

In *Navajo Nation et al. v. U.S. Forest Service* (2008), the Ninth Circuit Court of Appeals sitting en banc (eleven Ninth Circuit judges), eclipsed a lengthy ruling by a three judge panel of the same circuit that had gone far, in its brief eighteen-month life, to advance the legal claims regarding sacred land by Native peoples, and which had drawn something of a line in the sand about whether Native sacred lands could ever be protected under legal regimes of the freedom of religion.[2] The three judge panel ruling, now reduced to a dissent, pays close attention to the religious freedom claims by the Navajo, Hopi, White Mountain Apache, Yavapai-Apache, Havasupai, and Hualapai nations in their effort to protect the San Francisco Peaks, a mountain sacred to each nation, from a proposal to boost the commercial viability of a ski area on the mountain by making artificial snow with treated sewage effluent from the city of Flagstaff. While First Amendment claims had failed to halt expansion of the ski resort in the first place in the early 1980s,[3] the tribes in this instance challenged the US Forest Service's approval of the sewage-to-artificial-snow plan as a violation of the broader statutory protections of the Religious Freedom Restoration Act (RFRA).[4] The en banc majority ruled that spraying treated sewage as artificial snow on a sacred mountain does not "substantially burden" religious exercise under RFRA and thus does not pass the threshold question that triggers RFRA's strict scrutiny standard of review of the government action in question:

> Where, as here, there is no showing the government has coerced the Plaintiffs to act contrary to their religious beliefs under the threat of sanctions, or conditioned a governmental benefit upon conduct that would violate the Plaintiffs' religious beliefs, there is no "substantial burden" on the exercise of their religion.[5]

Instead, the en banc court found, since the ski area comprises only 1 percent of the surface of the mountain, and because there would be no limiting of access or physical destruction of plants or sites on the ski slopes, the "sole effect of the artificial snow" is on the Native Americans' "subjective spiritual experience," amounting merely to diminished "spiritual fulfillment":

> That is, the presence of the artificial snow on the Peaks is offensive to the Plaintiffs' feelings about their religion and will decrease the spiritual fulfillment Plaintiffs get from practicing their religion on the mountain. Nev-

ertheless, a government action that decreases the spirituality, the fervor, or the satisfaction with which a believer practices his religion is not what Congress has labeled a "substantial burden"—a term of art chosen by Congress to be defined by reference to Supreme Court precedent—on the free exercise of religion.[6]

In June 2009, the Supreme Court declined to hear the case, denying a certiorari petition that had asserted incongruous interpretations by various circuit courts of the meaning of "substantial burden" to religious exercise in RFRA.[7]

Consider the rhetorical force of reducing complex and corporate religious practices involving this mountain—seen as necessary to the well-being and peoplehood of six plaintiff Native nations—to the individualistic, interior, and sentimentalized terms of Native American *spirituality* and *spiritual fulfillment*. *Navajo Nation* involves a strained interpretation of Congress's intentions in RFRA, one that is now out of step with the interpretive posture toward ambiguous language in RFRA subsequently taken by the Supreme Court in *Burwell v. Hobby Lobby Stores, Inc.*[8] The 2008 en banc decision produces a disturbing result for the specific Native peoples involved, one reminiscent of the patterned, often ritualized, desecration by one group of another group's sacred sites. The *Navajo Nation* decision further impoverishes the language with which courts understand Native religions generally, and very likely the religious exercise of other communities that Congress intended to protect under RFRA.[9] *Navajo Nation* rests on the court's reduction of six different but equally sophisticated tribe-specific complexes of religious narrative, duty, and ritual practice to a common concern vaguely and inaccurately construed as Native spirituality.[10] At issue here is something more complex than simply to observe, along with the dissent and other critics of the decision, that all religion is inherently subjective.[11] I want to call attention to the alchemy by which the discourse of spirituality first denatures the accepted factual findings about the collective claims of Navajo, Hopi, and the other Native nations in such a way as to minimize the appraisal of the burden on their exercise, and then naturalizes this denaturing by appeal to conventional wisdom about Native spirituality. The court's rhetorical move is as weighty as it is subtle, embedded problematically in a discourse of "spiritual, not religious," which has more to do with broader therapeutic and consumerist trends in contemporary American religion than with the accepted factual findings about the Native claims at hand. The substantial burden analysis that follows is troubled as a consequence.[12]

FIG. 3.1. San Francisco Peaks
The San Francisco Peaks is one of the four sacred mountains that define Navajo homelands.
The massif is the home of ancestral spirits of the Hopi and the namesake of the White
Mountain Apache. Federal approval of a plan to use treated wastewater from nearby Flagstaff,
Arizona, to make artificial snow for a ski area on the massif generated litigation, but six
Native nations failed to convince courts their religion had been substantially burdened.
(Cococino National Forest/Photo Deborah Lee Soltesz)

The San Francisco Peaks and Navajo and Hopi Traditions

I'll return shortly to the Ninth Circuit majority's analysis in support of its
holding on RFRA, but first I want to turn to the detailed findings of fact elicited by the trial court regarding the indispensable place of the San Francisco
Peaks to the religions of the six Native peoples. My analysis need not proceed
beyond the factual findings that emerged from the testimony of Native spiritual leaders themselves, especially since those factual findings were agreed on
by all parties and accepted in full by the en banc Ninth Circuit.[13]

For the more than one quarter million Diné people of the Navajo Nation,
the San Francisco Peaks massif is Dookʼoʼoosłííd ("shining-on-top," in reference to its snowcap), the westernmost of the sacred mountains that define the
precincts of Navajoland and that orient disciplines of Navajo prayer and daily
life alike.[14] The mountain is understood to be the site of the creation of the
Navajo people, is regarded as alive, and is referred to as "Mother," the Navajos'

"essence and their home," their "leader," and a source of power for living and healing. Navajos regard the mountain as the place where the deity Changing Woman resided and went through puberty in the first *kinaalda* ceremony, which is replicated as a rite of passage to Navajo womanhood, one that is also a ritual renewal of community and cosmos.[15] The Peaks massif is a location for the ritualized gathering by *hitaali* (singers, or medicine men) of specific plants, medicines, and other items necessary for the creation and renewal of the medicine bundles that anchor healings and other ceremonies of Navajo life.[16] The mountain is not only an ecological niche for the flora necessary to these ritual practices, it is also a place whose power is related to the effectiveness of those medicines, a place for ritually regulated practices of gathering on the mountain. As Joe Shirley Jr., then president of the Navajo Nation put it, one "cannot just voluntarily go upon this mountain at any time. It's—it's the holiest of shrines in our way of life. You have to sacrifice. You have to sing certain songs before you even dwell for a little bit to gather herbs, to do offerings."[17] Such practices, because they are crucial to the generative and healing power that benefits all life, are not pursuits of individuals for their own spiritual edification; they are obligatory facets of ceremonies like the Blessingway, which brings healing, well-being, and cosmic renewal. Indeed, the Peaks are prayed to by name in the Blessingway, and because the Blessingway serves as a ritual coda of sorts to other ceremonial complexes, the sacred presence of the mountain is invoked in virtually every Navajo ritual event. In all these respects, it is clear that for Navajo people, the San Francisco Peaks massif is not simply a place for meditation, ritual activity, or a landmark on the horizon; it is a fundamental point of orientation and source of power for a Navajo way of life.

For the Hopi, the Peaks are also among the holiest of places, but for reasons that pertain to entirely different cultural traditions, narratives, codes of duty, and ritual practices.[18] As for the Navajo, for the Hopi the Peaks are a holy focal point orienting all life. The Peaks are the home of the *katsinam*, or kachinas, spirits who bring rain and blessing and on whom all life depends. Sacred narratives specify the Peaks as the place where Hopi ancestors went, after emergence from the underworld, to receive instructions from and establish a covenant with Maa'Saw, a key deity who teaches the Hopi how to live well on earth. The Hopi people maintain numerous shrines and make ritual pilgrimages on the Peaks; like the Navajo, they have scores of prayers and ritual practices that reference and revolve around the Peaks and foster the right relations with spirits on the Peaks. It would be hard to find a more religiously specific and necessary sacred place for the Navajo or Hopi, or to adequately describe all aspects of the Peaks' holiness, meaning, or urgency to Native people, much less to identify an adequate analogy for the shape of their significance to Native lives from monotheistic traditions.

For the Havasupai and Hualapai, the Peaks are the center of the world: a site where a female ancestor alighted following a cataclysmic flood and conceived by the water on the mountain the next generations. Ritual pilgrimages to the Peaks require complex spiritual preparation. Water from the Peaks is ceremonially necessary for healing and purification.[19]

For the White Mountain Apache, the San Francisco Peaks massif is one of the four "holy" mountains and the White Mountain that is the people's namesake. A conscious distinction between the language of the "sacred" and the language of the "holy" emerged in the testimony at the trial court, a distinction that suggested that "sacred" was insufficient to evoke the sacrosanct presence of the San Francisco Peaks, apart from the memories or ritual activities associated with it. Apache leader Vincent Randall said in response to a line of questioning that insinuated all Apache land was sacred, or that the Peaks were sacred like any number of sites in the region:

> That's your term "sacred." That's not my term.... There are other places of honor and respect. You're looking at everything as being sacred.... There is honor and respect, just as much as the Twin Towers is a place of honor and respect. Gettysburg. Yes there are places like that in Apache land, but there are four holy mountains. Holy mountains.[20]

Given such consistently rich and detailed testimony in the trial, it is perhaps unsurprising that the Ninth Circuit, like the trial court, accepted the factual findings about the religious practices associated with the mountain. So what was formally at issue was not whether the Native claims were religious or sincere, but whether Native peoples were "substantially burdened" in their religious exercise under RFRA.

The Legal Issue in Navajo Nation: "Substantial Burden"

A nearly unanimous Congress passed RFRA in 1993 to restore a robust strict scrutiny approach to religious freedom that placed the burden of proof on governments to show they had a "compelling state interest" and had found the "least restrictive means" in accomplishing government aims that placed a "substantial burden" on religious exercise. But RFRA does not define precisely what would constitute a "substantial burden" to that exercise.[21] Indeed, as Alex Tallchief Skibine puts it, RFRA remains "ambivalent" about how to regard such a burden, with a stated purpose that is difficult to reconcile with many of the findings in the Congressional Record.[22] The Ninth Circuit's en banc holding rejected an approach that would accept the term's plain meaning, or its meaning under the Dictionary Act.[23] The court also implicitly rejected the approaches of other circuit courts and its three dissenting judges that RFRA intended a more robust restoration of the reach of the free exercise of religion after *Smith*.[24] The dissent construed "substantial burden" to mean "preventing [the plaintiff] from engaging in [religious] conduct or having a religious experience." The dissent would have held that the Ninth Circuit precedent on the meaning of "substantial burden" had always been "according to the *effect* of a government action on religious exercise rather than particular mechanisms by which this effect is conceived."[25] The en banc majority insisted instead that "substantial burden" is a term of art developed in the Supreme Court's First Amendment precedents prior to *Smith*, applying "only when individuals are [1] forced to choose between following the tenets of their religion and receiving a governmental benefit ... or [2] coerced to act contrary to their religious beliefs by the threat of civil or criminal sanctions."[26]

Here the Ninth Circuit majority confined a "substantial burden" to the particular mechanisms of government interference in the two landmark Supreme Court cases of pre-*Smith* Free Exercise law, *Sherbert v. Verner* (1963), and *Wisconsin v. Yoder* (1972), although the specific construction "substantial burden" appears nowhere in those cases:[27]

> The dissent would have us ignore this Supreme Court precedent and, instead, invent a new definition for "substantial burden" by reference to a dictionary. This we cannot do. Rather, we must presume Congress meant to incorporate into RFRA the definition of "substantial burden" used by the Supreme Court.[28]

Crucially, the en banc majority bolstered that construal with broad appeals to Supreme Court decisions involving Native American religious freedom in *Lyng v. Northwest Indian Cemetery Protective Association* (1988), in *Bowen v. Roy* (1986), and in the 1983 DC Circuit decision in *Wilson v. Block*. While each was decided prior to *Smith*, and thus considered by the Ninth Circuit majority to be proper precedents for delimiting "substantial burden," they are hardly *Sherbert-* or *Yoder*-era decisions; indeed, *Lyng* and *Roy* were instrumental to the undoing in *Smith* of the strict scrutiny approach to the

Free Exercise Clause framed by *Sherbert* and *Yoder*.[29] *Lyng* and *Roy* served this purpose by articulating a presumed slippery slope that some on the Court reasoned had set in under *Sherbert* and *Yoder*, and who concluded that granting any religious freedom claim by any particular Native individual invites a potential judicial chaos where there is "no stopping place."[30]

The question of the relevance of the Supreme Court's precedent in *Lyng* is at the heart of the reasoning in *Navajo Nation*. In *Lyng*, the Supreme Court reversed a Ninth Circuit's holding that had been favorable to the Yurok, Karuk, and Tolowa tribes, and ruled that a logging road through high country precincts sacred to those nations did not sufficiently "prohibit" the tribal member's religious exercise under the First Amendment to trigger the strict scrutiny protections of *Sherbert*. Much has been written about *Lyng*, and I will not fully treat it here;[31] suffice it to say that *Navajo Nation* is effectively framed in terms of *Lyng* as a Native sacred land case, and that this asserted comparison mutes the contrast between resolving such claims under RFRA and under the First Amendment. I agree with Alex Tallchief Skibine that this contrast is a glaring one. Although *Lyng* admits of two different interpretations that, in turn, lead to two different views as to whether RFRA overturns *Lyng*, RFRA does not simply override *Smith* in favor of *anything* before *Smith*; rather, RFRA also must be considered in light of *Smith*-era decisions that raised the threshold and shrunk the reach of protected religious exercise.[32] For example, pre-*Smith* First Amendment cases had narrowed the scope of "substantial burden" analysis by requiring that the burdened religious exercise demonstrate a certain level of centrality to a religious system, and RFRA, as amended on this point by RLUPA in 2000, undid this standard of centrality by explicitly extending the definition of *exercise of religion* to include "any exercise of religion, whether or not compelled by, or central to, a system of religious belief."[33]

A Brief Interlude in Light of Burwell v. Hobby Lobby

The Supreme Court in *Burwell v. Hobby Lobby Stores, Inc.* has indeed taken this overarching view of RFRA—Congress intended in RFRA not simply to restore, but to extend beyond, the First Amendment Free Exercise jurisprudence prior to *Smith*. Because there had been no Supreme Court First Amendment case where a for-profit corporation had been recognized as having religious free exercise rights, the particular intention of Congress in RFRA with respect to that body of pre-*Smith* jurisprudence was key to the Court's conclusion that closely held for-profit corporations were "persons" capable of protected religious exercise under RFRA.[34]

In *Hobby Lobby*, the Court responded to the government's claim that RFRA did "no more than codify this Court's pre-*Smith* Free Exercise Clause precedents"—a claim that prevailed in *Navajo Nation*—and "because none of those cases squarely held that a for-profit corporation has free exercise rights, RFRA does not confer such protection."[35] To this view, and based on its over-all appraisal of RFRA as a "very broad" statute, the *Hobby Lobby* majority asserted that "nothing in the text of RFRA as originally enacted suggested that the statutory phrase 'exercise of religion under the First Amendment' was meant to be tied to this Court's pre-*Smith* interpretation of that Amendment."[36] The Court went on to espouse a view that had prevailed in the Ninth Circuit's three judge panel ruling in *Navajo Nation* but that was ultimately dismissed by the en banc ruling in that case. The *Hobby Lobby* majority wrote:

> If the original text of RFRA was not clear enough on this point—and we think it was—the amendment of RFRA through RLUIPA surely dispels any doubt. That amendment deleted the prior reference to the First Amendment and neither HHS nor the principal dissent can explain why Congress did this if it wanted to tie RFRA coverage tightly to the specific holdings of our pre–*Smith* free exercise cases. Moreover, as discussed, the amendment went further, providing that the exercise of religion "shall be construed in favor of a broad protection of religious exercise, to the maximum extent permitted by the terms of this chapter and the Constitution."[37]

"It is simply not possible," the *Hobby Lobby* majority concluded, "to read these provisions as restricting the concept of the 'exercise of religion' to those practices specifically addressed in our pre-*Smith* decisions."[38]

Justice Ginsburg's spirited dissent in *Hobby Lobby* gained wide acclaim for its defense of women's access to health care, but it turned legally on her disagreement with the majority's view that Congress, in RFRA, intended much more than what the Supreme Court had held under the First Amendment prior to *Smith*. Justice Ginsburg wrote, "persuaded that Congress enacted RFRA to serve a far less radical purposes, and mindful of the havoc the Court's judgment can introduce, I dissent."[39]

The *Hobby Lobby* decision reopens a number of questions about what might be termed collective or group religious freedom rights.[40] But more immediately, *Hobby Lobby* opens the door for rethinking the Ninth Circuit's interpretive posture in *Navajo Nation*: that Congress in RFRA narrowly meant to restore pre-*Smith* First Amendment jurisprudence, and thus that *Lyng* is a reliable controlling decision for the substantial burden analysis in the case.

No "Substantial Burden" on Native American Spiritual Fulfillment

Whatever should befall the substantial burden analysis modeled in *Lyng* and elaborated under RFRA in *Navajo Nation* in terms of what interpretive criteria to apply to the ambiguities of RFRA in light of *Hobby Lobby*, a still deeper question is begged by the Ninth Circuit's en banc decision, a question of how courts construe the *religiousness* of Native American sacred site claims, for a court's determination of what burdens are "substantial" and what are merely minor or incidental, are not determinations solely of burden, but determinations of the reach and extent of religious exercise.

Part of whether spraying treated sewage as artificial snow on a sacred mountain rises to the level of a substantial burden on religious exercise involves how the court chooses to gauge the religiousness of the Native American exercise in question. A proper analysis of this case cannot narrowly be about which theory of statutory interpretation should prevail or simply a threshold question about where a substantial burden begins but also a question of where protected religious exercise ends.[41] Thus, there is a substantive question about how the courts regard the distinctive shape of Indigenous religions, whose profound orientation to land and collective nature requires intellectual precision and rigor that the conceptual field of "spirituality" does not elicit. I turn now to the cultural history of that conceptual field of spirituality and its relations to the imagining of Native American spirituality. Thus equipped, we will see better how the Ninth Circuit, following the Supreme Court in *Lyng*, does not merely turn to the discourse of spirituality for aid in understanding the spatial orientation of Native religions, but draws on that seemingly natural semantic shift to distinguish the merely spiritual from the properly religious. In the doing, this filters out the sharper edges, not to mention what Kristen Carpenter has called the internal limiting principles, of the religions at hand.[42]

Religion as Spirituality in the Courts

It may seem like the words roll off the tongue today, but the usage "Native American Spirituality" is anything but a natural construction, and consideration of its cultural history can offer insight into the workings of its usage in

Navajo Nation. While this may pass as a seemingly natural and neutral way to describe those aspects of Native religious traditions that lay outside the typical semantic range of the concept *religion*, spirituality here is rooted in rhetorical strategies and valuations that pervert a proper understanding of the religious exercise at stake in *Navajo Nation.*

The cultural history of spirituality as a concept is a broad one, part of a narrative arc that includes the Enlightenment, Pietism, Romanticism, the Western encounter with colonized others, and 1960s counterculture. It cannot be exhaustively treated in these pages.[43] Here, I want simply to establish that the "spiritual fulfillment" that the Ninth Circuit regards as "decreased" in *Navajo Nation* ensconces by reference to *spirituality* a broadly American, rather than specifically Native American—much less Navajo, Hopi, or Apache— understanding of religion. Furthermore, this rhetorical move blurs the very boundaries that Congress, in RFRA, sought to maintain against the grain of the Supreme Court's First Amendment jurisprudence. The move from "religion" to "spirituality" asserts a distinction, if not opposition, that many Americans insist on in the oft-heard claim: "I'm spiritual, not religious." This opposition privileges *spiritual* in dualities like inner/outer, authentic/organized, experience/doctrine, even as it reduces *real* religion to a private subjective sphere of the self that makes few if any demands on the public square.[44]

Sociologist Robert Wuthnow has framed the phenomenon in terms of a tectonic shift in the second half of the twentieth century from an American religiosity of "dwelling" to one of "seeking." Fueled by rapid changes in mobility, technology, and globalization, American religion has gone from being typified by members of stable, enduring local religious communities in which they dwell to being typified by seekers, whose eclectic spirituality traverses geographical, cultural, and historical boundaries on a quest for fleeting "sacred moments" and new "spiritual vistas."[45] Wuthnow doesn't let the distinction between religion and spirituality stand, but interrogates it to find two highly contrasting types of piety, contrasting in ways that disclose deep contrasts in social theory on religion between Émile Durkheim and Max Weber:

With Durkheim, a spirituality of dwelling pays considerable attention to ways of distinguishing sacred habitats from the profane world and to rituals that dramatize these differentiations. With Weber, a spirituality of seeking pays virtually no attention to the contrast between sacred and profane, or to the use of spatial metaphors, but concentrates on that mixture of spiritual and rational, ethical and soteriological, individual and collective activities whereby the person in modern societies seeks meaning in life and tries to be of service to others.[46]

A legitimate quarrel with the binary nature of the contrast suggested here between Weber and Durkheim need not stop us from considering what a shift toward a spirituality of seeking means for a sense of the sacred and in particular to sacred places. "A spirituality of dwelling requires sharp symbolic boundaries to protect sacred space from its surroundings; a spirituality of seeking draws fewer distinctions of such magnitude," writes Wuthnow. Citing Max Lerner, he continues:

> One might agree with Durkheim that "the contrast between sacred and profane is the widest and deepest the human mind can make." Yet for myself I find all sorts of things ... to be sacred. Rather than being in a place that is by definition spiritual, the sacred is found momentarily in experiences as different as mowing the lawn or viewing a full moon.[47]

In another major study of the conscious turn toward spirituality in the remaking of American religion, sociologist Wade Clark Roof found that "talk about spirituality was often rambling and far-ranging," but among the themes that emerged as patterns were the self-authored search, looking inward, and journeying in search of growth.[48] For many, "journey involved extended mental trips, voyages into other traditions, imaginary movement across time and space in search of spiritual resources available to the self."[49]

Roof and others have called attention to the consumptive patterns of American religiosity as a "spiritual marketplace," and to the therapeutic turn in American religion from communal norms of self-discipline to individual possibilities of self-fulfillment.[50] Wuthnow describes the transformation of American religion in terms of a shift from "spiritual production to spiritual consumption." Religious Americans, he writes, "used to produce offspring for their churches and synagogues, send out missionaries ... to convert others, and spend their time working for religious committees and guilds; they now let professional experts—writers, artists, therapists, spiritual guides—be the producers while they consume what they need in order to enrich themselves spiritually."[51]

Market analogies may have their drawbacks, but they draw useful connections between the semantic range of *spirituality* as it is used in contemporary parlance and a concern for a piety whose authenticity relies on the self's ability to range freely across religious and cultural boundaries to find its fulfillment. This state of affairs urges the deregulation of a spiritual marketplace and the maximization of choices, even as it offers incentives for aggressive marketing and branding of a spirituality industry, in no small part through a thriving book trade where, it would seem, the term *spirituality* far outsells the term *religion*. Word searches on Native American religion produce books whose authors are typically familiar to this scholar of religion: a search of books under the rubric of Native American spirituality produces books largely authored by non-Native, nonscholarly writers, including authors with names like Cinnamon Moon.[52] Scholarship on what has come to be called the "plastic shaman" phenomenon has documented how the marketplace and consumption metaphors for spirituality have been particularly apt for understanding how a spirituality industry has trained spiritual hunger on representations of Native American religiosity.[53]

Native/Nature Spirituality

The cravings of a "spiritual, not religious" appetite for Native American traditions stem from deep in American culture and history. Philip Deloria has shown just how enduring has been Americans' penchant for "playing Indian," from the Boston Tea Party to Grateful Dead concerts, a penchant tied to deep ambivalence about American identity.[54] But a hunger for romanticized images of an emotional, aesthetic Native view that "everything is sacred" is also related to Wuthnow's observation of a shift to seeker spirituality. Seekers' desire to connect, to collect fleeting sacred moments, and to take in new spiritual vistas has led many Americans to a nature spirituality of which Native American spirituality might just be the apotheosis. Just as nature spirituality seeks to find a subjective home absent a stable objective one in emotive experiences of "Nature," "Nature" itself, like its corollary "wilderness," emerges as an abstraction increasingly unmoored from necessary connections to particular places. The history of American nature religion has often seen Deep Ecologists, Neo-pagans, Wiccans, and other activists seeking not only political alliances but also spiritual direction from Native people, and to be sure many Native people have been more than willing to find common ground.[55]

But to view Native American religions as the apotheosis of nature spirituality is to denature those traditions. Native religious traditions are highly diverse, involving many hundreds of distinct peoples speaking more than two hundred distinct Indigenous languages, and profoundly local—that is, profoundly tied to particular, specific places in complicated and sophisticated ways that are as obscured as they are clarified by the relatively wooden term *sacred*. Some places are so sacrosanct that traditions forbid anyone to go there; others are sacred but also open to other uses, such as for economic livelihood; still others are sacred at certain times of year.[56] These relationships to place, as heartfelt and emotive as they can be at a subjective level for individual members of a Native people, are not best understood through approaches to religion as individual conscience or subjective emotion. Even Judge Fletcher's otherwise able dissent in *Navajo Nation* turns on a criticism that the en banc majority had failed to see the subjective nature of all religion. Citing William James's definition of religion as "the feelings acts and experiences of individual men in their solitude, so far as they apprehend themselves to stand in relation to whatever they may consider the divine," Fletcher asserts that "religious exercise sometimes involves physical things, but the physical or scientific character of these things is secondary to their spiritual and religious meaning. The centerpiece of religious belief and exercise is the 'subjective' and the 'spiritual.'"[57] Fletcher's view surely pertains to many contemporary religious phenomena but does not speak with precision about the misrecognition of Native religious claims in the case.[58]

Scholars of Indigenous religions in particular have long struggled with the ill fit between religion as an analytical category emerging in the modern West and the practices and beliefs that characterize the local, oral traditions of Native peoples. But the term *spirituality*, which clearly some intend as a better suited analytic category, is not synonymous with religion; it only exacerbates the difficulties of religion as an analytical category. In the shift from the analytical frame of religion to that of spirituality, Indigenous traditions that often cannot be divorced from visible and outward signs of peoplehood, community, norms, duties, and disciplines are transmuted into a universal piety of nature religion, transportable to virtually any setting and viewing everything as sacred.[59]

I want to insist on an important distinction between tribe-specific religious traditions and a universal piety of nature that is blurred in the concept of spirituality as it is used here. Traditional Native American religions are profoundly local, tied to particular places not simply through deep feeling and aesthetic appreciation, or through religious practices that take place on them, but also through a whole range of narratives, ritual disciplines, and sophisticated moral codes related to particular places. As I elaborated above, the San Francisco Peaks are, for the Navajo, not just a pristine and beautiful natural place for meditation and spiritual edification; the Peaks orient all aspects of Navajo life as the westernmost of the sacred mountains designating Navajo space. The Peaks are the object of daily prayer disciplines and the sustaining source of healing power in medicine bundles that empower Navajo ceremonial life. For the Hopi, contamination of the Peaks is not just an encumbrance on Hopi spiritual experience on the Peaks but is a violation of a "spiritual covenant that the Hopi clans entered into with the Caretaker … Ma'saw and the other deities … and the Katsina that reside in the Peaks."[60] Desecration of the mountain would cause the Katsinam dance ceremonies that punctuate the Hopi year to lose their religious value, reducing them from effective "religious efforts" to "performances for performance sake."[61]

Similarly, for the Hualapai to bury a portion of a child's placenta on the Peaks after a difficult labor is not to seek spiritual fulfillment but to obey spiritual direction for the furtherance of the health of the child and mother.[62] Such traditions are not only specific to the respective tribes and keyed to specific religious narratives and beliefs, but they are also counted as duties more than as fulfillment. Such local religions, demanding disciplines of this specificity, are not generalizable into a universal spirituality of nature seeking to reenchant a disenchanted world.

The Discourse of Spirituality and the Legal Issue of Substantial Burden

We saw in chapter 2 how "Native American spirituality" has become regularized recently in the legal context of prisons. Its specific usage in the *Lyng* and *Roy* decisions mark not only the more important moments of the concept's legal history but also its rhetorical place in a judicial containment strategy concerning the reach of Native religious freedom claims to sacred lands that drives the Ninth Circuit's conclusion that spraying treated sewage on a sacred mountain for recreational skiing does not "substantially burden" religion under RFRA.[63]

The en banc majority of the Ninth Circuit affirmed the district court's recognition that the asserted beliefs of the Navajo, Hopi, and others are sincere. But it concluded that "no plants would be destroyed or stunted; no springs polluted; no places of worship made inaccessible, or liturgy modified" by the proposed sewage snowmaking:

Thus, the sole effect of the artificial snow is on the Plaintiffs' subjective spiritual experience. That is, the presence of the artificial snow on the Peaks is offensive to the Plaintiffs' feelings about their religion and will decrease the spiritual fulfillment Plaintiffs get from practicing their religion on the mountain.[64]

The majority goes on to distinguish "decreased spiritual fulfillment" from religious exercise that could be "substantially burdened" by the conduct in question:

> Nevertheless, a government action that decreases the spirituality, the fervor, or the satisfaction with which a believer practices his religion is not what Congress has labeled a "substantial burden."[65]

"Under Supreme Court precedent," the Ninth Circuit majority concludes, government action that results in "the diminishment of spiritual fulfillment—serious though it may be—is not a 'substantial burden' on the free exercise of religion."[66] This apparently clear distinction between diminished spirituality and burdened religion draws extensively—decisively—from the determination in *Lyng* that the threshold for First Amendment religious free exercise protection was not reached in a matter of interference with a "private person's ability to pursue spiritual fulfillment."[67] The en banc majority closes its logical circle in *Navajo Nation* by paraphrasing the Supreme Court's carefully worded conclusion in *Lyng*:

> No matter how much we might wish the government to conform its conduct to our religious preferences, act in ways that do not offend our religious sensibilities, and take no action that decreases our spiritual fulfillment, no government—let alone a government that presides over a nation with as many religions as the United States of America—could function were it required to do so.[68]

Indeed, though the Ninth Circuit speaks of *Lyng* merely as "on point," *Lyng* functions as the controlling analogy for determining the threshold of what will constitute burdened religion beyond mere diminished spiritual fulfillment.[69]

Further on I will revisit the Ninth Circuit's insistence on *Lyng's* relevance despite the intervening passage of RFRA, and its subsequent amendment in 2000. Here, I want to consider the cultural history of spirituality and Native American spirituality in order to address the crucial rhetorical turn to language of spirituality and its decreased fulfillment in the logical steps in *Navajo Nation*. Again, at issue is not merely the assertion that all religion is inherently subjective, and that, therefore, burdens on Native religious exercise centered on the San Francisco Peaks are no less substantially burdened for being subjective in nature. I want to query just how agreed on factual findings about the various ways that desecration of the San Francisco Peaks impairs the exercise of multiple highly sophisticated, complex Native religious traditions, most of which are not meaningfully confined to the subjective sphere of religious experience, become summarized in terms of "spiritual fulfillment." This rhetorical shift from religion to spirituality is no mere heuristic technique to understand beliefs and spatial practices associated with a sacred mountain. The shift to spirituality serves to undermine the force of the factual findings about the collective claims of Navajo, Hopi, and other nations by figuring them as the individual search for spiritual fulfillment that supposedly takes place on the mountain itself, claims that are potentially protean and limitless in nature. The support for this view is not an explicit treatment of the beliefs and practices themselves, but an implicit appeal to a romanticized view that Native Americans, particularly when it comes to sacred land, are spiritual, not religious.[70]

The *Navajo Nation* majority insists, following the logic of *Lyng*, which it cites on this point, that it is granting the sincerity of the Native religious claims and is cognizant of the full reach of the harm. In a revealing exchange of footnotes with the dissent on the question of the subjective nature of religion, the Ninth Circuit majority voices its agreement that "spiritual fulfillment is a central part of religious exercise," adding that "the Indians' conception of their lives as intertwined with particular mountains, rivers, and trees, which are divine parts of their being, is very well explained in the dissent."[71] The exchange continues to mangle the factual findings of sincere religious exercise with further spirituality-speak:

> For all the rich complexity that describes the profound integration of man and mountain into one, the burden of the recycled wastewater can only be expressed by the Plaintiffs as damaged spiritual feelings. Under Supreme Court precedent, government action that diminishes subjective spiritual fulfillment does not substantially burden religion.[72]

The "profound integration of man and mountain into one"? Where does such a construction come from if not straight out of some bookstore's New Age Spirituality shelf? To call San Francisco Peaks the "Mother" or "Leader" of the Navajo people, or to "pray to the peaks and visit them spiritually daily" as part of the discipline of being a good Havasupai, or to regard the desecration of the mountain as related to social and cosmic ills, is not to be in a mystical union of man and mountain, but rather to discipline one's thinking and behavior to conform ritually and ethically and doctrinally to the narratives, ethical teachings, and ritual duties of discrete religious traditions. This is true of many religious traditions, not simply Indigenous ones. Devout Muslims pray in the direction of Mecca not to be profoundly integrated or one with Mecca but because God commands such conduct. What counts is the fulfillment of the duty, not the height of the spiritual fulfillment. Consider the place of San Francisco Peaks in the Navajo Tribal Code, amended in 2002 to place the edifice of the code atop traditional foundations of law: "Diné Natural Law declares and teaches that ... the six sacred mountains [including 'Dook'o'oosłííd,' the San Francisco Peaks] must be respected, honored and protected for they, as leaders, are the foundation of the Navajo Nation"; and that "The Diné have the sacred obligation and duty to respect, preserve, and protect all that was provided, for we were designated as the steward for these relatives through our use of the sacred gifts of language and thinking."[73] Curiously, neither the Ninth Circuit majority nor dissent made reference to this formulation of a Navajo natural law obligation to the Peaks.[74]

I do not mean to deny any subjective dimension or inner spirituality to Navajo engagement with the mountain, or that of the other Native nations involved; my point is that the conceptual filter through which the Ninth Circuit court has supposedly granted the sincerity of those claims—"spiritual fulfillment"—has obliterated the complexities and details of more than ninety factual findings concerning these discrete traditions that assert any number of distinctions in their practices and beliefs related to the Peaks and reduce those religions to a singular emotional subjective spirituality of "man and mountain into one." If that's all that is really on the line, then of course, all that results is "damaged spiritual feelings." One can go find another beautiful mountain to be one with. But that's not how these Native religions work. For all the diversity of specific ways that specific Indigenous religions relate to specific places, a common thread through all is that specificity.

A brief consideration of two other cases involving Navajo religion in federal district courts can help illustrate the inaccuracy of the Ninth Circuit's construal of the factual findings about Navajo religion and the Peaks as merely subjective in nature, or matters of individual spirituality. First, a 1996 case in the District Court for New Mexico clarified that the medicine bundles—whose power is tied to and renewed by the ritualized gathering of medicines on San Francisco Peaks by authorized Navajo *hitaali*, or singers—are properly understood as cultural patrimony belonging to Navajo clans or the larger collective, and thus not alienable by a Navajo individual.[75] The case upheld the constitutionality of the criminalization of trafficking in such cultural property under the Native American Graves Protection and Repatriation Act and convicted Richard Nelson Corrow, a non-Native enthusiast of Navajo religion, who paid $10,000 for a number of medicine bundles from the widow of a *hitaali* he had come to know and even study with, only to flip them (after making inquiries of their worth on the private collector market) for $50,000 to a law enforcement officer posing as a collector.

Such medicine bundles, or *jiish*, are crucial to Navajo healing, blessing, and ceremonial traditions and are regarded as alive. That is, they are not simply "keepsakes" from Navajo singers' meditative experiences on San Francisco Peaks and elsewhere but draw on the power of the place to bring healing to the collective. *Hitaali* Harry Walters testified that "there is no such thing as ownership of medicine bundles," adding the *"jiish* belongs to the Navajo people because they are the only people that can get full benefit from that."[76] Admitting that some Navajos would say a singer's widow would own a bundle, Walters explained that "it would be sacrilegious to sell the [medicine bundle] to an individual who intended to remove [it] from the four corners of the Navajo Nation," making reference again to the sacred space delimited on the West by San Francisco Peaks.[77] *U.S. v. Corrow* illustrates how the practices associated with ceremonial gathering on the Peaks are not just about activities that happen on the Peaks, thus challenging the argument of the ski resort owners in *Navajo Nation* that such practices could continue apace even with the snowmaking scheme.

A second federal district court decision, this one from 1990, clarifies in no uncertain terms the distinctively collective nature of traditional Navajo religion with respect to sacred places.[78] In *Attakai v. U.S.* a group of individual Navajos brought a Free Exercise Clause challenge to a federally funded, Hopi approved fence project for range restoration in the "Joint Use Area" of the Hopi Reservation, which is occupied by both Navajo and Hopi people. The District Court for Arizona found individual Navajos had standing to bring claims about compromised access to sites of religious significance to their individual piety, but they did not have standing to bring a First Amendment claim about the compromised access to Star Mountain, the principal site in question, because it is a shrine of "tribal interest."[79] The First Amendment analysis did not compel this distinction; it was admittedly idiosyncratic to Congress's purposes in the Navajo-Hopi Land Settlement Act, which allows only the tribes, and not individuals, to litigate to help minimize the contentiousness of that long-standing dispute.[80] But the court nonetheless readily found reason to recognize and articulate an important and useful distinction between religious claims of collectives/tribes and the personal claims of individual religious practitioners. "In these proceedings the parties have drawn a distinction between 'tribal' religious sites, those which are generally identified and more widely known and which have significance to the tribe (i.e., Star Mountain), 'regional' local sites, those which are known and have significance to persons residing in a particular area (i.e., a special ceremonial site), and 'individual' sites, those which are known and therefore have significance only to individual members of the tribe (i.e., a burial site of an ancestor)."[81] Because Congress recognized the significance of certain religious shrines to each tribe, and intended that these tribal interests be considered in the context of the intertribal land dispute, the court held that "individual members of the respective tribes do not have standing to bring actions involving denial of access or interference with Tribal religious shrines."[82]

Neither *U.S. v. Corrow* nor *Attakai v. U.S.* finds its way into the arguments put forward in *Navajo Nation*, in part because the distinctions asserted in the two cases admittedly emerge in the context of statutes other than RFRA. Yet the distinctions made sense in those contexts because they make sense in terms of Navajo religion. Notwithstanding the subjective, emotional, experiential aspects of Navajo religion, the religious significance of the San Francisco Peaks is not principally an individual matter of interior states but a collective matter of duties, ceremonies, peoplehood. This would extend, by analogy, to the findings of fact concerning Hopi, Havasupai, White Mountain Apache, and other plaintiff tribes' religiosity. Justice for Native American religious freedom requires that there be room for courts to make reasonable distinctions of the sort the district courts of Arizona and New Mexico did in these cases. These are not distinctions whereby courts establish the centrality or sincerity of a given religious exercise; they are instead reasonable distinctions among registers in which religious exercise can be found.

As Kristen Carpenter has noted, there are sources in existing First Amendment scholarship that embolden the making of such distinctions and the recognition of group rights to Native American religious freedom.[83] Despite the assumed liberal basis of constitutional free exercise rights as an individual right of conscience, some scholars argue for group rights to free exercise of congregations, sects, and other collectives, not merely as derivative of the sum of individual rights involved but as matters of congregational autonomy, of rights to association, or of what Ronald Garet termed the "groupness" of religious groups existing importantly between the state and the individual.[84] Carpenter rightly observes that there are considerable "pragmatic, concep- tual, and doctrinal differences that distinguish American Indians from other theories of groups or institutional rights, and other instances of deference to church autonomy," especially in the context of federal Indian law's recogni- tion of the distinctive political, rather than religious or racial, status of In- dian tribes. But there are suggestive respects in which the literature on group rights to religious freedom makes potential judicial distinctions such as the kind seen in *Attakai* and *Corrow*, or in a variety of administrative accommo- dations for collective tribal religions, which seem consistent not only with federal Indian law but also with religious freedom law.[85]

Neither the Ninth Circuit majority nor dissent engaged the religious claims of the tribal plaintiffs in *Navajo Nation* as collective claims, in part no doubt because the principal Supreme Court First Amendment cases involving Na- tive American religious traditions had not engaged them as collective claims. I turn now to those pre-*Smith* cases.

Spirituality in Lyng v. Northwest Indian Cemetery Protective Ass'n. *and* Bowen v. Roy

Lyng, and by extension, *Bowen v. Roy*, are key to the Ninth Circuit rhetorical move from the register of religion to the register of spirituality. The 5-3-1 deci- sion in *Lyng* reversed lower court rulings and permitted construction of the logging road through high country sacred to the Yurok, Karuk, and Tolowa nations, finding no constitutional prohibition on the free exercise of their "religion." "Whatever may be the exact line between unconstitutional pro- hibitions on the free exercise of religion and the legitimate conduct by gov- ernment of its own affairs," Justice O'Connor writes, "the location of the line cannot depend on measuring the effects of a governmental action on a reli- gious objector's spiritual development."[86]

The *Lyng* majority could reason thus by drawing on *Bowen v. Roy* as its controlling precedent. In that case, decided two years previous, the Supreme Court found unpersuasive the claims of an Abenaki man that the govern- ment's use of a Social Security number assigned to his daughter in its admin- istration of public assistance benefits violated his First Amendment Free Ex- ercise rights.[87] Relevant to our discussion, the distinction between the facts of *Lyng* and those of *Roy* suggests something along the lines of the distinction between religion and spirituality. The Supreme Court in *Bowen v. Roy* did not

overtly question the sincerity of Roy's belief that his daughter's soul would be
damaged by use of the assigned Social Security number, but it did determine
that the religious exercise at issue was the furtherance of an individual's "spiritual development," a hindrance to "prevent her from attaining greater spiritual power."[88] In *Bowen v. Roy*, the Court held:

> Never to our knowledge has the Court interpreted the First Amendment
> to require the Government itself to behave in ways that the individual
> believes will further his or her spiritual development or that of his or her
> family. The Free Exercise Clause simply cannot be understood to require
> the Government to conduct its own internal affairs in ways that comport
> with the religious beliefs of particular citizens.[89]

It is revealing of the judicial propensity to draw from broader popular cultural ideas about Native Americans that the Supreme Court could find *Roy*
a compelling precedent to rule on the facts of *Lyng*. No ethnohistorians or
anthropologists were brought in, much less testimony from Native spiritual
leaders, to determine the depth or breadth of Roy's individual and rather idiosyncratic belief about Social Security numbers and soul robbing. Thus, the
Supreme Court justices could read the lower court's summary of Roy's claim
as follows: "he asserts a religious belief that control over one's life is essential
to spiritual purity and indispensable to 'becoming a holy person.' Based on
recent conversations with an Abenaki chief, Roy believes that technology is
'robbing the spirit of man.' In order to prepare his daughter for greater spiritual power, therefore, Roy testified to his belief that he must keep her person
and spirit unique and that the uniqueness of the Social Security number as
an identifier, coupled with the other uses of the number over which she has
no control, will serve to 'rob the spirit' of his daughter and prevent her from
attaining greater spiritual power."[90]

Implicitly under the analogy that both *Roy* and *Lyng* are Native American
cases, Justice O'Connor's majority opinion extends the holding in *Roy* to
the facts in *Lyng*: Government action in both would "interfere significantly
with private person's ability to pursue spiritual fulfillment according to their
own religious beliefs."[91] "However much we might wish that it were otherwise," O'Connor's writes, "government simply could not operate if it were
required to satisfy every citizen's religious needs and desires."[92] "Spiritual fulfillment" as a species of religious exercise can be hindered without violating
the Constitution, a potentiality that cannot serviceably define the realm of religious freedom protection because it implies no "stopping place." And where

O'Connor could see no stopping place under the First Amendment, the Ninth Circuit dissent sees in the en banc majority's view of RFRA no "starting place" for any meaningful protection of land-based Native religions.

In *Lyng*, O'Connor's rhetorical shoehorning of voluminous accepted factual findings of sincere and non-negotiable Native religious claims into the "spiritual fulfillment" or spiritual development of a "religious objector" abstracts the time-honored practices necessary to these Native nations into the hypothetical claims of several individuals seeking pristine meditative experiences of nature religion. It identifies them as "objectors" to government action, reversing the *Sherbert*- and *Yoder*-era position that it is government actions that effectively object to religious exercise that need to show their compelling interest and least restrictive means of doing so.

O'Connor's opinion bears a skeptical undertone, on the one hand identifying entire Native nations with the relatively ungrounded claims of *Roy* about Social Security numbers and, uprooting the meaningful, grounded, and fairly restrained and reasonable claims of practitioners of local religions into the hypothetical space of an expansive Native spirituality, where slippery slope reasoning can set in: that Native religious freedom claims to sacred lands, were they to succeed anywhere in the courts, would open the floodgates to any individual claiming any sincere belief having a "veto power" over any government action on public lands. The heft of the rhetorical move is belied by O'Connor's clarity that the Court was challenging neither the sincerity of the Native religious claims nor the adverse effects on their practice. But as Justice Brennan's strongly worded dissent avers, the framing of the facts in terms of *Roy* is sufficient to disregard the reach of the religious claims without disregarding their sincerity.[93]

Returning now to the legal issue in *Navajo Nation*: the Ninth Circuit majority saw *Lyng* as "on point" by a parallel set of facts—Native claims to sacred sites on public lands admitting of multiple uses—and by what it asserted to be a congruent legal issue, the question of what triggers an unlawful burden on religious exercise given those facts. But the rule by which *Lyng*'s analogous facts are assimilated derived from a very problematic precedent in *Roy*. The controlling analogy that these are both Native American cases trumps what common sense would find patently obvious: that the claims of one Native American man that a Social Security number will rob his daughter of her spirit—and apparently the only Native person to have come forward with this issue—carries the same force as concerns of entire Native peoples about the destruction of a sacred precinct where the cosmos is ritually renewed, where visions are sought, and where medicines are gathered, in order to construct a "marginally useful" road.[94] Applying the precedent of *Roy* to *Lyng* leads to what Justice Brennan called the "cruelly surreal result" that "governmental action that will virtually destroy a religion is nevertheless deemed not to 'burden' that religion."[95]

"Cruelly surreal" also aptly describes the result in *Navajo Nation*, where findings of fact establish the pivotal place of San Francisco Peaks for so many practitioners of so many tribes but do not deter government approval of spraying treated sewage on the mountain to facilitate recreational skiing for arguably fewer individuals. This result can work, we learn in *Navajo Nation*, in no small part because of the history of litigation, and in particular the 1983 rejection by the DC Circuit's, in *Wilson v. Block*, of the tribes' challenge to an expansion of the ski area on First Amendment grounds:

> Although the court noted that the proposed upgrades would cause the Indians "spiritual disquiet," the upgrades did not impose a sufficient burden on the exercise of their religion: "Many government actions may offend religious believers, and may cast doubt upon the veracity of religious beliefs, but unless such actions penalize faith, they do not burden religion."[96]

In referencing this earlier case, the Ninth Circuit hastens to affirm the district court's finding in *Navajo Nation* that the "tribes have continued to conduct religious activities on the Peaks ever since" the loss in this earlier litigation.[97]

The cited terminology of "spiritual disquiet" is not coincidental to the Ninth Circuit majority's reasoning in *Navajo Nation*. It attempts to contain the damage implied by desecration of the mountain to the diminishment of personal spiritual fulfillment on the mountain, and it suggests that Native American peoples' protean "spirituality" simply cannot be fully accommodated on public lands in a pluralistic nation.[98] The shaping force of reducing facts delineating complex contours of religious exercise by six distinct Native peoples to a watered-down form of nature religion known as Native American spirituality appears as well in several parenthetical observations in the decision, which are anything but peripheral to its reasoning.

To inform its contention that Native claims to spiritual fulfillment would have no stopping place, the Ninth Circuit majority noted that the Coconino National Forest in question involves "approximately a dozen" mountains sacred to various tribes as well as other landscapes "such as canyons and canyon systems, rivers and river drainages, lakes, discrete mesas and buttes, rock formations, shrines, gathering areas, pilgrimage routes and prehistoric sites."[99]

The decision also floated the observation that the White Mountain Apaches, one of the plaintiff tribes, had made snow at Sunrise, a ski area they operate on a mountain on their reservation, with water from a lake that includes discharged treated wastewater. The district court judge observed that one witness testified that Apaches held the entire White Mountain Reservation to be sacred, and also that the ski area was one of the two major ski areas in Arizona and potentially in competition with the Snowbowl on San Francisco Peaks. Thus conflating all mountains and all landscapes as sacred to the White Mountain Apaches, and blending all the complicated distinctions in belief and practice made by a sophisticated religious tradition into a single claim of Native spirituality that all nature is sacred, and hinting that some claims could be opportunistic or disingenuous, the district court could dispute the reach of religious exercise burdened by the Forest Service's action on the San Francisco Peaks.

Further Implications

The six Native nations appealed the case to the Supreme Court, citing the discrepancy between the Ninth Circuit's approach to the interpretation of "substantial burden" and that of the Tenth Circuit, which was invoked by a federal district court in Oklahoma to affirm RFRA protections for a Comanche sacred land claim.[100] But the Supreme Court denied the petition and, at the time of this writing, has yet to weigh in on such a discrepancy in the context of RFRA.[101] I have argued that the Ninth Circuit interpretation of "substantial burden" is centrally equipped, not just informed, by its transmutation of accepted factual findings about distinctive religious exercise involving the San Francisco Peaks by the six plaintiff tribes into matters of diminishable spiritual fulfillment. "Under Supreme Court precedent," the decision reads, making particular reference to *Lyng*, "government action that diminishes subjective spiritual fulfillment does not substantially burden religion."[102]

The Ninth Circuit's narrow interpretation of "substantial burden" is equipped by this shift from religion to spirituality in two problematic respects. First, spirituality is used ostensibly as a synonym for religion, even a "natural" synonym to encompass everything about Native American religions that does not easily fit the category of religion. I have shown, however, that spirituality is no neutral synonym for religion; it emerges in plain late twentieth-century parlance as a conscious departure from "religion." Nor is "Native spirituality" a natural construction; it is made, in relation to the development of spirituality and a spirituality industry, and deeply informed by an American cultural history of romanticizing the inherent spirituality of the noble savage.

Second, the court uses spirituality as a lens for viewing the facts of Native religions that are difficult to understand in conventional religious terms; it also draws on that lens because the *Lyng* decision, the authoritative text by which the court chooses to assimilate the facts pertaining to the San Francisco Peaks, describes the bundle of claimed religious obligations in terms of "spiritual fulfillment," to finesse the suturing of *Bowen v. Roy* in a *Smith*-era effort by the Supreme Court's conservative majority to contain the reach of religious free exercise protection where it conflicts with government and market interests. Recall that the *Lyng* claimants were charged with trying to effect the imposition of a "religious servitude" on public lands, a claim that hardly reflected the reasonable position of the Native claimants there, or in *Navajo Nation*.

The procedural logic of American law thus ensconces as substantive, and controlling, interpretations of Native religions that are cooked up under very different legal issues than the ones in play under RFRA. In *Navajo Nation*, however, we also see just how authoritative the category of spirituality has become as a frame for the courts' analysis of Native American religious freedom—so much so that it authorizes the spraying of treated sewage on a sacred mountain to make artificial snow for recreational skiing. Equipped by broader trends of American religion from the religiosity of "dwelling" to the religiosity of "seeking," and informed by a romanticized discourse of pure, "everything is sacred" Native American spirituality, the Ninth Circuit could believe its own conflation of the highly specific, highly particular religious claims of Navajo, Hopi, White Mountain Apache, Yavapai Apache, Havasupai, and Hualapai into a shared ethos of nature spirituality. Along the way, this manner of construing Native American religions handily contains the implications of those claims on public lands by interiorizing, privatizing, and aestheticizing them into a spiritual fulfillment that is diminishable without being protected under the freedom of religion.

One could argue, following Winnifred Fallers Sullivan, that there is a basic "impossibility of religious freedom" that afflicts constitutional and statutory protections of religious freedom qua *religion*, and that applies as consistently to the RFRA interpretation of the Ninth Circuit in *Navajo Nation* as it would to jurisprudence on either the Establishment or Free Exercise Clauses.[103] No doubt the decision in *Navajo Nation* is caught up in these larger discourse is-

sues. Still, there are indeed distinctive contours of Indigenous religions, substantively in terms of their basis in sacred lands, but also legally in terms of
the distinctive political status of federally recognized tribes like the six litigants in *Navajo Nation*. As valuable as Sullivan's appraisal is of the problems
accompanying minority religious communities' claims to justice under the
discourse of religious freedom, the particularities of Native American religious
claims such as those brought forward regarding the San Francisco Peaks embolden me to think that the impossibility of religious freedom, provocative
as it is, overstates the case here. In these instances, courts can make reasonable distinctions between claims of individual belief and interior piety and
the claims to collective duties and practices pertaining to Native nations as
collectivities. Lower courts had made such reasonable distinctions in *U.S.
v. Corrow* and *Attakai v. U.S.* Indeed, if religious freedoms, constitutional or
statutory, are to apply equally to Native peoples, courts must engage in such
distinctions, or we will continue to have results that discriminate against Native American religious freedom claims.

In light of the fact that the Supreme Court declined to review *Navajo Nation*, a number of other efforts have been brought forward by Native peoples.
The Hopi brought a suit against the city of Flagstaff on a public nuisance claim,
but there has been little as yet gained thereby.[104] And as we will explore in the
final chapter, tribes have registered formal complaints in a variety of international law forums, drawing on the United Nations Declaration on the Rights
of Indigenous Peoples. Despite these efforts to garner international law attention, the Snowbowl ski resort has proceeded to make artificial snow with
treated wastewater from Flagstaff, and as of July 24, 2014, was seeking a long-
term contract with the city of Flagstaff.[105] Absent some specific administrative or legislative fix in response, the final outcome in the San Francisco Peaks
case reveals the power of the discourse of spirituality to erode any meaningful American commitment to religious freedom to Native peoples.

If this particular case appears to be legally resolved, an ember of possibility
for RFRA protection of Native sacred places has begun to glow again, oxygen-
ated by the Supreme Court's recent holding in *Hobby Lobby* (2014) that RFRA
in no uncertain terms extends beyond the limits of First Amendment Free Exercise Clause jurisprudence prior to *Smith*,[106] and that, as Judge Fletcher's dissent averred in *Navajo Nation*, the holding in *Lyng* need not control substantial burden analyses in future cases.[107] In any event, judicial considerations
downstream from *Hobby Lobby* of sacred land claims under RFRA ought to
remember that while many contemporary Americans profess, with apparent

pride, that they are "spiritual, not religious," most such sacred land claims, at least those made by Native nations, are better understood as "religious, not spiritual."

Conclusion: Sacred Land as Prison Religion

When I first conceived of these two initial chapters, I felt I was going out on a limb in aligning a discussion of prisoner free exercise victories in court with the losses on sacred lands. But the two are not just joined by reference to the Native American religious traditions that animate them; they are also joined by a prevailing view of these traditions as Native American spirituality. The idea came into sharper focus when I read the opinion in the second phase of the Dakota Access Pipeline litigation, the phase involving religious freedom claims. The tribal claims here, though, turned largely on an argument that their position was closer to that of the prisoners seeking sweat lodge access in *Yellowbear* and *Haight*, which succeeded in federal appellate courts, than that of the Navajo, Hopi, and other nations in the San Francisco Peaks case.

The prevailing view of Native American spirituality that shapes the reception of the prison and sacred lands cases is certainly deeply related to what Winnifred Sullivan argues courses through "spiritual governance," the law on the ground that never makes it to the courts because religion as spirituality is no longer problematic. This spirituality is a naturalized, and thus unmarked, religion that is highly individualized, interior, subjective, and that everyone has by virtue of being human. So as we consider legal arguments for religion as *religion*, it is perhaps not unsurprising that such a presumption about religion as spirituality would pervade the case law related to Native claims. But the prevailing view of spirituality is turbocharged when it comes to Native religions.

As we saw in chapter 1, the romance with a naturalized Native American spirituality has its own particularly deep history, one that is rooted in a consistent ambivalence about the American project that results in a long history of *playing Indian*. The view toward Native American spirituality was entirely consistent with the violence of Assimilation Policy and the criminalization of Native religions in the Civilization Regulations. Through strategic essentialism, it became a point of considerable leverage for Peyotists and Pueblo leaders trying to make room for their traditions in the land of religious freedom, and as we will see in the next chapter, it helped fill the sails for the strategic movement in the 1970s and 1980s that would bring AIRFA and NAGPRA.

But all along, this romance with a naturalized Native American spirituality has denatured Native peoples' religious claims. Appropriating Native spirituality while denying its force as religion is no mere symptom of "spiritual, not religious" America, it afflicts Native efforts at redress in the courts with alarming consistency.

The second phase of the Dakota Access Pipeline court battle is a case in point. In January, 2017, days after taking office, President Trump directed the Army Corps of Engineers to abandon the environmental and historic preservation review process reopened in December 2016, and to give the green light to pipeline completion, crossing the Missouri River one-half mile upstream from the Standing Rock reservation.[108] In response, the Cheyenne River Sioux Tribe, Standing Rock's downstream neighbor, filed suit seeking a preliminary injunction to halt construction citing religious freedom. Cheyenne River had joined as a plaintiff in the lawsuit as early as August 2016, citing religious concerns in its own initial complaint, but neither plaintiff, Cheyenne River nor Standing Rock, cited religious freedom violations in their complaints at that time, instead seeking a halt to construction based on an argument that the Army Corps had failed to properly consult the tribes under the regulations of the National Historic Preservation Act. Judge Boasberg summed up the religious freedom claims in the second phase as follows:

> The Lakota people believe that the mere existence of a crude oil pipeline under the waters of Lake Oahe will desecrate those waters and render them unsuitable for use in their religious sacraments.... The Lakota people believe that the pipeline correlates with a terrible Black Snake prophesied to come in the Lakota homeland and cause destruction.... The Lakota believe that the very existence of the Black Snake under their sacred waters in Lake Oahe will unbalance and desecrate the water and render it impossible for the Lakota to use that water in their Inipi [sweat lodge] ceremony.[109]

The temporary restraining order and preliminary injunction sought from the court are difficult to attain, what precedent refers to as an "extraordinary remedy," requiring a showing of "a likelihood of succeeding on the merits," and "irreparable harm in the absence of preliminary relief."[110] The court rejected the motion, finding Cheyenne River's religious freedom claims were too little and too late to prevail. Or rather too late and too little. The district court found that the tribes' request for a preliminary injunction was nullified by laches, a designation for legal tardiness, since the tribes did not bring the

RFRA claim a half year earlier in their initial motions for a preliminary injunction.[111] But the court also found that the RFRA claim would be unlikely to succeed on the merits despite forceful arguments that *Hobby Lobby* had rendered *Navajo Nation* and *Lyng* no longer controlling precedents for such cases.[112]

Cheyenne River had argued first that, unlike *Navajo Nation*, the spiritual contamination of the only ritually pure water available for Lakota ceremonies would "foreclose" the practice of Lakota religion. Because the United States "has systematically deprived the Tribe of access to other water sources as a function of its more than 200 yearlong campaign to dispossess the Lakota people of their aboriginal lands and resources," Cheyenne River argued, "the Tribe and its members here are more closely analogous to the prisoners whose only options in the exercise of their religion are closely controlled by the government."[113]

Cheyenne River also argued that where the *Lyng* Court "could not vindicate Indian religious adherents' challenge to a government sanctioned project on the government's own land because to do so would imply 'de *facto* beneficial ownership of some rather spacious public property,' " the Lakota tribes had an "*actual* legal ownership interest in the waters of Lake Oahe," and the United States had "a fiduciary responsibility in the protection of those waters for the Tribe's benefit." [114] Finally, and most importantly, Cheyenne River took pains to argue *Navajo Nation* was "no longer good law" in light of *Hobby Lobby* and *Holt v. Hobbs*, for reasons previously argued.

The District Court for the District of Columbia rejected these arguments, instead finding a direct line from *Navajo Nation* and especially *Lyng*, in which the court found a tight analogy: "incidental, if serious impact on a tribe's ability to practice its religion because of spiritual desecration of a sacred site."[115] Remarkably, Judge Boasberg found additional support for the analogy with *Lyng* in the fact that the land in question under Lake Oahe was plainly "federal land,"[116] obscuring the treaty claims, court protected water rights,[117] and the elephant in the room: flooding of hundreds of thousands of acres of reservation lands, and the implicated federal trust responsibility that other courts, in other contexts, had taken into account over and again.[118] The court cited multiple authorities for the applicability of *Lyng* to RFRA cases and held that *Hobby Lobby* and *Holt*, while extending RFRA's religious freedom beyond the constraints of First Amendment law prior to *Smith*, did not do so in a manner that would advance Cheyenne River's specific claims.[119] *Hobby Lobby*, the court agreed, showed that Congress intended in RFRA "to effect a complete separation from First Amendment case law" with regard to the definition of

"exercise of religion," but the court held *Hobby Lobby* did not change anything about the "substantial burden" analysis, and thus doesn't change the result because the tribe "here faces no such coercion or sanction."[120] And where
Holt had made clear that Congress in RLUIPA meant to lower the standard
for a substantial burden under First Amendment analysis,[121] the district court
held, this "does not impliedly overrule *Lyng* or otherwise undermine its relevance here."[122]

Cheyenne River had argued had there was a clear distinction between their
case and *Navajo Nation* and *Lyng*. In *Navajo Nation*, Cheyenne River argued,
"the court held that the burden imposed upon the Indian's religious practice
was too weakly connected to the government regulation."[123] In *Hobby Lobby*,
by contrast "the real question that RFRA presents is whether the [government
regulation] imposes a substantial burden on the ability of the plaintiff[s] to
[act] in accordance with their religious beliefs, not whether the religious belief asserted in a RFRA case is reasonable."[124]

The illogic of making any tidy distinction between subjective, emotional
experience and substantially burdened free exercise, Cheyenne River argued,
is borne out even more clearly in the prisoner cases:

> Unless one is an observant Jew, the burden of being forced to eat food that
> is not prepared in a kosher kitchen must seem subjective and emotional,
> rather than objective and rational. Yet the courts ... did not apply a test of
> whether the belief was objective and rational to determine whether it sub-
> stantially burdened prisoners forced to choose between eating non-kosher
> food or violating their religious beliefs.... To apply such a test would be to
> question the validity of keeping kosher or observing halal practices, which
> the law does not permit.[125]

If this line of reasoning didn't work at the trial court level in *Standing
Rock II*, the religious obligation standard signaled anew by *Holt v. Hobbs* could
yet be a game changer for how sacred lands claims can pass the threshold
of the substantial burden analysis, when there are—and there usually are—
compelling accepted facts of religious obligation akin to those accepted in
the *Navajo Nation* case. This would be especially significant in a case that
should arise in a different circuit, perhaps especially within the Tenth Circuit,
where *Comanche Nation v. U.S.* applies a more expansive view of substantial
burden than in the Ninth Circuit's *Navajo Nation* case.[126] But even within judicial circuits holding the Ninth Circuit's view of substantial burden, the Supreme Court's recognition in *Hobby Lobby* of the religious exercise of a closely

held for-profit corporation could propel a view toward sacred land claims, or other claims advanced by Native nations, as matters of collective rights.

This chapter has tracked the consistency with which Native claims to sacred sites, when made in the register of collective religious obligation, are misrecognized as individual spirituality, failing to qualify those claims as protected religious freedom. Religion as religion becomes religion as spirituality. But there is nothing deterministic about this. Where others can conclude from such an analysis that any religious freedom claim to sacred lands is foreclosed, for me the indeterminacy of religion remains, potentially anyway, generative for strategic claims in the land of religious freedom.[127] The sacred lands cases also bespeak how damaging can be the romanticized image of Indians as naturally spiritual to Native claims to religious freedom in the courts, especially so as organized, modern engagement of legal and political processes on behalf of those traditions has struck that romanticized imagination as oxymoronic or, worse yet, disingenuous. Still, the romanticized image has helped and not just hindered attempts by Native peoples to secure statutory protections specific to their claims. But first we turn in the next chapter to a discussion of Native efforts made in light of the failure of religious freedom protections for sacred lands, efforts to articulate those claims instead in the language of cultural resource.

4

Religion as Cultural Resource

ENVIRONMENTAL AND HISTORIC
PRESERVATION LAW

Introduction

The last two chapters explored arguments to protect Native religions as *religion*, claims to sacred lands and practices made in the legal language of religious freedom that have been legible to courts thus far in terms of mere spirituality. If religious freedom has some as yet untapped potential, the courts have shown it thus far only to have been an imperfect tool. But the courts are emphatically not where most Native claims to protect sacred lands are advanced and adjudicated, and where the outcomes are felt. Partly because of the enumerated failures of religious freedom law, Native claims to protect sacred places, practices, and objects are at this point made mostly in terms of culture.

This chapter explores what results when Native peoples articulate religious claims in the language of culture and cultural resources under environmental and historic preservation law. A glance at the procedural history of the sacred land cases explored in chapter 3 would suggest I have the order of my chapters wrong: in each of those First Amendment and RFRA cases, the environmental review and consultation under cultural resource laws had failed to produce outcomes satisfactory to the tribes—in fact, in all those cases, federal agencies did very little to change their plans in light of those procedural protections. Yet cultural resource laws in the years since have become more fruitful in two respects. First, there is more emphatic insistence on government-to-government consultation between federal agencies and tribes. Second, in 1990, National Historic Preservation Act regulations were clarified by designating "Traditional Cultural Properties" as eligible for listing on the National

Register of Historic Places and in 1992, that law was amended to formally engage tribal governments in the review process. In light of these developments, protection under the categories of *culture* and *cultural resource* have proved more capacious for distinctive Native practices and beliefs about sacred lands, but it has come at the expense of the clearer edge of religious freedom protections, while still being haunted, and arguably bedraggled, by the category of religion from which these categories ostensibly have been formally disentangled.

I will argue, following Thomas F. King, that in the ideal, the procedures established under cultural resource law are remarkably promising, creating conditions for consultation with all stakeholders affected by government actions and promoting mutual problem solving and agreement. In theory, Native nations can take their rightful place at the table in discussions of the impact on them of government projects, and they can do so without having to make public the details of their traditional claims to sacred places and practices and without having to squeeze those claims into the confining language of religion. In actuality, though, these procedural protections by and large have not delivered on their promise, and I will explore two key reasons why in the case of the Dakota Access Pipeline. First, they lack sufficient legal teeth. They have become the routinized purview of professional consultants under contract with federal agencies, typically paid for by the private sector promoters of development. Unsurprisingly, then, these review processes often tilt toward approval of proposed actions, and the courts have surprisingly few cards to play to ensure equitable consideration.[1] Second, the processes of environmental and historic preservation review have difficulty robustly protecting cultural resources because of indeterminacies of culture, and because of inconsistent application of the law in decisions asserting clear lines among the gray areas of these indeterminacies.

The concerns of this chapter warrant their own book-length treatment. I will keep to a more modest aim, claiming my authority as one yet uninitiated into the guild of cultural resource management to query the assumptions of valuation that underlay the language of resource and to weigh advantages as well as limitations of protecting religion as *culture*. My focus will be on the two key laws, the National Environmental Policy Act (NEPA) and the National Historic Preservation Act (NHPA), although there are a number of other cultural resource laws germane to the concerns of this book.[2] One example is the American Antiquities Act (1906), under which a president can set aside lands for protection as national monuments. I will return to the

Antiquities Act in the conclusion in a brief discussion of the highly contested Bears Ears National Monument. But the national monument designation is a tool unavailable to most Native peoples. A focus on NEPA and NHPA is, in this sense, fitting.

Under NHPA as it has evolved in the decades since its passage in 1966, Native sacred sites and traditional cultural properties, including intangible elements of Native cultures, can be considered resources of national historic value to the United States. The threshold question for historic preservation protection is whether and how a property is historic in this sense of being consequential to the nation's history, determined in terms of its eligibility for listing on the National Register of Historic Places. Originally, eligibility was a function of a property's value to architectural history or scientific value to archaeologists. As NHPA evolved, Native peoples have had more avenues for claiming the national historic significance of their cultural resources and gaining the law's protection, but resource valuation remains stubbornly rooted in archaeological surveys. Perhaps especially vexing is the power of government agencies to ultimately adjudicate competing valuations.

In the environmental review process under NEPA, consideration of cultural resources must accompany considerations of natural resources because NEPA mandates that agencies consider impacts on the "human environment." Sometimes these include considerations of purely cultural resources—sacred sites, for example. Typically, though, environmental review considers impacts on natural resources, like water or wild rice or wolves, which for Native people can also be cultural resources. But the "human environment" is far more difficult to measure than the natural environment. So, while NEPA review arguably carries more legal cards to play for Native peoples making sacred claims, it is also the form of review for which the more difficult to quantify elements of culture and cultural value can be an awkward addition, even an afterthought, to the scientific work of reviews.

Considering Religion as Culture

The boundary between what we call *religion* and what we call *culture* is as porous as it is vexing. For at least forty years, scholarship in religious studies and in anthropology has tried to rethink these organizing terms following their critical explosion.[3] Anthropologist Ronald Niezen speaks of "a central irony associated with judicial use of the culture concept" in that it corresponds with an emerging consensus among anthropologists that "dismisses its value as a category of 'thing,' as a noun that can be identified described, compared with others, displayed in museums, presented at conferences, and by extension, decided upon in courts."[4] Courts and legislatures and administrative agencies struggle regularly with what these terms are to mean.

In the United States, folding the religious into the cultural for purposes of protection presents its own challenges under religious freedom law, risking government accommodations that run afoul of the First Amendment's prohibition on government establishment or endorsement of religion. Indeed, NHPA formally excludes places from eligibility for the National Register of Historic Places if their significance is primarily religious and not also historic or cultural. For many cultural resource managers, the line between religion and culture is a bright line. But at the foundation of historic preservation law is a legal concept of cultural property that first emerged, not on one side of a bright line between the cultural and the religious but in the gray area between them. The first major recognition of cultural property was an 1896 Supreme Court ruling in favor of the protection of Gettysburg Battlefield. The Court ruled that there was indeed a bona fide "public use" to the nation when the government condemned private lands crossing the battlefield that were to be developed by the Gettysburg Electric Railway.[5]

This case originated the notion of cultural property in US law, and Gettysburg, like the Vietnam Memorial and Ground Zero, has become a sacred site of American civil religion.[6] Government managers protect not only the integrity of such sites but also the integrity of the visitor's contemplative experience, even cataloging and safekeeping offerings left by visitors, much as pilgrims leave tokens of sacrifice or thanksgiving at explicitly religious shrines. Government management plans at such places often involve religious communities quite routinely as more than stakeholders, and often as co-managers of sites where the religious and the cultural are entwined, such as San Antonio Missions National Historic Park.

This is in ironic contrast to Native peoples' efforts to find protections for sacred places under religious freedom law, which have largely failed in the courts, in key moments failing because they arguably aren't "religious" enough. In the first of a series of cases foreclosing First Amendment protections for Native sacred land, the Sixth Circuit found that Cherokee challenges to Tellico Dam's destruction of sacred sites failed to rise above the merely cultural to the protectably religious under the First Amendment.[7] *Sequoyah v. T.V.A.* involved a First Amendment challenge to the Tellico Dam on the Little Tennessee River by Cherokee individuals who had been removed from the region in the Trail of Tears. They claimed the dam would flood their "sacred homeland ... along the river, which will result in destruction of "sacred sites, medicine gathering sites, holy places and cemeteries, [and] will disturb the sacred balance of the land."[8] Noting that some of the Cherokee plaintiffs had challenged the building of the dam "as early as 1965," but only recently asserted religious freedom claims,[9] the court held that:

> Cherokee objections to the Tellico Dam were based primarily on a fear that their cultural heritage, rather than their religious rights, would be affected by flooding the Little Tennessee Valley.[10]

Religion as Culture in Theory

Congress passed NHPA (1966) and NEPA (1969), endowing the landmark statutes with broad purposes. But most of the legal contestation has focused on the intricacies of the review processes established by these laws and elaborated under their regulations. Under Section 106 of NHPA, government agencies are to consult, identify, and seek agreements with stakeholders to mitigate adverse effects of federal undertakings on "historic properties," those places eligible for listing on the National Register of Historic Places. Under the better-known NEPA, federal agencies are to "take into account" how proposed government actions impact "the human environment" and provide reasons to the public for environmental impacts of the decisions they make. Although the review processes under the two laws have different outcomes, Memoranda of Agreement under NHPA Section 106 and agency Records of Decision under NEPA, the reviews are often conducted in tandem.[11] What follows are sketches of the review process under each as they have been elaborated over time, especially with regard to tribal consultation and Native claim-making.

National Environmental Policy Act

NEPA is typically regarded as a *natural* resource law, the one estimating parts per million of pollutants in Environmental Impact Statements. But it is also very much a cultural resource law. NEPA explicitly requires the federal government to consider impacts of its actions, including governmental licensure and permitting of private projects, on the "the human environment," which the law defines as "the natural and physical environment and the relationship of people with that environment."[12] Thomas King has pointed out that more expansively than NHPA, NEPA seeks to address "the sociocultural environment writ large," and the environmental law construes cultural resources beyond historic sites to include any number of tangible and intangible resources of cultures.[13] While NEPA, like NHPA, is a procedural law, requiring of agencies only that they identify and manage impacts, or give their reasons for not doing so, King points out that the procedures under NEPA equip communities living closely with those possible impacts more legal cards to play.

The Review Process under NEPA

NEPA regulations involve variations for different federal agencies, but in common they involve determining which actions, like hiring or purchasing file cabinets, may simply be checked off as "Categorical Exclusions," because they are completely uncontroversial, and which might be considered a "major federal action significantly affecting the quality of the human environment" (MFASAQHE). Before taking what could be a MFASAQHE, agencies must undertake an Environmental Assessment, or EA, a sort of preliminary, lower-level review to gauge whether there will be significant environmental effects. These preliminary assessments lead either to a "Finding of No Significant Impact," in which case no further review is required, or they lead to the more comprehensive and costly procedure of study and review that must consider a number of alternatives to the favored action and that culminates in an Environmental Impact Statement (EIS) by the agency. In practice, agencies that anticipate significant effects often proceed directly to an EIS.[14]

Determining what counts as a significant effect on the human environment is clarified in the regulations as being a matter of "context" (local, national, physical, human, short term, long term) and "intensity," or severity of impacts. The regulations enumerate several kinds of intensity: those "unique characteristics such as proximity to historic or cultural resources," effects on places eligible for the National Register of Historic Places, or those that "may cause loss or destruction of significant scientific, cultural, or historical resources," or that "are cumulatively significant impacts."[15] Courts have held agencies accountable in the preliminary stages of environmental review to a standard of what the Supreme Court in 1972 said was "taking a hard look at the environmental consequences before taking an action," and the *hard look* standard has been itself further elaborated by courts.[16] The Supreme Court in 1983 also clarified, in a legal challenge to federal licensure of Three Mile Island, based in part on the psychological stress that the nuclear plant placed on neighboring residents, that merely psychological effects of actions would not themselves rise to the significant impact requiring an EIS. This important precedent contained the reach of how far the NEPA requirement to consider impacts on the "human environment" would go. The Court found:

> NEPA does not require an agency to assess every impact of its proposed action, but only the impact on the physical environment. Although NEPA states its goals in terms of sweeping terms of human health and welfare, these goals are the ends that Congress has chosen to pursue by means of protecting the physical environment.[17]

Emphatically, this does not mean that subjective impacts need not be considered along with other impacts on cultural resources; only that a more exhaustive EIS review is not inevitably required if the impacts are psychological but not also physical.

Because the process leading to an Environmental Impact Statement for those actions with significant effects is so costly and time-consuming, agencies often actively consult stakeholders and agree, as part of the preliminary EA process, to plans that mitigate the impacts, in order to stay below the threshold of significant effects. As I'll discuss below, this was the approach of the US Army Corps of Engineers and Energy Transfer Partners in the Dakota Access Pipeline project. The Corps issued a "Mitigated Finding of No Significant Impact," first in November 2015 as a draft, and then in July 2016 as a final EA.[18] It was the publication of the final EA, in spite of the protests by the Standing Rock Sioux Tribe and others that a fuller EIS be undertaken, that sparked the camps and the litigation. And the lack of a fuller EIS was the specific reason for the Corps' December 2017 reversal of the easement enabling the pipeline to cross the Missouri, under pressure from President Obama. President Trump's reversal of the policy after taking office the next month declared the EA sufficient, reissued the easement, and greenlighted the plan.

Environmental Impact Statements

The fact of having to do an Environmental Impact Statement alone does nothing to ensure a federal agency will withhold its approval for projects with significant effects on the quality of the human environment, but it does require identification of alternatives and a process of scoping, consulting, conducting scientific analysis, and incorporating public comment, and thus puts federal agencies in a position of having to make public reasons for their decisions that have harmful effects.

The EIS is the "detailed statement for Major Federal Actions Significantly Affecting the Quality of the Human Environment." An EIS involves filing a public notice initiating "scoping" to identify the stakeholders, issues, time-table, and array of requirements beyond NEPA that need to be addressed in the EIS. Then the study proper commences, often conducted by consulting firms under contract with the agency. These firms may or may not have exper-tise, or deep interest, in the more difficult to quantify, and thus costlier to as-sess, impacts on cultural resources. After the agency issues a Draft EIS assess-ing the impacts for a number of alternative actions, and incorporates public comment into that study, it issues a Final EIS and ultimately issues a Record of Decision (ROD) in light of the EIS. Shaped by the data and analysis, but also informed by the political pressure elicited through the process, the ROD selects from the alternatives and can identify how the environmental impacts are to be managed.

Importantly, NEPA doesn't require the federal agency to protect the human environment in all its actions, or even to manage its impacts, and the consul-tants who oversee the process report to the agency but are often selected and paid by project proponents. But government is required in the early stages of the NEPA process to answer for any finding that its action will have no sig-nificant environmental effects to require the deeper level of review, and in the case of a Record of Decision, to offer reasons for the agency's course of ac-tion. Finally, the process time frame itself enables public scrutiny of proposed actions, sometimes producing political climate changes that shape develop-ment more than the NEPA procedures themselves. The Council on Environ-mental Quality is the federal agency within the Executive Office of the Presi-dent that is responsible for the regulations.

The Review Process under NHPA Section 106

Where NEPA's Environmental Impact Statement process is quite well known, the other major cultural resource law and review process carries little public name recognition: the National Historic Preservation Act, typically known as "Section 106" review by the professionals who manage it, and typically un-dertaken concurrent with the environmental review under NEPA.

The NHPA review process as it has developed holds considerable promise for places of religious significance to Native peoples. It requires consultation with stakeholders, including especially officials of federally recognized tribes at various stages, and consideration with those parties of adverse effects on any sites of historical and cultural significance to them, and it aims to result not in a governmental Record of Decision but in a Memorandum of Agreement signed by all the stakeholders. Specifically, the law requires:

> The head of any Federal agency having direct or indirect jurisdiction over a proposed federal or federally assisted undertaking in any state and the head of any Federal department or independent agency having authority to license any undertaking shall, prior to the approval of the expenditure of any federal funds on the undertaking or prior to the issuance of any license, as the case may be, take into account the effect of the undertaking on any district, site, building, structure or object that is included in or eligible for inclusion in the National Register. The head of any such Federal agency shall afford the Advisory Council on Historic Preservation (ACHP) ... a reasonable opportunity to comment with regard to such undertaking.[19]

If Register-eligible properties are identified, either by consensus of the parties and the State Historic Preservation Officer (SHPO) or the Tribal Historic Preservation Officer (THPO), or with the weigh-in on the part of the Keeper of the National Register, another set of judgment calls ascertains whether the federal undertaking involves any "adverse effects" on them. If there are adverse effects, then consultation ensues between the agency and parties, typically involving the Advisory Council on Historic Preservation (ACHP), and proceeds toward mitigating the adverse effects, resulting in a Memorandum of Agreement or, more rarely, termination of consultation.

Although Section 106 regulations include the potential for the ACHP to comment to heads of federal agencies what decisions are being made in their field offices, and although courts have given shape to the reach of some judgment calls under NHPA, as with NEPA, the decision-making power remains solidly in the federal agency's hands.[20] The statute only requires the federal agency to "take into account the effect of the undertaking" on historic places. But the process does mandate consultation, places some constraints on the planning process, and creates incentives for planning to account for and even to mitigate ill effects on historic properties.

Religion as Historically Significant

The threshold determination for proceeding with Section 106's adverse effect analysis, consultation, and mitigation is, of course, a site's listing on, or since 1970, eligibility for listing on, the National Register of Historic Places. Efforts to protect places and practices that are religiously significant to Native Americans as cultural resources under NHPA involve at some level an appeal to their public value to the American nation as a whole.

Under NHPA's regulations, properties that meet one or more of the following four criteria are eligible for listing on the National Register:

(A) The property must be associated with events that have made a significant contribution to the broad patterns of our history.

(B) The property must be associated with the lives of significant persons in our past.

(C) The property must embody the distinctive characteristics of a type, period, or method of construction, represent the work of a master, or possess high artistic values, or that represent a significant and distinguishable entity whose components may lack individual distinction.

(D) The property must have yielded or may be likely to yield, information important in history or prehistory.[21]

The regulations also exclude properties from eligibility if they no longer retain "integrity" in terms of their Register-eligible significance or if they can be classified in terms of enumerated exclusions:

Ordinarily cemeteries, birthplaces, graves of historical figures, properties owned by religious institutions or used for religious purposes, structures that have been moved from their original locations, reconstructed historic buildings, properties primarily commemorative in nature, and properties that have achieved significance within the past 50 years shall not be considered eligible for the National Register.[22]

Several stipulated exceptions to this rule are important to our purposes. "A religious property deriving primary significance from architectural or artistic distinction or historical importance" can be eligible, as can a property achieving significance within the past fifty years if it is of exceptional importance." Finally, properties that on their own might be excluded can be Register-eligible "if they are integral parts of *districts* that do meet the criteria."[23]

Even a quick glance at these regulations suggests the difficulty Native peoples would face in successfully articulating their claims to a given place's religious or traditional significance in terms of the narrative of significance to the American nation. Among other things, most Native places have continuous significance that predates the United States. And while it might seem that the exclusion of sites whose historical significance is not documented beyond the last fifty years would pose no problem for sites of ancient significance, that significance may only have been dimly understood by missionaries, agents, traders, or ethnologists who shaped the written record, or obscured by the forcible interruption of those traditions by dispossession or displacement.

The identification of Register-eligible properties is to Thomas King often the most contentious part of the process, and rife with misunderstandings about what NHPA actually requires. First, evaluation of eligibility for listing on the Register is not to be conflated with downstream parts of the process, like the questions of effects or the weighing the public good of the agency action. Indeed, identification of historic properties does not preclude any contemplated agency action, only action without consideration of the effects on such places. Furthermore, evaluation of Register eligibility is a matter of parties applying the stated criteria, not the product of a formal determination by the Keeper of the National Register or any agency official alone. What is often called a "consensus determination" of eligibility is actually not a formal determination but rather an agreement among the agency, the SHPO, and the THPO that the criteria are sufficiently met.[24] If there is no such agreement, the regulations call for a formal nomination and determination of eligibility by the Keeper of the National Register.

When Register-eligible historic properties are identified, the Section 106 process moves to the adverse effect analysis. "An adverse effect," according to the regulations, is found when:

> An undertaking may alter, directly or indirectly, any of the characteristics of a historic property that qualify the property for inclusion in the National Register in a manner that would diminish the integrity of the property's location, design, setting, materials, workmanship, feeling or association.[25]

A charged phase of the process is the determination of the Area of Potential Effect (APE). A narrowly drawn APE reduces the exposure of an undertaking to adverse effect analysis. For example, a proposed government building can have a narrow APE that includes its footprint, construction area, and the area shaded by the building, but if the building eclipses a prominent or significant view of, say a sacred mountain, then the viewscape arguably is part of the APE. Strategic use of the APE, as we will see, can make or break the effectiveness of Section 106 in safeguarding the integrity of cultural resources.

Where adverse effects are determined to obtain, the process moves to the crucial step of consultation with stakeholders to consider alternatives or to mitigate those effects. "The section 106 process," its regulations announce, "seeks to accommodate historic preservation concerns with the needs of federal undertakings through consultation among the agency official and other parties with an interest in the effect of the undertaking on historic properties, commencing at the early stages of project planning."[26]

Consultation about adverse effects ideally results in a Memorandum of Agreement (MOA), although again Section 106 only requires an agency to "take into account" adverse effects to historic properties and allow the Advisory Council on Historic Preservation an opportunity to comment on any final agency decision. If MOA is not in the cards, parties can terminate consultation, and the ACHP's comment is presented to the top official of the agency.

In its earlier years, NHPA was not particularly helpful in the protection of Native sacred places. NHPA had been the ken of professional architectural historians and archaeologists, for whom the public value of cultural resources to the nation was mainly one of aesthetic or scientific value. As Register-eligibility consideration came to embrace the cultural significance of places for the many distinct communities that compose the American nation, the managerial discourse was still haunted by the language of "ethnographic resources" as a moniker for those cultural resources that are of value to living communities. Even though NHPA review underwent changes in 1990 that strengthened the hand of all Native communities and in 1992 for federally recognized tribes, Section 106 continues to inscribe a power relation of academic knowers and Indigenous knowns in administrative judgments of value.

Religion as Culturally Significant: Traditional Cultural Properties

In response to the frustration resulting from the fact that places of significance to Native peoples and other living American communities were not being properly served under NHPA, *National Register Bulletin 38* (1990) formally recognized as eligible for National Register inclusion what it designated a "Traditional Cultural Property," or TCP.[27] Eligibility here, and thus the threshold trigger for Section 106 protections, need not be a function of a property's archaeological importance, or even ethnographic importance, but because of its

> association with cultural practices or beliefs of a living community that a) are rooted in that community's history, and b) are important in maintaining the continuing cultural identity of the community."[28]

Bulletin 38 and its TCP designation was a profoundly creative bureaucratic intervention by Thomas King, then a top official for the Advisory Council on Historic Preservation, and his late wife, Patricia Parker of the National Park Service, to reclaim NHPA review from the narrow concerns of archaeologists and architectural historians in determining which places count.

According to King, it was the failure of the Section 106 process to satisfactorily resolve the dispute between the Forest Service and tribes that led to the failed First Amendment challenge in the Supreme Court's *Lyng* decision. It was also the failure of Section 106 review to get the Forest Service to recognize the traditional cultural importance of San Francisco Peaks in the earlier expansions of the Snowbowl ski resort in the 1980s.[29] There, the Forest Service's consultants, contenting themselves with archaeological surveys, found insufficient evidence confirming the tribes' claims to the mountain's significance. While the TCP designation has come to seem synonymous with Native sacred place claims, *Bulletin 38* stipulates that it should not be taken to "imply that only Native Americans ascribe traditional cultural value to historic properties."[30] *Bulletin 38* also makes clear that it doesn't create a new category of Register eligibility, arguing that what it calls traditional cultural properties had been "listed and recognized as eligible" for the Register from the beginning. Still, the organized attention *Bulletin 38* gives to TCPs, and guidance on how to evaluate them and incorporate them in planning, has helped Native nations and other living communities engage the Section 106 process to protect places important to them.

Specifically, the TCP designation shapes a reading of NHPA's criteria for Register eligibility that was more open to the incorporation of places of ongoing cultural significance. Importantly, even as it reads well as a work of analysis and narrative, *Bulletin 38* is a clarification of the NHPA regulations. It is thus part of the body of administrative law.

The "integrity" standard, for example, would apply to TCPs differently than it would to an archaeological site or architectural structure alone, and it would begin from the perspective of the community, not the specialist. Recall that Register eligibility involves places that "possess integrity of location, design, setting, materials, workmanship, feeling, and association. The integrity standard can disqualify many places of ongoing significance to living communities, especially so in cases where a community can still regard TCPs as significant even if they are no longer pristine or bear the marks of dispossession and even desecration. So *Bulletin 38* frames the question of integrity in terms of the integrity of the "relationship to traditional cultural practices or beliefs" and whether the "condition of the property" is such that "the relevant relationships survive," even if the places has been substantially modified. "Cultural values are dynamic," *Bulletin 38* says, "and can sometimes accommodate a good deal of change."[31]

With this approach to the integrity standard, *Bulletin 38* turns to evaluation of Eligibility Criterion A, places "associated with events that have made a significant contribution to the broad patterns of our history." Here, *Bulletin 38*'s TCP designation makes specific room for considerations of Dakota, or Ojibwe, or Chinese American history, heading off at the pass a procedural judgment call about whether those particular histories are significant to the nation. Plenty of judgment calls in ascertaining this history are required, but *Bulletin 38* clarifies that a full range of evidence be considered and guards against an objectivist historicism with regard to Indigenous understandings of the past. *Bulletin 38* states:

> It would be fruitless to try to demonstrate, using the techniques of history and science, that a given location did or did not objectively exist in a time whose own existence cannot be demonstrated scientifically. Such a demonstration is unnecessary for purposes of eligibility determination; as long as the tradition itself is rooted in the history of the group, and associates the property with traditional events, the association can be accepted.[32]

With regard to Criterion B, "those associated with the lives of significant persons in the past," *Bulletin 38* offers a reading of "significant persons" to include spirits or demigods or culture heroes associated with oral traditional pasts. This interpretive move made room for recognizing a sizeable number of timbers lying at the bottom of a Lake Superior bay as a TCP for local Ojibwe peoples for their association with the work of the Anishinaabe Trickster in enabling them to interrupt the ravages of the logging industry.[33]

Bulletin 38 clarified as well how the NHPA "Criteria Considerations," which exclude properties from Register eligibility, are not to be applied rashly to TCPs. Because Indigenous peoples do not tidily distinguish the religious from the cultural, or supernatural "religious" events from merely natural or historical ones, many places that communities might speak of in plainly religious terms should not hastily be seen as excluded under the "religious exclusion":

> Applying the "religious exclusion" without careful and sympathetic consideration to properties of significance to a traditional cultural group can result in discriminating against the group by effectively denying the legitimacy of its history and culture. To exclude from the National Register a property of cultural and historical importance to such a group, because its significance tends to be expressed in terms that to the Euro-American observer appear to be "religious" is ethnocentric in the extreme.[34]

Similarly, the "graves" or "cemetery" exclusions for Register eligibility are framed in terms of the many TCPs that will involve ancestral burials.[35]

Finally, in its discussion of exclusion from Register eligibility those properties "achieving significance within the past fifty years," *Bulletin 38* affirms that a significance ascribed to a property only in the past fifty years cannot be considered traditional, but also cautions against rash judgments about the ineligibility of properties that have gone unused for long periods of time. The bulletin takes as important context for such determinations the widespread displacement and/or interruption of place-based Indigenous traditions and acknowledges the difficulty of finding documentary or physical evidence attesting to historic activities at many TCP sites.

Thomas King's later work calls attention to a range of challenges to managers as they face determinations at the edges of what will count as a TCP. Among these are what will count as "traditional" and *who* will count in speaking for a community about what's traditional. But King hastens to add that these indeterminacies need not be feared altogether. One example King gives is the Enola Hill case, where a Forest Service timber sale to selectively log diseased trees near Oregon's Mount Hood was delayed for almost a decade because of the unsettled question as to whether a hill that an individual Native man used for vision quests could count as a TCP.[36] Rip Lone Wolf's claims to Enola Hill as a sacred site were supported by the Yakama Nation, but the Confederated Tribes of Warm Springs, which agreed that the proposed targeted logging was in the interest of the forest's health, wrote that they "oppose the voices of those individuals about the importance of Enola Hill."[37] The case went to court in 1993, and logging was authorized by congressional action two years later.

1992 NHPA Tribal Consultation Amendment

In 1992, following on the heels of NAGPRA and the other statutory affirmations in the cultural realm of tribal sovereignty and the federal trust relationship, Native leaders persuaded Congress to amend NHPA to require agency consultation when any federally recognized tribe identified potentially affected sites of "traditional religious and cultural significance" whether or not the sites are on tribal lands. *Bulletin 38* had been on the books, but three federal agencies important to Native nations—the Bureau of Land Management, the Forest Service, and the Bureau of Indian Affairs—had not thoroughly embraced the bulletin into their policies, and the tribes, according to King, wanted to ensure that some gains of *Bulletin 38* be written into NHPA itself.[38] The amendment also ensured the ACHP would include at least one Native member and importantly bolstered a system of Tribal Historic Preservation Officers (THPOs) to complement the SHPO system for the consultation process whenever recognized tribes are stakeholders. The amendment specifically reads:

> Properties of traditional religious and cultural importance to an Indian tribe or Native Hawaiian organization may be determined to be eligible for inclusion on the National Register.... In carrying out its responsibilities under Section 106, a federal agency shall consult with any Indian tribe or Native Hawaiian organization that attaches traditional and cultural significance to such properties.[39]

Although this amendment pertains only to recognized tribes and acknowledged Native Hawaiian Organizations—remember the TCP designation includes unrecognized Native nations, tribes, and communities—and although the amendment stopped short of automatically rendering Register-eligibility to sites claimed to be of traditional religious and cultural importance by tribes, the amendment did hardwire Tribal Historic Preservation Officers into eligibility evaluation processes. In its implementation of the amendment, the ACHP also strongly advised agencies to factor in AIRFA and President Clinton's Executive Order 13007 on American Indian Sacred Sites, "which may impose obligations, independent of Section 106 and NHPA, with regard to Indian sacred sites that do not meet the National Register criteria."[40]

Relationship between NEPA and NHPA

Although they vary in the respects identified above, NEPA's and NHPA's respective regulations promote coordination of concurrent reviews under the sibling laws. While both laws concern cultural resources, the common shorthand refers to Section 106 for the cultural resource studies and NEPA for the natural resource studies. And typically the Section 106 review is often presented as part of the Environmental Assessment or Environmental Impact Statement. The Dakota Access Pipeline review is a good example, as the cultural resources report is included as an appendix to the Environmental Assessment.[41]

Advantages of Religion as Culture in Practice

Ideally, the procedures established by NHPA and NEPA foster timely planning, substantive consultation with Indigenous stakeholders, and mutual problem solving and agreement, or at least the procedures make government agencies account for the effects of their decisions. As the case of the Dakota Access Pipeline makes clear, however, in the real world of practice, NHPA and NEPA review has all too often become perfunctory, overseen by consultant contractors often paid by the project developer. Taken alone, these statutes lack robust opportunities for judicial review that would shape negotiation conditions more favorable to Native peoples, but combined with other federal directives from treaty-based Indian law, and the growing heft of consultation with federally recognized tribes, cultural resource protections under them have become more fruitful.[42]

I turn now to explore the positive and negative implications of efforts to protect religion as culture under the rubrics of environmental and historic preservation law. Some of these implications are philosophical and abstract; others are more technical and legal, but in any case are part of the felt consequences of Native efforts to protect religion as culture. To illustrate these consequences, I'll draw on a number of concrete examples, paying particular attention to that of the Dakota Access Pipeline.

Involving Native Peoples in Decision-Making

Thinking first of religion as culture for the purposes of legal protection can enable more voluble access by Native peoples to government decision-making processes and—ideally anyway—do so earlier in those processes to make a difference. Although there are clearly limitations even in theory to the processes established in NEPA and NHPA review, they can offer more avenues to effectively persuade decision-makers and shape development than merely to make the all or nothing declaration "*this is sacred*" required of effective claims in the arena of religious freedom. To make the declaration "this is sacred" can promote adversarial postures between government agencies and Native peoples and inclines toward win-lose litigation. The cultural resource discourse, by contrast, ideally factors into government and development planning the protected concerns of Native peoples through processes of consultation, negotiation, compromise, and in the case of NHPA, agreement between agency and stakeholders. Even NEPA, which requires no such agreement, formalizes consultation and publicizes the fruits of that consultation, and compliance can be factored into feasibility and strategy for development interests and government agencies in a manner that can give Native peoples stature in decisions that otherwise might utterly overlook impacts on them if all agencies had to worry about were the high standard for religious freedom protections. Thomas King understands these sensitivities well. "In the interest of 'sacred site' protection itself," King warns of the danger of insisting on every TCP as a sacred site:

> The result, I'm afraid, will be that a very few, tightly defined "sacred sites" will be absolutely protected from physical destruction, while [a] tremendous number of places that aren't amenable to narrow definition aren't protected at all, and effect[s] other than direct physical damage aren't considered even on "sacred sites."[43]

In this view, TCPs and the broader processes of cultural resource management, by contrast, offer more possibilities in a culturally and religiously plural democracy to negotiate for places that matter to them. Native peoples may speak of places or practices in terms of the sacred but may negotiate plans to mitigate adverse effects of private development and government actions that they agree to for whatever reasons they choose. For example, Section 106 Memoranda of Agreement can include negotiated agreements that stop short of utter protection of a TCP, but that land exchanges, compensation, or other compromises that enable other priorities to prevail. Cultural resource discourse can enable Native peoples to be more nimble at the helm to safeguard places and practices they hold sacred.

Can enable. *Can* offer. *Can* create. When commending the possibilities for protections under cultural resource discourse, one must speak with precision in such terms because the legal frameworks of NHPA and NEPA *can* work if their original purposes and required processes are carried out fully and in good faith. This is a big "if," as will be clear from our consideration of the Dakota Access Pipeline case. And despite a number of court cases that set parameters for fuller compliance, courts have not consistently held government's feet to the fire in terms of NHPA and NEPA compliance.[44] But especially given the failure of religious freedom claims in the courts to date for protection of Native sacred sites, adept Native tribes and communities have engaged these processes to considerable effect.

Cultural Resources Are Often Also Natural Resources

Another advantage of the cultural resource discourse of NEPA and NHPA is the entwinement of cultural and natural resources. This is especially true of NEPA in requiring government to take a hard look at the impacts of its actions on the human environment. Because NHPA and NEPA reviews often proceed in tandem, they involve consideration of impacts on plants, animals, and the places they need to survive as impacts on culture and not simply nature. Consideration of adverse impacts on salmon or wild rice, for example, are not merely in terms of their status as natural resources but also in terms of their cultural or religious significance. There is good reason to believe that the professional firms that do most of the work of NHPA and NEPA reviews emphasize the natural over the cultural; natural resources and impacts on them are, to be sure, more handily measured. Yet when properly done, review processes can consider the significance to a people of Wolf or Bear, not just populations of wolves and bears.

There is, to be sure, a basic disconnect in speaking of spiritual beings as resources; to do so may effectively concede that the specific cultural significance of a natural resource is vaporous compared to the measurable physical, natural resource.[45] This remains a concern shared by Thomas King even as he promotes the possibilities of cultural resource management done well. King thinks "'heritage' is a better word than 'resource' to refer to such things ... it seems less loutishly materialistic." But he sticks pragmatically with the term because "we seem to have stuck ourselves with resource."[46]

The linking of the cultural and the natural does usefully integrate considerations of cultural significance to living communities into the hard looks of environmental review. Government management of populations of timber wolves in Minnesota or bison in Yellowstone National Park have been constrained to factor in cultural significance of these species to Native nations into what would otherwise be purely natural resource considerations.[47]

The Secular Purposes of Cultural
Resource Management of the Sacred

A discourse of cultural resource has at least two more distinctly *legal* advantages. First, resource language implies a property interest of sorts and it thus triggers elements of the federal fiduciary responsibility for managing the resources of recognized tribes. This applies not only to cultural resources on the lands in trust on reservations but also to the many off-reservation cultural resources on traditional territories. Second, reasoning in the discourse of cultural and natural resource management can help shield from constitutional challenges those accommodations made by government agencies to protect Native peoples' sacred lands, waters, plants, and animals. Not simply because of federal trust responsibilities to acknowledged tribes, but because of the language of cultural, rather than religious, resources, such accommodations can be justified against claims they violate the Establishment Clause.

A good example is Cave Rock, a formation that rises dramatically from the Nevada shore of Lake Tahoe. The Washoe nation considers Cave Rock to be profoundly sacred and voiced concerns about threats to the place from public recreation there. The Washoe were concerned with alterations made by climbing enthusiasts: permanent hardware pounded into the rock, alterations to caves to promote better climbing, and other behavior seen to desecrate the place. Cave Rock was recognized by the Forest Service as a Washoe TCP, and the climbing alterations were seen as adverse effects to its Register eligibility. In the 1990s, the Forest Service developed a management plan banning climbing on the rock, and a climbing advocacy group, the Access Fund, challenged the policy as an unlawful privileging of the religion of one group on public lands in violation of the Establishment Clause.[48] But the Forest Service persuaded a federal judge, later affirmed by the Ninth Circuit, that the policy, in pursuit of protection of cultural and natural resources under NHPA and NEPA, was motivated by a "secular purpose" and neither advanced nor hindered Washoe religion. The appeals court held that "the Establishment Clause does not bar the government from protecting an historically and culturally important site simply because the site's importance derives at least in part from its sacredness to certain groups."[49] As important as federal appeals court cases are, perhaps their greatest significance is how they dramatize, punctuate, and further shape the everyday decisions made by resource managers in the big land-managing federal agencies: the Forest Service, the National Park Service, and the Bureau of Land Management. For public officials in the field force of these agencies, *cultural resource management* is a language they can feel emboldened to engage in terms of secular purposes relative to the management of sacred places. This is not to say there aren't problems in translation from religion to culture, or pretense in managing the sacred.[50] But it matters that government officials can feel emboldened to make accommodations, in the name of cultural resource management, for practices and places that are meaningfully religious.

Culture *as an Intellectual Starting Point for Indigenous Traditions*

Compellingly, under the rubric of *culture*, there is more room for the legal consideration, even protection, of Indigenous traditions that don't easily fit the category of religion. On the one hand, there is more room for place-based traditions of Native peoples inadequately served by religious freedom law for consideration of significant places that might be both religious and economic—traditional fishing grounds, for example—and for consideration and mitigation of impacts on those places and practices. On the other hand, there is under environmental and historic preservation law no requirement to establish the religiousness of a claim. Native peoples need only demonstrate historical and cultural significance. Adherents to universal religions like Christianity and Islam may be accustomed to making such showings, indeed welcome such opportunities as witness to their faith, but these can present difficulties for practitioners of *local* religions. Under NHPA and NEPA processes, Native peoples need not prove a place rises to the high standard of being a sacred place.

NHPA's TCP designation creates space for communities rather than academics to determine what was of value to them, and the designation importantly allows for the fuller range of ways that the spiritual significance of places may be regarded by Native peoples. Where religious freedom discourse conventionally can admit only a dichotomy between sacred/profane or religious/secular—and under which Native claims to the sanctity of particular places are seen to contradict claims elsewhere that all land is held to be sacred, the TCP-inflected cultural resource discourse allows for the finer grain of specific Indigenous religious relationships to specific places. As King writes, some places are pilgrimage sites, others are so sacrosanct that no one is allowed to go there, other places are sacred at certain times of year, other places are embodiments of stories or clan identities.[51] Still others may be used for Indigenous economic development or other purposes without profaning them.

Part of the challenge of making a showing of *religion* in legal processes for Indigenous peoples is going public with traditional knowledge that is proprietary or secret or even dangerous outside its culturally prescribed limits. Cultural resource consultations with governments of recognized tribes have evolved in practice to include the sealing of sensitive knowledge. Some Native nations, like the Navajo, have published information on at least some of their traditional cultural properties in order to help systematize their protection.[52] Others retain cultural resource surveys, testimony, and other materials sealed from public view. In any event, the strategic choice is in the hands of Native peoples.

A federal court case involving NHPA and Sandia Pueblo clarified the importance of this point even as it strengthened the consultation provisions of Section 106 through judicial review.[53] The case involved a proposed improvement in the early 1990s of a road up Las Huertas Canyon in New Mexico's Cibola National Forest. In its NHPA consultation, the Forest Service sent officials at Sandia Pueblo a form letter with a request to map all TCPs in that canyon to inform their planning.[54] Although the canyon was awash in shrines, medicine gathering sites, and other places of religious and cultural significance, as its governor and others had formally told government officials, Sandia Pueblo did not comply with the specific request to map those places. Pueblo communities have won the reputation for maintaining rigorous protocols to delimit who has access to ceremonial and cultural knowledge. The Forest Service consequently determined there were no potential adverse effects on any historic properties. After an unsuccessful appeal in the Forest Service's internal process, Sandia Pueblo sued in federal court. The Ninth Circuit Court of Appeals reversed a lower court decision and found the Forest Service had violated Section 106, failing to have made a "reasonable and good faith effort" to identify historic properties through its perfunctory consultation and discounting Pueblo statements about the canyon's numerous TCPs that would be adversely affected. The court specifically cited *Bulletin 38*'s acknowledgment that proper consultation should factor in sensitivities around publicizing sacred knowledge.

Federal Recognition Not Required

Native peoples need not be federally recognized to count in the review processes under NEPA and NHPA. While federal agencies are obligated by the federal trust responsibility to conduct government-to-government consultations with recognized tribes in their NEPA and NHPA reviews, and while this federal recognition can matter in agency decision-making, NEPA and NHPA do not make categorical distinctions between communities based on this status. Under NHPA, as yet unrecognized Native peoples can have TCPs just like their federally acknowledged counterparts and can factor into NEPA review, especially as populations who may be facing potentially disproportional impacts in considerations of environmental justice.[55]

Although NHPA's 1992 Amendment bolsters the possibility of Register eligibility to properties declared religiously or traditionally significant by federally recognized tribes, the broader reach of the TCP does not thus require federal recognition for designation as such.[56] A good example involves the Mattaponi people of Virginia and their concerns about the proposed King William Reservoir. The Mattaponi had been signatories of colonial-era treaties with the British and were recognized by the Commonwealth of Virginia but not by the federal government until 2018. For decades before that, the Mattaponi resourcefully fought the reservoir, which would supply water to nearby cities but which also would block shad runs and treaty-protected hunting and gathering practices, destroy archaeological, cultural, and sacred sites, and disproportionately impact the nearby Mattaponi reservation. Much of the legal challenge occurred in Virginia courts, but because of an effect on wetlands, US Army Corps of Engineers permits under Section 404 of the Clean Water Act were required, and thus the Corps was obligated to conduct the necessary NEPA and NHPA reviews.[57]

As Allison Dussias's analysis shows, the case played out over decades and was legally and politically complex.[58] Although it did not agree with all the Mattaponi claims, the local Corps office initially found that adverse effects on Mattaponi cultural resources and on other natural resources, especially in environmental justice terms, outweighed the reservoir's benefits. But local and state officials disagreed and the matter was referred to regional divisional Corps officials, who granted a permit in 2005. The EPA, which previously joined in opposition, did not stand in the way of the newly granted permit, as it was entitled to under the Clean Water Act. Further legal challenges on treaty rights failed in Virginia courts, which distinguished the stature of treaties under the Supremacy Clause of the Constitution and treaties made with only state-recognized tribes.[59]

By 2009 the dispute had made its way to a federal court, which found in favor of environmental groups joined by the Mattaponi, though the decision was based on "environmental principles in general rather than on considerations unique to the Mattaponi Tribe, such as the threat that the project presented to its cultural, spiritual, and archeological values."[60] Newport News, one of the cities seeking a water supply, withdrew its plans for the reservoir, and the project was tabled.[61] If the court victory itself did not hinge on the Mattaponi specific claims, the original Corps determination about adverse effects on Mattaponi TCPs and recognition of the environmental justice problems posed by the proposed reservoir did depend on the capacity of NHPA and NEPA review processes to work for the Mattaponi as they might for a federally recognized tribe.

The Ends and Means of Delays and Costs

The Mattaponi case exemplifies what may be most valuable about NEPA and NHPA protections: the reviews take time. Proponents of development, including those in the political branches of government, can decry the cost and hassle of the red tape, and perhaps even rightly rue how the review processes can make their own weather, so to speak, in generating opposition. But even if NEPA and NHPA lack robust legal teeth, the red tape itself can create time for government and stakeholders to stop, look, and listen. When Native concerns are at stake, this tempo shift is especially important; it buys time to organize, study, and articulate their concerns and for the public to engage them. Better alternatives can emerge in the process, often ones that even development proponents can live with. And while there's certainly little in the laws or their regulations or the routinized conduct of reviews that compels outcomes acceptable to Native nations, their place at the table can be asserted as a matter of stipulated process—or threatened protest.

Native nations have made ample and resourceful use of the protest strategy. A good example is the Mole Lake Sokaogon Chippewa nation's successful thwarting of a proposed mine on their traditional lands in Wisconsin.[62] From the 1970s, investors had been pursuing a copper and zinc mine that threatened tribal natural and cultural resources with toxic discharges into water. In this case as in others where NEPA and NHPA review processes are helpful, their use was coordinated with other legal tools at hand. Here, Mole Lake successfully asserted its sovereignty in setting stringent water quality standards that, under 1995 amendments to the Clean Water Act, were to be treated like standards set by states and thus capable of requiring upstream compliance.[63]

A report by anthropologists Larry Nesper, Anna Willow, and Thomas King helped document TCPs in a cultural landscape under threat by the proposed mine, much of it outside the political boundaries of the of the Mole Lake reservation.[64] In this case, the Army Corps of Engineers responsible for the Section 106 review defined the Area of Potential Effect as the mine site for archaeological studies, but without a boundary for potential traditional cultural properties.[65] On the NEPA side, the tribe hired a team of its own scientists to challenge the models used by the Corps' consultants. Larry Nesper describes the strategy as "death by a thousand cuts."[66]

Thus equipped, and drawing on alliances with non-Native opponents, Mole Lake was able to make the project costly and prickly enough to compel the sale from the original mining companies, Exxon and Rio Algom, to another international firm, the chief executive of which was persuaded of Mole Lake's resolve. Ultimately, the tribe was able to buy the mine site, and it has not developed its own mining operation.

As the better advisers and consultants involved in cultural resource management will attest, sober anticipation of costs and delays of environmental and historic preservation review can lead agencies to better and earlier consultation and planning with Native nations. If they don't, or if they blindly follow the advice of consultants and attorneys who sell themselves as able to reduce exposure and "streamline" review, developers and agencies can be confronted by mounting costs, delays, and headaches. The chapter will conclude with an assessment of the outcome of the Dakota Access Pipeline controversy: general failure in courts but an iconic warning to others about how to approach NEPA, NHPA, and the resolve of Indigenous peoples to *defend the sacred*.

Drawbacks to Religion as Culture in Practice

NEPA and NHPA Lack Strong Legal Teeth

The discourse of cultural resource management has become the lingua franca of most Native efforts to safeguard sacred places, but despite the promise of that discourse on paper, in practice NEPA and NHPA have lacked the legal teeth to fully deliver on that promise. And courts have been reluctant to forcefully commend the teeth already there. In this legal environment, agencies, corporations, and the professional consultants who manage the process can approach NEPA and NHPA review as little more than a routine exercise in minimal compliance. They can do more, and they sometimes do, but much rests on the good faith of any given public official and/or Native peoples' resolve and resources to make the most of the review processes.

Courts have differed in addressing whether NHPA provides a legal cause of action under the statute itself, or whether challenges under the law, like those under NEPA, must be made under the Administrative Procedures Act (APA), where courts act within standards of deference to agency decisions, where burdens of proof are higher, and where all administrative remedies must first be exhausted, often pushing challenges beyond the time window in which interventions can be made to protect sacred places.[67] In a major sacred land case involving Apache claims that Forest Service approval of a telescope on Mount Graham violated NHPA, the Ninth Circuit found no cause of action directly under NHPA, agreeing with two other circuits.[68]

Judicial review of agency decisions claimed to have violated NHPA in threats to Native sacred sites, when put under the APA, is halting at best.[69] The APA empowers courts to set aside an agency action when found to be "arbitrary, capricious, an abuse of discretion, or otherwise not in accordance with law" or "without observance of procedure required by law."[70] But courts have been largely deferential to agency decision makers, stepping in to set aside decisions only in cases of egregious procedural flaws by agencies. The legal doctrine known as *Chevron deference* insists that courts will not replace an agency interpretation of a statute with their own more stringent one.[71] For all the promise in theory, in practice courts have not stepped in to ensure that NHPA's protections for Native sacred sites are maximized. This is also in part because the APA requires all administrative remedies be exhausted prior to a legal action under it, and in many cases, by the time they have been exhausted, the damage is already done.

Good arguments have been made that federal agencies can be arbitrary and capricious even when acting in their usual realm of discretion if they fail to live up to their trust responsibility to Native nations.[72] But in the case of environmental laws and other laws of general applicability, courts have not found cause to judicially enforce the trust responsibility under the APA.[73]

THE DAKOTA ACCESS PIPELINE LITIGATION

The Dakota Access Pipeline controversy makes the legal ineffectiveness of NEPA and NHPA abundantly clear in the failure to win over courts of law even as Native opponents of the Dakota Access Pipeline gained favor in courts of public opinion. If the second round of *Standing Rock Sioux Tribe v. U.S. Army Corps of Engineers* (*Standing Rock II*) failed to persuade a judge the tribes had a religious freedom argument for blocking the pipeline's completion, the initial strategy was to challenge under NHPA. In July 2016, days after the Army Corps of Engineers released its Environmental Assessment and "Mitigated Finding of no Significant Impact," the Standing Rock Sioux Tribe, joined shortly by the Cheyenne River Sioux Tribe, filed its initial suit, challenging the Corps' final decision on grounds of NHPA, NEPA, the Clean Water Act, and the Rivers and Harbors Act.[74] In August, Standing Rock filed for an expedited hearing in their effort to gain a preliminary injunction to halt completion of the pipeline.[75]

Even as the American nation was paying attention to the arguments on the ground in the Water Protector camps, the legal arguments were languishing in court. In September, federal judge James E. Boasberg released the first decision in the case, finding no violation of NHPA Section 106 sufficient to warrant a preliminary injunction on pipeline completion, and this ruling was affirmed on appeal to the DC Circuit Court.[76] I'll discuss this initial decision shortly under the heading of consultation. A third decision, in June 2017, marked something of a victory for the tribes. In *Standing Rock III*, Judge Boasberg found sufficient gaps in the NEPA review to require the Army Corps to fill three specific ones.[77] The court stopped short of requiring the fuller Environmental Impact Statement, which would compel consideration of other alternatives to this crossing of the Missouri, and also refused Standing Rock's request to halt the flow of oil as the remand process played out, showing how Pyrrhic was any victory claimed by Standing Rock's lawyers.[78] First, the judge found that the Corps had failed to fully consider "the degree to which the pipeline's effects on the quality of the human environment are likely to be highly controversial" and required the Corps to make a showing to justify an EA would suffice in light of controversies about the scope of the impact raised by Standing Rock's own experts.[79] Recall how one of the threshold criteria requiring a fuller EIS is the likelihood of a government action to be "highly controversial," later clarified in the courts to "cases where a substantial dispute exists as to the size, nature, or effect of the major federal action rather than to the existence of opposition to a use."[80] Second, the judge cited the tribe's treaty-protected rights to fish and game in the Missouri River and required the Corps to consider the impact of a potential toxic spill on those rights.[81] Third, the judge held the Corps to account for failing to fully factor in environmental justice impacts on the Standing Rock Nation.

Still, Judge Boasberg denied Standing Rock's request to enjoin the continued flow of oil while the Corps addressed these review oversights, and his justification for the refusal (*Standing Rock IV*), bespoke the likelihood that the Corps could handily answer the court's objections without facing a full-fledged EIS. On affected treaty rights under spill scenarios, the judge indicated the Corps presumably would only need to "connect the dots" of data it already had.[82] Similarly, as to whether the Corps had adequately treated the "highly controversial" estimate of the pipeline's crossing effect among experts of the different parties, the judge faulted the Corps for not saying anything to refute the tribes' expert opinions. "Correcting this flaw," the judge writes, "does not require that Defendants begin anew, but only that they better articulate their reasoning below."[83] What the judge said about the continued question of environmental justice is telling:

> There is no doubt that our nation's history is replete with examples of Native American tribes bearing the brunt of government action. And Chairman Archambault is eloquent on why the Tribes believe that this pipeline embodies another transgression. Yet the court's role here is not to determine the wisdom of agency action or to opine on its substantive effects.... Instead, it must consider only the Corps' likelihood on remand of fulfilling NEPA's procedural environmental-justice requirements and justifying its prior decision.[84]

Unsurprisingly, with such modest judicial pressure, the Corps in August 2018 issued a two-page memorandum concluding there were no hunting and fishing treaty rights or environmental justice concerns and concluded that no formal reconsideration of its original EA and Finding of No Significant Impact was needed. When the fuller report providing reasons for the Corps decision was released several months later, Standing Rock redoubled its legal efforts. In August 2019, Standing Rock filed a motion for summary judgment that the Army Corps had failed to meaningfully respond to its concerns in the remand process, relying on the pipeline operator for all the relevant information and shutting Standing Rock out of the process.[85] Standing Rock seeks the court to remedy this by vacating the easement authorizing the pipeline's crossing of the Missouri and halting the flow of oil pending a fuller EIS.

At the time of this writing, that proceeding is still underway, but so is the massive flow of oil beneath the Missouri River, which the pipeline's operators propose to double. And while there's always hope that an appeal might produce a different outcome, the DC Circuit already affirmed the trial judge's opinion in *Standing Rock I*.

DAKOTA ACCESS PIPELINE AND
THE WEAKNESS OF NHPA AND NEPA

The relative weakness of NEPA and NHPA in this case is not simply related to those statutes but to relaxed rules governing pipeline infrastructure. The vast majority of the Dakota Access Pipeline, as the company boasted, crossed private land and consensually so. Crossings of any navigable waters implicated the Corps, but almost all of those crossings were bundled through a so-called nationwide permit under Section 404 of the Clean Water Act, a process streamlined to relieve parties of an endless cycle of permit requests where the agency sees few or no adverse effects.[86] The key legal issue at Standing Rock was the crossing of the federal land beside and under Lake Oahe. Indeed, after more than a thousand miles of pipeline were already in place, what might seem like eleventh-hour timing of the litigation is in reality simply Standing Rock's immediate response to the Corps' release of its final EA in July. The heavy lifting in terms of compliance had been done with relative ease through the nationwide permit.

Quite aside from the specific provisions of NHPA and NEPA, and no matter how compelling the facts and the mounting attention raised by the protest, the legal burden for obtaining a preliminary injunction was nearly insurmountable. And an emergency injunction was the only legal remedy that made sense at that last stage of the pipeline's construction. It should be said that NHPA and NEPA inadvertently hand agencies and pro-development interests these temporal advantages. If project delays related to NEPA and NHPA are some of the strongest cards available to Native nations facing threats to what they consider sacred, agencies and industries promoting such development can structure their reviews accordingly.

Consultation and Its Wide-Ranging Standard

In the absence of strong legal teeth, NEPA and NHPA are most effective for Native peoples when consultation is genuine, timely, and respectful. Consultation is required at various points under both NEPA and NHPA, and while federal agencies are directed by Executive Order 13175 to step up their consultation with tribes, there is surprising variation among government officials—and courts offering judicial review of their actions—as to what constitutes sufficient consultation. We have already considered the Las Huertas Canyon case, where the Forest Service initially contented itself with sending form letters to tribes asking them to identify any sites of religious and cultural significance on survey maps. A federal court in that case, *Pueblo of Sandia v. United States*, chastened this approach as woefully incomplete and insensitive to Native protocols concerning cultural knowledge.[87] This has mattered, especially for government officials eager to fulfill the spirit of NHPA and NEPA. But the impact of such cases in lower federal courts, or the extensive discussion of best practices in consultation with Native nations found in *Bulletin 38*, is unimpressive.[88] To some government officials, and particularly in agencies or local units that for whatever reason do not emphasize rigor in this regard, consultation has become either a routinized term of art for pushing paper or a volatile problem to be carefully managed.

To illustrate, let's return to the Dakota Access Pipeline case. The first round of litigation turned on Standing Rock's position that the Corps had failed its legal consultation obligations under NHPA, including following procedures that "predate amendments to the NHPA that significantly broaden the role of Tribes in the Section 106 process" and that "have never been approved by the ACHP."[89] These allegations in turn met a forceful response by the United States, and Judge Boasberg's decision rejecting the preliminary injunction revealed the "he said, she said" quality that can characterize disputes about the adequacy of consultation. "After digging through a substantial record on an expedited basis, the Court ... concludes that the Corps has likely complied with the NHPA."[90]

In its July 2016 "Mitigated Finding of No Significant Impact," the six-page document that secured approval of the pipeline's crossing of the Missouri River, the Corps acknowledged the opposition of the tribes to "the pipeline and its alignment," but maintained that "the EA establishes that the district made a good faith effort to consult the tribes and that it considered all tribal comments." The judge correctly summarized the Section 106 regulations for consultation, including the determination of the Area of Potential Effect by the agency and the SHPO that set the terms of the historic preservation review. He cited Dakota Access's diligence in crafting a route that "almost exclusively tracked privately held lands and, in sensitive places like Lake Oahe, already existing utility lines" to minimize potential impacts—but failed to mention here Dakota Access's reconsideration of an original crossing upstream from Bismarck, after widespread opposition in North Dakota's second-largest city and the seat of state government.[91]

The judge also noted how Dakota Access undertook cultural surveys on a 400-foot corridor for pipeline and construction through the Dakotas and that "the pipeline workspace and route was modified to avoid all 91 of these stone features and all but 9 of the other potentially eligible sites."[92] He did not mention that these cultural surveys were merely archaeological ones, conducted by consultants considered by Standing Rock to be ill-equipped to sufficiently identify cultural sites of significance to them. Recall that *Bulletin 38* made clear that archaeological evidence is not required, and thus cannot be the only meaningful data for identifying TCPs.

The judge noted that Dakota Access met with the Standing Rock's Tribal Council on September 30, 2014, and had reached out subsequently to the Tribal Historic Preservation Officer, including about Standing Rock's own cultural survey, with no apparent response.[93] The Corps stepped in with formal Section 106 consultation in October 2014 when Dakota Access needed the Corps' approval to explore the feasibility of conditions for underground drilling at the Missouri River. The judge indicated that the Corps never received a response from Standing Rock when sent information about the proposed work and cultural sites, including sites "that the Corps considered to be outside the projected area of effect."[94]

The THPO may not have responded in a timely way to every request, but the larger context couldn't be clearer. Standing Rock unambiguously opposed the pipeline crossing and rejected the terms set by the Corps for consultation, specifically the narrowly delineated Area of Potential Effect. As Justin Richland has ably shown in the context of federal consultation over a proposed National Forest land sale involving off-reservation ancestral sites with the Hopi Cultural Preservation Office, Native engagement with federal consultation can reflect a candid appraisal of whether the consultation will matter. Often consultation ensues after significant commitments to the proposed action have been made, foreclosing Native options to recommend no action or alternative actions. Noting that the Hopi were the only affected Native nation that engaged in consultation, Richland observes the lack of response from the other nations may have been "motivated by something other than the lack of organizational competence that the archaeologists claim it was":

> Perhaps it was a form of much more present absence, a refusal, or a deferral, that holds open certain possibilities (maybe freedoms) for later engagement in a way that cannot so easily be appropriated to the ends of the state.[95]

In the Dakota Access case, the judge was nonetheless surprised that "Standing Rock took a different tack" than other tribes that chose to engage the Section 106 consultation to identify cultural properties and work to mitigate adverse effects. Instead, Standing Rock "urged the Corps to redefine the area of potential effect to include the entire pipeline and asserted that it would send no experts to help identify cultural resources until this occurred."[96]

Judge Boasberg acknowledged that Standing Rock had responded in a timely fashion to a Draft EA, which the Corps released in December 2015. Timely indeed: part of their concern was that the Draft EA and preliminary Finding of No Significant Impact failed to incorporate any discussion of Standing Rock at all. The tribes' comments challenged the Corps' failure to live up to its own standards for "active and respectful dialogue … before decisions are made and actions are taken," and noted that the Corps relied on some surveys conducted before the 1992 NHPA amendments that hardwired tribes and their THPOs into processes of historic property identification. Presumably, the Corps was using surveys completed in the early 1980s for the natural gas pipeline running parallel to the Dakota Access course. Standing Rock commented that they counted "at least 350 known sites within the project corridor in North Dakota alone." And they pushed for the higher-level cultural surveys to identify significant properties.[97]

There were seven meetings between Corps officials and the tribes from January through May, including meetings held at the proposed Missouri crossing site, where the Standing Rock chairman "pointed out areas of concern and explained the tribe's issues with the pipeline project."[98]

When the Corps sought to conclude its Section 106 process in April 2016, with the North Dakota SHPO's concurrence that there were "no historic properties subject to effect," Standing Rock's Chairman David Archambault formally objected: "To date, none of our requests for consultation or Class III Cultural Surveys has been honored."[99]

In early September, a former THPO for Standing Rock was allowed by a private land owner to do a cultural survey along the pipeline route cleared for construction. The court noted that he "observed several rock cairns and other sites of cultural significance inside the pipeline corridor," and sites "that he believed to be of great cultural note nearby, including a stone constellation used to mark the burial site of a very important tribal leader about seventy five feet from the pipeline corridor," that were nonetheless not fenced or protected.[100] But the court denied a temporary restraining order on continued construction to preserve any such sites while the lawsuit awaited decision.[101]

While the judge advised "that it is not a dispute of fact that the Standing Rock nation voiced its opposition to the routing of DAPL from the beginning," he found unavailing the tribe's claims that the Corps violated its Section 106 consultation obligations. "Suffice it to say," Judge Boasberg snapped, "that the Tribe largely refused to engage in consultations. It chose instead to hold out for more—namely the chance to conduct its own cultural surveys over the entire length of the pipeline."[102] Judge Boasberg was consistent with other courts in his reluctance to stretch the legal tools. Injunctive relief is "an extraordinary remedy" that the Supreme Court had said required a plaintiff to establish (1), that he is likely to succeed on the merits; and (2), that he is likely to suffer irreparable harm in the absence of the preliminary injunction.

This was combined with the judge's estimate that Standing Rock could not make its necessary showing of "irreparable harm" from the absence of a preliminary injunction. Legal hairsplitting to be sure, but hairsplitting citing relevant case law. The sought-after preliminary injunction and the action under the APA indeed presented high legal standards to meet, and these were conscripted to try to block the final couple miles of construction of a 1,200 mile pipeline already built. Ambiguities in NHPA were sufficient, particularly those that set the terms of review by defining the Area of Potential Effect. As we'll explore in the next section, the APE for this Section 106 consultation and review involved a postage-stamp-sized staging area for the drilling of the underground crossing of the Missouri and its construction access road: not the pipeline's route through deeply significant sites at the juncture of the Cannonball and Missouri, not even the pipeline's route beneath all the federal land controlled by the Corps, and certainly not the crossing of the Missouri River itself. And it made little legal difference that the ACHP weighed in against the Corps' approach and execution of its consultation commitments under Section 106.[103]

The same day as Judge Boasberg's released his decision in *Standing Rock I*, the heads of three federal agencies, including the Department of the Army that oversees the Corps of Engineers, signed a statement halting construction pending further review.

When the review processes of NHPA and NEPA work for Native peoples, it is because consultation is done according to the spirit of the laws: earnestly, early, and often. When Native nations are respectfully approached, they can be empowered to negotiate what they can live with. This seldom happens, I'm convinced, because government agencies stoke their own irrational fear that Native nations will veto all development, even when they are warned that stopping, looking, and listening before acting is precisely what NEPA and NHPA are there to ensure.

In the course of research for this book, it has also become clear that different federal agencies foster different cultures of consultation. It is not insignificant that the Section 106 policies and procedures directing the Army Corps officials have not been updated since the 1992 NHPA Amendments. The Corps, for example, is a problem-solving agency filled with engineers and those thinking that problems have solutions, facts are facts, archaeological facts are plain, and oral traditional facts or Indigenous interpretations of facts are less plain. And despite people of good will occasionally occupying seats of power within it, and despite a chain of command culture, recall that this is the agency that ran roughshod over Standing Rock, Cheyenne River, and others in the development of the Pick-Sloan dams, that tried to ensure the tribes did not have a stake in the revenues from the dams that were built at their expense, or in the management of the water levels since. Standing Rock leaders don't need to be reminded of this history. Judge Boasberg may refer to it as "holding out for more," but perhaps this deep historical experience indicated the perilous nature of accepting the terms for consultation offered by the Army Corps of Engineers.

There are other, more hopeful stories of government agencies doing right by the aspirations and standards of NEPA and NHPA when it comes to tribal consultation. Indeed NEPA and NHPA can be procedural on-ramps for the kinds of robust consultation that can result in better outcomes for Native nations trying to protect what they hold sacred without going public and going to court. I don't mean to discount those stories. But, as *Standing Rock I* makes clear, there are few legal tools to hold agencies accountable to these norms. I'll return to this thread in the final chapter on Indigenous rights in international law, where expectations of government consultation with Indigenous peoples are raised to a standard of "free, prior, and informed consent." Indeed, these cultures of consultation are ripe for an upgrade in light of newly clarified and developing norms of international law for Indigenous rights.

Ambiguities to Reduce Cultural Resource Review Exposure

It would be naive to insist that NEPA or NHPA, even their regulations, be so clear that there be no room for interpretation. Still, reliance on these review processes to protect Native sacred heritage must contend with two significant ambiguities in the laws that have been particularly problematic in review, especially under NHPA. First, there are ambiguities about the *scale* of review, about which aspects of a proposed project are to be subjected to NHPA or NEPA review. Second, there are ambiguities around how precisely to consider *cumulative effects*. These ambiguities are available to project proponents to reduce their exposure to review and make the system work for them. While each ambiguity is in some sense understandable, as illustrative examples show, they have worked consistently against Native American claims to religion as *culture*.

AMBIGUITIES OF SCALE

Dakota Access and the Corps were able to persuade the judge they had adequately consulted under Section 106 because NHPA, like NEPA, allows determinations of scope or scale to be made by agencies, equipping those agencies to set the terms of the process. Much of the dispute was about scale, and this in two specific legal respects pertaining to NHPA and NEPA. For Standing Rock, the federal undertaking requiring Section 106 review and consultation was the broad Army Corps approval of a nationwide permit for the pipeline at hundreds of crossings of navigable waters throughout many states, and at the very least the indirect approval of the pipeline throughout their traditional lands made possible by the Corps' permitting of the Missouri crossing. Standing Rock also maintained that the many reviews involving the Corps along the 1,700 miles of pipeline in four states should, for NEPA purposes, be treated as one federal action involving a bundled review. For the Army Corps, the undertaking subject to Section 106 review was merely the Corps' consideration of an easement across land it manages near and under the Missouri River, and its approach to segmenting environmental review was well within its agency prerogative under NEPA regulations.[104]

Dakota Access and the Corps had a good deal of law on their side here. NEPA and NHPA reviews themselves defer much to a government agency's prerogative to set the terms for consultation through "scoping" under NEPA and defining the "Area of Potential Effect" under NHPA. Under NEPA, scoping involves determining the "range of actions, alternatives, and impacts to be considered." Thomas King observes that "too often scoping is reduced to a public meeting or two—often highly structured and formulaic, perceived merely as regulatory hoops through which to jump rather than as opportunities to reason together—and exchanges of correspondence with regulatory agencies."[105] King suggests that scoping should be informed by background

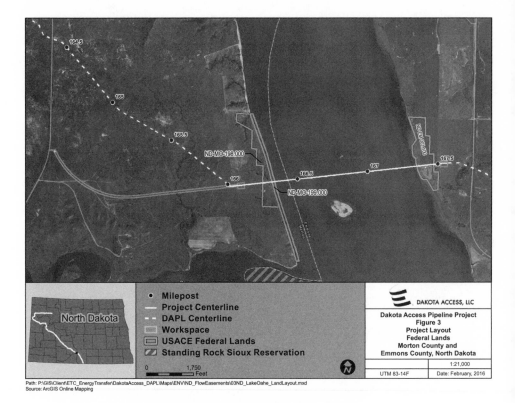

FIG. 4.1. Area of Potential Effect for DAPL
This Map from the Dakota Access Pipeline Environmental Assessment highlights the
access road and drilling construction zone, which defines the Area of Potential Effect
for the environmental assessment for the crossing of the Missouri River.

research and consultative in nature. "Up-front investment in planning identification will pay for itself many times over in research efficiency and improved
relations with affected communities."[106]

Under NHPA, the agency establishes the Area of Potential Effects (APE)
for identified historic properties. In the Dakota Access case, the Corps, or the
firm hired to conduct the review, drew a stunningly small APE—one that
didn't even include the Missouri River it was so controversially crossing—to
narrow the scope of consultation and reduce exposure to opposition. Although Standing Rock maintained that the "confluence of the Cannonball
and Missouri Rivers is sacred ground" and that "industrial development of
that site for the crude oil pipeline has a high potential to destroy sites eligible
for listing," it asserted the Corps had defined the APE for the river crossing

"exceptionally narrowly to include only a tiny parcel immediately surrounding the horizontal directional drilling pits on each side of the river and a narrow strip for an access road and 'string area.'"[107]

The Corps could content itself on good faith consultation with Standing Rock to identify places of significance to them within the size of a standard suburban house lot at the entrance and exit of the underground tunnel, together with the narrow road to the site for construction equipment. In many cases of TCPs, the APE can and should include auditory ranges and view sheds going well beyond the narrow area of a government action, and other indirect effects of the government action. But in *Standing Rock I* the court was unpersuaded that the APE was too narrowly established to consider the adverse effects asserted.[108]

In effect, the consultation extended to Standing Rock was rigorously delimited to this APE. True, the Corps could claim as part of its good faith consultation three site visits with Standing Rock officials to the APE that involved a glimpse at the surrounding sacred landscape, but the judge agreed that sacred landscape was outside the Area of Potential Effect and not subject to further consultation or mitigation. Who defines that area of potential effect can define the terms of the conversation, and the courts in this case as in others defer.

CUMULATIVE EFFECTS

Another crucial ambiguity of cultural resource law is that of *cumulative effects*. Seldom for Native peoples is any given government action an isolated event. What matters is the cumulative effect on Native resources that any given government action might add. Along with direct and indirect effects of alternative actions considered, NEPA requires considerations of an action's cumulative effect, defined as:

> the impact on the environment which results from the incremental impact of the action when added to other past, present, and reasonably foreseeable future actions regardless of what agency (Federal or non-Federal) or person undertakes such other actions.[109]

In its discussion of principles of cumulative effect review, the Council on Environmental Quality notes that while review of effects is ordinarily done from the perspective of the action taken, cumulative effect analysis "requires focusing on the resource, ecosystem, and human community that may be affected."[110]

Absent in the Dakota Access Pipeline EA was any serious discussion of cumulative effects of the pipeline's crossing of the Missouri at Lake Oahe. Rather chillingly, the long history of the Army Corps creation of the reservoir, of displacement and desecration of Standing Rock and Cheyenne River lands and sites and cemeteries, is utterly absent. And chillingly as well, there is no mention of the cumulative effect in any of the court opinions in the Dakota Access litigation, even in the passages where the court speaks in vague terms of the "tragic" history of the federal treatment of the tribes.

Cumulative effects are easier to determine when the focus is on a species of fish or plant; such effects are more difficult to measure in the context of cultural resources.[111] Still, the regulations call for consideration of cumulative effects on the human environment. What is more, in many cases, an action that is strategically planned to minimize exposure to impacts and further review can ironically add to the cumulative effect. Dakota Access said it chose the particular crossing of the Missouri because there were existing utility lines and a natural gas line crossing the river at that point, and this was commended by the judge as evidence of the company's care in minimizing effects. But from Standing Rock's perspective, this was not only adding insult to injury, it was potential injury on injury, doubling the sources for potentially devastating leaks in the river. And concerns raised with the Corps about the adequacy of the review conducted for the Northern Borderline Pipeline project in the 1980s and thus prior to *Bulletin 38* and the 1992 NHPA amendment engaging recognized tribes in the identification of religiously and culturally significant places, were received as unnecessary.[112] Such ambiguities in cultural resource review have tilted the law against them. We turn now to the related ambiguity of the culture concept itself.

Indeterminacies of Culture: What Counts as Cultural Significance and Who Decides?

Protecting religion as *culture* can simply defer the presenting problem of religion's indeterminacy to that of culture. And courts have not gone far to help adjudicate competing interpretations of what counts as culture, who gets to say, and what kinds of evidence are accepted to establish historical significance—again the threshold for protecting religion as culture under NHPA.

Bulletin 38 represents a strenuous effort to clarify how *culture* is to be regarded and especially who is authorized to determine cultural significance. Recall that *Bulletin 38* makes room within a historic preservation regime privileging places of architectural and archaeological interest for places of value to living communities, to culture in the present tense. According to *Bulletin 38*, culture "is understood to mean the traditions, beliefs, practices, lifeways, arts, crafts, and social institutions of any community, be it an Indian tribe, a local ethnic group, or the people of the nation as a whole."[113] *Bulletin 38* seems clear enough on its face that communities are able to say what places are of traditional cultural significance to them, and that oral traditional, "mythical," revelatory, and other distinctive forms of Indigenous knowledge are to count as evidence in support of those claims. But as Thomas King argues in multiple works, *Bulletin 38* has been inconsistently applied by consultants and government managers who are professionally trained archaeologists and historians and who bring views about historicity and culture that are often at odds with how Indigenous peoples think about such things.[114]

First, although *Bulletin 38* makes clear that professional archaeologists and historians are not the only ones to assign cultural significance to historic properties, many cultural resource professionals are trained archaeologists and regard the cultural surveys so important to Section 106 review as exercises in archaeology. To be sure, plenty of consultants, including archaeologists, have expanded their methodologies to ask Native peoples about places of ongoing significance to them; King himself is an archaeologist. But to interview community members and listen for subjective significance takes more time, resources, and a different set of skills than to walk a charted course in the field and make test digs at periodic intervals.

The issue is not only cost. Many cultural resource professionals are shaped deeply by a scientific approach to culture that can view claims by living communities as weak if not corroborated with material evidence in the field or academic evidence in the library. Scientists trained in archaeology can view claims in contested places skeptically as merely a tool to oppose development. To be clear, there is nothing in archaeological training that prevents a cultural resource manager from engaging with living communities, and many have reimagined the relationship with Native peoples.[115]

Analysts as Proponents

It is no secret that while NEPA and NHPA obligate government agencies to oversee reviews, the work is done largely by professional consultants who conduct the analysis and shape much of the conversation through their recommendations in scoping, defining APEs, research designs, and the like.

Consultants are typically chosen and paid by the project proponents themselves, and are factored into the costs of business. This is perhaps as it should be: taxpayers should not have to subsidize reviews that would primarily benefit a company promoting its project. But in my view this is troubling in the absence of the kind of robust professional licensure and ethical review process that, say, lawyers have in the American Bar Association. Under NEPA regulations, federal agencies are to "insure the professional integrity, including scientific integrity, of the discussions and analyses in environmental impact statements."[116] But there is no system in place to do so, beyond expectations that consultants have graduate degrees in relevant fields of archaeology, history, architectural history, or a combination of an undergraduate degree and experience.[117]

Thomas King titles his discussion of this arrangement "The Analyst as Proponent," and I think it is worth pondering those implications for the strengthening of NEPA an NHPA as protections.[118] King finds it as unhealthy as it seems natural that "a proponent's project really does mean 'the world'—that is, survival" to environmental and cultural resource management firms:

> Most people who work for such companies and who run them have spent most or all their professional lives working within this system. Advancing our clients' interests, acting as part of our clients' planning teams, is simply understood to be the way the game is played.[119]

King doesn't charge consultant colleagues with blatant abuses; the rigging of the system is subtle, accruing from everyday decisions. "The impacts we identify," King writes, "depend substantially on where we look, what we look at, how we look, what conceptual and analytic tools we use.... It's ridiculous to think that our decisions ... aren't influenced [by] the interests of those whose financial support means the world to us."[120]

Of course, firms speak of their independence conducting reviews and can take pride in their professionalism. And there are professional membership organizations: the National Association of Environmental Professionals and the American Cultural Resources Association (ACRA) help advocate for member firms and for better cultural resource management. Each organization has a code of ethics and professional responsibility for its members, but membership in both is open, and there are no apparent disciplinary mechanisms.[121] Professionalization of the field of cultural resource management is a good thing, as the work of review for any given project can be done more effectively and efficiently based on professional experience. But it can, as King repeatedly points out, lead to a routinized compliance culture.

CONSULTANTS AND THE
DAKOTA ACCESS PIPELINE REVIEW

Standing Rock included in its original complaint an argument that the consultants hired "to do cultural surveys are not equipped to suitably assess the potential cultural significance of sites in this area. The Tribe has never had the opportunity to discuss protocols for cultural surveys or participate in the surveys that were conducted."[122] This wasn't explicitly because of the systemic issues or just because their work was paid for by the Dakota Access developers; it was primarily because the consultants' expertise in archaeology and the archaeological methods they chose to use to identify cultural resources did not factor Native voices into the equation. This is precisely why *Bulletin 38* was required to put Traditional Cultural Properties on the map of Section 106 review: there may not be evidence of the sort an archaeological survey would encounter to suggest a place is of significance to a living community. Tim Mentz, a former Standing Rock THPO, identified the problem thus:

> On another project I conducted with the Zuni tribe, I watched as elders explained to the archaeologists excavating a site in the path of a new Arizona highway that they had placed a survey flag in a semicircle of rocks— which was likely a shrine used to bless and protect the ancient village. When it comes to traditional practices, Native Americans see what archaeologists overlook.[123]

The Dakota Access Pipeline is a good example of the systemic problem inherent when project proponents select and compensate the consultants who do the legwork of the environmental and cultural review, especially when a federal agency lacks the will or resource base to intervene. The cultural resource surveys for Dakota Access were conducted by Gray and Pape, a Houston, Texas, firm, along with Alpine Archeological Services and Merjent Inc.[124] These are established firms; the first two have sponsored the American Cultural Resource Association.[125] Such firms rely on professional expertise, general training in archaeology and history, and knowledge of how to conduct Section 106 and NEPA reviews in a way that bears fruit. But such firms market themselves to the project proponents that pay for their services. Alpine's web page includes the following: "We believe that the best way to help clients realize their project goals is to offer expert services, delivered in a timely and cost-effective manner."[126] Merjent's self-marketing even more boldly appeals to project proponents. Its web page includes a banner, "We promote an environment where people and projects succeed." And the "What We Do" page

FIG. 4.2. Page from Dakota Access Pipeline Environmental Assessment
Page from an appendix to the July 2016 Environmental Assessment and Mitigated Finding of No Significant Impact of the Dakota Access Pipeline's crossing of the Missouri River, release of which ignited the lawsuit filed in August. The study's appendixes included industry-produced documentation, including this page on the Grundo Ram Pneumatic Pipe Rammer, part of horizontal directional drilling technology.

includes a banner proclaiming, "Our staff help propel clients' multi-million dollar projects from feasibility to operation."[127]

Were these firms prepared, or predisposed given the professional-client relationship they were in, to anticipate and shape the review process in a way that fully engaged the Standing Rock Sioux Tribe early and often? Were they too acclimated to a business model that promised their clients a streamlined review process—efficiently produced surveys, unduplicated efforts, manageable areas of potential effect to reduce exposure—to properly anticipate what could happen if their pipeline clients or the Corps did not more effectively engage Standing Rock leaders?

Put another way, streamlining doesn't always pay, and this became all too obvious to Dakota Access investors. Troy Eid, a former US Attorney appointed by George W. Bush whose law firm advises energy and pipeline industries, hastens to point out the costs of not engaging tribes in good faith consultation early in a development process. Eid tallied at least $750 million in the costs of the Dakota Access pipeline for not having engaged more directly the tribal consultation required under NEPA and NHPA.[128] A more thorough study by a University of Colorado research center placed the cost of delays and additional costs specifically to the Dakota Access investors of between $1.8 and $2.2 billion. This study also factored in the additional bank divestment and reductions in stock price and estimated the total costs of the Dakota Access debacle to be $7.5 *billion*.[129] Whatever the precise figure, perhaps the most lasting implication of the Dakota Access case is that investors in similar development projects will look more closely at the costs of not engaging tribal consultation and NEPA and NHPA review.

Conclusion

Protecting religion as cultural resource makes considerable intellectual sense, and environmental and historic preservation review can offer Native peoples a place at the table in matters affecting their religions and cultures in meaningful ways. But the Standing Rock litigation shows the overall statutory weakness of procedural laws like NEPA and NHPA to effectively protect Native American sacred places.

The overall lack of success here is not directly because religion as culture is intellectually problematic. Even though it defers the indeterminacies of religion onto the indeterminacies of culture, there have been efforts, like *Bulletin 38*, that go a long way to shape a reading of culture that is open to living communities. And to be sure, when the process works well, with good faith consultation in more than name only, Native peoples can shape the projects that impact their lives.

In sum, the cultural resource review process required by NEPA and NHPA is most certainly *a card* to play for Native peoples seeking to protect their sacred places, but this is not to say it is *the card* to play. As part of broader strategies of protection, cultural resource law surely has its place. Taken alone, NEPA and NHPA lack robust opportunities for judicial review that would shape negotiation conditions more favorable to Native peoples. But other federal directives from treaty-based Indian law concerning formal consultations with tribes have strengthened the process and made cultural resource protections more fruitful. And with emerging norms of Indigenous rights in international law, the available processes established in NEPA and NHPA can better accomplish the spirit of the law.

5

Religion as Collective Right

LEGISLATING TOWARD NATIVE
AMERICAN RELIGIOUS FREEDOM

Introduction

Because the language of religious freedom, with its presumptions to universality, has been only dimly effective for Native sacred claims in the courts, we have seen in the last chapter that Native advocates have increasingly articulated sacred claims, especially to sacred lands, in the language of cultural resource protection. But the protections for religion as culture, too, have proved halting and procedural at best. We turn now to consider how Native people drew on the rhetorical power of American religious freedom to bolster the legal protection of religions specifically of Native peoples. We found in chapter 1 how Native leaders in the early twentieth century turned to the language of religious freedom to protect dance ceremonies and ritual Peyote use from the scourge of the civilization regulations. We considered how this strategic appeal to religious freedom came with trade-offs. The Native religion that was legible to American law was an individualistic religion, one limited to the interior lives of Native people and tinted with the aura of the Native spirituality that anthropologists and other seekers of the era saw. It was also set off from other features of Native culture and economy that had been part of a thick weave of collective life. Close attention to these historical developments highlights how American religious freedom discourse functions to exclude the religions of Native peoples but also how that discourse authorizes Native peoples to appropriate it for their own purposes.

These next two chapters pick up after the last chapter's discussion of disappointments with the procedural safeguards of cultural resource law. Looking at efforts to legislate Native religious freedom over the last forty years, this chapter tells the story of the remarkable accomplishments of the 1978 American Indian Religious Freedom Act (AIRFA), and the next chapter tells the related story of the 1990 Native American Graves Protection and Repatriation Act (NAGPRA). Informed by interviews with Suzan Shown Harjo—journalist, poet, and strategic advocate of Cheyenne and Hodulgee Muscogee descent who was centrally involved in passage of these laws—this chapter also gives it a fresh reading. The history I offer here follows these interviews closely but is also something of a constructive history, at least in the sense that I try to make explicit what sometimes is implicit, that when Harjo and other actors appealed to the discourse of religion and religious freedom, they intended to be speaking about collective as well as individual religious freedom.

Where courts and even common sense have seen AIRFA as a religious freedom statute—as an extension of the legal protections of the First Amendment into the distinctive terrain of Native American traditions—I suggest a different view. Together with a handful of other statutes and executive orders, AIRFA (like NAGPRA) carries the rhetorical force of religious freedom into the legal shape of federal Indian law, with its recognition of treaty-based group rights and the United States' nation-to-nation obligations to Native nations. And the story starts at a sacred place.

"Consecrated on Sacred Ground": Bear Butte, 1967

In June 1967, a twenty-something Suzan Shown Harjo drove with her toddler daughter from New York City to South Dakota to attend Cheyenne summer solstice ceremonies at Bear Butte. Harjo was at the time working as an arts producer at "Free Speech" radio station WBAI. It was a full creative life in Greenwich Village, airing poetry by William Burroughs and memorably broadcasting a full hour of the composer Philip Glass boiling water. But she got a call, and went.

For the Cheyenne, or Tsitsistas, Nation, it was originally at Bear Butte, which they call Nowah'wus (Holy Mountain), where they were taught how to be Tsitsistas/Cheyenne, to live as a people in right relationship with one another, with creation, and with the spirits. The prophet Sweet Medicine was called by the Creator to receive instruction at Bear Butte about the Cheyenne way, and the power of those teachings was conferred on the people through the gift of four Sacred Arrows. The Arrows have quite a story in their own

FIG. 5.1. Bear Butte

Moonrise from Bear Butte. According to Suzan Harjo, the movement that produced
AIRFA and NAGPRA was commissioned at the conclusion of Cheyenne
summer ceremonies in 1967. (Photo courtesy Greg Johnson)

right, and today they are part of a medicine bundle associated with Tsitsistas peoplehood. Although the Cheyenne have lived at some remove from Holy Mountain, split into the Northern Cheyenne in Montana and the Southern Cheyenne in Oklahoma, Tsitsistas people make annual pilgrimages to renew the Sacred Arrows, the community, and the world in summer ceremonies.

The 1967 ceremonies continued as mandated, but the spiritual leaders had been increasingly emboldened by ceremony to challenge the long legacy of injustices leveled at Native peoples and their religious traditions. There were concerns about specific desecrations at Bear Butte, where proper ceremonial access was hampered by management policies of the South Dakota State Parks and where the aquifer and nearby lake and sacred springs were disturbed. But the concerns were also very much about desecrations of other sacred places, about ancestral remains and sacred items held hostage in museums, about ongoing grave robbing and dehumanizing displays of Native body parts in museums and roadside curio shops. An Arrow Keeper of the Cheyenne, James Medicine Elk, joined by Lakota Sun Dance leader and medicine man Pete Catches Sr., called for a meeting following the ceremonies.[1] In attendance were a few invited people from outside the Cheyenne, Arapaho, and Lakota peoples, among them the noted Muscogee spiritual leader Phillip Deere and a Mandan elder, Old Man Baker. "Our elders told everyone not to leave," Harjo remembered, "when they came for ceremonies in June of '67, not to leave because we're going to talk about all of these things, and to be prepared to stay for several days." As Harjo recounted it:

> Word just goes out. When you come, be prepared to stay. Now, when Cheyenne say, "Be prepared to stay," that usually means four days. So, we had our four days of ceremonies and then, this was another four days. We just camped out there at Bear Butte and I had my daughter with me—she was two years old. She was the youngest person but I was the youngest adult who was there. There were some teenagers but mostly older people and just a handful of us who really were kind of in that active age and looking for direction or needing direction. When you're in your early twenties and you're just looking for people to put you to work. You want people to tell you, "This is important, do this." We were all figuring these things out and I was the only writer there—people would say, "Write that up!" They didn't mean "make a note of it," they meant, "do something about this!" ... So, my work orders were: "you tell them" and "write this up."[2]

Harjo wrote up what elders said in the proceedings and organized the text under four rubrics:

1. "Leave them alone"	Protect Sacred Places and Ancestors
2. "Give them back"; "Put them back"	Repatriation
3. "A new way"; "we can do it right"	Museum Reform
4. "Stop treating us that way"	Respect[3]

From Bear Butte, Harjo traveled with Raymond Spang, her husband Frank Ray Harjo, and others to Zuni Pueblo, at the invitation of Governor Robert E. Lewis, a leader of the Cultural Committee of the National Tribal Chairmen's Association. Thereafter, they went by invitation to Hopi, Santo Domingo, San Felipe, and Taos Pueblos, to the Yakama Nation and to the Confederated Tribes of the Warm Springs Reservation.[4] "We went all around the country and who we were changed depending on who could go."[5] Ironically, it was Nixon's Bureau of Indian Affairs that unwittingly financed this travel and the capacity it helped build. "They still refused our requests for help with laws or administrative actions for religious freedom, repatriation, and our cultural center in front of the Capitol, but they gave us books of government travel requisitions, Harjo recounted. "One book was good for a year of heavy airline travel and enabled us to meet in more tribes' territories and to understand better the size and shape of the legal door we were trying to construct."[6]

Eventually, Harjo would go on to serve in the Carter administration, and subsequently as the executive director of the National Congress of American Indians, the Washington voice of tribal governments, and the story of this chapter is in many respects a Washington, DC, story. But crucially, the accomplishments to which we turn are rooted more deeply than simply in the US Constitution and a savvy awareness of the three branches of US government established long after Sweet Medicine had received the Cheyenne Way and the Cheyenne Nation received its law and its religion.[7]

We need not know the details of the ceremonies at Bear Butte to grasp an important truth here. Legal and political efforts by Native advocates to engage the discourse of religious freedom began with ceremony, not politics, at the initial direction of traditional spiritual leaders and elders, not lawyers or generally, for that matter, of elected tribal officials. And while every paragraph of this chapter suggests the strategic creativity of Native people like Harjo to advance this agenda in the language of American law and policy, the advocates began in 1967 with more Indigenous categories:

> In 1967 when we first started talking about repatriation law, we didn't talk about it in terms of law and we didn't use the word repatriation. So when we formed the coalition ... we didn't even have a slang for it. We didn't have a catchphrase. We were talking about protection of our sacred places, museum reform, getting our dead relatives out of these museums, getting them off the highways from these curio places. So, we were looking at all of this. The baby cords and the beaded pouches that shouldn't be in museums. Human remains of all kinds and our sacred objects. So, we were talking about repatriation in terms of "put 'em back, give 'em back, stop doing what you're doing, stop showing us,"—so, we had to develop a way of talking about this. And repatriation came later—that term.[8]

Similarly, from the beginning a cultural center was imagined "that would stand in the face of Congress so that policymakers in the U.S. Capitol would have to look us in the eyes when they made decisions about our lives."[9] These ideas, Harjo reflected nearly forty years later, were becoming strategic, but for her it was crucial that the efforts were rooted in ceremony, in the sacred:

> We consecrated [the coalition's strategic work] on sacred ground, so it was as good as done, and it was left to those of us who were young and strong to carry it out. And we are not finished yet.[10]

Strategic Engagement with Religious Freedom

By no means am I the first to tell the story of these legislative efforts. But those who have told the story as an agonistic struggle for *religious freedom* without querying that category have missed an important point. Native leaders strategically used religious freedom discourse to secure rights that are more complicated, more collective, and more Indigenous than *religious* in any conventional sense of that term. Their efforts have thus been misrecognized as more naive, more plainly religious so to speak, leading to hastier pronouncements of victory or failure in that agonistic struggle.[11] Although his discussion of sacred land traditions and legal controversies is nuanced, Peter Nabokov's *Where the Lightning Strikes* takes as its starting point the author's appropriate dismay about AIRFA given four prominent rejections in appellate courts of AIRFA-based claims to protect sacred lands.[12] "For a fleeting moment," he remembered, "the topic of American Indian sacred places commanded the nation's attention. It felt like a great success on behalf of more than fifteen thousand years of Indian presence, prayer and practice in this land. But it was not."[13]

In their engagement with the language of religion, I contend, Native leaders demonstrably drew on the discursive field of religious freedom and were no doubt faced with the co-optation that came with that engagement, but they also pushed the subjective, individualized terms of that discourse rhetorically and legally in the direction of the collective rights of Native nations. Individuals as citizens and members of those nations carry a distinctive political and legal status that makes them far more than legal individuals with civil rights, or members of religious or racial minority groups.

Religious Freedom in the Courts

Efforts to make the language of religious freedom work for Native claims in the "courts of the conqueror," as we have seen, have had disappointing results.[14] The literature on Native American religious freedom, in legal studies and in religious studies, has largely been fed by analyses of the two key decisions where the Supreme Court reversed lower court holdings and crushed any meaningful possibility for court-enforced First Amendment protections, either to Native American sacred lands, as in *Lyng v. Northwest Indian Cemetery Protective Association* (1988), or to ceremonial practices that are effectively prohibited by "neutral laws of general applicability," like drug statutes, wildlife protection laws, or prison dress codes in the case of the second decision, *Employment Div. v. Smith* (1990).

Notably, it was Native American claims in *Lyng* and *Smith* that occasioned the Rehnquist Court to actively rewrite First Amendment Free Exercise jurisprudence, and this has captured the attention of comparative religionists like Huston Smith and Robert Michaelson eager to show how diverse must be the palette of "religion" if the United States is to be a fully inclusive diverse democracy.[15] Just after the Court's holding in *Lyng*, Robert Michaelson wrote of the dashed hopes surrounding AIRFA:

> The Act has been interpreted by the courts to add nothing substantial to Indian rights and protections under the religion clauses of the First Amendment, rights and protections enjoyed by all Americans. And the Congress has done nothing since the passage of AIRFA to counter that view.[16]

Set in the register of tragedy, Native claims lose out to the religious tastes of the American majority. More curious is how indexical these two decisions have become for the limited possibilities of Native rights qua "religion freedom" in the scholarship on federal Indian law, or within the broader canvas of Indigenous studies. A major casebook on federal Indian law has contained questions of religion largely to analyses of these two cases, in turn overlooking the highly religious nature of other claims found elsewhere in the casebook: claims to jurisdiction, sovereignty, land, water, or traditional fishing and hunting practices.[17]

The Religious Freedom Restoration Act: Everything but the Indians

Even when Congress reinstated by statute what the Supreme Court had largely removed in terms of judicial review of government actions burdening religious exercise, the protections of the Religious Freedom Restoration Act (RFRA) have largely failed Native claims in the courts. Out of a sense of shared outrage with the holding in *Smith*, First Amendment organizations came together from across the culture wars spectrum—from the ACLU to Pat Robertson's ACLJ (American Center for Law and Justice) and everything in between: American Jewish Congress, Joint Baptist Religious Freedom Coalition, National Association of Evangelicals, Jehovah's Witnesses, and so on. They won passage of RFRA in 1993, reapplying what the *Smith* decision had taken away—the "strict scrutiny" standard of judicial review of government actions that "substantially burdened" religious exercise, whether or not those actions were neutral laws of general applicability.[18]

When the Supreme Court found RFRA unconstitutional as applied to the states in *Boerne v. Flores* (1997), Congress passed in 2000 the more narrowly tailored Religious Land Use and Institutionalized Persons Act, which, among other things, amended RFRA's definition of "religious exercise" to include "any exercise of religion, whether or not compelled by, or central to, a system of religious belief."[19] And finally, RFRA's constitutionality with regard to federal laws remained intact, and thus held considerable promise for Native American religious challenges to the many actions of federal government regulating their lives.

But even with the leg up offered by RFRA and its expanded definition of "religious exercise," Native claims to sacred land protection under RFRA have generally failed, with the Ninth Circuit's decision against the tribes in the San Francisco Peaks case seeming to control current cases and encouraging other courts to misrecognize claims to collective obligations and practices merely as the flattened spirituality of individuals.[20] If, as I have argued, the romanticized image of Indians as naturally spiritual hurt Native people's efforts to show the burden on their religion in the courts, the romanticized image perhaps has helped as much as it has hindered attempts by Native peoples and advocates to secure statutory protections specific to their claims. We now turn in the direction of those remarkable statutory accomplishments and to particular ways in which Native religions have come to be defined through those legal processes. But first, we should briefly remind ourselves of developments in the 1970s shaping self-determination and the federal trust responsibility that provided the legal architecture for legislated Native American religious freedom.

Self-Determination and Federal Trust Responsibility

In the 1970s, the United States formally adopted policies of Indian self-determination, and a series of court decisions firmed up a legal basis for that policy, elaborating on two principles, Native treaty rights and federal trust responsibility, that went deep into the legal past. The specific government-to-government obligations spelled out in over 370 different treaties with what the courts recognized as "domestic, dependent nations" were interpreted as a special federal trust relationship with those tribes, likened to that of a guardian to a ward. Although it is not surprising that such a paternalistic approach as the federal trust responsibility has provided a source of federal power, including a source of power to intervene in tribal affairs to protect the rights of individual tribal members,[21] it can also serve as a source of tribal rights, especially when courts have held the United States accountable to the "highest fiduciary standards" in its trustee role.[22] And while the federal trust responsibility applies in fairly plain legal fashion to the fiduciary management of natural and economic resources, it has also been understood to extend to cultural resources: languages, cultures, and religions of tribes.[23]

Rooted in treaties and the recognition that tribal governments are the third sovereignty in US law, aside from the federal and state governments, the trust relationship also distinguishes federal relationships to federally recognized tribes from its treatment of other minority populations. In a number of important rulings in the 1970s, the Supreme Court established the position that policies benefiting members of federally recognized tribes, like the Bureau of Indian Affairs hiring preference, could pass muster under civil rights challenges when they were tailored to the political, rather than racial, ethnic (or religious) status of those members.[24] As the Court put it in 1979, laws that "might otherwise be constitutionally offensive" might be acceptable if they are enacted pursuant to the United States' trust relationship.[25] The approach has broadly safeguarded other federal Indian law supporting tribal self-determination, such as the 1975 Indian Self-Determination and Education Assistance Act, which recognized the tribes as contractors, akin to states and local governments, for federal programs, and the Indian Child Welfare Act (1978) that privileged adoption and foster placement of Native children within tribes.[26]

Legislating toward Native American Religious Freedom

When read in the light of legal elaboration of self-determination and the federal trust responsibility, the legislative gains in the American Indian Religious Freedom Act (1978), National Museum of the American Indian Act (1989), the Native American Graves Protection and Repatriation Act (1990), and the 1994 "Peyote" Amendment to AIRFA, appear not simply as narrowly *religious* freedom gains but as gains toward a particular species of religious freedom for tribes as collectivities. This view of collective religious protections remains wedded to the notion that Native Americans enjoy a special political and legal status that can render their rights differently from those civil liberties of other American citizens.

In 1970, President Nixon championed and signed legislation returning 48,000 acres surrounding the sacred Blue Lake to Taos Pueblo. For more than sixty years, Taos Pueblo challenged President Theodore Roosevelt's 1906 executive action that had confiscated established Taos lands for the Carson National Forest. Taos even rejected the monetary settlement suggested by the Indian Claims Commission; they wanted the sacred lake back. At the signing ceremony, Nixon said the return of Blue Lake represented "justice," because it returned Indian lands unlawfully taken; "respect for religion," because Taos people had been worshipping at Blue Lake for at least seven hundred years; and "a new direction for Indian Affairs," one of "cooperation rather than paternalism and self-determination rather than termination."[27] In 1972, Nixon signed an executive order restoring to the Yakama Nation 21,000 acres of Washington's Mount Adams, including the summit of its sacred mountain.[28] The land had originally been surveyed as part of the reservation, but was erroneously later incorporated into a national forest.

Nixon's return of Blue Lake and Mount Adams were symbolic of a new policy direction, but isolated and ad hoc in nature. By and large, the formal Indian policy of self-determination, first championed by the Nixon adminis-tration and elaborated by Congress through the subsequent Ford adminis-tration, took as its focus economic development and political development, especially the building of tribal capacity to act as contractors rather than con-sumers of federal services. Suzan Harjo suggests neither the Nixon nor Ford administrations was particularly supportive of broader special protections for Native religious and cultural rights, viewing such an approach as uncon-stitutional and saying they would veto any such bill a Democrat-controlled Congress would send them.[29]

In 1975, Congress established the American Indian Policy Review Com-mission, which made hundreds of recommendations toward fuller self-determination. This commission took a similar approach, stipulating in detail recommendations about jurisdiction, economic development, and human services, but avoided religious concerns altogether. In a section of that report called "General Problems," the commission noted that it had not adequately plumbed questions of cultural matters, listing fourteen categories of culture from architecture to folk art to performing arts to sports, but still shying away from religion. The report elaborated on the work of cultural preservation, but in the folklorized register of academic studies, museum collections, and eth-nic heritage funding programs.[30] Its related recommendations did not call for a review of the overall impact of federal policy on Native cultures, languages, and religious traditions, instead calling for more culturally sensitive and robust grant support programs of the National Endowment for the Humanities and the Smithsonian.[31]

According to Harjo, the vision going back to 1967 had always conjoined the various religious and cultural issues to the broader self-determination agenda: return of deceased Native people and sacred items from collections, freedom to conduct ceremonies without interference, access to and protec-tion of sacred sites, and a more visible and visibly sovereign presence in American life. From this perspective, the more political and economic ele-ments of self-determination policy were incomplete if the linguistic, cultural, and religious traditions that make Native peoples distinct weren't part of the equation.

Especially as executive director of the National Congress of American Indians, Harjo was at the center of advocacy for land recovery and other elements of the self-determination agenda. But even within those leadership circles, she continued to emphasize action on Native religious and cultural concerns. Harjo considered such work "atmospheric" for the broader agenda:

> I worked on all the big stuff. And this is part of the big stuff, and it's foundational, it's fundamental, it's atmospheric, it's contextual to everything else. If the traditional Indians stop being the traditional people, and our religions and cultures and languages cease to exist, there are no more Native people. There are simply more brown White people.[32]

The American Indian Religious Freedom Act

As a presidential candidate, Jimmy Carter caught the eye of Harjo and other leaders as one who might advance Native religious and cultural rights, and Harjo joined his campaign. She recounts Carter departed from her script at a meeting with tribal leaders to say he would support a bill supporting Indian religious and cultural rights "because my Bible tells me so." Harjo became part of President-Elect Carter's transition team, and after a stint as legislative liaison at the Native American Rights Fund in the time leading up to AIRFA's passage, she was asked to join the Carter administration as a special assistant for Indian legislation and as a liaison with tribal leaders. Among her tasks was orchestrating the policy review across dozens of federal agencies required by AIRFA and coordinating the president's Report to Congress on American Indian Religious Freedom.

The legislation that became AIRFA was made possible by strong support from the Carter White House and was sponsored by Senators Edward Kennedy (D-MA) and Barry Goldwater (R-AZ), together with Representative Morris Udall (D-AZ) in the House. But the effort faced powerful opposition from other congressional leaders concerned about the potential disruptive impact on public land use by extractive industries.

Native leaders sought a broad declaration formally disclaiming policies that had expressly criminalized Native religions or that had the unintentional effect of infringing on their practice in the years since. AIRFA's formal restatement of policy reads as follows:

> On and after August 11, 1978, it shall be the policy of the United States to protect and preserve for American Indians their inherent right of freedom to believe, express, and exercise the traditional religions of the American Indian, Eskimo, Aleut, and Native Hawaiians, including but not limited to

access to sites, use and possession of sacred objects, and the freedom to worship through ceremonial and traditional rites.[33]

To the policy declaration was added a process for federal agencies to "evaluate their policies and procedures in consultation with [N]ative traditional religious leaders in order to determine appropriate changes necessary to protect and preserve Native American religious and cultural rights and practices," calling for an executive branch report to Congress after the first year.[34]

But the formal congressional findings in "whereas" clauses (and which make up the bulk of the act's wording) are crucial to the overall arc of AIRFA. AIRFA anchors the policy statement to the broader discourse of religious freedom: "Freedom of religion for all people is an inherent right, fundamental to the democratic structure of the United States and is guaranteed by the First Amendment of the Constitution." AIRFA also acknowledges that "abridgement" of Indian religious freedom has occurred under federal policies that either overtly "banned" ceremonies or that placed "religious infringements" "resulting from the lack of knowledge or insensitive and inflexible enforcement of federal policies and regulations premised on a variety of laws," including laws "designed for such worthwhile purposes as conservation and preservation of natural species and resources but were never intended to relate to Indian religious practices and, therefore, were passed without consideration of their effect on traditional American Indian religions." What is more, AIRFA specifies some of the distinctive contours of Native religions that have been denied by US policies: "access to sacred sites required in their religions, including cemeteries" and "use and possession of sacred objects necessary to the exercise of religious rites and ceremonies."[35]

AIRFA as a Religious Freedom Law

AIRFA may be read as a statute to bolster the First Amendment's Free Exercise Clause, a clarification that the First Amendment, if it were to protect traditional Native religions, would necessarily apply protections for "access to sacred sites, use and possession of sacred objects, and the freedom to worship through ceremonial and traditional rites." And to be sure lawyers representing claimants in its first ten years advanced such a reading, that AIRFA grafted a variety of Native claims to Free Exercise Clause jurisprudence and should secure for their clients clear First Amendment rights to sacred lands or to sacred practices. Although there were some hopeful signs elsewhere in the lower courts, most cases claiming that AIRFA clarified First Amendment rights wound up failing in the appellate courts.[36]

The Supreme Court's holding in *Lyng* put the final nail in the coffin to this reading of AIRFA. Quoting AIRFA's policy statement and finding that the Forest Service's "solicitude" to the tribal concerns about a logging road through their sacred places were fully "in accord" with that policy statement, Justice O'Connor took pains to disagree that AIRFA went further:

> Nowhere in the law is there so much as a hint of any intent to create a cause of action or any judicially enforceable individual rights. What is obvious from the face of the statute is confirmed by numerous indications in the legislative history.... Representative Udall emphasized that the bill would not "confer special religious rights on Indians," would "not change any existing State or Federal law," and in fact "has no teeth in it."[37]

AIRFA: A Finer-Grained Reading

That courts found AIRFA held no water as a statutory enactment of First Amendment religious freedom protections for Native Americans has led many commentators to conclude that AIRFA was a legislative failure, one more empty congressional promise made in a paternalistic manner to Native people, who were again tragically undermined. For example, in an otherwise more nuanced treatment of sacred site management, Andrew Gulliford wrote under the heading "The Failure of the American Indian Religious Freedom Act": "With the vote on AIRFA, Congress recognized Indian religious beliefs but made no real effort to protect those beliefs and practices. Legislators passed a useless law."[38]

Gulliford's view is apt in part. Even as the advisory, procedural resolution of Congress that the *Lyng* Court said it was, AIRFA was not taken particularly seriously by the two Reagan administrations, and arguably others. But the Native leaders pursuing the broader tribal sovereignty agenda of which AIRFA was a part were hardly duped, or particularly surprised. As Harjo put it, "When the Court said the Religious Freedom Act doesn't provide a cause of action for sacred places, we thought, well, *newsflash!*—I mean, no one should ever have said that it did. It was clear on the record, clear on the house floor."[39] There were powerful legislators who would remove their support for AIRFA were it to include a legal cause of action. Representative Tom Foley (D-WA), as chair of the House Agriculture Committee, was congenial to the concerns the timber industry had about a stronger law. In the Senate, James Abourezk (D-SD) was vehement that sacred lands language would not affect the Black Hills so crucial to his state's tourism industry and said he would kill any further-reaching AIRFA bill before passage. So it was a strategic decision to move forward with an AIRFA even without the teeth. Harjo recounted the choice:

> [Rep. Morris] Udall talked to several of us, and he said, so we can pull it and go back and try to do something else … or we can have the policy statement and then get the specific cause of action afterward. So, we all went with the something rather than nothing view, that you get the policy statement first.[40]

Harjo later recalled that Native leaders vigorously sought that cause of action between 1989 and 1995, "but Department of Interior politicos, Department of Justice lawyers, and White House pollsters opposed it."[41]

Even without success in adding that legal cause of action amendment, AIRFA as it reads has been hardly the failure that this common reading of it suggests. In at least the following four respects, AIRFA has proved itself to be a weighty legislative accomplishment.

First, even as the federal courts were raising the standards to which the federal trust responsibility would be held accountable, AIRFA incorporated into the trust responsibility specific concern for the religious and cultural rights of recognized tribes. In keeping with the common law tradition of fiduciary responsibility of a trustee, the federal trust responsibility for the tribes had largely been elaborated in terms of maximizing the value of real property and tangible economic property, but that responsibility was beginning to apply as well to the cultural resources of the tribes, and AIRFA's acknowledgment of the vagaries of assimilation policies and the continued, often inadvertent, ill effects of government actions on the traditions of the Native nations helped chart this new course. This was explicit in AIRFA's wording: US policy would "protect and preserve *for American Indians* their inherent rights." This policy redirection was no small matter, especially in light of its acknowledgment that the United States had formerly pursued policies expressly designed to undermine Native religions. For Harjo, this meant, "It's a whole different world. Then all sorts of things are possible. You don't have an act of Congress just so you can have a pow-wow. You have an act of Congress because there are still barriers that have been erected and still stand in the way of people trying to exercise their religious practices."[42]

Second, AIRFA mandated the thorough policy review in various federal agencies, opening up for scrutiny policies and procedures that had long proceeded with no regard for their impact on the religious and cultural rights of the tribes. Tapped to oversee this process, Harjo secured a contract for a parallel study and implementation project by the Native American Rights Fund and the American Indian Law Center, which was able to more thoroughly survey and consult in the field with the religious leaders and tribes. From its consultation, the study identified the following key issues where federal policies infringed on Native religions: (1) preservation of and access to sacred sites; (2) the right to religious use of Peyote; (3) the right to recover religious objects; (4) the right to cross borders freely for religious purposes; (5) the rights of incarcerated Indians; (6) the right to religious privacy; (6) the rights of Indian students; and (7) the right to traditional hairstyles in schools, prisons, reformatories, and military service.[43] Within a couple years of AIRFA's passage, the public record included formal recognition of the range of religious infringements that government actions directly, but also inadvertently, placed on Native peoples, laying the groundwork for the subsequent legislative and administrative accommodations on sacred sites, ceremonial Peyote use, repatriation of human remains from museums and scientific collections, and return of ceremonial items.

Third, even if it was largely disregarded under Reagan, AIRFA created language for subsequent administrations to breathe meaningful life into its provisions, and to relate it to other review and consultation processes, such as those under environmental and historic preservation laws, to form a thicker weave of serious government consideration of tribal claims. In 1996, out of a concern to expand minimal readings of AIRFA's policy directives, President Clinton signed Executive Order 13007, mandating that those agencies managing federal lands:

(1) accommodate access to and ceremonial use of Indian sacred sites by Indian religious practitioners and (2) avoid adversely affecting the physical integrity of such sacred sites. Where appropriate, agencies shall maintain the confidentiality of sacred sites.[44]

For all the variation in how different administrations and different federal agencies have engaged the consultative framework established by AIRFA, as Todd Morman has ably shown, we should not gainsay its significance at ground level for Native nations working to protect specific sacred places through administrative accommodations.[45]

Finally, the formal consultations with Native religious leaders mandated by AIRFA did their part to help establish the tribal consultation structure that gives shape to the broader government-to-government relationship. Harjo credits the momentum from AIRFA's passage with helping win the government-wide statutory, not just regulatory, tribal consultation provision in the 1979 Archaeological Resources Protection Act[46] and in an amendment to NHPA's Section 106, requiring federal consultation with tribes that assert a religious or cultural claim to a significant place.[47] Later in 2000, President Clinton signed Executive Order 13175, "Consultation and Coordination with Indian Tribal Governments," which extended and clarified what proper consultation with sovereign tribes should look like as a matter of policy.[48]

In sum, a plain reading of AIRFA, or one that is overly shaped by the courts' interpretation of it, suggests that it lacks legal "teeth" for the full-fledged protections of religious freedom. But AIRFA set in motion a procedural mechanism for federal respect and accommodation of religious and cultural concerns of sovereign tribes as collectivities.[49] As Harjo reflected twenty-five years after passage, "today, there is every reason both to celebrate the American Indian Religious Freedom Act and to complete its unfinished business."[50]

To be sure, in the absence of specific legal causes of action, and thus judicial review, such procedural mechanisms rely for their effect more on the good will of the federal agency involved and under various administrations that may or may not consider Native rights a priority.

Still, AIRFA put considerations of Native religious and cultural rights on a footing quite other than that of the individual civil liberty basis on which religious freedom had generally been seen to rest. These considerations direct the federal government to consult and ultimately to make agreements with tribal governments to accommodate what practices, places, objects, and beliefs those nations indicate are urgent to them without having to prove religiousness under religious freedom law or having to expose sacred places, practices, beliefs, or objects to unwelcome voyeurism on the public record, one of the issue areas of friction identified through the AIRFA review process between Native religions and federal agency policies.

AIRFA Report to Congress, 1979

AIRFA mandated a review of federal agency policies and a report to Congress the following year. The three-hundred-page report documented the consultations undertaken by the agencies and those undertaken by the Native

American Rights Fund and the American Indian Law Center throughout Indian Country.[51] It also used language important to understanding the often collective nature of Native religions. A lengthy historical introduction distinguishes traditional Native religions and "Western" religions, including a general disinterest among Native religions in proselytizing or making pronouncements of universal truth. Recommendations on sacred lands, objects, and ceremonies and traditional rites speak of certain contested federal actions not simply as violations of individuals' religious freedom but as outright violations of Native American *religious law*. "Ceremonies and traditional rites" are introduced not as spiritual experiences but as "religious obligations" "detailed" under "tribal and societal customary law."[52] "Tribal traditional law" can "decree" duration, preparation, appropriate attire, and proper conduct. It can also mandate attendance, "set standards for exclusions," and "may proscribe conversation concerning details of certain ceremonies." "Failure to observe these laws may hold severe consequences for the individual practitioner or the group as a whole."[53]

Federal policies affecting access and integrity of sacred lands are also framed in terms of the violation of religious law: "There are specific religious beliefs regarding each sacred site which form the basis for religious laws governing the site":

> These laws may prescribe, for example, when and for what purposes the site may or must be visited, what ceremonies or rituals may or must take place at the site, what manner of conduct must or must not be observed at the site, who may or may not go to the site and the consequences to the individual, group, clan or tribe if the laws are not observed.[54]

The issue of sacred objects, too, is framed by the report in terms of Indigenous law. "Equally elaborate concepts of personal property have developed in both Native American and western legal traditions," the report observes. "The problems presented by the presence of Native American sacred objects in museums will be resolved only" through an appreciation of "these conflicts between culturally distinct systems."[55] Especially in the case of sacred items, the report elaborates, "the Native American equivalent of legal ownership is reserved in the tribe or group as a whole and the interest of the individual owner or keeper resembles physical custody."[56]

Although these references in the report do not amount to a fuller assertion of comparative law at play on the issues concerned, they do lay claim within the context of a formal government utterance that Native traditions differ from other religions not only in terms of theology and ritual but also in the sense that they are collective matters of obligation and law, and that federal accommodations must not only take this into account but also recognize "the integrity of internal discipline which the Indian tribal traditions emphasize."[57]

AIRFA's 1994 Peyote Amendment

If AIRFA was not to be a legally binding clarification that the First Amendment would apply to the distinctive contours of Native religions, the distinctive contours of AIRFA as a policy statement of the federal trust responsibility to the tribes proved that it was friendlier terrain for protecting Native religious concerns than broader religious freedom law. Recall that it was shared outrage at the Supreme Court's stripping of the First Amendment's Free Exercise protection in *Employment Division v. Smith* that unified a coalition of religious groups across the culture wars spectrum and secured near unanimous support for RFRA. But the statutory rebuke to the Supreme Court's *Smith* decision notably stopped short of reversing the specific issue in the case. RFRA did not reinstate the broad rights to ceremonial Peyote use won so ably by practitioners of the Native American Church in dozens of state statutes and through a broad range of court-backed protections of Peyotism.[58] In the words of James Botsford, a Wisconsin attorney representing members of the Native American Church: "We took the hit and were not in the huddle."[59] Harjo remembered:

> They wanted us at the meetings as token Indians to show that their coalition was broad, but they didn't want us there in a substantive way so that there wouldn't be any cause of action for Native religious freedom interests.... And we of course, Native people got the entire blame for the *Smith* decision.... They didn't want to be dragged down by the Indians.[60]

The legislative history of RFRA does not reveal as much in so many words. But in the House report on the bill, the Judiciary Committee made clear that RFRA did not specifically address the injustice of the *Smith* decision for Smith, or the tens of thousands who were practicing the Peyote religion:

> In terms of the specific issue addressed in *Smith*, this bill would not mandate that all states permit the ceremonial use of peyote, but it would subject any such prohibition to the aforesaid balancing test.... It is worth emphasizing that although this bill is applicable to all Americans, including

Native Americans and their religions in keeping with the Congressional policy set in the AIRFA of 1978, the Committee recognizes that this bill will not necessarily address all First Amendment problems by itself. Native Americans have unique First Amendment concerns that Congress may need to address through additional legislation.[61]

A Proposed Native American Free Exercise of Religion Act

Wizened by the experience with the RFRA coalition, and perhaps seizing on the spirit of the nod from the House, the Native religious and cultural rights coalition that gathered as part of the AIRFA policy review began to pursue, on their own, a legislative response to *Lyng* and *Smith*. In May 1993, Senator Inouye introduced S.B. 1021, the Native American Free Exercise of Religion Act of 1993 (NAFERA).[62] The bill rested on findings that the Supreme Court had "created a chilling and discriminatory effect on the free exercise of Native American religions" not only in *Smith* but also in *Lyng*. The bill made provisions for Peyote protection, Native religious exercise in prisons, religious exercise involving eagles and other animals and plants protected under other statutes, and a detailed set of provisions for sacred site protection. Most important among them was a legal cause of action, and a definition of *Indian* that could encompass Native practitioners beyond those who were members of federally recognized tribes.[63]

The Peyote Amendment to AIRFA

NAFERA did not garner the support the coalition had hoped it would, perhaps encouraged as they were by the support for RFRA, and it never made it out of the Senate Indian Affairs Committee. Even the Clinton Justice Department opposed a legal cause of action for sacred sites.[64] That said, NAFERA's exemption for Peyote had gained traction with the Clinton administration, perhaps persuaded of the immense burden raised by the *Smith* decision and hearkening toward that decision's nod that it should be Congress, not the courts, that should recognize such religious exemptions to generally applicable laws. As Harjo described it, "we went with what we could get support for and that was just Peyote use and that was just so ironic because the RFRA people had said you will never get anything through that says Peyote and that was the only thing we could get through in 1994.[65]

The subsequent legislation was not a Native amendment to RFRA but a Peyote Amendment to AIRFA. Having already begun specifically to consult with leaders of the Native American Church as part of the policy review mandated by AIRFA, and desiring to make any Peyote protection "Scalia-proof," as James Botsford put it, the strategy was to "make it an Indian right, rooted in the trust relationship" and resting on the distinctive legal and political status of the tribes and their members, and that would also immunize it from equal protection challenges under civil rights law.[66] The 1994 amendment, as Congress passed it, provided:

> The use, possession, or transportation of peyote by an Indian for bona fide traditional ceremonial purposes in connection with the practice of a traditional Indian religion is lawful, and shall not be prohibited by the United States or any State. No Indian shall be penalized or discriminated against on the basis of such use, possession or transportation, including, but not limited to, denial of otherwise applicable benefits under public assistance programs.[67]

Its definitions section made clear that "Indians" referred to members of federally recognized tribes and that "Indian religion" meant any "religion ... which is practiced by Indians, and ... the origin and interpretation of which is from within a traditional Indian culture or community."[68]

Such definitional language was crafted to persuade Congress there would be no slippery slope to rampant Peyote use. It was also expressly keyed to the logic of federal Indian law's recognition of the special political and legal status of members of tribes with rights based on the treaty and trust relationship. This logic could be undone, the coalition feared, by opening the door to those claiming *only* religious freedom rights to Peyote use. And to be sure, there are any number of others claiming religious freedom exemptions to controlled substance laws that have had their eyes on AIRFA's Peyote Amendment for similar equal protection sustenance of their claims.[69]

Statutory Protections for Native Languages and Arts

Congress affirmed a federal trust responsibility to preserve and protect Native American cultural traditions in a number of additional statutes in the 1990s as "follow on" laws in the wake of AIRFA and the policy review that AIRFA set forth.[70] These steps to preserve, protect, and even promote languages indigenous to what became the United States and to protect and promote Indigenous art-making are certainly each worthy of more sustained attention than is allowed here, even as they don't at first glance concern religion. But at the risk of paying them only lip service, they are noteworthy for the way they illustrate how integral are Native languages and art-making to the practice of Native religious traditions. On the face of it, this point is made by the fact that they emerged from the nexus of concerns at Bear Butte in 1967 and that were identified in the AIRFA policy review consultations. But Native peoples have increasingly insisted on the necessity of their art-making and original languages, often regarded as spiritual gifts, to ongoing and efficacious religious practice and to community and cosmic well-being.

In 1990, Congress passed the Native American Languages Act. The 1990 act began, as did AIRFA, with a list of findings that the federal government's policies, particularly the English-only directives during the boarding school era, were key drivers of the suppression of Native languages, that there is continued potential for policies to continue to have ill effects that conflict with a policy of self-determination, that Native Americans have a "special status" and "distinct cultural and political rights, including the right to continue separate identities," and that traditional languages are "an integral part of their cultures and identities and form the basic medium for the transmission, and thus survival, of Native American cultures, literatures, histories, religions, political institutions, and values."[71] Like AIRFA, the law included a declaration of policy to "preserve, protect, and promote the rights and freedom of Native Americans to use, practice, and develop Native American languages," and concluded with a one-year federal agency review to evaluate whether existing policies conformed to the policy statement. The law also made specific provisions for protection and promotion of Native languages, including the making of exceptions to teacher certification requirements for federally funded projects to enable elders and others qualified on traditional grounds to teach those languages, encouragement to educational instruction in Native languages, and insistence that Native languages be treated on a par with foreign languages in terms of credit and proficiency standards by federally funded higher education institutions. In 2006, the Esther Martinez Native American Language Preservation Act created more programmatic support for development of tribal language revitalization plans and for immersion programs of Native language instruction under the Administration for Native Americans within the Department of Health and Human Services.[72] A number of other funding programs have emerged, among them a provision under the 2015 Every Student Succeeds Act that supports schools engaging in language revitalization programs as an integral part of educational success.[73] Native nations and organizations themselves have been pouring resources into a wide range of language preservation and revitalization efforts, for the revitalization of Native languages is not only an important educational issue, but also, centrally, a cultural and religious issue.[74]

Also in 1990, Congress passed the Indian Arts and Crafts Act, less directly as a "follow on" to AIRFA but similarly aligned in terms of the federal government's responsibility to preserve and protect Native cultures and religions.[75] The 1990 law dramatically updated a 1935 law promoting Native arts and crafts and amended the federal criminal code to specifically outlaw the display or sale of any good "in a manner that falsely suggests it is Indian produced, an Indian product, or the product of a particular Indian or Indian tribe or Indian arts and crafts organization, resident within the United States," and to create a legal cause of action for Indian artists or organizations to bring lawsuits under the act. An amendment in 2010 extended enforcement of these provisions beyond the FBI to include other federal law enforcement agencies, including especially the Department of the Interior.[76] The 1990 act also defines "Indian" in the familiar federal trust responsibility terms of members of federally recognized tribes, or "Indian artisans" designated by recognized tribes, but the law also includes state-recognized tribes. While the Indian Arts and Crafts Act can be seen as an economic development law, it also can be seen to extend the federal trust responsibility to preserve and protect the cultural traditions of tribes in its promotion of cultural artistic practices that are often also religiously significant.

Conclusion

Faced in the courts with what Walter Echo-Hawk has described as "heartbreaking" failures of religious freedom protections of the First Amendment and RFRA, Native leaders in the 1970s, 1980s, and 1990s energetically sought Native-specific legislative protections and regulatory accommodations for beliefs and practices of tribes.[77] National leaders like Echo-Hawk, Vine Deloria Jr., and Suzan Harjo, and their coalition of Indigenous elected officials, intellectuals, and lawyers, not to mention the many local tribal officials and spiritual leaders asked to testify in hearings or who consulted with federal officials, proved adept at speaking the language of religion freedom in the halls of power to make their case with intelligibility and urgency. And as evidenced by Echo-Hawk's choice of "heartbreaking" to describe losses in the First Amendment cases, by the plain language of AIRFA and by the tabled language of the Native American Free Exercise of Religion Act of 1993, these leaders in no small part put their faith not only in the rhetorical power of that language but also in the scope of its protection for their concerns. But theirs was no naive faith in the American language of religious freedom—how could it be after the workings of "religion" in the Civilization Regulations or in the RFRA coalition's remarkable exclusion of Native American religious freedom in its efforts to override a Supreme Court holding about Native American religious freedom?

The omission of Native people and their concerns from the coalition that produced RFRA illustrates the broader exclusion of how the "consensus" view of "religious freedom" could marginalize collective claims of Native American peoples, not simply for the intellectual distinctiveness of their religions, but also because any specific statutory expansions of religion's effective definition to Native collectivities would have no place. Thus even RLUIPA's acknowledgment that "land use" by religious communities could be expressly considered protected religious exercise would have no analogical extension to religious land use by Native American peoples.

So Native advocates engaged religious freedom as a discourse, fully aware of how it had excluded some in the act of including others in the name of universal rights. Crucially, they inflected the language of Native American religious freedom, speaking it in the register of the distinctive status of Native peoples as sovereign nations predating the United States and its Constitution, on the one hand, and on the other, in the register of the distinctive federal trust responsibilities to protect and preserve Native peoples' collective rights to land, resources, cultures, languages, and religions, as well as the rights of members of these nations.

Many interpreters of these legislative accomplishments—including in key moments, the courts—have too hastily read the appeal to the discourse of religious freedom without seeing the inflections that integrate these laws into the body of federal Indian law (and increasingly Indigenous international rights law), and not simply into the body of religious freedom law. I have read these efforts to secure religious freedom in terms of their place in the larger effort to strengthen and advance the self-determination of sovereign nations. As Suzan Harjo put it, such cultural and religious rights are not marginal matters, but are "atmospheric" of other collective rights to land, peoplehood, and tribal self-determination, and should be read carefully for the way they are woven into the logic of those collective rights, not simply because they might be "Scalia-proof" as a matter of strategy, but because they better accord with the distinctive contours of Native American religious traditions.[78]

6

Religion as Collective Right

REPATRIATION AND ACCESS
TO EAGLE FEATHERS

Introduction

The coalition that persuaded Congress in 1994 to pass the Peyote Amendment to AIRFA was successful in part because it was largely the same circle of
advocates, lawyers, tribal spiritual and political leaders, and allies who had
recently won congressional passage of two repatriation statutes: the National
Museum of the American Indian Act (NMAI) in 1989 and the Native American Graves Protection and Repatriation Act (NAGPRA) the next year. This
chapter tells the story of Native-led efforts to secure these two laws and, like
chapter 5, offers an interpretation of them not as religious freedom laws—
though they do secure ancestral remains, funeral objects, and sacred items—
but primarily as additions to federal Indian law that encompass religious and
cultural heritage. The chapter concludes with a consideration of court recognition of collective rights to Native American religions in case law related
to a contested exemption in eagle protection laws to accommodate Native
American access to ceremonial eagle feathers.

Repatriation Legislation

For more than a century, Native peoples had struggled against the robbing
of their graves and against the display of their sacred items. While each state
had its own cemetery protection laws on the books that otherwise recognized the dignity of the lives of deceased human beings and those who honor
them, Native American graves did not count.[1] Museums and government sci-

entists endeavored to collect anything and everything Indian they could find before Native cultures vanished, as Euro-American ideology assured they would.[2] The desire to collect Indian bodies and artifacts of Indian cultures ran deep, and stunningly went hand in hand with the desire to erase living Native people and their cultures, for the heyday of amassing Native artifacts and bodies in collections coincided with Assimilation Policy.[3]

By the late twentieth century there may well have been bodies of more Native American individuals in museums and research collections than there were living in the United States. Estimates vary, but there were remains of as many as 2.5 million Native individuals. The Smithsonian alone had the remains of 18,500 Native people and the skulls of another 4,500, part of a medical collection related to the Army Medical Museum's Indian Crania Study that included decapitated heads from victims of the 1864 Sand Creek Massacre.[4]

Harjo relates that while members of the 1967 Bear Butte coalition were traveling throughout Indian Country to hear concerns, numerous people spoke of the ill effects of their ancestral remains and sacred items locked up in museums or paraded in public. Although Harjo said she never had nightmares, she began to have a recurring dream of a little Cheyenne dress that she had seen while visiting the Heye Museum of the American Indian in upper Manhattan with her mother. It was "a buckskin dress with a bullet-hole right where the belly had been. It was a distinct bullet-hole with the blood patterns from it":

> I dreamed of the little Cheyenne girl in this beautiful buckskin dress—how it had looked before it became this stiff thing and before she was shot. She said a few things and one of them was, "I'll walk this way until my spirit's returned." So, that's a pretty powerful thing. I saw her image a lot. Now how often, I don't know but, pretty often—once a month, every two months—often. Until we got the second repatriation law passed and then, I haven't seen her since then—since 1990. And I miss her, I mean she became a companion in my dreams—a fixture in my dreams. Usually wouldn't say anything, she would just be there. Something else would be going on in the foreground and in the background, seated on a limb on a tree or walking by, not really talking, just observing.[5]

Concerns about Native human remains, related burial items, and sacred objects had animated the coalition seeking AIRFA in the first place and were well documented in the *American Indian Religious Freedom Task Force Report* mandated by AIRFA. AIRFA's federal agency policy review actually resulted *child of time*

a child of time, naked and weeping
walked one night in my dreamless sleep
she came to claim my word of honor
the promise she heard me make to keep
her voice when she spoke
was the sound of the wind
first howling, then moaning and sighing
the sound of a storm without end

she knew of my early mourning visit
to the museum of indian dead
where i had stared at her small torn gown
of leather and beads, all stained with red
blood should mean something more than this
blood flows and lives and gives again
but here, only dead rust patterns surrounding
a bullet hole where her belly had been

to most it was merely a dress on display
placed next to the ancient Navajo loom
lighted and indexed for all the curious
patrons of this bone-chilling public tomb
this dress of dried blood does not belong here
it should be saged and secretly burned
and now, with the dawn, her voice on the wind
"I'll walk this way 'til my spirit's returned."

hush, now, my pretty, there's work to be done
sleep on the earth, i'll give your heart ease
your name will be claimed, now quiet the storm
and come to me next as a soft, gentle breeze

—SUZAN SHOWN HARJO, 1965

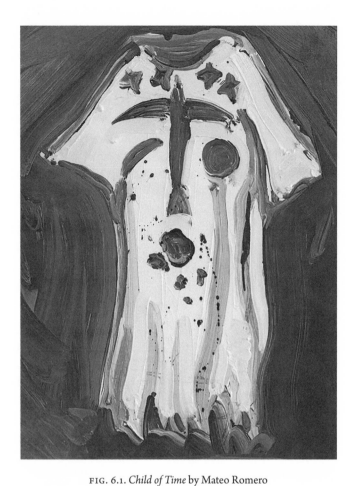

FIG. 6.1. *Child of Time* by Mateo Romero
Child of Time, by Mateo Romero (Cochiti Pueblo) was inspired by Suzan Shown Harjo's 1965 poem telling of the dream visits of the spirit of a Cheyenne girl whose dress bore the red tinge of a bullet hole to the belly. Compelled to work toward repatriation, Harjo said the dream visits ceased after 1990 passage of NAGPRA. (Photo Seth Roffman, courtesy Mateo Romero)

in the first repatriation policies for "cultural patrimony" within the Department of Defense and Smithsonian Institution. Other private museums like Harvard's Peabody Museum were involved in repatriation proceedings of certain high profile items like the Sacred Pole of the Omaha, especially where the provenance of such items rendered a museum's title to them unclear.[6] But prior to NAGPRA such repatriations were retail matters, not wholesale ones, and under AIRFA alone, federal agencies viewed their repatriations more as matters of good faith than as legal obligation.

All this changed dramatically in 1990 when President George H. W. Bush signed NAGPRA into law. The detailed legislative history of NAGPRA has been well chronicled by Greg Johnson, beginning in February 1987 in a hearing before the Senate Committee on Indian Affairs on a prototype bill introduced as the Native American Cultural Preservation Act.[7] Johnson pays close attention to the Indigenous voices in the hearings from this beginning point on and helps us understand how their religious speech in such legal and political spaces could be at once faithful and strategic.[8] The road to NAGPRA, we learn, was paved brick by persuasive brick by these resourceful Native spiritual leaders. What Johnson's ground-level account of NAGPRA's legislative history leaves out is a series of strategic choices made at a different altitude by national Native leaders like Harjo, Vine Deloria Jr., and organizations like the Native American Rights Fund to secure passage of the legislation. From this vantage point, NAGPRA was almost a follow on law to the original repatriation statute, the National Museum of the American Indian Act passed a year earlier in 1989. The NMAI Act yoked the repatriation provisions that had been the dream since Bear Butte in 1967 to the storied transfer of more than 800,000 objects from the New York City's then decrepit Heye Museum of the American Indian to the Smithsonian Institution. The nationalization of this collection occasioned the creation of the monumental National Museum of the American Indian on what was then the last open tract along the Washington Mall, and the one closest to the Capitol. But perhaps the equally monumental accomplishment was the incorporation of a repatriation provision. The flagship museums of the Smithsonian were to inventory, identify, and consider for return to lineal Native descendants or to culturally affiliated tribes the thousands of Native human remains in their collections, along with a range of specified kinds of objects.

Where there is a remarkable result, there is often a remarkable story, and there is a story here—Harjo being the one to tell it more fully[9]—of political theater, luck, and, among other things, rat-infested warehouses, an all but manufactured bidding war for the museum collection involving Texas billionaire H. Ross Perot, and some serious political hardball with the Smithsonian. As Harjo put it, "we couldn't build a dream of a museum out of the nightmares of the stuff that were the reason for repatriation. You had to have them both. You couldn't have your dreams if you were building them on nightmares."[10] An example of those nightmares, Harjo related in a congressional hearing, were the "beetle rooms" at the Smithsonian, where bones of Native American individuals were cleaned by flesh-eating beetles.[11]

Native leaders had successfully identified New York's Heye Museum of the American Indian as a national treasure sufficiently threatened to engage Congress and the Smithsonian in acquiring it, but they were still having difficulty tying repatriation provisions to the collection exchange. Attorneys at the Native American Rights Fund and elsewhere were building significant litigation pressure on federal agencies and private museums—Harjo recalls roughly forty distinct challenges.[12] The tide of litigation drew on property law principles to challenge the precarious title museums and agencies often held to Native ancestral remains, sacred objects, and cultural items of significance to Native peoples: the common law principle that there ultimately can be no property interest in deceased human beings and the principle that an individual could not alienate or sell title to objects that could be shown to belong to a community. As early as the 1970s attorneys from the Native American Rights Fund helped Zuni Pueblo members challenge the Denver Art Museum's title to three Ayahu:da, or War Gods, and the museum returned them within several years.[13] Further cases emerged in the 1980s. The Native Village of Larsen Bay was readying to file a lawsuit with the Smithsonian, a place that it could justly refer to as the Larsen Bay cemetery, since there were more of its dead in Smithsonian storage rooms than in the village cemetery itself in Alaska.[14] According to Harjo, attorneys for Larsen Bay wanted to continue in court rather than compromise on repatriation provisions in the NMAI legislation.[15]

The force of such property law arguments and the cost, much less possible outcome, of mounting litigation was not lost on museums with major Native American collections. But according to Harjo, Smithsonian leaders favored engaging repatriation as a matter of good faith discussions between museums and claimant communities about specific items, not as a blanket obligation established by law. Harjo credits supporters in Congress for holding out on passage of the NMAI Act and thus the funded transfer of the collection from New York to Washington, until the repatriation matters could be encompassed.

Key support in the Senate came from Senators Daniel Inouye (D-HI) and Ben Nighthorse Campbell (D-CO). Members of the New York delegation like representatives Barber Conable (R-NY) and Charles Rangel (D-NY) and civic leaders David Rockefeller and Charles Simon were keen to support the repatriation provisions of the NMAI Act in exchange, having gained support of Native leaders for a continued presence of at least part of the collection in New York City. Exhibit space was ultimately sited in lower Manhattan's historic Customs House.[16]

Harjo remembers the moment quite clearly when Robert McCormick Adams, the Smithsonian director, agreed to a deal linking the NMAI transfer of the collection to repatriation requirements, and this at the eleventh hour. Reading documents while flying out to a reception to be hosted jointly by the NCAI and the Smithsonian in Santa Fe, Harjo came upon bills of lading for the transport to Washington of skulls from decapitated Cheyenne bodies at Colorado's 1864 Sand Creek Massacre. When she related this finding in a phone call later that day to Adams, then at his home in Colorado, it seemed to make a difference—as Harjo learned later, Adams had realized he was about to meet in Santa Fe with three Cheyennes—Harjo, Richard West, and Senator Ben Nighthorse Campbell. Adams told Harjo they had a deal for the Smithsonian's support of the NMAI Act. When he suggested she and Vine Deloria Jr. join him to celebrate the agreement over dinner at his favorite Santa Fe restaurant, Harjo noted the fitting irony: the Coyote Café may as well have been referring to the cunning Trickster behind the result.

Native American Graves Protection and Repatriation Act

But perhaps the bigger story is what the tense NMAI Act negotiations with the Smithsonian enabled: swift passage the following year of a remarkable NAGPRA statute extending the repatriation process to all federally funded museums and government agencies, extending the items to be inventoried, identified, and considered for return beyond human remains and burial objects to several other categories of cultural items. These categories, later added to the NMAI Act, most notably include "sacred objects," defined as those "needed by traditional Native American religious leaders for the practice of traditional Native American religions by their present day adherents," and "cultural patrimony," defined as "an object having ongoing historical traditional, or cultural importance central to the Native American group or culture itself, rather than property owned by an individual Native American, and which therefore, cannot be alienated, appropriated, or conveyed by any individual." Also created was the category of "unassociated funerary objects," items found to have been removed from a burial site even if a collection didn't include the associated human remains.[17]

NAGPRA required "expeditious return" of human remains, associated funerary objects, and the three other specified classes of cultural items (sacred objects, objects of cultural patrimony, and unassociated funerary objects) from the collections of museums and agencies to lineal descendants, in those cases where a clear line of descent could be drawn to human remains and associated funerary objects, or to "culturally affiliated" tribes and Native Hawaiian Organizations that could show "cultural affiliation by a preponderance of the evidence."[18] In civil law, a "preponderance of evidence" is a relatively low standard, more the tipping of a scale than a bright line and involving factors such as the quality of evidence and not simply the quantity. And the statute made explicit that such evidence to be weighed was not limited to scientific evidence, but could include oral tradition: "a preponderance of the evidence based upon geographical, kinship, biological, archaeological, anthropological, linguistic, folkloric, oral traditional, historical, or other relevant information or expert opinion."[19]

To these remarkable provisions was added the criminalization of trafficking in the protected items and tribal control of any human remains and cultural items subsequently excavated on federal or tribal lands, with tribal lands defined broadly as lands within the exterior boundaries of reservations whether or not controlled by tribes. Finally, the law established the NAGPRA Review Committee, including appointees from both tribal and scientific communities, to adjudicate between competing claims.

Talk about competing claims! It is hard to overstate the ramifications of NAGPRA for museums, archaeology, physical anthropology, land development, and other interests that saw the proverbial writing on the wall with the NMAI negotiations and that took what might be identified as a containment strategy to ensure NAGPRA took their interests to heart in a balanced way. Greg Johnson likens the strategy to a "controlled burn" whereby museums and scientific professionals acknowledged the clear human rights basis for Native claims items and human remains whose cultural affiliation could be straightforwardly ascertained, but making "time depth" the operative boundary, or "fire line" to maintain against a perceived limitless series of kinship claims asserted by Native peoples.[20] In the period of legislative history following passage of the NMAI Act, NAGPRA received support from the American

Association of Museums, the Society for American Archaeology, and the American Association of Physical Anthropologists in exchange for their own participation in the process. According to Harjo, it was the Department of the Interior that was the hardest sell on key provisions, opposing in particular the classification of "sacred objects" and the reference to aboriginal territory in the cultural affiliation determination provisions.[21] Ultimately, Interior's National Park Service was agreed on as the lead agency to administer NAGPRA and its Review Committee.

It is hard to overstate the enormity of the cultural and religious possibilities and challenges that repatriation presented to American Indian, Alaska Native, and Native Hawaiian peoples.[22] I will not here undertake the fuller treatment warranted by NMAI and NAGPRA, and particularly by the complex struggles over the regulations, the indeterminacies of evidentiary weight, and the ongoing work of the NAGPRA Review Committee. Such a treatment would require a second volume of this book and I could in any case add little to very fine book-length treatments that treat NAGPRA not merely as a "legal event," in the words of Kathleen Fine-Dare, but as a "cultural and political process."[23] Religious studies scholar Greg Johnson does much of the work for us, bringing theoretically informed attentiveness to the "making of religion," the generative articulation of tradition unleashed and occasioned by the legal and administrative processes of NAGPRA (though distinguishing his analysis from the presumptions of the "invention of tradition"). In his book *Sacred Claims: Repatriation and Living Tradition*, Johnson reviews NAGPRA's legislative history but also takes a deep dive into the proceedings of its Review Committee and perceptively attends to the trove of Native American religious speech he finds there as evidence of the vitality of and complexity of Indigenous religions. Johnson discerns a pattern whereby Native religious speech moves resourcefully between two registers that pertain to the larger concerns of this chapter. Native practitioners lay claim, on the one hand, to the unique minority specific obligations, practices, and beliefs of their traditions, and to the universally applicable human rights discourse on the other.[24] Insofar as Congress deferred detailed elaboration on "sacred objects," "cultural affiliation," and other terms to the rule-making process and the Review Committee, the entire process set in motion what Greg Johnson described as "an effulgence of religious expression" alongside scientific, archaeological, and historical claims that NAGPRA "cannot begin to contain, channel, or otherwise manage in predictable ways."[25]

Generativity of Religious Speech in the NAGPRA Process

Needless to say, the determinations under NAGPRA required for repatriations to proceed are complex. On account of the "rip-and-run" nature of much of the collecting and grave-robbing that accumulated the collections in the first place, many items have accession records too unspecific to be culturally identifiable. A category of "culturally unidentifiable human remains" had been identified in NAGPRA's statutory charge to the Review Committee to compile an inventory of unidentifiable human remains in federal agency collections and to recommend actions "for developing a process for disposition of such remains."[26] Twenty years into the NAGPRA process, amid the criticism that museums and institutions were moving at a glacial pace, a new rule was finally agreed on to guide disposition of such culturally unidentifiable remains.[27]

But if indeterminacies could prolong the fairly clear legislative intent of NAGPRA to secure the repatriation of human remains and classified items in accord with Native traditions, the process of addressing those indeterminacies could be generative for Native traditions, prompting Native peoples to seek out their traditional knowledge keepers and to articulate what is important to them going forward. Determinations of "cultural affiliation" often invoke competing narratives about origins of Native American communities— scientific narratives of archaeologists and linguists on the one hand and Native American oral traditions on the other. They even can invoke varied oral traditions of Native peoples that each make claims to cultural affiliation. Greg Johnson writes:

> Religious testimony under the law has at times served the role legislators anticipated, tipping the balance of "preponderance of evidence" in favor of Native claims. At other times it has played a far greater role in advancing Native claims than was forecast, persuading audiences of claims in ways that eclipse consideration of other forms of evidence. At still other times religious discourse in a traditional key has hindered Native efforts, particularly when nonnative audiences have been confronted by competing and conflicting religious assertions.[28]

If this is remarkable for the volubility of religious speech in legal processes that runs against the secular grain of modern liberalism, it is also remarkable for the nonchalance with which that speech is included in a larger conversation about evidence, for the way that religious speech in Native peoples is not just *religious* speech, but one of the key registers in which Native peoples reckon their histories, their relations to lands, their economic practices, and their law.[29]

Generativity of Repatriation and Reburial

Beyond the proliferation of religious speech in the NAGPRA process, the actual repatriations of ancestral remains and sacred items have been generative of, and not just referential to, Native religiousness. Welcoming ceremonies of storied sacred bundles and reburial ceremonies have contributed to the trend of healing and have inspired Native peoples to claim their distinctive traditions with renewed vigor. As an example from the Omaha Nation shows, this is perhaps the most important respect in which the NAGPRA process has been religious.[30]

Although its repatriation predated NAGPRA, the return of the Omaha Sacred Pole illustrates how repatriation does not just settle past wrongs but also can fuel cultural and spiritual renewal. The Omaha call their Sacred Pole *Umon'hon'ti*, the "Venerable One" or "the Real Omaha." Like so many sacred items, *Umon'hon'ti* is not an object but a spiritual presence with agency and even gender—not an *it*, but a *he*. Indeed traditional Omaha life literally revolved around *his* sacred presence at the center of the Omaha camp circle, analogous perhaps to the Tabernacle that accompanied the nomadic Israelites as recounted in the Hebrew Bible book of Numbers. Perhaps the better analogy is the burning bush on Mount Sinai in Exodus, since according to oral tradition, *Umon'hon'ti* came to the people from a fiery bush that wasn't consumed. In the 1880s, as a dwindling land base and buffalo population threatened the viability of the traditional Omaha way of life, *Umon'hon'ti*'s keeper, Yellow Smoke, made what must have been a difficult decision to entrust his preservation to others outside the Omaha nation. In a complex story involving anthropologists Alice Fletcher and Frances La Flesche, who was himself Omaha, Harvard's Peabody Museum came to hold *Umon'hon'ti*' in its collection. The Omaha people never forgot where he was.[31] In part, no doubt, because *Umon'hon'ti*'s accession was well documented and involved implicit, if not explicit, language about the museum's role as trustee, not owner, but also because of the relationships that developed with Omaha spiritual and political leaders and Peabody officials, Omaha tribal chairman Doran Morris was able to persuade the museum to repatriate *Umon'hon'ti*. A film, *Return of the Sacred Pole*, tells the story of the repatriation. Beginning scenes show the Sacred Pole as a lifeless object in the low oxygen rooms in the basement of the museum, and later in a restoration room where "it" was meticulously measured, photographed, and crated for transport. But "Venerable One" appears as more than a mere object when *Umon'hon'ti* returns to the community in a ceremony in summer 1989. Cayoni (Joe Johns), a traditional Creek woodcarver who worked at the Peabody as a building manager and as an artist in residence, was chosen to carry *Umon'hon'ti* into the dance arena, and he later told a filmmaker about the incredible power he felt in his arms, likening it to a father holding his child for the first time.[32] The film documents the subsequent ceremony wherein a spiritual leader performs a ritual purification and addresses *Umon'hon'ti* in the Omaha language, and after an invitation over the loudspeaker, the gathered community was invited to "welcome him home." The film silently tracks a procession of ordinary people as they line up and touch *Umon'hon'ti*. What is most affecting is when two women attendants help those who can't themselves reach out and touch *Umon'hon'ti*—the withered and stiff hand of an elderly man in a wheelchair and the tiny fingers of a swaddled baby.[33]

This is just one instance of a remarkable phenomenon NAGPRA unleashed over the last three decades. More typically in private ceremonies, behind and around and through each repatriation or reburial can be something profoundly generative of Native religion. There is certainly an element of closure; in rites of purification items and remains of individuals are ceremonially cleansed from the untold harm done to them by their alienation and isolation and display. But there is not simply closure; there can be awakening, renewal, a forward act of healing from historical trauma, and new imaginings of traditional futures.

NAGPRA in the Courts: Religion v. Science?

Greg Johnson observes that NAGPRA events "cut against the grain of modern liberalism" not only because Indigenous peoples are positioned in unelaborated terrain between the state and the individual, but also because "in principle they affirm rather than reject the role of religion (and tradition) as a form of evidence."[34] The insistence on the part of Native proponents that cultural affiliation need not be determined with scientific certainty but by a preponderance of the evidence that engages distinctive indigenous modes of reasoning and affiliation was crucial. But it was emphatically not a specific appeal for the elevation of religion in the NAGPRA process. Instead, Native proponents understood it as a restoration of a level playing field after a chilling history of dispossession in the name of science that many provenance records show often amounted to grave robbing and looting.

Unsurprisingly, there has been no small amount of litigation related to NAGPRA, and court interpretations have given shape to the ultimate reach of its various provisions.[35] But in perhaps the highest profile challenge to the protections of NAGPRA, *Bonnichsen v. United States*, a physical anthropologist claimed that a federal decision to repatriate the 9,300-year-old remains of so-called Kennewick Man, found in 1996 on federal land along the Columbia River, to a group of area tribes who considered him "the Ancient One," an ancestor by Indigenous reckonings of kinship, violated the statute itself.[36]

The scientist won. In its affirmation of district court Judge Jelderks's 2002 holding in favor of the scientists, the Ninth Circuit Court of Appeals acknowledged that scientists and museums, not just tribes, had standing to sue under protections of NAGPRA, and agreed that the oral traditional evidence presented by the tribes could not reasonably outweigh the scientific evidence placing the remains several thousand years before the tribes in question had arrived in the region. Indeed, part of the public intrigue of the case was the conjecture that the skeletal remains were potential evidence of people related to Europeans whose presence in North America predated ancestors of contemporary Native Americans. *Time* magazine depicted an artistic rendering of Kennewick Man's face that was memorably likened to Star Trek's Captain Jean-Luc Picard, played by Patrick Stewart. As fantastical as the public discussion appeared to be, the original federal court decision in the litigation combined the claims of Bonnichsen and the scientists with a separate motion by the Asatru Folk Assembly, a legally incorporated church representing what it described as "one of the major indigenous, pre-Christian, European religions."[37] In his initial 1997 ruling, Judge Jelderks affirmed that the scientists had standing to bring a claim under NAGPRA, disagreeing with the government's contention that Congress passed NAGPRA to protect interests of Native Americans, not of scientists. The judge did not settle the substantive issues, but vacated the previous decisions made by the Army Corps of Engineers and remanded to the government's administrative apparatus to reevaluate all the evidence, and attend to a set of questions. By an interagency agreement with the US Army, the Department of the Interior did so, and determined early in 2000 that the remains were "Native American" and in September of that year found that despite some evidence of cultural discontinuities, "the evidence of cultural continuity is sufficient to show by a preponderance of the evidence that the Kennewick remains are culturally affiliated with the present-day Indian tribe claimants."[38]

Bonnichsen and the other scientists challenged the government's final decision, and two years later, Judge Jelderks held in a second decision that the remains were not "Native American" for the purposes of NAGPRA and using the statute's own definitions and therefore not subject to repatriation.[39] Remarkably, the case turned on a narrow reading of the present tense of the NAGPRA definition—"Native American" means "of, or relating to, a tribe, people, or culture that *is* indigenous to the United States." Because the court could not find what it considered sufficient evidence to establish a cultural affiliation of the remains to the current tribes of the plateau—this, too, rested on a very narrow reading of the plain language of the statute's expansive provision on what evidence could count for determining cultural affiliation—it found no cultural affiliation between the remains of a man who *was* Native American to the claimant tribes who *are* Native American.[40] As remarkably perhaps, the Ninth Circuit Court of Appeals affirmed the holding.[41]

The Ancient One's remains stayed under control of the Army Corps of Engineers and resided at Seattle's Burke Museum of Natural History and Culture under a contract where scientific research on his remains could continue, without public display and subject to NAGPRA Review Committee oversight. The original team of anthropologist plaintiffs made three visits to conduct their research, and spiritual leaders from the tribes came to conduct ceremonies and to advocate for the Ancient One's return.[42] In 2014, Douglas Owsley, a physical anthropologists who was one of the plaintiffs, published findings that Kennewick Man was more closely related to Pacific groups like Polynesians or the Ainu of Japan.[43] A story in *Smithsonian Magazine* set for simultaneous publication was rather immodestly titled, "The Kennewick Man Finally Freed to Share His Secrets."[44] But freed from *what*: from 9,000 years of buried obscurity or from the needless red tape of an antiscience statute? A sentence in the article's introduction clarifies: "If it weren't for a harrowing round of panicky last minute maneuvering worthy of a legal thriller, the remains might have been buried and lost to science forever."[45]

Owsley's findings were based on morphological analysis of the bones, but a team of Danish scientists led by Eske Willerslev sequenced the Ancient One's genome and compared it with various populations, expressly including

Ainu and Polynesians. Published in *Nature*, the Danish scientists concluded, "Kennewick Man has ancestry proportions most similar to those of other Northern Native Americans, especially the Colville, Ojibwa, and Algonquin."[46] This finding renewed tribal efforts under NAGPRA to reclaim his remains for reburial, expedited by congressional legislation in late 2016.[47]

A few months later, in February 2017, a group of religious leaders from the tribal coalition reclaimed the Ancient One's remains and conducted them in a cortege to the Columbia Valley for a private reburial in an undisclosed location. Chuck Sams, a spokesperson for the Confederated Tribes of the Umatilla Reservation, told a Seattle reporter that the ceremony would no doubt be unlike the original one 9,000 years previous, since elements were from the Washat religion brought to the region by the prophet Smohalla. "But the songs we sing," he said, "are very close and have been sung throughout the Columbia Plateau for thousands of years."[48]

If the reburial finally brought the long-sought closure for the coalition of Native peoples, Judge Jelderks's decision and its affirmation by the appeals court brought a very different kind of closure in terms of NAGPRA's reach going forward. The courts dealt a hard blow to the capaciousness of NAGPRA's process for determining cultural affiliation, and to the agency of Native nations in that process. The cultural affiliation of the majority of human remains in museum and scientific collections, and no small number of the cultural items for that matter, is hard to ascertain. The holding in *Bonnichsen* suggested NAGPRA had gone too far in valorizing "religion" over secular science.

The narrative that carried public understanding of NAGPRA was the narrative that the law pitted religion against science, despite the utter inconsistency with NAGPRA's clear evolution out of AIRFA as a human rights law and as keyed to federal Indian law, and thus resistant to equal protection or establishment clause challenges. As David Hurst Thomas put the issue in his book on the controversy, "if archaeologists surrender the right to study ancient human bones and artifacts, will the scientific community have to fear continual censure by the religious beliefs of a few?"[49] Thinking about the complex relationship between science and religion in terms of the metaphor of warfare, as perceptive scholars of both have pointed out, often has more to say about the anxieties of the moment than about the facts on the ground.[50]

The controversy over Kennewick Man seen through the familiar lens of the battle between science and religion cemented a view of NAGPRA as decidedly religious. Consider, for example, a model lesson plan sponsored by the

National Endowment for the Humanities that teaches the Kennewick Man controversy but that frames it in terms of "Kennewick Man: Science and Sacred Rights," asking students if they see any strategy for reaching a compromise between the claims of religion and those of science.[51] The narrative has also shaped legal studies scholarship on NAGPRA. Steven Goldberg, for example, considers the passions and emotional investment of both sides in the litigation and likens it to the "emotional investment" of the creation science and intelligent design controversies. "Scientists brought suit in the Kennewick Man case just as science teachers challenged the ban on teaching evolution in Arkansas," Goldberg writes, in an apparent effort to recognize that it is scientists as well as "Native Americans and Biblical creationists who care deeply about our origins."[52]

Clearly, the religion versus science narrative stuck because it emplotted the complex and varied struggles between Native peoples, many scientists, and museum professionals, in terms familiar to late twentieth-century audiences that had seen the Christian right assert biblical reasoning into educational standards, curricula, and textbooks with considerable success. This made for a good story, even if it asserted a false equivalence between politically ascendant evangelical Christians and dispossessed Native peoples reclaiming the humanity of their ancestral dead from archaeological resourcehood.

But another reason for this narrative's appeal was its strategic usefulness to those scientists and museum professionals keen to curtail the demands of NAGPRA. First, it reduced the complex field of specific Native concerns and interests—this sacred bundle and not that woven basket; this particular way of asserting kinship with ancestral dead in particular places—into a singular and irrational religious opposition to science. Spun as a "religious" statute, NAGPRA thus could be framed as a problem requiring sensible containment in rule-making and dispute resolution under the terms of the statute itself. Second, identifying NAGPRA as an enactment of purported religious opposition to science could render Native claims both unreasonably totalizing and naive to the complexity of implementation. This was far from the case for those Native leaders advocating for NAGPRA; they well knew the myriad ways that hundreds of different Native peoples would address thousands of specific instances of plundered bodies and cultural items.[53]

So while there are elements of the NAGPRA process that suggest its texture as a religious freedom statute—the religious speech strategically engaged by Indigenous peoples in the hearings leading up to NAGPRA's passage or in the deliberations of its Review Committee, or the clear religious flourishing that has been fed by repatriated items like the Omaha Sacred Pole, or the return and reburial of Native ancestors at home—judicial interpretations, too, have stressed NAGPRA's religious leanings.

NAGPRA: A Finer-Grained Reading

Yet as with AIRFA, a closer reading of NAGPRA requires us not only to distinguish, as Greg Johnson has, between "strategic" universal appeals to an American discourse of religious freedom and the culture specific funerary and ceremonial traditions of burial, but also to see how the combination of those two religious discourses has been grafted legally onto the discourse of collective rights under federal Indian law. It is in this sense like the Peyote Amendment was after the wizening process of AIRFA's narrow reading by the courts and the RFRA coalition's exclusion, strategically placed not as an amendment to RFRA, where the logic of religious freedom would place it, but as an amendment to AIRFA, where the logic of federal Indian law and the special status of members of recognized tribes made it not only "Scalia-proof" but also a cultural/religious facet of a broader agenda promoting tribal sovereignty.

First, NAGPRA on its face is hard to view primarily as a religious freedom statute. Native proponents were careful to regard it as a basic human rights law for its fundamental acknowledgment of the humanity of deceased Native American persons, regarded hitherto in the American Antiquities Act of 1906 and the 1979 Archaeological Resources Protection Act, as so many "archeological resources."[54] This was no small thing, the rhetorical and legal assertion that Native skeletons were Native American human remains, because among other things it demonstrated how protections of the dead in common law, not to mention statutes in every state, had failed to apply equally to Native American dead. Harjo notes that this turn of phrase from resource to human being was resisted by many in the archaeological community from the beginning. It was not that archaeologists had resisted the notion that the remains belonged to humans, but that their status as persons tied to Native nations rather than resources belonging to the nation undid the pretense that scientists could exert control of them on behalf of the Native peoples as well as on behalf of scientific discovery of the nation.[55]

Second, in the taxonomy of legal studies, NAGPRA is regarded as a cultural property law, not a religious freedom law, one that ultimately questions the clarity of the title that federally funded museums or agencies could ever have under common law to human remains, or under the terms of contract and property law to items of cultural patrimony. As Greg Johnson observes, a turning point toward NAGPRA's passage was testimony by the Native American Rights Fund: "Where cultural affinity can be demonstrated, a tribe or tribal group has property rights in human remains and associated grave goods superior in the law to the asserted property rights of either federal government or public or private institutions."[56] These arguments were largely adopted in the report commending Senate passage of NAGPRA by the chair of the Senate Committee on Indian Affairs, Daniel Inouye.[57] Harjo notes that the ability to go to court on the basis of these property claims, even without the repatriation statutes, was part of what brought antagonistic interests to the table in shaping the legislation.

Third, the very terminology of repatriation references the internationalist language of *patria*, nations, and the return to *nations* of origin of what can be said rightfully to belong to them. Repatriation has its roots in the return of war dead, but the term came to prominence in international conventions under the purview of UNESCO beginning in the mid-twentieth century. Suzan Harjo indicates than in the years following 1967, she and others in her coalition contemplated return of plundered human bodies and inappropriately displayed sacred items in terms linked to the other issues identified in AIRFA as religious freedom, not in terms of repatriation. But the language of repatriation, with the light it casts implicitly on de-patriation, and with its endorsement of cultural patrimony that individuals cannot themselves alienate, presented itself as a compelling way to assert interests that were in some respects religious but not merely religious, and that would not in any event go far under the mere language of religious freedom.

Fourth, the procedural approach to federally recognized Indian tribes and recognized Native Hawaiian Organizations aligns NAGPRA and the NMAI Act with the federal trust responsibility to protect and preserve the cultures, religions, and traditions of tribes, and to consult tribes in a manner befitting the nation-to-nation relationship. NAGPRA is unambiguous here about the unique nature of the repatriations contemplated: "This Act reflects the unique relationship between the Federal Government and Indian tribes and Native Hawaiian organizations and should not be construed to establish a precedent with respect to any other individual, organization, or foreign government."[58] Under both NMAI and NAGPRA, the only operative entities for repatriations beyond lineal descendants are "Indian tribe[s]" and Native Hawaiian

Organizations, and "Indian tribe" is defined in terms of federal recognition elsewhere in federal law:

> "Indian Tribe" means any tribe, band, nation, or other organized group or community of Indians, including any Alaska Native village, which is recognized as eligible for the special programs and services by the United States to Indians because of their status as Indians.[59]

Federally Recognized Native American Religions?

It is true that in tailoring protections to conform to the unique political status of federally recognized tribes and their members, NAGPRA, like AIRFA, privileges protections for those with this status, and Native Americans from outside this circle can be justly critical: what kind of religious freedom protection can legislate such distinctions in the land of universal religious freedom? This certainly was not the vision at Bear Butte in 1967, nor the desire of those advocating these statutory protections for Native American religious freedom. Indeed, in some regards, it is an artifact of the compromise process that almost inevitably comes with legislation. Tailoring the reach of protection to federal recognition satisfies concerns about potential exposure to equal protection and no establishment claims that such accommodations to special groups would violate the Constitution.

It is also true that Harjo and other advocates were mindful of and trying to minimize, where possible, the exclusions of religious protections for the many nonrecognized Native peoples and the many individuals who are not members of federally recognized tribes. AIRFA did not expressly define Indian or American Indian."[60] More importantly, according to Harjo, is that AIRFA expressly identifies its consulting class to extend beyond recognized tribal governments and their representatives: Section 2 directs agencies to evaluate their policies "in consultation with native traditional religious leaders," and this language was deliberate to effect consultations with the right voices in Native communities, whether or not they were the elected leaders of the entities of federal recognition, the tribes themselves.

In its effort to broaden the circle of federal agencies' consultations on Native religious freedom matters, the 1979 Report to Congress mandated by AIRFA took pains in its recommendations section to elaborate. "Important to the issue of consulting class" under AIRFA was not only the definition of American Indian and the federal relationship but also "the distinction, where it exists, between Native governments recognized by the United States and Native traditional governments, which may or may not be federally-recognized."[61] The report identifies the slippages between definitions of Indian, from membership and citizenship in a tribe to various kinds of federal programs, "directed at the purposes for which the definitions are suited—political, property or services." "None is suitable for the purposes of the American Indian Religious Freedom Act, which is designed to protect the cultural and religious interest of individual Native Americans and Indian tribes and Native groups as cultures, rather than simply as political entities. Perhaps the best approach to definition is to view the matter within the functional cultural context: individuals who are accepted as Indian in the community in which they live."[62]

If the AIRFA Report appears to oscillate some on this sensitive matter, it is hardly surprising given the complexities of Indian identity in different registers, and the exacerbation of attendant tensions by the settler-colonial state.[63] At one point in its effort to enlarge the consulting class federal agencies should engage, the report avers that "for the purposes of AIRFA, the political relationships between the tribe and the United States, as governments or between the tribe as a government and an individual tribal citizen are clearly irrelevant."[64] The relevant considerations, the report continues, "would appear to be whether an Indian is sincerely attempting to exercise a First Amendment right which is a matter of federal law and, where applicable, whether an individual Indian is authorized to perform a particular ceremony or possess a certain sacred object which is a matter of tribal law or custom."

But this does not mean the report suggests AIRFA is a clarification of First Amendment rights alone or a dismissal of a collective religion. The report references elsewhere Native religions as individual and collective matters and in terms of religious and customary law. Instead, such a remark stems from the report's effort to integrate religious freedom and the nation-to-nation logic of federal Indian law, and seems particularly concerned to enlarge federal consultation beyond the government representatives of recognized tribes. At that time before self-determination developments had more fully settled in, tribal governments didn't uniformly speak for the protection of traditional cultures. Listen to how the report navigates this:

> In many instances, federal policy has created a political stalemate within the Indian tribes. The federal government recognizes and deals exclusively with the constitutional form of government, which controls tribal land

and resources, formal political institutions, law and order systems and service delivery agencies. At the same time on many reservations, the effective authority in the life of the tribe—filling most of the traditional roles of religious, political and social control—is still an outgrowth of the traditional Indian culture, which makes little distinction between religion and other aspects of human life. In these traditional cultures, all laws are spiritual and form the foundation of government.[65]

A decade later, even though many tribal governments had begun to redraw their constitutions and address the sensitive issues raised, the NMAI Act and NAGPRA continued to follow AIRFA's lead in terms of the consulting class. Here again was an effort to distinguish the authority relative to Native religious traditions from the authority of the tribes as recognized political entities, or more accurately, to extend the circle of recognized authority where appropriate beyond leadership of the tribes, as the AIRFA Report directed. The NMAI Act directs the Smithsonian to inventory and identify human remains and cultural items "in consultation and cooperation with traditional Indian religious leaders and government officials of Indian tribes."[66] NAGPRA specifies the inventories are to be "completed in consultation with tribal government and Native Hawaiian organization officials and traditional religious leaders."[67] Still, repatriations themselves under both statutes are to be made only to federally recognized tribes and the Native Hawaiian Organizations delimited by the laws.[68]

Importantly, this restriction to recognized tribes applies only when lineal descendants cannot be identified, and here is one place where a lack of federal recognition does not get in the way of repatriations to Native people who are not members of recognized tribes. For in NAGPRA's priority order of ownership or control of Native American human remains and associated burial objects, lineal descent trumps the claim of a culturally affiliated tribe. And "Native American," as we have seen, is statutorily defined as "of, or relating to, a tribe, people, or culture that is indigenous to the United States," so a lineal descendant need not be a member of a federally recognized tribe for the status under the statute.[69] At least one critic has called attention to this facet of NAGPRA together with the identification of Native Hawaiian Organizations as indications that the law fails to pass constitutional muster in the face of an equal protection challenge that it discriminates in favoring one group over other citizens.[70] But in the common law tradition, lineal descendants of deceased people are generally accorded control over their relatives' bodies.

The NAGPRA process writ large could draw on silences or ambiguities in statutory language to encompass possibilities for nonrecognized Native peoples unforeseen in the statute itself. While NAGPRA surely privileges federally recognized tribes, "nothing in NAGPRA prevents a museum or agency from including a non-federally recognized Indian group in the consultation process or a non-federally recognized tribe from participating in decisions about Native American human remains or cultural objects."[71] The Wanapum Band of Priest Rapids, for example, was part of the coalition with the recognized Confederated Bands of the Colville Reservation and others seeking return of the Ancient One/Kennewick Man. The Wanapum's strategy was to make a joint claim.[72] The Mashpee Wampanoag in Massachusetts ultimately received federal recognition in 2007, but had resourcefully formed the Wampanoag Repatriation Confederation with the Assonet Band of the Wampanoag and the federally recognized Wampanoag Tribe of Gay Head, and worked with museums for the successful repatriation of many ancestral remains for reburial.[73] Some museums, like the Peabody working with the nonrecognized Nipmuc tribe in central Massachusetts, even worked to repatriate human remains where a cultural affiliation was clear and the recognized tribes in the region voiced their approval, even without the statutory requirement to do so. Indeed, the final rule on culturally unidentifiable human remains codified the possibility that consultation could include officials and religious leaders of tribes that were not federally recognized, and that transfer of control may go to those groups if supported by recognized tribes involved and subject to the formal approval of the NAGPRA Review Committee and the Secretary of the Interior.[74]

While not entirely exclusive of the claims of Native people who are not members of federally recognized tribes, NAGPRA, the NMAI Act, and AIRFA are tailored to the nation-to-nation logic of federal Indian law, and thus steer clear of challenges that they violate constitutional equal protection standards. This also applies to NAGPRA's overtly religious provisions about sacred objects. With definitions grounded in federal Indian law, the statute makes only culturally affiliated federally recognized tribes and Native Hawaiian Organizations eligible for sacred object repatriations. And the NAGPRA regulatory procedures for making determinations about what items constitute sacred objects and their disposition, too, can proceed without plainly violating the First Amendment's Establishment Clause.

The implications of federal recognition come into sharp relief through strenuous federal efforts to accommodate Native access to eagle feathers for ceremonial use while enforcing the eagle protection purposes of the Bald and Golden Eagle Protection Act. We turn now to consider the case law elaborating these implications.

Eagle Feathers and Court Recognition of Collective Rights

Sacred mountains that become playgrounds for downhill skiers or climbers; ancestral remains buried in the ground that call out the artifice of a property owner's title—it is uncanny how Native American religious freedom claims so consistently confront American identity at its most pronounced symbolic extensions and trigger deeply rooted American reactions. In fact, the symbolic weight of what's at stake is perhaps an enormous part of the difficulty of finding sufficient legal remedies. As cultural theorists from Gramsci to Bourdieu have argued, our world is defined more often by the exercise of symbolic power than by overt displays of military or economic might.[75] Perhaps we should not be so astonished, then, that there should arise so much litigation over legal protections for the bald eagle, at once preeminent symbol of the American nation and a powerful spiritual presence for Native American nations.

Since its original passage in 1940, the Bald and Golden Eagle Protection Act (Eagle Act) has prohibited eagle hunting, possession, and trafficking with stiff fines and up to a year in prison.[76] Even with the delisting of bald eagles under the Endangered Species Act in 2007, courts have held the line on relaxing the rules. As one court put it, "The bald eagle would remain our national symbol whether there were 100 eagles or 100,000 eagles."[77]

Since its amendment in 1962, the Eagle Act has accommodated Native religions by exempting possession of eagle feathers and other parts "for the religious purposes of Indian tribes."[78] To maintain eagle populations while also enabling access to feathers for Native Americans, the government created a permit process that restricts access to members of federally recognized tribes who participate in "bona fide tribal religious ceremonies."[79] The National Eagle Repository near Denver estimates that applicants can expect to wait two years for a whole bald eagle, or three to six months for sets of loose feathers.[80]

These two stated interests of the Eagle Act have triggered a storm of litigation—I have pored over at least two dozen cases in five of the eleven US circuits.[81] What's fascinating is that the court cases don't generally align in terms of a contest between Native American religious freedom and the national interest in protecting eagle populations as the national symbol. The legal divide that structures most of the litigation concerns instead two competing ways of

FIG. 6.2. National Eagle Repository
This facility outside Denver receives, processes, and distributes eagle feathers, bone whistles, and other body parts to qualified applicants who are members of federally recognized Indian tribes using them for bona fide religious purposes. The distribution and permitting system has generated much litigation. Interior photographs are forbidden as directd by Native nations.

imagining or defining Native American religions: on the one hand, as religions in the conventional sense of individual belief and practice and on the other as an integral and necessarily collective part of the heritage of Native American nations with whom the United States has a special legal and political relationship. Because courts in these cases have consistently, if unwittingly, affirmed the collective dimensions of Native religions and because the stories behind the cases illuminate the particular difficulties of squaring the distinctive contours of Native American religions into the analytical and legal boxes of religion, it is tempting to devote an entire additional chapter to the subject of Eagle Act litigation. Because I tell the fuller story elsewhere, I will here summarize the major findings.[82]

It's hard to overstate the sacred significance of eagles for Native peoples even as it's hard to generalize about that significance from how hundreds of distinct Native religions variously construe it. Eagle feathers can be passed on through generations, awarded ceremonially to people who have earned them, and buried with the dead in some funerary practices. Particular feathers can carry blessings of spiritual mentors, help concretize the religious lineages in which ceremonial practices are grounded, and can exhibit ritual power to those in their presence. Feathers are common also to intertribal traditions: powwows, smudging, and talking circle ceremonies.

Feathers are also sought by increasing numbers, it seems, of non-Native practitioners of Native spirituality. To make several long stories short, the First, Ninth, Tenth, and Eleventh Circuit Courts of Appeals have upheld the government's restriction of permits to practitioners of Native religions who are members of federally recognized tribes.[83] The case law agrees that the permit issuing exceptions to the Eagle Act are not simply matters of accommodating the religious freedom of individuals practicing some universal Native American religion, but are in furtherance of the federal trust responsibility of "fostering and protecting the culture and religion of federally recognized Indian tribes."[84] These courts found this responsibility to be a sufficiently compelling government interest in the restrictive permit process to outweigh the excluded individual's religious freedom claims, sincere and robust as they were.

The First Circuit case from Maine illustrates how important can be the distinction between a religious identity as a practitioner of a Native religion and a political identity as a member of a recognized tribe who practices Native religion. Because ceremonial demand for eagle feathers far exceeds the supply, this distinction serves to protect Native religions from non-Native appropriations that detract from efforts by Native nations to protect what they consider sacred. In the case *Rupert v. Director*, a white pastor of an "all race" church that follows Native American religious customs had organized it as a "tribe," the "Tribe of the Pahana." When a permit application citing his tribal identity as Pahana was turned down, he challenged the Eagle Act accommodations as a violation of the Establishment Clause, citing an unconstitutional "denominational preference" for some groups practicing Native American religions over his own.[85] The First Circuit affirmed a lower court ruling against Rupert.[86] In the case of the other three circuits, courts rejected the religious freedom claims of sincere practitioners who were either lineal descendants of Native people, like Firebird Gibson,[87] a member of a Canadian First Nation, like Leonard Antoine,[88] or non-Native people with deep connections to Native communities, including tribally enrolled children.[89]

While aspects of these decisions ought appropriately to trouble those concerned with the religious freedom of all Native peoples and not simply of those who are citizens/members of federally recognized tribes, I want to call attention to the way the Ninth and Tenth Circuits legally distinguish between the religious freedom claims of individuals, keyed to universal discourses on religious beliefs and rights of private conscience, and those asserted by association with the distinctive political status of federally recognized tribes and the cultural and religious heritage that are woven into peoplehood. In *U.S. v. Wilgus*, part of a complex case that had gone up and down the federal court ladder several times, a three judge panel of the Tenth Circuit reversed a lower court's holding on remand to affirm that the permit scheme was the least restrictive means to operationalize the federal government's trust responsibility and outweighed the religious freedom claims of Wilgus, a sincere practitioner of Native religions who was demonstrably connected to Paiute people in Utah though non-Native himself.[90]

The court's key move was its choice of one of two alternatives for interpreting the government's compelling interest with regard to protecting Native American religion cued up by competing prior rulings. The 2011 decision opted for "the protection of the culture of federally recognized Indian tribes" as the controlling construal of the trust responsibility, rather than the language in the majority opinion of its earlier holding in the case: that of "preserving Native American culture in-and-of itself" potentially "as a thing separate and apart from those Indian tribes to whom the government owes a trust obligation."[91]

The *Wilgus* court found this not only in better keeping with an initial ruling in the litigation and the special legal federal relationship with the tribes[92] but also with its interpretation of the Eagle Act itself, noting the statute authorizes permits "for the religious purposes of Indian Tribes" when it could have read "for the purposes of Native American religion":

> From this we infer that Congress saw the statutory exception not as protecting Native American religion qua religion, but rather as working to preserve the culture and religion of federally recognized tribes.[93]

In 2014, the Fifth Circuit disagreed, finding it could not "definitively conclude that Congress intended to protect only federally recognized tribe members' religious rights in this section."[94]

In this case, a member of the federally unrecognized Lipan Apache who leads a congregation that engages renewal of Native American traditions brought a religious freedom challenge that a district court found consistent with the case law considered above.[95] But on appeal, the Fifth Circuit reversed and remanded, requiring the government to show how the permit process was tailored narrowly enough to pass muster in light of a new test for RFRA's least restrictive means analysis introduced by the Supreme Court in *Hobby Lobby*.

But it wasn't a complete departure. The Fifth Circuit took pains to align its recognition of the individual's rights in terms of his membership in the Lipan Apache Tribe. While the tribe is not currently federally recognized, the court noted that Texas State Senate by reference to an 1838 treaty had recognized the Lipan Apache to "have had a 'nation to nation' relationship with the Republic of Texas, the State of Texas, and the United States government."[96] Ultimately, a settlement agreement enabled specific named members of the church to possess feathers, putting an end to further legal proceedings that might have resulted in a change in course to the case law in the other three judicial circuits.[97]

The controversy over which practitioners of Native religions can have access to eagle feathers for religious purposes also points to the importance of prosecutorial discretion on such matters and how uniform—or not—has been the enforcement across federal agencies and even within the Justice Department's field of US attorneys.

In 2010, an "Eagle Feather Working Group" of the National Congress of American Indians met with the White House and various agencies to better coordinate federal administration and enforcement.[98] President Obama responded with a new policy to "ensure a consistent and uniform approach" to enforcement, specifically directing US attorneys to exempt from prosecution, even in the absence of a permit, members of federally recognized tribes who found or possessed or gifted feathers and parts. The policy also encouraged federal prosecutors "to consider allowing 'particular cases' to be handled by tribal prosecutors.[99] Noting its basis in the "special relationship ... with federally recognized tribes," the policy was explicit that it was not to change how prosecutors should handle cases involving either "non-Indians or members of state-recognized tribes or other groups or organizations."[100] Still, it affirmed that "the traditional elements of federal prosecutorial discretion" should apply to such cases, and stressed a federal priority "to focus wildlife enforcement resources on those cases involving illegal activities that have the greatest negative impact on protected species," like killing protected birds and engaging in unlawful commercial activities with them.[101]

Conclusion

The Eagle Act accommodations have given rise to court recognition of a collective right to Native American religious freedom, a judicial affirmation, albeit indirect, of Native efforts to assert religious freedom through statutes like AIRFA and NAGPRA that correspond to the collective logic of federal Indian law and the trust responsibility. Courts may seem ham-fisted in the way they distinguish the collective rights to religion that are the object of the federal trust responsibility to recognized tribes from the rights of religious individuals, but they do broadly agree on the messy result, and this is significant. To be sure court recognition of these collective rights comes through the back door, not in direct rulings on tribal religious freedom claims, but in terms of to whom the trust responsibility obligates the federal government. In this respect, the affirmation remains yoked to the vagaries of federal acknowledgment, with its plain exclusion of so many Native American people and peoples whose collective religious freedom ought to count too. The logic is also keyed to the federal trust responsibility, which surely can be a source of Native power, but not empowerment, mediated as it is by the historic paternalism of the trust relationship and subject to shifts in policy.

So, as important as these admittedly messy court affirmations are to the analysis of this book, it will be refreshing to turn in the next two chapters to consider affirmations of collective rights to Native religions and cultures through the front door logic of inherent sovereignty and peoplehood. We look in the next chapter to case law affirming treaty rights to traditional practices like whaling and salmon fishing, practices whose reassertion is every bit as sacred as it is economic and political.

7

Religion as Peoplehood

SOVEREIGNTY AND TREATIES
IN FEDERAL INDIAN LAW

ON THE PACIFIC Ocean just off the northwestern tip of Washington, amid a noisy flotsam and jetsam of protest boats with loudspeakers, media helicopters, onlookers, and a German film crew, a group of whalers chosen by the Makah Nation that had undergone months of spiritual, mental, and physical preparation paddled a traditional canoe toward a particular gray whale, harpooned it, and later euthanized it with a rifle. As the Makah understood it, the whale had chosen them and offered itself up to them, part of an exchange between Makah people and whales since time immemorial. The night before, an elder gave them a song that he said had been given to him in a dream.[1]

It was May 1999, the first time in seventy years that a whale had been sought and given itself to the Makah, a people whose entire culture orbits around the reciprocal relationship with whales. In the 1855 Treaty that ceded much of their homeland to the United States, Makah leaders explicitly retained their "right of taking fish and of whaling and sealing at usual and accustomed grounds and stations."[2] As Janine Bowechop (Ledford) notes, Makah people had been hunting whales for thousands of years, and had managed hunts by limiting them to a portion of the population at two seasons of the year. When whale populations dwindled under a ravaging commercial whaling industry, the Makah faced increased difficulty in subsistence hunting. But it was also out of a deep sense of obligation to whales that the Makah scaled back. Bowechop (Ledford) finds that between 1913 and 1921 possibly only two whales were hunted and consumed. By the 1920s, the Makah had voluntarily ceased hunting whales.[3] Only after the gray whale was delisted from Endangered Species Act protections in 1994 did the tribe pursue legal authorization from the International Whaling Commission (IWC) to take a small number of whales for ceremonial and subsistence purposes. They could do so because of a crucial series of court victories in the late 1970s affirming the reserved rights of Washington tribes in similar treaties to take salmon at their "usual and accustomed grounds and stations." At every step, the Makah met stiff opposition from animal rights organizations, and after two decades of further environmental review and litigation, have yet to be authorized to take another whale, although several Makah individuals, impatient with the legal delays, killed a whale in a 2007 hunt condemned by the tribal council.

In 1999, when the whale was brought to a spot on the shore where Makah hunters had brought whales historically, the community came out singing ancient songs to honor her for her sacrifice and adorn her with eagle down. Blubber and meat were carefully distributed and a potlatch concluded the hunt, with Makah relatives and supporting nations up and down the coast attending. Especially given the long legal struggles and spiritual preparation, the whale hunt was like oxygen to the Makah, for whom the seventy-year period without whales had been characterized by consistent hardship: first coercive policies of assimilation, later economic and social marginalization, historical trauma, and disease.

Detractors, especially environmental groups led by the Sea Shepherd Conservation Society, stressed discontinuity between modern Makah life and the traditional past as evidence against a legitimate hunt. To critics, the Makah no longer needed whales for subsistence and, worse, they had lost their cultural competence to hunt in the traditional manner at the time of the treaty signing. Detractors argued "real Makah" would oppose, not support, modern hunting of such majestic animals. The argument bespoke how critics were seeing the Makah relationship to whales through the rose-colored romanticized lens of Native spirituality as a matter of sentimental love rather than a reciprocal relationship. They certainly argued that a Makah proposal to use a high-powered rifle to bring a safer, swifter, and more humane death to any harpooned whale introduced clear evidence of the hunt's inauthenticity.

But such presumed constraints on authenticity are not the conditions in which cultures live and move, and certainly not how the sacred works. As a former Makah chairman put it: "It's a war out there, and we know it ... they want us in the museum. They'd rather we just said, 'Oh the Makah were great whalers,' and leave it at that. They want us to have a dead culture. But it's been our way of life. We look at the ocean and we feel we not only have a legal right but a moral right to whale."[4]

Indeed it is in the reassertion of rights to such traditional practices that interrupted traditions can be awakened and restored. The assertion of treaty rights here was not only an exertion of Makah sovereignty; it was a powerful restoration of a sacred relationship between whales and people. Traditional knowledge returned to the Makah people, informed by ethnographic and archaeological research, but especially through the practical and ancestral knowledge that only comes from prayerful doing.[5] The renewed rigorous practices of ritual and spiritual preparation transformed Makah individuals and the entire Makah community.

"The umbilical cord that connects us to our whaling tradition has remained unbroken and continues to nourish and strengthen our communities," writes Nuu-chah-nulth (Nootka) scholar Charlotte Coté.

> The tradition is in our family names, in the names of the land we live on, and in the names of waterways we subsist on. It has continued to live on through the stories contained within our oral traditions, through our cere-monies, songs, and dances, and through our artistic expression. We have always been known as a whaling people; as former Makah Whaling Com-mission Chairman Keith Johnson maintains, "It's who we are."[6]

Religion as Peoplehood in Federal Indian Law

The last chapter followed strategic efforts to fashion through legislation what courts have been unable to produce in the sacred lands cases: full throated protections for Native American religious practices as matters of collective right. AIRFA and NAGPRA draw on the power of religious freedom dis-course but tailor the protections in terms of the nation-to-nation relationship of federal Indian law. The next two chapters follow that logic beyond Native efforts to engage religious freedom to broader-brush assertions of people-hood, of sovereignty. In these two chapters, Native nations rely not on the rhetorical force of religious freedom but pursue protections for what might be called *religious* under the aegis of their broader sovereignty and self-determination as peoples. The Makah whale hunt is a fine example. For all its ritualized protocol and religious generativity, the modern-day assertion of a traditional whale hunt did not turn on "religious freedom" but on the solemnity of its 1855 treaty, and the specifically reserved rights to take whales in usual and accustomed places. To argue for religion as peoplehood, Native Americans spare themselves of making distinctions about which places and practices necessary for their full peoplehood are sacred or for making a showing of how they are sacred by articulating them as religious. No external determination is needed about what will count as religious, whether it is grounded as an aboriginal or authentically traditional practice, or whether it has changed with time. Sacred or secret knowledge need not be publicly aired in court or in public.

Chapter 8 will take this up in the context of the discourse of *Indigenous rights* in international law, an emerging discourse that remains considerably aspirational even as it is rapidly helping clarify other legal orders. This chapter concerns claims to the religious in federal Indian law as part of broader claims made in the register of sovereignty. It follows a number of crucial cases that concerned the shape of treaty-protected rights to fishing, hunting, and gathering off-reservation, notably those in the Great Lakes region and the salmon cases in the Pacific Northwest, rulings that cleared the way for the Makah whale hunt. I argue these cases are not simply about political sovereignty or about the economic value of the treaty rights but also about the religious and cultural importance of those sacred practices and how the practices themselves constitute peoplehood. At the conclusion of each of these chapters, I will also signal where protecting religion as *peoplehood*, under international law and especially under federal Indian law, can have its limits, particularly in the short term.

Sovereignty and Federal Indian Law

Sovereignty is, to say the least, a complex concept. The sovereign under the divine right of kings was the individual ruler who stood in for the body politic and who was immune from lawsuits. In Enlightenment thinking and American nation-building, sovereignty transferred to "the people."[7] But in the United States, which people? Federalism posits two sovereigns: the various states and their federation as the United States. The Constitution's Commerce Clause allocates to Congress the power to regulate commerce between the states and among the Indian tribes and effectively recognizes Indian tribes as the third sovereign. Indian tribes, like states and the federal government, have sovereign immunity.[8]

As used by and about Native nations, sovereignty discourse is not simply one of politics and law. Within its aura lies considerations of dignity and respect and cultural survival—collective self-determination in a fuller sense.[9] Indeed, some of the higher-profile judicial decisions affirming tribal sovereignty that form the basis of this chapter have not been mere matters of legal jurisdiction, economic development, territory, or taxation but matters of cultural practices of peoplehood like whale hunting. This has led some to think first of treaty claims or assertions of tribal sovereignty to protect what they hold sacred, instead of religious freedom law or of cultural resource law. With Wallace Coffey, the Yaqui legal scholar Rebecca Tsosie has framed the approach as one of "cultural sovereignty," but it might, too, be extended in our case to be called something like religious sovereignty.[10]

If for Indigenous peoples, there is no *one* word for religion, a similar poverty of meaning applies to such secularized modern Western categories as law, politics, economy, and jurisdiction. By considering crucial Supreme Court cases of federal Indian law affirming inherent sovereignty and specific treaty rights, my aim is not simply to say that these treaties protect the religious elements of such practices as Makah whaling, though that is certainly true. Instead, I wish to show that assertions of political and legal sovereignty are perforce assertions of cultural sovereignty, and that the cultural, even the religious, elements of the peoplehood asserted are crucial, not incidental, to sovereignty's fuller realization. Along the way, I wish to show that Native assertions of treaty rights in these cases are generative of the religious, integral to the spirited renewal of interrupted traditions and peoplehood.

Under federal Indian law, the sovereignty of Native peoples is a limited sovereignty. In the eyes of US law since *Cherokee Nation v. Georgia* (1831), Native peoples are "domestic, dependent nations" exercising what courts have since come to call "quasi-sovereignty."[11] Tribes exercise sovereignty over some aspects of their lives—courts have identified these as internal matters—but even that sovereignty has been limited, and the doctrine of congressional Plenary Power, affirmed in *Lone Wolf v. Hitchcock* (1903), shored up a view that Congress has the power to define the quasi in quasi-sovereignty, to circumscribe as it sees fit, subject only to a "good faith" version of the federal trust responsibility.[12]

The paradox of *Cherokee Nation v. Georgia* is a contradiction at the heart of federal Indian law. Even as one hand of the US legal system acknowledges the inherent sovereignty of tribes as Native nations, the other hand emphasizes their "domestic, dependent" status, and the broad legal power of Congress to legislate their affairs in the manner of a guardian.

This core instability has made for a highly contingent body of law, subject more perhaps to political winds of the moment than are other fields of law.

An increasing number of legal scholars, Walter Echo-Hawk and Robert Williams among them, question whether it is possible incrementally to (re)build full legal sovereignty from legal materials that remain saturated with the overt racism of the past. For Echo-Hawk, there is no *Brown v. Board of Education* equivalent to answer the counterparts to *Plessy v. Ferguson* in federal Indian law:

> The Court needs to find some theory other than conquest, colonization, or racial superiority to justify its decisions. That change would entail a paradigm shift in American legal thinking similar to that which prompted the Court to overturn the legal bases for segregating America.... Until change is demanded by society at large, the Court will continue to apply outmoded rules to Indians that "the Courts of the conqueror cannot deny."[13]

There will continue to be efforts to push beyond the oxymoron of quasi-sovereignty and the limits of federal Indian law, but the state of affairs discussed in this chapter begs questions addressed in the following chapter on international law. By turns, the fullest realization of international law norms comes through the reform of domestic laws. The reader is invited to regard this chapter as the first part in a couplet on religion as peoplehood.

Although there are important moments when US courts have recognized an *inherent sovereignty* of Native nations predating the Constitution and informing how treaties are to be understood, federal Indian law takes the cue from *Cherokee Nation v. Georgia* and follows a domestic law trajectory rather than an international law one. From much of the federal Indian law perspective, it is treaties and the Constitution's Commerce Clause that compels recognition of the internal sovereignty of Native nations.[14] As courts have tried to find the boundary line between the quasi- and the sovereign, they have looked to the specific terms of relevant treaties themselves. While canons of construction, the reserved-rights doctrine, and other elements of federal Indian law jurisprudence shape how courts interpret treaties, it is the terms of treaties themselves that often provide structure for Native legal claims, including claims to the sacred. This chapter follows successful efforts by Native nations to defend the sacred by asserting their treaty rights, especially where rights are specifically spelled out and reserved in treaties.

Treaties and the Sacred

When they negotiated treaties, leaders of Native nations took pains where possible to reserve rights to what they held sacred. But consistent with the theme of these chapters, *religion as peoplehood*, the language of the sacred need not have been raised in treaty negotiations, and the integration of land, practices of living on the land, and religion need not be distinguished. As Suzan Harjo put it:

> Religion was so basic and fundamental and atmospheric and contextual that for the most part people didn't discuss it. It was assumed that no one would try to interfere with the Native people being the Native people.[15]

For example, in those land cession treaties where Native nations reserved portions of their homelands for reservations, they often chose to secure their places of ancestral burials and certain of their sacred sites. Almost any such treaty implies this.[16] A classic example is the 1868 Fort Laramie Treaty, in which the Sioux Nation explicitly reserved the Black Hills and its holy environs. Article 16 provides that "the United States hereby agrees and stipulates that the country north of the North Platte River and east of the summits of the Big Horn mountains shall be held and considered to be unceded Indian territory, and also stipulates and agrees that no white person or persons shall be permitted to settle upon or occupy any portion of the same; or without the consent of the Indians, first had and obtained, to pass through the same."[17] Of course that article was violated by American gold seekers and their military protectors, led by George Armstrong Custer, and in response to his defeat at the Battle of Greasy Grass, the Black Hills were cut out of the Great Sioux Reservation by Congress in 1877, and the reservation was reduced even further by Congress in 1889.[18] Notably, it was the 1889 act that unilaterally stripped the unceded lands crossed by the Dakota Access Pipeline. Although the Supreme Court in 1980 found these treaty violations "rank," and set aside a considerable escrow fund of monetized damages, member tribes of the Sioux Nation have yet to cash the check. They want instead a restored relationship with the land.[19]

Even as they ceded territory in treaties, many Native nations expressly reserved rights to hunting, fishing, and gathering on off-reservation homelands. Especially because courts have largely upheld these rights when asserted, they have been one of the success stories in the hard work of defending the sacred. These practices can be considered sacred to the nations for whom they express peoplehood and for whom they affirm religious as well as economic and cultural relationships with the plants and animals of the land and water. Again, Suzan Harjo:

> Even when people talk about fishing rights or hunting rights, they're talking about religion. When you talk about land, you're talking about religion.

When you talk about gathering, you're talking about not just the ability to go out and shoot a deer or get a salmon or pick a berry; you're talking about the song that is the first salmon song that goes before the fishing season; or the song that prepares the land, the prayers ... asking for the buffalo to allow themselves to be taken or for the huckleberries to return, for stripping the bark that becomes the basket that will hold a particular kind of plant.[20]

This chapter will elaborate on the successful protection under treaty law of off-reservation traditional practices: of salmon fishing and whaling in the Pacific Northwest and of fishing and gathering wild rice in the Great Lakes.

Solemn Treaties as the Law of the Land

"We are all Treaty People"

Historical accounts show that treaties were consistently made in the context of ceremonious practices of diplomacy. They often continue to be spoken of by Native parties as sacrosanct covenants. In certain moments, including those discussed in this chapter, courts too have spoken of treaties as solemn. In such a view, treaties are not simply lifeless legal documents detailing specific provisions of agreements made in the past; they are living arrangements in that they establish and recognize continuing nation-to-nation relationships between the United States and Native nations. Unless they are expressly abrogated, they remain the law of the land. Various acts in US law and in tribal law continue to affirm and breathe new life into them.[21] Treaties are covenants, solemn agreements; how they were originally understood, documented and remembered on both sides, matters.

Native nations have their own legal traditions of diplomacy, of making and consecrating and documenting and upholding treaties. This topic alone, considered in the context of one people, the Haudenosaunee Confederacy, could fill several volumes. Suffice it here to say that treaties remain multilateral affairs, ritualized relationships, and that Native memory of treaties matters to their ongoing interpretation. It needs to be said also that the United States didn't just become what it is through treaties in the past; as with slavery, its continued prosperity and might rely on the continued benefit treaties have provided. In this respect it is not only Native peoples who are treaty people; as Pamela Klassen richly explores in the Canadian context, "we are *all* treaty people."[22]

The Status of Treaties

From its infancy, the United States assumed the obligations of treaties made between the British Crown and Native peoples. Going forward, the United States committed itself to honorable treatment and diplomacy with Native peoples. In the Northwest Ordinance (1787), the United States declared:

> The utmost good faith shall always be observed towards the Indians, their lands and property shall never be taken from them without their consent; and in their property, rights and liberty, they never shall be invaded or disturbed, unless in just and lawful wars authorized by Congress; but laws founded in justice and humanity shall from time to time be made, for preventing wrongs being done to them, and for preserving peace and friendship with them.[23]

The United States made more than 370 different treaties with Native peoples through 1871, when the United States ceased calling subsequent agreements *treaties*.[24] Under the Constitution's Supremacy Clause, once ratified by the Senate, treaties are "the law of the land" and along with other federal laws, have legal priority over conflicting state and local laws.[25] This much is unambiguous.

But the body of federal Indian law interpreting treaties is beset with ambiguities, fueled largely by shifting winds of federal Indian policy and especially in the period of Assimilation Policy. These ambiguities also stem from the tensions of the foundational Marshall trilogy of decisions. Chapter 1 introduced the starkly theological basis of *Johnson v. M'Intosh* (1828), and I have just referenced the oxymoronic quasi-sovereignty of *Cherokee Nation v. Georgia* (1831). The trilogy is incomplete, though, without consideration of *Worcester v. Georgia* (1832), especially as this case serves to anchor the jurisprudence of treaty rights.

Worcester v. Georgia is a crucial comment and corrective to *M'Intosh* and *Cherokee Nation*, clarifying the inherent sovereignty of Native nations and the full force of treaties with Native nations, reiterating the federal government's nation-to-nation relationship with Indian peoples and that any guardian/ward language (explicitly not used by Marshall in this decision) does not nullify that relationship.

The case involved a Vermont Baptist missionary, Samuel Worcester, who was sentenced to four years of hard labor by Georgia authorities for living without a state license on lands of the Cherokee Nation, which had granted him permission. It was what we might now identify as a civil disobedience action, because for a white man on Cherokee land to qualify for a license, he had to take a loyalty oath to the constitution and government of the state of Georgia.[26] Technically, it was a habeas corpus action to bring his case into federal court, but it was brought as a test case to settle whether Georgia could enforce its laws on Cherokee lands, and that question rested on the Court's view of the continued force of the 1785 Treaty of Hopewell and the 1791 Treaty of Holston, which recognized continued Cherokee sovereignty on their lands.

The Supreme Court held against Georgia, nullifying its laws on Cherokee lands and finding the laws in question "repugnant to the constitution, laws, and treaties of the United States." Justice Marshall's opinion pulled few punches:

> When the United States gave peace, did they not also receive it? Were not both parties desirous of it? ... Did the Cherokees come to the seat of the American government to solicit peace; or did the American commissioners go to them to obtain it? The treaty was made at Hopewell, not at New York. The word "give," then, has no real importance attached to it.[27]

The case underscored the ongoing force of treaties because the Cherokee Nation has inherent sovereignty.

> The Indian nations had always been considered as distinct, independent political communities, retaining their original natural rights as the undisputed possessors of the soil from time immemorial.... The words "treaty" and "nation" are words of our own language, selected in our diplomatic and legislative proceedings by ourselves, having each a definite and well understood meaning. We have applied them to Indians, as we have applied them to the other nations of the earth. They are applied to all in the same sense.[28]

Marshall did incorporate the logic of discovery and law of nations from his *M'Intosh* opinion and the dependency of Native nations from *Cherokee Nation*, but cited them if only to caution that dependency and protectorate should be regarded as limits on, not simply authorization of, US power, and that even a weaker state "may place itself under the protection of one more powerful without stripping itself of the right of government and ceasing to be a state."[29] Tensions among these opinions notwithstanding, Marshall's three opinions established the rudiments of continued treaty-making and the legal recognition of inherent, if limited, tribal sovereignty. That would change dramatically later in the century.

Judicial Blows to Sovereignty

In 1871, as part of a broader assault on "tribalism," Congress determined there would no longer be diplomatic treaties but only agreements made with Native peoples.[30] Recall from chapter 1 that the guiding principle of Assimilation Policy was that Native collectives and the treaties made with them were a thing of the past. Even for self-styled "Friends of the Indian" reformers, a progressive future was the assimilation of Natives as individuals toward full citizenship and protection as individuals under the law. A number of court cases sought to square the new approach with the established law on treaties. In *U.S. v. Kagama* (1886), the Supreme Court found constitutional Congress's assertion in 1885 of federal jurisdiction over murder, rape, and other major crimes committed by Indians against Indians on reservations.[31] Ambiguity abounded, because the Supreme Court had just in 1883 affirmed the jurisdictional dimension of sovereignty on reservations, and there seemed no constitutional basis (yet) for this assertion of jurisdiction.[32] The *Kagama* Court found no grounding in the Constitution and appeared to struggle for a legal logic to Congress's brash action:

> It seems to us that this is within the competency of Congress. These Indian tribes *are* the wards of the nation. They are communities *dependent* on the United States.... The power of the General Government over these remnants of a race once powerful, now weak and diminished in numbers, is necessary for their protection.[33]

Kevin Washburn has called this the "It Must be Somewhere Doctrine" of federal Indian law. The Indian tribes are dependent on the United States as wards to a guardian, "so it must have this power."[34]

In this vein, it was the Supreme Court's decision in *Lone Wolf v. Hitchcock* (1903) that earned the dubious distinction as the *Dred Scott* decision of federal Indian law.[35] In *Lone Wolf*, a savvy Kiowa traditionalist challenged forced allotment of reservation lands in Oklahoma secured in the 1867 Treaty of Medicine Lodge.[36] Extending the logic of *Kagama*, the Court recognized Congress's power to unilaterally abrogate a treaty. Congress was empowered to exercise "Plenary Power," trumping the Supremacy Clause and subject only to the limitations of good faith.[37] The *Lone Wolf* Court even concluded that Congress had always enjoyed this power and that treaties were always provisional in this regard.[38] While courts have since asserted limits on this congressional power, *Lone Wolf* remains valid precedent, securing for Congress the continued legal authority to abrogate terms of treaties when its statutes (or their legislative history) show its intent to do so.[39] The Supreme Court has even recognized as lawful "quiet abrogations" of treaty terms in cases where Congress passes laws of generally applicability, such as with the Bald and Golden Eagle Protection Act or the Endangered Species Act.[40]

Sovereignty Affirmed

There have been other, more recent, decisions in the line of *Lone Wolf* that have narrowed the scope of sovereignty.[41] But a countervailing thread of case law has, in turn, maintained or expanded those rights in certain contexts, first in assimilation-era holdings supporting tribal jurisdiction and customary law, but especially in the realm of off-reservation hunting, fishing, and gathering rights.[42] We turn now to these cases, for they involve reserved rights to maintain traditional practices and the spiritual relationships with lands and waters that are necessary to those practices.

U.S. v. Winans, 1903

Astoundingly, in the same year as *Lone Wolf*, the Supreme Court sided with Yakama treaty rights to access traditional salmon grounds. The Winans brothers, who operated fish wheels on the Columbia River for mass harvest of salmon, had excluded Yakama people from crossing their Homestead Act property to access the river for traditional salmon fishing. The brothers argued they bought the land from the United States without any knowledge of an easement for tribal members. The Court reversed lower court decisions and sided with the Yakama, concluding that their "reserved right" in the 1859 Treaty with the United States to off-reservation fishing "at all usual and accustomed places, in common with citizens of the Territory" outweighed any property rights to exclude them.[43] In *Winans*, the Court identified a crucial truth about the nature of treaties, one often mistaken by those who view Native peoples as special populations "given" special rights by the United States.

> The treaty was not a grant of rights to the Indians, but a grant of rights from them—a reservation of those not granted.[44]

This "reserved rights doctrine" helps understand how "reservations" are not simply the land bases set apart in treaties, but are also bundled with other unspecified rights that are not expressly extinguished in treaties.

LIMITED INHERENT SOVEREIGNTY

How were courts to square such decisions as *Kagama* and *Lone Wolf* with the Marshall decisions of the 1820s and 1830s and with *Winans*? On what basis could the US Indian policy affirmations of sovereignty and self-determination make legal sense from the 1970s forward? An answer lay in the game-changing work of a government lawyer, Felix Cohen, whose *Handbook of Federal Indian Law*, first published widely in 1942 as a government document, synthesized the unwieldy body of federal Indian law and made it comprehensible in terms of principles of limited sovereignty laid out in the Marshall cases that were qualified but not quashed by subsequent decisions. According to Charles Wilkinson, Cohen "effectively stemmed the tide of opinions that threatened to bury the doctrine of tribal sovereignty in the name of changed circumstances."[45] Cohen's 1942 position is worth quoting as it has been regarded as "the single most influential passage ever written by an Indian law scholar":[46]

> Perhaps the most basic principle of all Indian Law is the principle that those powers which are lawfully vested in an Indian tribe are not, in general, delegated powers granted by express acts of Congress, but rather inherent powers of a limited sovereignty which has never been extinguished. Each Indian tribe begins its relationship with the Federal Government as a sovereign power, recognized as such in treaty and legislation. The powers of sovereignty have been limited from time to time by special treaties and laws.... What is not expressly limited remains within the domain of tribal sovereignty.[47]

Solemn Treaties and Salmon

The Boldt Decision and Canons of Construction

Contemporary treaty rights were deeply strengthened by a 1974 decision in favor of Native nations' reserved fishing rights vis-à-vis the state of Washington's power to regulate salmon. In a complicated stream of decisions, federal district judge George H. Boldt's holding in favor of reserved treaty rights for traditional fishing and its justification under the "canons of construction" were affirmed by the Ninth Circuit and by the Supreme Court in a related proceeding in 1979,[48] but it is often Judge Boldt's original opinion that is cited.[49] Indeed, the Boldt Decision has been crucial to the Makah whaling and Anishinaabe cases to which I'll turn shortly. The decision combined claims of more than a dozen distinct Native nations who were successors to the treaty signatories, including the Makah and Yakama.

When they ceded vast parts of their territory to the United States in the 1850s, leaders of these nations insisted on retaining rights to fishing at "usual and accustomed places," but even with theoretical protection by courts of those rights in *Winans*, treaty rights were routinely overridden on the ground, with Native fishermen arrested for fishing without a license, out of season, or for violating other state regulations.[50]

Something Religious at Stake

Clearly more was at stake than economic livelihood for these Native nations, whose very peoplehood is interwoven with salmon in mutual relations of support and respect. So traditional fishing practices are economic, but they are also matters of community health, and governed by ethical and ritual obligations of religion. From 1964 on, Indigenous activists led by Billy Frank Jr. had been conducting *fish-ins*, using their bodies to assert treaty rights to take salmon in traditional ways despite the state of Washington's aggressive enforcement of regulations favoring commercial and recreational fishing interests. With pressure building—Frank was himself arrested more than fifty times—the United States filed suit, joined by tribes, in a treaty-based challenge to how Washington regulated salmon fishing and habitat.[51] In the years leading up to the 1974 decision, both sides exhaustively engaged anthropologists, linguists, historians, and biologists to help inform the Judge Boldt's ambitious goal "to determine every issue of fact and law presented and, at long last, thereby finally settle ... as many as possible of the divisive problems of treaty right fishing which for so long have plagued all of the citizens of this area, and still do."[52]

Boldt's ruling didn't turn on religious rights to salmon, but it did pay more than lip service to the ceremonial and ethical obligations related to traditional fishing:

> The first-salmon ceremony, which with local differences in detail was general through most of the area, was essentially a religious rite to ensure the continued return of salmon. The symbolic acts, attitudes of respect and reverence, and concern for the salmon reflected a ritualistic conception of the interdependence and relatedness of all living things which was a dominant feature of the native Indian world view. Religious attitudes and rites

FIG. 7.1. First Salmon Ceremony at Lummi Nation
Elaborate First Salmon Ceremonies of Pacific Northwest peoples conclude
with the return of the first salmon's uneaten parts to the sea out of respect
and reciprocity. Judge Boldt referred to the ceremonies in his decision
affirming treaty rights to fish. (Photo Courtesy Lummi Nation)

insured that salmon were never wantonly wasted and that water pollution
was not permitted during the salmon season.[53]

More than an isolated single ritual, the annual ceremony reiterated sacred
narratives, dramatized ethical teachings, and renewed a reciprocal relationship between people and salmon. "The Yakimas continue as a religious rite
not only the first salmon ceremony," the court elaborated, "but the basic, un-
dying salmon culture existing in this northwest area, and this religious concept of the interdependence and relatedness of all living things is a dominant
feature of their life-style."[54] The court noted how such religious and cultural
commitments found expression in contemporary Indigenous self-regulation
of fishing on their reservations and of their members off-reservation. If fisheries could not sustain commercial fishing, Yakama self-regulation prioritized ceremonial fishing, followed by subsistence fishing, over commercial
fishing.[55]

Such observations by the court took their place alongside inquiries into
locations of traditional waters for fishing, historical accounts of treaty negotiations, and the like, but those about the religious and cultural importance of

salmon to Native peoples helped underscore the urgency with which Native leaders reserved their rights to continue their salmon-related lifeways and obligations. Appeals to the religious beliefs and practices helped affirm for Judge Boldt what was at stake for Native peoples in the solemn treaties in question. And when the Supreme Court weighed in to reaffirm Judge Boldt's decision, it noted the religious relationship between salmon peoples and salmon:

> Religious rites were intended to insure the continual return of the salmon and the trout; the seasonal and geographic variations in the runs of the different species determined the movements of the largely nomadic tribes [*sic*]. Fish constituted a major part of the Indian diet, was used for commercial purposes, and indeed was traded in substantial volume.[56]

Canons of Construction

The legal question in *United States v. Washington* was the proper meaning of a phrase common to a series of treaties negotiated in the 1850s between Isaac Stevens, governor of the Washington Territory, and fourteen Native nations:

> The right of taking fish, at all usual and accustomed grounds and stations, is further secured to said Indians, in common with all citizens of the Territory, and of erecting temporary houses for the purposes of curing.[57]

The state of Washington maintained that "in common with all citizens of the Territory" meant that any subsequent Indian fishing would be subject to regulations applying commonly to all citizens. The United States and the tribes maintained that the phrase had been understood by Indigenous signatories as the continuation of shared fishing among Native and non-Natives without interference from the other party and this view prevailed.

Judge Boldt's decision drew on a mass of academic research assembled surrounding the treaty negotiations. Few of the Native participants spoke English, and the Chinook Jargon, a trade pidgin of sparse vocabulary, was the medium by which the legal fine points were related to them. The court found nothing in the archives "to indicate that the Indians were told that their existing fishing activities or tribal control over them would in any way be restricted or impaired by the treaty."[58] Judge Boldt applied the canons of construction, principles of interpretation of treaties that considered translational and other inequities at play in the proceedings.

The canons of construction incline courts to apply these three principles of interpretation to treaties with Native peoples:

(1) Ambiguous expressions must be resolved in favor of the Indian parties concerned.[59]

(2) Indian treaties must be interpreted as the Indians themselves would have understood them.[60]

(3) Indian treaties must be liberally construed in favor of the Indians.[61]

Given the level of scrutiny of the scholarship the case involved, and the scrutiny of Judge Boldt's decision by the Ninth Circuit on appeal, and later, in a related action, by the Supreme Court in 1979, *United States v. Washington* served to bolster the canons of construction and frame them anew for subsequent treaty rights litigation. The Supreme Court affirmed the resounding result of Judge Boldt's interpretation:

> By dictionary definition and as intended and used in Indian treaties and in this decision "in common with" means *sharing equally* the opportunity to take fish at "usual and accustomed grounds and stations": therefore nontreaty fisherman shall have the opportunity to take up to 50% of the harvestable number of fish that may be taken by all fishermen at usual and accustomed grounds and stations and treaty right fisherman shall have the opportunity to take up to the same percentage of harvestable fish, as stated above.[62]

Fish caught for ceremonial or subsistence purposes, or those caught on reservation grounds, were not to be counted as part of the tribal share. Judge Boldt's decision ordered the state to regulate nontreaty fishing accordingly, which it so haltingly did that he called on the Coast Guard to help enforce the court order. Even with the Ninth Circuit's affirmation of the ruling and the Supreme Court's rejection of Washington's request for a hearing of the case on appeal, nontreaty fishermen's groups and Washington state were not in compliance. Boldt received death threats.

Several years later, the Supreme Court agreed to hear a related proceeding to settle the matter and affirmed Judge Boldt's holding that tribes would receive up to 50 percent of harvestable fish at their usual and accustomed places and agreed with the rationale: "it is the intention of the parties, and not solely that of the superior side, that must control any attempt to interpret the treaties."[63] "The treaty must therefore be construed," the Supreme Court continued, "not according to the technical meaning of its words to learned lawyers, but in the sense in which they would naturally be understood by the Indians."[64]

River by River

The Supreme Court emphasized that 50 percent of the harvestable fish was a ceiling, not a minimum allocation, and applied a standard of "some apportionment that assured that the Indians' reasonable livelihood needs would be met."[65] The Court also noted that salmon populations are variable and thus "the share was to be calculated on a river-by-river, run-by-run basis," which introduced enormous complexity in real-time decisions about what treaty rights to take fish look like in any given year for any given nation. Litigation has settled, among other things, disputes about whether and how to count hatchery-bred fish in the allocations.[66]

Unsurprisingly, litigation has continued apace in the years since *United States v. Washington*.[67] Every case brought before the courts must pay careful attention to factual details on which the legal formulation of the allocation of treaty-based resources will rest.[68] Rooted in the Boldt Decision, which included some orders related to upstream salmon spawning grounds, there has been further litigation concerning sensitive salmon habitat and obstructions to rivers.

Indeed, as I was drafting this chapter in June 2018, the Supreme Court weighed in yet again on the issues of Judge Boldt's decision. In yet another *United States v. Washington* case, commonly known as the "Culverts" case, the Supreme Court split 4–4, leaving in force a Ninth Circuit holding that "the State violated the Treaties when it acted affirmatively to build roads across salmon bearing streams, with culverts that allowed passage of water but not passage of salmon."[69] Washington is now obligated to replace, at considerable expense, those culverts such that salmon can pass through to reach their spawning grounds.

Makah Whaling

A Whaling People

The Makah, the southernmost community of Nuu-chah-nulth (Nootka) people, have always been a whaling people. A recent archaeological dig at Ozette confirmed their oral traditions and showed evidence of Makah whaling for several thousand years, and whale use at other sites for more than twice that.[70] Their sense of peoplehood has been grounded in their relationship with whales, and this relationship has always been a deeply spiritual one. We learn from Charlotte Coté that the Nuu-chah-nulth language word for whale, *iihtuup*, means "big mystery." Sacred stories tell of the Thunderbird's first hunt for a whale with lightning, and family lineages retain their own stories of ancestral links with whales and whaling. Naming practices make clear that many of their sacred sites are associated with storied whales of the past. Elaborate songs and ritual practices accompany the spiritual preparations for whaling.

At the heart of the reciprocal relationship between whales and the people has been the tenet that the whale chooses the whaler. "A whaler believed that a specific whale gave itself to him, through a mysterious power," writes Charlotte Coté:

> Prayer and cleansing the mind and body made the whaler worthy of the great whale's gift of life. When the whaler went out to sea and reached the place where thousands of whales were migrating up the coast, when he got there he didn't harpoon the first whale he saw, he identified the one that he was intended to kill. That one was looking for him, too. They recognized each other. The whale gives himself to the hunter who has been praying and who is clean.[71]

The spiritual preparation could involve months of bodily regimens and disciplined contemplation. As Richard Umeek Atleo put it, "the great personage of the whale demanded the *honor* of extended ceremony."[72] *Oo-simch* is ritual bathing in cold water and typically scrubbing with evergreen boughs, together with its associated songs and prayer and regimens of abstinence from sex, intoxicants, and certain foods. Coté glosses *oo-simch* as a matter of being careful in the presence of supernatural power; she notes it is about cultivating inner ethical and ritual purity as well as outward bodily purity. Paying respects at familial shrines and performing rites that have been specifically handed down within lineages has also been part of these traditions. And the whalers were not alone obligated by these practices. While the whalers themselves undertook these practices, their wives, families, and the entire community had spiritual labor to do as well.[73]

A Seventy-Year Gap

When Makah leaders ceded much of their homeland to the United States in 1855, they insisted on the rights to continue to hunt on the sea, especially whales. Article 4 of the treaty enshrines the Makah's "right of taking fish and of whaling and sealing at usual and accustomed grounds and stations."[74] The Makah continued their ancient traditions of subsistence whaling, sealing, and fishing, even as formal policies of assimilation all but banned the ceremonial potlatch that culminated and celebrated their whaling hunts—for their Nuu-chah-nulth relatives in Canada, potlatches were explicitly outlawed in an 1884 amendment to the Indian Act.[75] But perhaps more than these constraints and settler encroachment, it was the commercial whaling industry that most interfered with their way of life. By the early twentieth century, commercial whaling, with its rapacious and wasteful search for whale oil, killed off the region's whale populations. The Makah hardly partook in the frenzy of commercial whaling, and out of a combination of a changing diet and concern for the depleted population of whales, the Makah voluntarily stopped whaling in the 1920s.[76] In the 1970s, gray whales were placed on the newly established list of endangered species, and their decline seemed indexical to Makah well-being. In this case correlation may be causation. One study related that "Elders and anthropologists trace the decline of the physical and social health of the tribe to the elimination of the whale hunt and its associated ceremonial and social rigors."[77] By the 1990s, unemployment on the Makah reservation was as high as 50 percent in summer and 75 percent in winter. In 1995, the average per capita income on the reservation was $5,200.[78]

The 1999 Whale Hunt

But a current brought tangible change. The salmon decisions of *United States v. Washington* had shored up the status of reserved rights to traditional practices in the usual and accustomed grounds and stations, with affirmation from the Supreme Court on the same body of treaties that included the 1855 Neah Bay Treaty reserving the right to hunt whales. And Endangered Species Act protection, along with considerable international efforts to restrict commercial whaling, had enabled the gray whale population to bounce back sufficiently to be delisted in 1994. Shortly thereafter, the Makah first notified the United States of their interest in a ceremonial and subsistence hunt, and with US approval, sought authorization from the IWC to hunt a small number of whales. Despite federal support, demonstration of "a continuing tradition" fell short for skeptical members of the commission and the Makah request was denied.[79] After changing its standards, the IWC by 1998 had authorized a five whale quota—one for each of the five Makah villages—over two years for ceremonial and subsistence purposes, requiring a Makah whaling commission to ensure a traditional and self-regulated hunt. All the careful plans of the Makah Whaling Commission—to have motorized safety boats on hand, to use a high-powered rifle to bring a swifter, safer, and more humane death to the harpooned whale, were included as part of the government approval process.

An environmental assessment (EA) concluded that the small amount of whales proposed for the hunt constituted a Finding of No Significant Impact, but opponents filed suit that the United States had violated NEPA in not requiring a fuller EIS. A federal judge ruled that the EA was sufficient and that the Makah proposal could go ahead.[80]

The Makah Whaling Commission selected a group of whalers representative of the "major Makah families" and evaluated their progress in physical, mental, and ceremonial preparation for the hunt. Understandably, many found the abstinence required tremendously challenging, but multiple accounts attest to the gradual transformation of the whaling crew and community as a result.[81] If *oo-simch* at its core is spiritual preparation to be respectful of mysterious spiritual power, accounts suggest the depth of their preparation, especially in light of the mounting opposition to their endeavor. Working through self-doubt that they could never live up to their ancestral Makah ideals, the whalers were reticent to speak in such terms, but the work, and transformation, was spiritual as much as physical and mental. After all, their tradition underscored the open question: would the whaler prove worthy enough to be chosen by a whale?

When the hunt was declared on, doubts intensified after two unsuccessful days with many watching.[82] But early on the third day, a whale was sighted and successfully harpooned "with a force that was aided by ancestral strength" and then brought to shore for a ceremonial welcoming and thanksgiving by over 1,400 Makah people.[83] Janine Bowechop (Ledford) chronicled the moment: "the whale was sung to, prayed over, and thanked for giving itself life in order that our community might thrive."[84] A feast similar to a potlatch later brought the Makah community together with guests from neighboring peoples. Meat, blubber, and oil were distributed to reservation families who tasted, many for the first time, their Makah soul food. Charlotte Coté has explored the effects in different registers of the return of whale products in the Makah diet: "because our traditional foods have cultural, social, and spiritual significance, the harvesting and sharing of these foods unite our communities while putting *nanash'aqtl* (health) food on our dinner tables."[85] "The real possibilities for the future of the Makah tribe are brighter than ever before," Janine Bowechop (Ledford) writes, "and much of this is because of the existence of the opportunity for whale hunting":

> At a local café a child of a friend of our family looked lovingly at his mother and said, "When I get big, Mom, I'm going to get you a whale."[86]

Legal Barriers to Makah Whaling since 1999

The taste for whale, and for the social and spiritual wholeness that the 1999 hunt brought, only grew sharper. A needs assessment for an application to continue the hunt involved a survey of the Makah membership. Ninety-three percent of respondents favored another hunt. More than half cited as the most important reason for continuing the hunt either "maintaining or restoring some aspect of cultural heritage or tradition" or "moral or spiritual benefits, such as changed lifestyle, better discipline, or increased pride."[87]

But outside opposition was gaining steam too. Since the 1999 hunt, the environmental laws typically used by Native nations to protect natural and cultural resources had been successfully used against any further authorized hunts. Just after the hunt was completed, the Ninth Circuit reversed the lower court ruling that had opened the way to that hunt. The Ninth Circuit said that an environmental review had improperly come on the heels, rather than in advance, of the US agreement with the Makah to support the hunt before the IWC.[88] A new EA was completed in 2001 and resulted in another Finding of No Significant Impact, since five gray whales per year for ceremonial and subsistence purposes was insignificant to an estimated population of 26,000.[89] Opponents filed suit again, but the same district court judge concluded that "the federal agencies had taken the requisite 'hard look' at the risks," finding no violation of NEPA or the Marine Mammals Protection Act (MMPA).[90] And again, the Ninth Circuit reversed on appeal, requiring a fuller EIS to take into account new science about gray whale populations and placing an injunction on any whaling in the meantime.[91]

Still operating within their IWC quota approval, in 2005, the Makah filed for a waiver under the MMPA to take up to twenty whales for ceremonial and subsistence purposes over any five-year period—up to five each year, one for each Makah village. Thus began another environmental review, resulting in a nine-hundred-page Draft EIS in 2008 finding no major impacts from the Makah proposal. But the effort was complicated in 2007, when five Makah men killed a whale with permission from neither the United States nor the Makah Council. The men were charged in tribal court and also in federal court and found guilty of criminal violations of the MMPA.

After further legal challenges, the government terminated its 2008 Draft EIS because of still new scientific information about whale populations, and only in March 2015 had a new Draft EIS been published for public comment. At the time of this writing, there is still no Final EIS for the granting of the exemption under the MMPA, and further litigation and negotiations have yet to clear the way for a return to the renewed whaling tradition begun twenty years previous.[92]

Anishinaabe Fishing and Ricing

Emboldened by the Northwest fish-ins and the Boldt Decision, Ojibwe and Odawa people (Anishinaabe) asserted their rights to take fish off-reservation under treaties ceding lands that became Michigan, Wisconsin, and Minnesota. And federal courts largely have backed their claims, beginning with assertions in the late 1970s of treaty claims to harvest fish in the Great Lakes by Michigan's Anishinaabe.[93] The focus here will be on Wisconsin in the 1980s and Minnesota in the 1990s. While the issues have been largely settled in courts, there remain ongoing negotiations in terms of resource co-management between the treaty tribes and the states and perennial challenges in terms of non-Native public opinion.

Where Food Grows on the Water: Anishinaabe Akiing

The Anishinaabe people (pl. Anishinaabeg) include the Ojibwe (Ojibwa, Chippewa) and their Odawa (Ottawa) and Potawatomi allies. Their vast traditional territory surrounds the western Great Lakes, stretching from Toronto on the east to Ontario and Manitoba to the north, to Michigan, Wisconsin, and Minnesota, and stretching on to the Plains in North Dakota and Saskatchewan. Never a single nation with a centralized government, the Anishinaabeg have been united by language, culture, and religion in a thick weave of relationships among clans and local communities. They have also been united by a collective calling to live well in right relationship with their traditional lands and waters. In the poetics of the Ojibwe language, their name for that vast territory, *anishinaabe akiing*, is grammatically reciprocal: it can be translated "the people's land" or "the land's people." The belonging goes both ways.

While historians consider Anishinaabe movement into the region to be a function of the fur trade, for Anishinaabe people, the story of their migration is all about the sacred: in obedience to prophetic visions, the Anishinaabe moved west from the Atlantic seaboard until they arrived where "food grows on the water."[94] That food, wild rice, or *manoomin*, rises above the shallow clear waters of the region's lakes and quiet rivers. Manoomin is traditional staple, but it is also an Anishinaabe sacred food. Manoomin is present at all feasts and ceremonies, the traditional first food for a baby and a traditional food for a "spirit plate" to feed the souls of the dead.[95]

The Anishinaabe traditional lifeway has also been in motion. Often called the seasonal round, the Anishinaabe lifeway of the western Great Lakes is calendrical, moving with the resource base of each season. From setting up sugar camps when the maple sap starts to run in early spring, to spear fishing at later spring spawning times, to gardening and fish netting at their summer lakeshore villages, to harvesting rice at early fall camps, and to harvesting manoomin and to big game and waterfowl hunting in fall and winter. Although keyed to each of these seasonal foods of the land and waters, this has not simply been an economy of maximizing resource potential or even just an elegant cultural ecology; the seasonal round has been tied in with ethical obligations to trees, fish, berries, wild rice, and deer, and ritual obligations to maintain proper relationships with the spirits behind them.[96] One might even call the seasonal round a *liturgical* calendar: each season with its organizing practice, each with its own sacred songs, stories, and ceremonial teachings. Indeed, the names of the lunar months of an Anishinaabe calendar evoke these themes: Maple Sugar Moon, Strawberry Moon, Wild Ricing Moon, Great Spirit Moon. To live well has had spiritual, moral, and aesthetic dimensions as well as economic and ecological ones.

Treaties and Retained Fishing/Gathering Rights

Accordingly, when faced with having to cede beloved homelands to become Michigan, Wisconsin, and Minnesota, Anishinaabe leaders commonly negotiated for provisions that retained their rights to hunt, fish, and gather in ceded territories. This was, after all, the way Anishinaabe people imagined *anishinaabe akiing*, territory imagined not in terms of property title but of rights to use. As Charles Wilkinson writes, they "came to the bargaining table with considerable sophistication. They not only loved their land, they knew it. They also knew the commercial uses that the white people wanted to make of the land, especially in terms of the surging timber and minerals industries."[97]

In the Treaty of 1837, Anishinaabe leaders retained "the privilege of hunting fishing, and gathering the wild rice, upon the lands, the rivers and the lakes included in the territory ceded ... during the pleasure of the President of the United States."[98] The 1842 Treaty of LaPointe similarly provides, "The Indians stipulate for the right of hunting on the ceded territory, with the other usual privileges of occupancy, until required to remove by the President of the United States."[99]

Even as they incorporated new elements into their ways and as their lives became largely confined to reservations, Anishinaabe people resolutely continued the practice of their seasonal round. And while they chose to reserve homelands that could support their lifeway, practices of the seasonal round often took them off-reservation to traditional ricing lakes, sugar bushes, and spawning grounds, places to which their leaders had taken pains to secure continued access in treaty negotiations.

But in the later nineteenth century, allotment and the taking of timber took a heavy toll on the ecosystems that sustained the seasonal round on the reservation. Immigrant settlement on ceded lands, and the developing apparatus of state conservation to ensure hunting and fishing of commodified game fish for sport, led to what ethnohistorian Bruce White has aptly called "the criminalization of the seasonal round."[100] Where killing deer, ducks, and fish for sport rather than necessity violated Indigenous ethical and spiritual commitments to deer, ducks, and fish, continued Anishinaabe practices were targeted as particularly primitive and unsportsmanlike, and prosecuted accordingly.[101] The Wisconsin Supreme Court—hardly the venue for a treaty rights decision—ignored the US Supreme Court's ruling three years earlier in *U.S. v. Winans* and found that Wisconsin statehood had abrogated Anishinaabe fishing, hunting, and gathering rights under the 1837 and 1842 treaties.[102]

So the treaty language still stood—the law of the land. But in the years of Assimilation Policy, the Anishinaabeg had few legal cards to play. Outlawed practices of the seasonal round became even more symbolically charged with peoplehood. Larry Nesper observes that "violating," the practice of asserting Indigenous hunting, fishing, trapping, and gathering rights, had grown in importance in Native communities in these years, an essential mark of manhood and even drawing on "warrior" discourse. Women, too, asserted sovereignty by boldly continuing to pick berries in the traditional manner on ceded lands.[103] Anishinaabe fishers in Michigan, then Wisconsin, then Minnesota asserted their treaty rights to take fish in traditional ways that violated state regulations about seasons, methods, and licensure, and often with full expectation of arrest.

Walleye Warriors

In 1974, Fred and Mike Tribble, members of the Lac Courte Oreilles Band of Lake Superior Chippewa, told Wisconsin game wardens that they planned to exercise their rights under the 1837 and 1842 treaties to spear fish off-reservation. As Walt Bresette, another "walleye warrior," told it, "they crossed the imaginary reservation line on frozen Chief Lake near Lac Courte Oreilles, cut a hole in the ice and speared a fish" until state game wardens rushed to arrest them.[104] Not only were they asserting rights to fish off-reservation, they also were fishing using traditional methods of spearing.

Thus began nine years of litigation.[105] As in the Pacific Northwest, the continued assertion of those treaty rights provoked an aggressive backlash. This was especially true after 1983, when the Seventh Circuit Court of Appeals affirmed treaty rights to hunt, fish, and gather on public lands off the reservation.[106] The Lac Courte Oreilles Band had brought suit, but members of Lac du Flambeau and other signatory bands also took to the lakes in early May, practicing a tradition deeply resonant with Anishinaabe identity. That tradition has involved going out to spawning beds in canoes at night, and spearing walleyes by torchlight. The very name Lac du Flambeau (Lake of the Torches), a translation of *waswaaganing*, references this practice.[107]

Opponents to the treaty rights assembled at Anishinaabe fishing sites with slogans that said "Save a Walleye, Spear an Indian" or even "Save Two Walleyes, Spear a Pregnant Indian." One poster depicted a frontal view of the barrel of a large handgun with the caption: "Spear This!" A company even issued beer in cans called "Treaty Beer," proceeds of which funded opposition to treaty rights. Even as they offered tobacco to the fish in thanksgiving, purified themselves for the onslaught with smudging sage and accompanied by prayers and drum songs, treaty fishers were spat on, threatened, and harassed as though they were smoking marijuana. Ceremony was recognized only as trouble-making and defiled by opponents of treaty rights. But as Larry Nesper argues in *The Walleye War*, the stage of the assertions of treaty rights helped produce awakened pride and freshly embraced identity as Anishinaabe people.[108]

Opponents' concerns were both highly symbolic and economic: symbolic because they concerned walleyes, the gold standard of northern Wisconsin

FIG. 7.2. Ojibwe Spearfishing, 1988
Lac du Flambeau's Mike Chosa showed Harold Jackson a walleye speared in a traditional Ojibwe manner on Wisconsin's Balsam Lake in April 1988. Lac du Flambeau is the French translation of the Ojibwe name for a reservation lake, referring to the seasonal practice of spearing fish from canoes by torchlight. (Photo Courtesy of Jeff Wheeler)

game fish, and economic because of the importance to the region of angling tourism. Opponents were thus politically well positioned to press the state of Wisconsin to vigorously defend what they saw as its rights to regulate fishing and hunting in the state, and in the face of decisions in favor of the treaties, to continue to constrain the reach of those rights.

"Complex Litigation"

The 1983 Seventh Circuit decision that opened the door to the controversy specifically held that the reserved off-reservation rights so clearly stated in the treaties of 1837 and 1842 were not, as the trial court had previously found, extinguished by the Treaty of 1854 or by an 1850 removal order by President Zachary Taylor. The appeals court found Taylor's order exceeded the authority of the executive branch under the treaties, and it drew on Supreme Court distinctions between aboriginal rights and treaty-recognized rights of use, where the treaty-recognized rights of use required a higher "degree of explicitness" for Congress to abrogate them.[109] This distinction informed how the Seventh Circuit regarded Wisconsin's claim that the treaties' usufruct rights were only temporary because they were qualified in the 1837 Treaty to be effective "during the pleasure of the President" and in the 1842 Treaty "until required to remove by the President." Applying the canons of construction, the court observed that the Indians understood these clauses to apply only if they misbehaved or harassed white settlers. And the Seventh Circuit disagreed with Wisconsin that the rights were extinguished by the Treaty of 1854, which made no mention of off-reservation rights even as it established reservations on the lands ceded in the 1837 and 1842 treaties. "Treaty-recognized rights cannot," the court held, "be abrogated by implication."[110]

The case was remanded down to the district court to work out details, and back up to the appellate court, for an impressive total of seven distinct rulings.[111] These details included determining on which public lands treaty rights remained in force, how to consider related hunting, trapping, and maple sugaring rights, and how to allocate harvest rights to walleye and other fish between treaty fishers and others. Because the Great Lakes treaties did not include the "in common with other citizens" language of the Pacific Northwest treaties, there is no straightforward 50/50 allocation, but rather sufficient allocation to treaty fishers to support "a moderate living."[112] Notable is the clear desire to regulate their own harvests, drawing on Indigenous knowledge and Anishinaabe ethical commitments to co-manage the fisheries with Wisconsin in keeping with those principles.

This is an interesting outcome of treaty rights litigation: the creation of compacts and agreements for co-management of natural resources and the emergence of treaty-based intertribal organizations to self-regulate tribal members. In 1984, eleven Anishinaabe bands across Michigan, Wisconsin, and Minnesota formed the Great Lakes Indian Fish and Wildlife Commission to support that co-management and bring traditional ecological knowledge together with conservation biology and resource management science. Similar groups have formed in Michigan and Minnesota.[113]

Anishinaabe court victories over Michigan and Wisconsin emboldened one of the 1837 treaty signatories in Minnesota, the Mille Lacs Band, to press its fishing, hunting, and gathering rights in spite of Minnesota's claimed rights to regulate those activities off-reservation. The circumstances in Minnesota differed somewhat, but *Minnesota v. Mille Lacs Band of Chippewa Indians* wound up in the Supreme Court in 1999, and thus brought the High Court's affirmation of the off-reservation reserved rights in the other Anishinaabe cases.[114]

Like the Wisconsin case, *Mille Lacs* involved complex litigation in multiple phases over questions of the continued force of the reserved rights on ceded lands in the Treaty of 1837. Mille Lacs persuaded the district court, and then, on appeal, the Eighth Circuit and ultimately the Supreme Court that the treaty rights to fish, hunt, and gather on ceded lands had not been nullified by a presidential executive order or Minnesota statehood.[115] Neither had those rights been nullified by a provision of the Treaty of 1855 that included seemingly plain language of relinquishment of all rights to other lands in Minnesota, but that was not found to be understood by Anishinaabeg to relinquish their usufruct rights.[116]

In *Mille Lacs*, the Supreme Court solidified off-reservation treaty rights, and has further inspired some of the region's Anishinaabe nations to insist not only on off-reservation rights under the 1855 Treaty but also to claim legal leverage in efforts to protect habitat for wild rice and fish on ceded lands. In Minnesota, at the time of this writing, the zigzag route of Enbridge Energy's proposed Line 3 pipeline replacement, carrying Alberta Tar Sands oil to ports on the Great Lakes, avoids reservations but traverses ceded territories under the 1855 Treaty where Anishinaabe claim off-reservation fishing, ricing, and hunting rights.

Treaty Rights to Environmental Habitat Protection?

While courts have largely backed treaty claims to off-reservation fishing, hunting, and gathering, courts also have also held that states may lawfully regulate those practices in instances of conservation necessity or "highly probable irreparable harm to species."[117] One occasion for the possible alignment of Native interests and those of states is a shared concern for species and habitat conservation. According to the 2005 edition of *Cohen's Handbook of Federal Indian Law*, "courts have not yet definitively determined whether reserved rights to fishing, hunting, and gathering include rights to habitat protection for the species subject to the rights … but several decisions indicate courts' willingness to consider habitat a necessary part of the tribes' reserved treaty rights."[118] In its affirmation of the key elements of the 1974 Boldt Decision, the Supreme Court rejected the state of Washington's claim that rights to fishing "in common with the citizens" meant that treaty-fishers had an equal opportunity of access to try to catch fish in those places, not a guaranteed right to any harvest of fish.[119]

Indeed, the productivity of traditional treaty fishing at usual and accustomed places on rivers had suffered greatly from commercial fishing at sea.

So it was recognized as a proportional right to *take*, not a right merely to *try*, in common with nontreaty fisherman.[120] And in the second phase of the initial *United States v. Washington* proceedings, the district court held that treaty-fishers' rights to "a sufficient quantity of fish to satisfy their moderate living needs" encompassed a "right to have the fishery habitat protected from man-made despoliation" in the case area.[121] The Ninth Circuit vacated in 1985 this habitat aspect of the decision.[122]

The Culverts *Case*

But in a more recent version of *United States v. Washington* before it, the Ninth Circuit went further.[123] In a case known as the *Culverts* case because the judgment binds the state of Washington to a multi-billion-dollar replacement of more than eight hundred culverts under state roadways shown clearly to obstruct salmon migrations, the Ninth Circuit extended the circumstances in which courts can affirm implied rights to habitat protection, or at least habitat access, for species involved in treaty protected rights. The court found about one thousand miles of upstream salmon habitat was blocked by the culverts, and that their replacement would mean several hundred thousand more salmon each year.[124] The Ninth Circuit also drew on a 1983 water rights decision in which it ruled a federal agency had to secure sufficient flow in the Klamath River to supply water to a marsh, the health of which was necessary for the Klamath Nation to enjoy any meaningful reserved treaty rights to hunt, fish, and gather on their reservation.[125]

The *Culverts* case is especially important because the US Supreme Court, which had agreed to hear an appeal, split 4–4, with Justice Kennedy recusing because as a sitting Ninth Circuit judge he had joined the opinion in the 1985 case. Although such a split does not produce an actual opinion to affirm, procedurally it lets the lower court decision stand. So while no court has "expressly found that tribes have a right to habitat protection that is implied from the treaty hunting, fishing, and gathering rights,"[126] the *Culverts* case goes far to suggest that in particular instances, where species stability is under dire threat, courts may feel emboldened.

Treaty Rights to Relationship

The as yet unsettled legal question of treaty rights to habitat highlights a truth: what animates Native assertions of treaty rights in each case considered in this chapter goes deeper than the assertion of legal and political sovereignty or of economic well-being, important as those dimensions are to Indigenous peoplehood. This something deeper, I would argue, can be called *religious*, and I mean this more than in the degree of urgency Native peoples feel about the political and economic issues. For these Native peoples, gray whales, salmon, walleye, and wild rice are not simply *resources*; they are relatives. And when Native people speak in such terms, they are doing so not simply out of a strategic poetics.

The point is made resoundingly by Frank Ettawageshik, director of the United Tribes of Michigan and fourteen-year tribal chair of the Little Traverse Band of Odawa. In speaking of the 50 percent property right to Great Lakes fish that courts assigned to Native signatories of the Treaty of 1836, Ettawageshik maintains that "the true treaty right" is not a quantifiable property right but a right to continued relationship to the fish:

> Our ancestors didn't say "those are our fish." Rather, they reserved the right to fish. That meant they reserved a right to sing to the fish, to dance for the fish, to pray for the fish, to catch and eat the fish but to live with the fish, to have a relationship with the fish.[127]

The relationship does not, of course, mean that Great Lakes fish, or water, are not *resources*: One legal implication of this understanding of the treaty right as relationship would insist that a 50 percent allocation of harvestable fish is meaningless if the fish are inedible because of pollution. But the treaty right to relationship runs deeper than a legal entitlement to a quantified resource; it has to do with a spiritual relationship and with peoplehood.

Conclusion: Religion as Peoplehood

In this chapter we have considered cases within the body of federal Indian law where the assertion of treaty rights has offered Native nations significant legal opportunities to protect traditional practices like fishing that I have observed are at once economic, cultural, social, and religious, and that threats to the continuation of those practices heighten their simultaneously religious and political valence. Even more than the protections under environmental and cultural resource law, protections under treaty rights have been important for Native nations pressing beyond the shut doors of religious freedom protection to articulate claims to practices and places important to them. As we have seen, federal Indian law has both qualified and affirmed treaty rights and Indigenous sovereignty. And to be sure not all Native people have treaties, or have treaties that reserve specific rights, like those of whaling and fishing considered above, that can serve as footholds for these kinds of claims. Still, especially where treaties expressly do reserve such rights, defending the sacred not in discrete terms of religion or even of cultural resource but in terms of peoplehood has brought considerable success.[128] The chapter concludes with four observations about the cases considered above.

Explicitly not Religious

First, the arguably *religious* aspects of traditional practices (whaling, salmon fishing, ricing) in these cases are elided into broader claims of peoplehood. That the claims do not turn on the religious nature of these practices, or the specific ceremonies that obtain, requires no showing of their genuine religiousness, no need to disclose the details of ceremonies in question, or to pass muster on some *substantial burden* analysis that has been produced in case law concerning Christianity, or to empanel elders and spiritual leaders to offer public interpretations of their meaning and reach.

What is more, in these cases any serious attention to the ceremonial nature of the claims may help lay rhetorical claim to the urgency of the cause, but legally it can be as much liability as asset. For example, when there are other claims, like treaty claims, to be made, bringing religious freedom arguments at the same time can cast aspersions on the whole affair. In *U.S. v. Dion*, the Supreme Court held against two Yankton Dakota men who were arrested under the criminal provisions of the Bald and Golden Eagle Protection Act for hunting eagles within the bounds of their reservation. The Supreme Court ruled that their otherwise valid treaty rights were abrogated, if quietly, by Congress's passage of the law.

When Dion initially brought suit, though, his challenges included not only his nation's inherent sovereignty to regulate hunting within reservation boundaries but also a First Amendment Free Exercise claim, one that was rejected by the Eighth Circuit even as it affirmed the treaty right because the taking of the four eagles, the court concluded, was primarily commercial, even though Dion was engaged in provisioning ceremonial users of the feathers.[129] Here the potential economic function of a practice tarnishes by association the sincerity of its asserted religiousness. Every case considered in this chapter has involved practices that are at once economic, cultural, and religious, but especially in the minds of detractors, religious and deep cultural claims are undercut by association with their economic benefit. A similar reticence to speak extensively of rights to ceremonial or religious freedom is striking in the salmon and Makah whaling cases. The First Salmon Ceremony is discussed in the Boldt Decision, but it is hardly elaborated there, or in the subsequent rulings. Below, behind, and around these diminutions of the religious claims is a presumption that animates other cases seen through this book. *Real* Native American religions belong, like other *real* religions but even more so, to a separate sphere insulated from the legal and political processes concerned with interpretations of treaties, or of estimates of fish and whale populations. Efforts to bring religion into those discussions can appear, to non-Natives anyway, as opportunistic, even disingenuous. If the Makah really were practicing their spiritual relationship with whales, according to this perspective, they wouldn't hunt them; they would hug them.

Freedom to Regulate

Relatedly, if Makah whalers and Anishinaabe walleye warriors are criticized by opponents as interest groups taking advantage of special rights and using appeals to the sacred to claim those rights as absolute and non-negotiable, and thus conversation stoppers, the assertion of those treaty rights is better understood as a conversation starter. The *freedom from* state regulation asserted under reserved treaty rights has always been for Indigenous peoples a *freedom to* regulate for themselves their traditional practices. This is a freedom to regulate in accordance with traditional cultural teachings and religious commitments at once ethical and ritual. It can be regarded as a right not only to regulate activities related to resources, but to reimagine what natural and cultural resources are from Indigenous perspectives. Indigenous resource management is often shaped by that discourse, but it is also accountable to traditional ecological knowledge, informed by sacred stories in the oral traditions, ritual and ceremony, and Indigenous authority structures.

This is important to reckon with fully in an effort to understand Indigenous religions on their own terms as highly disciplined religions and not simply as the free-ranging individual spiritualities that to a romanticizing imagination are the opposite of "organized religion." My students are repeatedly surprised at how "strict" Native traditions can seem in terms of ethical and ritual rigor. Kristen Carpenter argues that these limiting principles internal to Native American traditions show how grossly exaggerated are judicial worries over slippery slope analyses of Native religious accommodations.[130] Native American religious freedom is, importantly, a matter of Native peoples' freedom to regulate themselves.

Religious Generativity

Larry Nesper has drawn careful attention to how the walleye wars were generative of ceremony and religious forms at the community level. "Cultural practices that had retreated to the relative privacy of extended family gatherings over the course of the century became realized once again at the community level," Nesper writes. "Large feasts and ceremonies bolstered and hardened the resolve of those who were taking the risk of reimagining Lac du Flambeau. Prophecy reemerged and played a key role in this unfolding drama."[131] Nesper begins his book not with the account of the Tribble brothers' initial assertion but with the Lac Du Flambeau Nation's refusal to accept a monetary settlement with Wisconsin to quiet the social unrest and extinguish their treaty claims in exchange for payments. Of course they refused, perhaps regarding their traditional practices as even more sacred than they had a decade earlier, not so much because they were threatened with desecration, but because they were productive and generative of an awakened sensibility for the beauty, spirit, and obligation of the Anishinaabe way of life.

Similarly, Charlotte Coté documents the generativity of the Makah whale hunt, the health and well-being and healing that can come from renewed relationships with whales and the sacred, and revitalized, traditions, language, and pride in Makah peoplehood. And as we have seen in the case of Makah whaling, recovery of the practice itself can teach the traditions. In a short documentary about the Tribble brothers, the Anishinaabe Lac Courte Oreilles Band members said that when they chose to become the test case to gain court recognition of treaty rights in Wisconsin, they had little idea how far-reaching would be the outcome:

> Mii'iw anishinaabe-izhitwaawin. Giishpin ani-bima'adooyaang miinawaa giga-mashkawizimin miinawaa.

> This is our way of life. If we follow this path again, we will be strong again.[132]

Plenary Power of Congress Looms

This chapter's stories, told in and through the law, are powerful stories, at once protective and generative of Native religious traditions. It would be prudent to note in conclusion, though, that their success owes much to the clarity of the specific reserved rights in the treaties in question. While reserved rights to, say, water need not be spelled out in the treaties themselves to be recognized as legally in force, salmon fishing and whaling rights in the Pacific Northwest gain traction because there are highly specific reserved right treaty provisions.[133] While the canons of construction enable courts to interpret treaties as Native peoples would have understood them, and while treaties are, in principle, the law of the land, looming above these cases is *Lone Wolf v. Hitchcock*—still regarded as *good law*, an operative precedent—that affirms Congress's power to abrogate provisions of any treaty subject to very little external scrutiny.

Courts have even upheld Congress's ability to "quietly" abrogate treaty protections, as in *U.S. v. Dion*. Citing that case as controlling precedent, courts have also found quiet abrogation through the Endangered Species Act of Seminole treaty rights to ceremonial, noncommercial hunting on their reservation. A federal court in Florida found lawful the arrest of Seminole tribal member James Billie for a ceremonial hunt on his reservation of a Florida panther, listed as an endangered species.[134]

It is perhaps a foregone conclusion under federal Indian law that tribal sovereignty will always be only "quasi-sovereign," for there are deep contradictions in its deepest roots, the Marshall trilogy. Where *Worcester v. Georgia* affirmed that treaties with Native peoples will continue to be the law of the land and solidified Cherokee internal sovereignty against state regulation by Georgia, *Cherokee Nation v. Georgia* sees to it that tribes will be "domestic, dependent nations," wards to the guardianship of the United States. And at the end of the day, the whole edifice rests on *Johnson v. M'Intosh* and the theological presumption—a contradiction if there ever was one for secular law—that absolute title belongs to the Christian discoverer and mere aboriginal rights of occupancy to the non-Christian Indigenous people. And after *Lone Wolf v. Hitchcock*, Congress's Plenary Power over Indian affairs looms. "In one grumpy afternoon," as Sam Deloria reportedly put it, Congress could do away with much of the apparatus of federal Indian law.[135]

The next chapter continues our exploration of legal protections for Native religions as peoplehood, stretching beyond these contradictions and constraints of federal Indian law, with its affirmation of a *qualified* tribal sovereignty into the discourse of *Indigenous rights* in international human rights law. In so doing, we will leave one set of constraints and possibilities for another.

8

Religion as Peoplehood

INDIGENOUS RIGHTS
IN INTERNATIONAL LAW

Indigenous peoples have the right to the full enjoyment, as a collective or as individuals, of all human rights and fundamental freedoms as recognized in the Charter of the United Nations, the Universal Declaration of Human Rights and international human rights law.

—ART. 1, UN DECLARATION ON THE RIGHTS OF INDIGENOUS PEOPLES

Introduction

We are in the early years of what promises to be a legal paradigm shift, as Native peoples increasingly articulate their sacred claims in the discourse of *Indigenous rights* and international human rights law. This possibility has been opened up by the United Nations Declaration on the Rights of Indigenous Peoples (UNDRIP), adopted nearly unanimously by the General Assembly in 2007, and endorsed by the United States with reservations in 2010.[1] The Organization of American States, to which the United States belongs, is also in the revision and consensus building process of its own Draft Declaration on the Rights of Indigenous Peoples.[2]

This chapter complements and completes the previous chapter's discussion of religion as peoplehood under treaty rights and domestic federal Indian law. It *completes* because international Indigenous rights presents the possibility of rising above the colonizing features of domestic federal Indian law: limited sovereignty, unilateral treaty abrogation, and congressional power over Indian affairs. It *complements* the previous chapter in that Native nations increasingly draw on both international Indigenous rights and federal Indian law to make their claims, because international law becomes most forceful when its norms suffuse domestic law. Indeed the nonbinding nature of the Declaration may commend this book's sustained case for recognition of the collective rights of Native American religious freedom under US law in the near term, while stressing the reconceptualization of these rights in terms of the Declaration.

I will not presume here to offer a full-on assessment of UNDRIP or its implementation; it is at once a nonbinding aspirational declaration and a crucial step in the development of norms and practice in customary international law and in the domestic policies of nation-states.[3] I also cannot offer a comprehensive discussion of the full range of international law instruments, or of the monitoring and reporting processes that are relevant to Indigenous rights. For that, I heartily refer the reader to James Anaya's *Indigenous Peoples in International Law*, a work as lucid as it is encyclopedic.[4] More modestly, my aim is to offer a close reading of UNDRIP and the human rights instruments it clarifies to show how the religious is absorbed into the cultural but ultimately folded into the larger bundle of collective rights associated with recognition of the world's Indigenous groups as peoples. Thus, religion as peoplehood. The religious, I will show, is in the Declaration everywhere and virtually nowhere at once in a manner that befits Native American traditions. And the Declaration's affirmation and elaboration of Indigenous self-determination extends to cultural self-determination in a manner that doesn't require Native nations to establish that their traditions count as religion. But because the Declaration insists that Indigenous peoples, not just people, carry human rights, I argue that religion can be read back into the Declaration as an important part of implementing UNDRIP in domestic US law. The ripening of the norms articulated in the Declaration and their implementation and enforcement largely depend on their recognition within domestic law and policy. This is important because where US law ensconces religion in the Constitution, one must look hard to find legal significance assigned to culture or cultural rights.

There is tremendous promise in this paradigm shift. Kristin Carpenter and Angela Riley frame the moment unleashed by UNDRIP as "jurisgenerative," rife with the creation of law.[5] Like the Amish and other strong communities, Indigenous peoples create law simply by living out their calling as religious peoples.[6] But Carpenter and Riley chart the energetic law-creation that, in the wake of UNDRIP, "is occurring at every level at which Indigenous peoples make and experience law: tribal, national, and international."[7] Walter Echo-

Hawk has argued that the norms of Indigenous rights elaborated in the UN Declaration offer a compelling international standard for addressing the "dark side" of federal Indian law and for commending court decisions that extend Native self-determination. Finally, the folding of claims to religion into claims to peoplehood helps resolve the central presenting problem of this book: the difficulty of trying to squeeze Indigenous traditions into the category of *religion*. This approach affirms cultural self-determination by which Indigenous communities themselves determine what matters to them for protection, and how. UNDRIP affirms Native peoples' right to restore, renew, and redirect their religions without calling into question their authenticity.

But even with a paradigm shift, law does not change overnight. For Native Americans in the United States, this elision of religion into culture, and finally into peoplehood, also risks losing the distinctive rhetorical and legal force of the language of religious freedom in US law. Although religious freedom rights figure into international law instruments, religion and religious freedom are hardly as salient in international law as they are in US law.

I will argue that making claims to religion as peoplehood, in the register of Indigenous rights in international law, may offer the best way forward in bringing existing domestic law, including religious freedom law, up to higher standards. I will also suggest how religion might be read back into Indigenous rights discourse in ways that will help its implementation in the context of the United States, where *religion* is a legal and rhetorical power word and *cultural rights* a legal footnote.

The prominence of the concept of religion is not in itself a concern; my goal here is not to argue for religion against all else. Still, as legal protections under Indigenous rights in international law grow in stature, and especially as Native peoples work to implement the norms of Indigenous rights from international law into domestic US law, there is value yet in the language of religion's specialness among other aspects of culture and as a driver of distinctive Indigenous connections to lands, waters, and resources.

Curiously, the specialness of religion, the distinctively spiritual nature of Indigenous rights, is as discursively prominent in Indigenous rights talk as it is legally negligible. Siegfried Wiessner regards the Indigenous rights movement as a "re-enchantment" of international law, a restoration of a holistic view of human rights. In contrast to the materialism and rationalism that Max Weber characterized as modernity's "disenchantment" of the world, "Indigenous peoples insist that they continue to live on the lands of their ancestors, in line with their ancient traditions. They are in particular need of protection as the survival of their languages, rituals, and cultural identities is often in moral peril."[8] Certainly, the discourse nourishing the growth of Indigenous rights has been decidedly spiritual in tone, not only refusing to reduce claims to territory, economic development, health, education, and political self-determination to secularized language but also drenching such claims in the sacred.[9]

The very category of *Indigenous* itself has been constituted in no small part by significant reference to attachments to place, territory, lands, and waters that are characterized by their spiritual nature and distinguishable from other strong connections to territories that even non-Indigenous peoples can have.

If so much of indigeneity is articulated in the register of the sacred, then some of this international law rings strangely hollow. In UNDRIP, the spiritual and religious appear often as adjectival markers of cultural matters: "religious and spiritual property" (Art. 11), "religious and cultural sites" (Art. 12), "spiritual relationship to lands to lands, territories (Art. 25). Where *sacred*, *spiritual*, and *religious* do appear in the Declaration as modifiers, they can be crucial modifiers to Indigenous cultures. This is seen especially in Article 25's recognition of Indigenous peoples' right "to maintain and strengthen their distinctive spiritual relationship with their traditionally owned or otherwise occupied and used lands, territories, waters, and coastal seas and other resources," a relationship that can be the basis of their "responsibilities to future generations in this regard" and that can serve to frame the distinctive contours of indigeneity with respect to land and the appropriate framework for the key recognition of collective rights to culturally inflected land ownership, occupation, tenure, or use. If the religious or the spiritual is only a qualifier, it is perhaps the qualifier that asserts distinction of kind, not degree.

UNDRIP is not a binding legal document, but this is not to say it is irrelevant to real questions of the legal protection of Native American religious traditions. Indeed, as James Anaya, Tonya Gonnella Frischer, Robert Williams Jr., Walter Echo-Hawk, Robert T. Coulter, Kristin Carpenter, and Angela Riley among others have argued, UNDRIP is a forceful enunciation of emerging norms of Indigenous rights and a powerful declaration that existing human rights long established in legally binding treaties and conventions must apply as collective rights if they are meaningfully to apply to Indigenous people and peoples.[10]

While this chapter will try to come to terms with the difficulties of implementation and enforcement of human rights norms of international law, and perhaps especially those emerging through an Indigenous rights movement that faces definitional and structural challenges to that implementation and enforcement, my goal is to follow James Anaya's and Walter Echo-Hawk's commendation of the Declaration's possibilities for rethinking domestic Indian law, and crucially, for rethinking religious liberty law as it is to apply to Indigenous peoples in the United States.

The Challenge of Indigenous Rights in International Law

There is irony in the emergence of Indigenous rights under international law. As James Anaya points out, it is a field of law that has its basis in the Law of Nations, which sought to settle competing European claims to Indigenous lands. It was the Law of Nations to which Chief Justice Marshall turned in *Johnson v. M'Intosh* (1823), incorporating the theological presumption of the Doctrine of Christian Discovery to settle a title dispute between Euro-Americans. But the same Law of Nations also deeply informed Marshall's opinion in *Worcester v. Georgia* (1832), the taproot precedent for affirmations of inherent tribal sovereignty and treaty rights.[11] As Walter Echo-Hawk has observed, these ironies open up, and don't simply foreclose, the possibility that federal Indian law can be rehabilitated on the surer foundation of the human rights principles of the Declaration.[12] The body of precedent resting on *Worcester* can be commended, while addressing the colonizing and racist underpinnings of federal Indian law that is the progeny of *Johnson v. M'Intosh*.[13] It was the effort to decolonize US federal Indian law in the first place that fueled the movement toward the UN Declaration by the World Council on Indigenous Peoples and later at the United Nations by the Working Group on Indigenous Populations from 1982 on.[14]

A second irony involves the emergence of Indigenous rights from within international law in a manner not suited by current structures of international institutions. Indigenous peoples are betwixt and between the two fundamental units of received international law and its institutions. Indigenous *peoples* are neither merely Indigenous *people*, individuals who are the bearers of human rights vis-à-vis the state, nor constituents of ethnic "minority populations" alongside other cultural, linguistic, and religious groups. But neither are they fully *peoples* in the sense of the other principal unit of international human rights law: member nation-states with what the UN Charter assigns inviolable rights to sovereignty, territorial integrity, and political independence.[15]

A third irony, if we call it that, stems from the first and second. International law can seem appealing because it presumably offers opportunity for redress after domestic efforts fail. But the legal and institutional capacity for granting and enforcing such redress, especially given American reluctance to engage international law, is more long-term aspiration than near-term possibility. "In the United States," writes Robert Williams Jr., "the pervasive belief is that international law doesn't work very well at all. Many lawyers and law students I know will say they think international law is a waste of time for Indian people."[16] If it seems unremarkable to assert that the enforcement mechanisms of international law are relatively weak vis-à-vis US domestic law, it is important to acknowledge in order to commend the ways that international law *can* be helpful for Indigenous rights in the United States. Take the San Francisco Peaks case, for example. After the Ninth Circuit decision in *Navajo Nation v. U.S. Forest Service* foreclosed protections under US law, the Navajo Nation Human Rights Commission brought concerns about the desecration of the mountain to the Special Rapporteur on the Rights of Indigenous Peoples.[17] Rapporteur Anaya, in turn, included attention to the San Francisco Peaks case prominently in his 2012 country report on the United States, observing that "desecration and lack of access to sacred places inflicts permanent harm."[18] Later, in 2015, the Navajo filed a formal petition to the Inter-American Commission on Human Rights to "declare the United States responsible for the violation of the rights to religion, culture, and judicial protection under the *American Declaration on the Rights and Duties of Man*" through its authorization of snowmaking with treated sewage on the sacred mountain.[19] Despite the abundant evidence of jurisgenesis involved with the Navajo Nation Commission, and thus the cultivation of international law norms involved, there is as yet no firm result. Snowmaking with the treated sewage effluent, in the absence of some extraordinary development, will continue apace.[20]

Religion as Peoplehood in International Law

The Road to UNDRIP

The strategy of seizing any available opportunity for legal protection that we have seen throughout this book characterized the earliest efforts by Native people to engage modern international law. In 1923, well before creation of the United Nations, the Cayuga leader Deskaneh brought concerns of the Haudenosaunee to the League of Nations in Switzerland. Deskaneh was challenging Canadian refusal to recognize the traditional Haudenosaunee government, so his claims weren't particularly religious, but his appeal to the international community was strategically positioned to capitalize on a romanticized regard for the plight of North America's Indians.[21]

In the 1970s, Haudenosaunee leaders went again to Geneva to get an international hearing concerning broken treaties. Their manifesto, *Basic Call to Consciousness*, underscored the reintegration of an Indigenous spiritual posture toward the economic, political, and environmental challenges facing the world:

> Traditional First Nations Peoples hold the key to the reversal of processes in Western civilization that hold the promise of unimaginable future suffering and destruction. Spiritualism is the highest form of political consciousness. And we, First Peoples of the Western Hemisphere, are among the world's surviving proprietors of that kind of consciousness.[22]

For all the historic importance of airing such claims in Geneva, the impact was limited in two respects. Structurally, Indigenous communities making the claims were, and still are, stuck between the principal units of the international law institutions—nation-states that are the members of those bodies and individuals who are the bearers of human rights. Secondly, Indigenous claims themselves straddle the operative conceptual divides of political, cultural, economic, and religious rights. As we have seen, rights to land, health, food, education, and self-determination can also be taken as implicitly religious concerns.

The formative triad of human rights law instruments—the Universal Declaration of Human Rights (1948); the International Covenant on Civil and Political Rights (1966, effective 1976); and the International Covenant of Economic, Social, and Cultural Rights (1966, effective 1976)—articulate both religious and cultural rights. But those rights were, for reasons of these structural incongruities, only partly of use to Indigenous peoples. At best, Indigenous peoples could register collective claims to culture, land, and religion as aggregations of rights-bearing individuals, or as "populations" claiming "minority rights."

Religion as Religion in International Law

Religious freedom is embedded in the key instruments of international human rights law. Article 18 of the Universal Declaration of Human Rights (1948) (UDHR) provides that:

> Everyone has the right to freedom of thought, conscience and religion; this right includes freedom to change his religion or belief, and freedom, either alone or in community with others and in public or private, to manifest his religion or belief in teaching, practice, worship and observance.

In contrast to the terse language of the US Constitution's First Amendment, the more privatized individual right of religious belief is here joined with language that makes room for public expression, manifestation, and practice. Article 18(1) of the International Covenant on Civil and Political Rights (ICCPR) takes the UDHR language and embeds it in the binding law of this covenant:

> Everyone shall have the right to freedom of thought, conscience and religion. This right shall include freedom to have or to adopt a religion or belief of his choice, and freedom, either individually or in community with others and in public or private, to manifest his religion or belief in worship, observance, practice and teaching.[23]

The United States ratified the ICCPR in 1992, committing the government to periodic reporting under the covenant, though ICCPR was acknowledged to be a "non self-executing treaty," a technicality that means it is generally not actionable in US courts.[24] Article 4(2) of ICCPR clarifies that rights of religious conscience, along with rights to life and freedom from slavery and torture, cannot be suspended even in states of national emergency. But ICCPR Article 18(3) qualifies that rights to "manifest" religious belief or conscience are not strictly speaking non-derogable: "Freedom to manifest one's religion or beliefs may be subject only to such limitations as are prescribed by law and are necessary to protect public safety, order, health, or morals or the fundamental rights and freedoms of others."

Importantly, UNDRIP clarifies that all existing human rights, including the religious rights provisions of ICCPR and UDHR, should be regarded as collective, not just individual, as they apply to indigenous peoples. In this, the Declaration provides a resounding legal affirmation of claims in earlier chapters of this book that Native American religious freedom rights be considered collective, not just individual. Curiously, as shot through as UNDRIP is with language of spirituality, it does not emphasize its own implications for existing human rights of religious freedom.

Religion as Spirituality in Indigenous Rights Discourse

So *religion* is named prominently in instruments of international human rights law, but in UNDRIP and in materials parsing and applying it, as concerns Indigenous peoples' traditions, the language of religion consistently dissipates into a language of spirituality, amenable to being understood more as an ethos or affect of culture than as a discrete category of religion. Although UNDRIP does not explicitly distinguish between spirituality and religion, Siv Ellen Kraft's study of a range of Indigenous rights publications demonstrates not only that spirituality is the preferred term, but that the distinction highlights something important about Indigenous rights to spirituality, and in spite of religion.[25]

For example, a periodic report from ECOSOC, the *State of the World's Indigenous People*, asserts, "it is important to recognize the difference between spirituality and religion." "Spirituality can be seen as an internal connection to the universe," the "sense of meaning and purpose in life," "cosmology," and "personal moral code" that infuses all life, while "religion could be defined as a specific practice and ritual that are the external expression of some people's spirituality."[26] But the report goes on to suggest that in the colonization of Indigenous peoples, missionization and conversion processes map onto that inner and outer distinction between Indigenous *spirituality* and colonizer *religions*. "Indigenous spirituality and belief systems have often been dismissed as being mere expressions of superstitious and irrational thinking," the report observes, "under constant assault from the large, dominant religions: Christianity, Islam, Hinduism, etc."[27]

Religion as Culture in International Human Rights Law

Prior to UNDRIP, Indigenous communities had gradually more traction available to them for religious rights within ICCPR's Article 27, the key instrument for the rights of ethnic minority populations in member nation-states:

> In those States in which ethnic, religious or linguistic minorities exist, persons belonging to such minorities shall not be denied the right, in community with the other members of their group, to enjoy their own culture, to profess and practise their own religion, or to use their own language.

Article 27 is emblematic of religion's conceptualization in international law. As a matter of individual belief or conscience, religion is enumerated among the rights of the highest, non-derogable order. But as a matter of community identity and collective practice or expression, this view regards religion as a species of culture, religious rights as a species of cultural rights. Perhaps this observation may seem both unremarkable and odd; unremarkable because of course religion is a facet of culture, odd because the discursive purchase religion has in the US political and legal context as a distinguishable domain is specific to US legal, political, and cultural history.

UNESCO and other cultural rights instrument in the later twentieth century emerged to protect cultural life and cultural "achievements," exemplary archaeological or historical built environments and the heritage of the world's civilizations for human posterity. The International Covenant on Economic, Social, and Cultural Rights (ICESCR), in Article 15, emphatically affirms "the right of everyone: (a) to take part in cultural life; (b) to enjoy the benefits of scientific progress and its applications; (c) to benefit from the protection of the moral and material interests resulting from any scientific literary or artistic production of which he is the author." The United States has not ratified ICESCR, but its broad endorsement internationally commends the weight of its norms as international customary law.

For Indigenous communities, cultural rights can be salient as rights to practice everyday activities of culture, not just as rights to benefit from scientific discoveries or fine arts. And culture is not so easily set apart from the other domains: the cultural is also the religious is also the economic is also the political is also the environmental. Uninflected with these resonances, cultural rights for Indigenous peoples had paled in comparison to those same rights for others.

But with the active lobbying of the Indigenous movement at the United Nations, these minority cultural rights were clarified to include Indigenous peoples and land-based traditional cultural and spiritual activities. In 1994, the UN Human Rights Committee commented on the ICCPR:

> With regard to the exercise of the cultural rights protected under Article 27, the Committee observes that culture manifests itself in many forms, including a particular way of life associated with the use of land resources, especially in the case of Indigenous peoples. That right may include such traditional activities as fishing or hunting and the right to live in reserves protected by law.[28]

The Human Rights Committee also clarified that states would have special obligations to protect Article 27 rights "towards ensuring the survival and continued development of the cultural, religious, and social identity of the minorities concerned." "These rights," the committee continued, "must be protected as such and should not be confused with other personal rights conferred on one and all under the Covenant."[29]

Importantly, such clarifications took pains not to shake up the basic structure of the ICCPR, arguably the most far reaching of the human rights instruments. Even as it acknowledged that Indigenous groups might have expansive claims under the rubric of cultural rights, the Human Rights Committee also made clear that Article 27 was strictly speaking about individual rights to group membership and as such not to be confused with ICCPR Article 1's rights of "peoples" to self-determination.[30] From this vantage point, even Indigenous groups were aggregations of Indigenous people, not *peoples* in the technical sense of international law; citizens of nation-states with minority population rights, but not nations in an international law system.

Peoples, not People or Populations

There is an immense difference between the legal force of *peoples* and *people*. Peoples have rights of collective self-determination; aggregations of people do not. Both the ICCPR and ICESCR begin with the same article:

> All peoples have the right of self-determination. By virtue of that right they freely determine their political status and freely pursue their economic, social and cultural development.

This right to a people's collective self-determination together with the collective pursuit of economic, social, and cultural development is thus the first word in international law, the counterpoint to the enumerated human rights enjoyed by all people, as individuals, within those peoples. But the right to peoples' collective self-determination has remained the province of the nation-states that drive the institutions and processes of international law. ICCPR Article 27 is emblematic of how Indigenous communities were ill served by a human rights discourse based on the tension between individuals and nation-states. For even the cultural, religious, and linguistic rights of minority communities were aggregated rights of the individuals belonging to the communities. Among the more important ways for ICCPR to become operationalized has been for grievances to come before the UN Human Rights Committee under the (First) Optional Protocol, signed by 115 states, but the grievance structure had included only those of individuals, not collectivities.[31]

Even the 1989 Indigenous and Tribal Peoples' Convention 169 of the International Labor Organisation (ILO), which served to highlight how unique Indigenous relationships with land should shape development, makes clear in its first article that "the use of the term *peoples* in this Convention shall not be construed as having any implications as regards the rights which may attach to the term under international law."[32] Amid criticism by governments, this was at the time the compromise position for Indigenous advocates intent on securing affirmation of further self-determination rights for Indigenous peoples.[33] The United States has yet to ratify the ILO convention, and so I will not explore it in further detail, but as James Anaya observes, Convention 169 lay important groundwork for UNDRIP and subsequent elaboration of the norms of Indigenous rights, and plays its part toward fuller acceptance of such norms as customary international law.[34]

The UN Declaration on the Rights of Indigenous Peoples

UNDRIP's passage in 2007 was in this sense a game changer: it clarifies that existing human rights, if they are to apply to Indigenous people, should be regarded as matters of *collective*, not just *individual*, rights. UNDRIP's Article 1 makes this plain:

> Indigenous peoples have the right to the full enjoyment, as a collective or as individuals, of all human rights and fundamental freedoms as recognized in the Charter of the United Nations, the Universal Declaration of Human Rights and international human rights law.

In what follows I will explore what the language of UNDRIP does to encompass the protean nature of Indigenous religion by weaving religious rights into the broader fabric of Indigenous rights to peoplehood. But first, it is important to contextualize that discussion with the aspirational nature of Indigenous self-determination in UNDRIP. Proponents and critics alike of UNDRIP agree that it creates no *new* rights. For critics keen to point out what UNDRIP has yet to accomplish in terms of Indigenous rights, this is a crucial point. The rights of a people's fuller collective self-determination described in Article 1 of ICCPR or ICESCR, or that compose the basic principles of the UN Charter—respect for the "sovereign equality," "territorial integrity," and "political independence" of the peoples that are member states—are potentially advanced to the degree that those states implement UNDRIP.[35] But while there are significant nods in this direction, there is yet no bold structural intervention in the institutions of international law to place Indigenous peoples on a nation-to-nation relationship basis with member states. UNDRIP's Article 46 bookends the Declaration with insistent clarity on this point:

Nothing in this Declaration may be interpreted as implying for any State, people, group or person any right to engage in any activity or to perform any act contrary to the Charter of the United Nations or construed as authorizing or encouraging any action which would dismember or impair, totally or in part, the territorial integrity or political unity of sovereign and independent States.[36]

For realist critics of UNDRIP, those who regard its aspirational language as aspirational only, this is where the rubber hits the road. But for scholars more familiar with the often halting advances of international law, this aspirational language can represent not simply a modest step but a profound intervention, because of the clarity of its declaration that Indigenous peoples have rights to exist as peoples, and that existing human rights must be also collective as applied to them.

Religion as Culture in UNDRIP

The Declaration directly engages the category of religion in its elaboration of collective Indigenous rights, but unlike the First Amendment religion clauses and other human rights instruments, the Declaration elaborates on what protection of religious traditions might entail in terms of the collective practices of Indigenous communities. UNDRIP extends the narrowly or plainly religious beyond its ordinary meaning. The provision that most clearly speaks to religious rights is Article 12:

> Indigenous peoples have the right to manifest, practice, develop and teach their spiritual and religious traditions, customs and ceremonies; the right to maintain, protect, and have access in privacy to their religious and cultural sites; the right to the use and control of their ceremonial objects; and the right to the repatriation of their human remains.

In its effort to follow religious concerns into every aspect of Indigenous cultures, UNDRIP does not content itself with a single religious freedom provision or a tight focus on religion as a power word or a term of art. The decidedly "religious" Article 12 follows a broader vision of cultural rights set out in Article 11, and one that includes a provision for redress:

> (1) Indigenous peoples have the right to practise and revitalize
> their cultural traditions and customs. This includes the right to

maintain, protect and develop the past, present and future mani-
festations of their cultures, such as archaeological and historical
sites, artefacts, designs, ceremonies, technologies and visual and
performing arts and literature.

(2) States shall provide redress through effective mechanisms, which
may include restitution, developed in conjunction with Indigenous peoples, with respect to their cultural, intellectual, religious
and spiritual property taken without their free, prior and informed
consent or in violation of their laws, traditions and customs.

Put simply, rights to religion are framed by, and folded into, more expansive
considerations of cultural self-determination, where economic, ecological,
juridical, and political matters can also have spiritual or religious facets and
urgency. Even in Article 12, where UNDRIP expressly discusses rights to religion, the term appears as an adjective: "spiritual and religious traditions," "religious and cultural sites." Where the protection, maintenance, and strengthening of Indigenous institutions and customs are concerned, the operative
term is not *religion* but *spirituality*. Article 34 provides that, "Indigenous
peoples have the right to promote, develop, and maintain their institutional
structures and their distinctive customs, spirituality, traditions, procedures,
practices, and in the cases where they exist, juridical systems or customs, in
accordance with international human rights standards."

Religious or spiritual considerations are explicitly enumerated in five additional UNDRIP articles protecting various elements of culture (Articles 25,
31, 34, 35, 36) and implicitly present in further considerations of rights to oral
traditions, philosophies, languages (Article 13), traditional medicine (Article
24), and traditional knowledge (Article 31).

If they blur the boundaries or dull the edges of "religion," these adjectival
enumerations of religious or spiritual considerations of other cultural protections are still consequential. Indeed such references can be drivers of what
can distinguish a range of Indigenous cultural rights as sacred, as urgent, or as
tantamount to peoplehood. Notable here is the explicit recognition of rights
to "maintain and strengthen" an Indigenous people's "spiritual relationship"
with traditional "lands, territories, waters and coastal seas and other resources
and to uphold their responsibilities to future generations in this regard."[37]
Thus Article 25 introduces a series of other articles regarding rights to traditional land and frames those rights at least in part in terms of relational "spir-

itual" responsibilities to the land itself and to future generations. Furthermore, a manual to help implement UNDRIP underscores the centrality of the religious to cultural rights:

> The concept of Indigenous spirituality is inherently connected to culture. Adopting policies that promote certain religions or prohibit Indigenous spiritual practices, or the failure of laws or other governmental institutions, such as the police and courts, to respect Indigenous spiritual practices, can undermine the right to culture.[38]

Religion as Culture in the OAS Draft American Declaration

The Organization of American States (OAS) Draft American Declaration on the Rights of Indigenous Peoples makes even more explicit the recognition of the interrelated nature of the religious with the economic and the political and social.[39] At the time of this writing, the draft is still in its consensus-building process, and so it is not a subject of deep engagement here. Still, the OAS Draft Declaration has fed off the UNDRIP process and can be seen as making clarifications of Indigenous rights norms more broadly.

The OAS Draft Declaration's Article XIII on "the Right to Cultural Identity and Integrity"—already agreed on by consensus in the draft process—provides that "Indigenous people have the right to the recognition for all their ways of life, world views, spirituality, uses and customs, norms and traditions, forms of social, economic and political organization, forms of transmission of knowledge, institutions, practices, beliefs, values, dress and languages, recognizing their inter-relationship as elaborated in this Declaration."[40] The OAS Draft Declaration goes beyond UNDRIP in making explicit the interconnection between religious rights and land rights, including a right to healthy Indigenous habitats:

> Indigenous peoples have the right to live in harmony with nature and to a healthy, safe, and sustainable environment, essential conditions for the full enjoyment of the right to life, to their spirituality, worldview and to collective well-being.[41]

The OAS Draft Declaration, too, includes spiritual considerations into provisions recognizing rights to health (Art. XVII), environment (Art. XIX), assembly (Art. XX), law and jurisdiction (Art. XXII), and property (Art. XXV).

Perhaps for related reasons, the OAS Draft Declaration references rights to Indigenous *spirituality* rather than religion in its article specifically referencing "spiritual" rights:

> Indigenous peoples have the right to freely exercise their own spirituality and beliefs and, by virtue of that right, to practice, develop, transmit, and teach their traditions, customs, and ceremonies, and to carry them out in public and in private, individually and collectively.[42]

Like UNDRIP, the OAS Draft Declaration will not be legally binding; it too is a clarification of how agreed-on human rights in legally binding treaties are to be applied to Indigenous peoples. Particularly relevant here are the OAS Declaration on the Rights and Duties of Man (1948) and the American Convention on Human Rights (1969), which the United States signed in 1977, but has yet to ratify. The Declaration on the Rights and Duties of Man provides "Every person has the right to freely profess a religious faith, and to manifest and practice it in both public and private" (Art. III). The American Convention on Human Rights protects "Freedom of Conscience and Religion" in a manner that signals the aggregative if not collective facet of the right. Article 12 provides: "Everyone has the right to freedom of conscience and of religion. This right includes freedom to maintain or to change one's religion or beliefs, and freedom to profess or disseminate one's religion or beliefs, either individually or together with others, in public or in private."

What Does UNDRIP Mean?
The Legal Force of International Law

Having considered the text of UNDRIP and the language for speaking the norms of Indigenous rights, what are we to make of the force of this language in law? In this next section, we turn in the abstract to consider the legal weight of various kinds of international law instruments, the better to understand what the UN Declaration means, or can mean, on the ground.

People often first think of international law as an effective arena for making claims when domestic law fails, either through making global news of grievances and leveraging the politics of shame and seeking changes of policy or law, or directly through seeking judgments in international courts. The possibilities for international adjudication of particular claims and grievances is limited, though. It is easy to overinterpret a provision without knowledge of the relative legal force of the document in question or of the broader context of international law's monitoring and enforcement mechanisms. A brief sketch of both can help us proceed with an awareness of the relative force of the law we're reading.

Elaboration of Norms

TREATIES/COVENANT/CONVENTIONS

Treaties, covenants, and conventions are binding law for the nations that ratify them, so norms found in conventions or treaties accordingly bear the most legal muscle. Key examples are ICESCR and the ICCPR, adopted by the UN General Assembly in 1966 and in force by 1976. The United States ratified the ICCPR in 1994, though the Senate's ratification included a provision finding that the ICCPR was a "nonself-executing" treaty, a distinction that introduces another variable in terms of the legal force of international law in the United States. Self-executing treaties present causes of action in US courts. Non-self-executing treaties, by contrast, require affirmative congressional action to gain legal force as causes of action. So the ICCPR's provisions cannot be raised in a US court except as part of a legal defense, or perhaps in an administrative proceeding. And as Navajo litigants found when they claimed their relocation under the Navajo-Hopi Land Settlement Act violated religious freedom and other rights under the UN Charter, federal courts found the UN Charter to be non-self-executing.[43]

Another relevant US-ratified convention that has been a source of Indigenous rights activism is the International Convention to Eliminate All Forms of Racial Discrimination (ICERD), which was approved by the General Assembly in 1966 and ratified by the United States in 1994.[44] ICERD provides for "the right to freedom of thought, conscience, and religion," but other non-discrimination provisions have been a source of considerable energy in the attendant periodic reviews for signatories like the United States.[45]

DECLARATIONS

The norms in such treaties and conventions, or in customary international law, are often clarified in declarations that, like UNDRIP, are not legally binding, even for the states that adopt them. But short of being legally binding, such declarations, especially those with such broad support, can be forceful elaborations of those norms. They can also exert a strong, if indirect, legal force as they clarify the meaning or reach of provisions in treaties, covenants, and conventions ratified by states. Because of this indirect force, UNDRIP is arguably a strong legal document as it insists that agreed-on human rights must apply to Indigenous peoples as collective, not just individual, rights.

CUSTOMARY INTERNATIONAL LAW

What makes such declarations as UNDRIP in effect more than mere declarations—and what can make treaties and conventions legally relevant to the domestic law of even nonratifying nations—is the role in establishing how the norms they articulate may already be functioning as customary international law, a form of law that the US Supreme Court has identified as binding in the common law.[46] In his discussion of the legal force of UNDRIP as a powerful statement of customary law, Walter Echo-Hawk observes that customary law "carries the same binding force, and equal authority, as [the UN] treaties."[47] Still, the determination of customary international law is a rather fluid one, since it emerges from the community of nation-states as a controlling consensus, to use James Anaya's words, and what other scholars speak of in the metaphors of crystallizing or ripening:

> Norms of customary international law arise when a preponderance of states and other authoritative actors converge on a common understanding of the norm's contents and generally expect future behavior in conformity.[48]

Cohen's Handbook of Federal Indian Law defines customary international law as "rules of behavior that originate in international custom not necessarily found in any specific document":

> Customary law is "the oldest and original source of international law," and consists of rules nations follow because they consider themselves to be legally obligated to do so. A customary law norm binds a nation even if it has not formally recognized the norm.[49]

US courts occasionally engage customary international law.[50] The lack of any formal document establishing the contours of a particular right or the failure of the United States to formally ratify a particular covenant does not necessarily mean that United States courts will always ignore the standard.[51]

Enforcement of Norms

Incorporation in domestic law and domestic courts can be the most effective enforcement mechanism for international law norms, but there is also a range of international enforcement mechanisms and modest remedies available in regional international courts. First, in signing certain conventions and treaties, states obligate themselves periodically to report and to be reviewed by international bodies. Notable here are obligations the United States has under the ICCPR for periodic reports to the UN Human Rights Committee, or under ICERD to the UN Committee on the Elimination of Racial Discrimination. The UN Human Rights Council also conducts a universal periodic review of member states on the range of human rights instruments. In addition to the official governmental reports for these reviews, international bodies can receive "shadow reports" from authorized NGOs like the International Indian Treaty Council to provide context and counterpoint to the governmental reports.

An important part of the development of Indigenous rights under the United Nations was its creation in 2001 of the office of the Special Rapporteur on the Rights of Indigenous Peoples, an official reporting to the UN Human Rights Committee who monitors Indigenous rights through country reports, hears specific cases, and promotes best practices toward the fuller realization of Indigenous human rights.

In addition to formal review and monitoring, complaints can be brought to international bodies like the UN Human Rights Committee or the Inter-American Commission on Human Rights. One relevant mechanism is the Optional Protocol for the ICCPR, by which the Human Rights Committee can receive formal grievances from individuals, including asserted violations of ICCPR Article 27 rights for minority populations. The Optional Protocol is so named because it is an opt-in feature of the ICCPR to which not all signatory nations, among them the United States, have committed themselves.

Finally, there are several international tribunals that rule on claims under international law. Most relevant is the Inter-American Court of Human Rights, which has heard important Indigenous rights cases within the Organization of American States system. The United States, while a member of the OAS, does not yet subject itself to the jurisdiction of international tribunals. Still, the Inter-American Court has rendered a number of decisions that have supported the normativity of collective Indigenous rights. Its *Awas Tingni* decision in 2001 has been generative for the broader acknowledgment of distinctively collective Indigenous rights.[52] The case concerned Nicaragua's leasing of ancestral lands of the Miskito, Rama, and Sumo peoples for logging with neither their consent nor compensation. The Inter-American Court found Nicaragua in violation of rights to property under the American Convention on Human Rights, ruling that the collective nature of Indigenous land holding did not exempt Nicaragua from its recognition under a domestic property rights system that does not recognize collective title. In its analysis, the Inter-American Court also strengthened the implications of Indigenous relationships with land. "The close ties of Indigenous people with the land," the court's majority wrote, "must be recognized and understood as the fundamental basis of their cultures, their spiritual life, their integrity, and their economic survival."[53]

Even before UNDRIP, the decision cleared space for other judgments in favor of collective Indigenous rights, and in particular for the legal recognition of collective cultural traditions of land holding.[54] *Awas Tingni* also opened the door for the Inter-American Commission on Human Rights, the OAS body distinct from the Inter-American Court, to issue a report in favor of the Dann sisters, two Western Shoshone women who, after having exhausted domestic remedies, challenged mining development on their ancestral Shoshone land in Nevada, including sacred sites.[55]

Kristin Carpenter and Angela Riley see in these cases a developing "jurisprudence of legally cognizable Indigenous rights under human rights instruments," adding, "the cases reach even further than they first appear, in that they acknowledge ongoing importance of the link between Indigenous peoples and their lands, despite historical dispossession and colonization."[56]

DOMESTIC LAW

Again, especially as regards developed nations with relatively robust rule of law, the most enforceable international law is that which becomes effective through the domestic law of nation-states. Bolivia imported UNDRIP's language and standards wholesale into domestic law and policy (noting that rule of law in Bolivia is not as robust as in other more developed nations where such a gesture would be far more exacting). International law instruments and/or customary law can offer causes of legal action in domestic courts, or at the least serve to interpret other facets of domestic law. The Belize Supreme Court in 2007 sided with Mayan Indian land claims based on Belizean law but also citing UNDRIP and ILO Convention 169 (to which Belize is not a party) as international customary law.[57]

Implementing UNDRIP Specifically

Structural challenges to Indigenous peoples' representation in international institutions like the United Nations remain, because Indigenous peoples are not recognized in the same manner that nation-state members are. But they are clearly more than the nongovernmental organizations that are registered with or that have consultative status at the United Nations. This representational challenge has been addressed through a range of bodies dedicated to the furtherance of Indigenous rights and specifically the implementation of UNDRIP: the Expert Mechanism on the Rights of Indigenous Peoples (EMRIP) and the Permanent Forum on Indigenous Issues. These are in addition to general efforts such as large-scale events like the 2014 World Conference on Indigenous Peoples or smaller, topical ones, like a 2015 expert seminar on Indigenous cultural heritage issues or an implementation manual produced by the UN's High Commissioner for Human Rights.[58]

In 2007, the Human Rights Council created EMRIP, a panel made up of experts on Indigenous rights and law representing geographical regions around the globe to provide "thematic expertise on the rights of Indigenous peoples" in the form of "studies and research-based advice" and to suggest proposals to the Council for its "consideration and approval." EMRIP has issued a number of topical studies: Right to Health, Cultural Heritage, Access to Justice, Right to Education, Right to Participate in Decision-Making, Languages and Cultures, and one focused on good business practices, and more recently, a study of free, prior, and informed consent.

In 2016, EMRIP received an expanded mandate that called on it to help member states on request to implement UNDRIP in their domestic laws and policies.[59] This has evolved not only into working with member states but also convening and facilitating dialogue with various stakeholders, including working with the private sector.

The United Nations has endeavored to address the problem of Indigenous structural representation through the Permanent Forum on Indigenous Issues. Formed in 2000 as an advisory body to ECOSOC, the UN body charged with processes related to ICESCR, the Permanent Forum is convened for ten days annually on a particular theme—the 2018 meeting concerned collective rights to lands, territories, and resources—with broad representation of Indigenous peoples across the globe. Apart from its advisory function and the thematic topic of its deliberations, the Permanent Forum serves the function of an Indigenous assembly.

Especially with a revised mandate that includes making targeted country reports, the Special Rapporteur has come to play a key role in the implementation of UNDRIP and the promotion of Indigenous rights norms more broadly. Special Rapporteur James Anaya conducted a mission to the United States and filed a report in 2012 after extensive fact finding, interviews with relevant officials, and extensive field hearings. Anaya concluded that Native peoples in the United States "face significant challenges that are related to widespread historical wrongs, including broken treaties and acts of oppression, and misguided government policies, that today manifest themselves in various indicators of disadvantage and impediments to the exercise of their individual and collective rights."[60]

The current Special Rapporteur, Victoria Tauli-Corpuz, recently completed a mission and 2017 Report on the United States. She cited as among her top human rights concerns the insufficiency of US consultation vis-à-vis UNDRIP's norm of free, prior, and informed consent, particularly in the energy development sector.[61] The report made detailed reference to the United States' failure to adequately consult Native nations on the Dakota Access Pipeline, which Tauli-Corpuz called emblematic of the experience of many Native peoples. The report also called attention to energy development projects endangering other sacred sites, such as Chaco Canyon, Mount Taylor, and President Trump's gutting of the Bears Ears National Monument.

Diplomacy and the Power of Words

Given the weakness of international enforcement of Indigenous rights norms in the United States through periodic review or the international tribunals to which the United States does not submit, I find it helpful to take a step back and regard international law in its aspect as a well-documented conversation. It is literally awash in words, bespeaking international law's roots in diplomacy, of settling differences in carefully chosen words and incremental processes toward agreement on those words. While the same could be said of law in general, international law grows less through decisions in adversarial venues than through the slow, methodical building of consensus. Accordingly, the language is stated, refined, and commented on by commissions, committees, and acknowledged experts in the idiom—and word count—of diplomacy. What makes any consensus on the norms of Indigenous rights in international law so important, especially when compared to domestic federal Indian law, is that the decades-long conversation is decidedly shaped by Indigenous voices.

Keeping this insight, however unoriginal, in view helps understand what UNDRIP means on the ground, to gauge both the plain limits in the short term of domestic enforceability of Indigenous rights norms and the enormous potential in the longer term of this growing conversation. In this sense, UNDRIP and Indigenous rights in international law are more than aspirational. It is, as veterans of federal Indian law like Walter Echo-Hawk have recently argued, the surer way to liberate Native American claim-making from the confines of domestic law, and, in turn, to redeem federal Indian law by reference to Indigenous rights norms.

Religion as Peoplehood in Domestic US Law

Having analyzed the provisions of UNDRIP and considered its emerging norms against the backdrop of the relative weakness of international law's enforceability in the United States, we turn now to what UNDRIP might mean for reform of the domestic law considered thus far: federal Indian law, cultural resource law, and religious freedom law. Few things in international law, much less law in general, are all or nothing propositions. The norms newly articulated in UNDRIP, even if they enact no new rights, create pathways for thinking anew about Native religious and cultural freedoms under US law. The norms clarified in UNDRIP present opportunities to reimagine the application of religious freedom law to Native communities as a matter of collective, not just individual rights. Even more, those norms help reconceive specifically religious or cultural rights in terms of Indigenous self-determination, of peoplehood. To illustrate, I will focus on UNDRIP's norm of free, prior, and informed consent so necessary to Indigenous self-determination, and how it should raise the standards for nation-to-nation consultation. Finally, I will suggest that domestic implementation of the Declaration may require more care in translating ambiguities in UNDRIP with respect to specifically *religious* rights and in identifying Indigenous religious self-determination as crucial to cultural, political, and economic self-determination.

Rethinking Domestic Law in Light of Indigenous Rights Norms

In addition to the possibility of enforceability in US courts as UNDRIP's norms become recognized as customary international law or its provisions align with existing treaty obligations, the standards of Indigenous rights in the Declaration can be summoned to measure and amend US law and policy.[62]

The norms of Indigenous rights in international law can commend elements of judicial precedent in the United States that support self-determination and can serve as standards for eradicating elements of precedent, like *Johnson v. M'Intosh*, that are still considered "good law" even as they remain based on colonialist and racist foundations. As Kristen Carpenter and Angela Riley show, the Declaration is jurisgenerative of law furthering and practicing Native nations' self-determination, including cultural and religious self-determination. Religion as peoplehood, indeed!

But realizing the aspirations of UNDRIP domestically is no small or easy task given a general reluctance to engage international law in US courts. It is decidedly a long game, perhaps not bearing fruit in the short term, and one that commends invoking the Declaration early and often in legal settings. Because "today's developing norms are tomorrow's settled rules of international law," Echo-Hawk writes, "once an Indigenous right becomes a norm, the domestic legal status of customary international law in the United States becomes significant: those norms are then enforceable as federal common law. As such, when rights in the Declaration constitute customary international law, they are enforceable by the courts."[63]

To get US courts in the habit of thinking of Indigenous rights norms, Echo-Hawk, Carpenter, Riley, and others underscore the importance of Native litigants raising principles from UNDRIP in their claims, of speaking forth the norms of the Declaration at every opportunity, regardless of the short-term efficacy of such claims. They recognize, of course, that lawyers ethically obligated to their client's best interest may regard citing the Declaration in complaints and briefs as a distraction for judges. Others commend a strategy of "pushing up" the norms of the Declaration from within tribal court rulings in the event they are reviewed in US courts.[64] As advocates and jurists engage in this effort, I want to make and briefly develop a number of observations that may help steer the implementation of UNDRIP in the United States toward productive ends as regards Native religious claims.

Cultural Integrity and Self-Determination in US Law

First, when it comes to religious concerns, we ought to think carefully of burying the lede by subordinating the religious to the cultural. Following the language of UNDRIP, important discussions of its implementation in the United States engage the religious as a modest subset of cultural rights. James Anaya discusses the core norm of self-determination as being elaborated through other norms: nondiscrimination, lands and resources, social welfare and development, self-government, and cultural integrity, a category that includes but that subordinates "religious freedom." This is good in that it joins cultural self-determination to political and economic self-determination as constitutive of self-determination affirmed in Article 3 of the Declaration. And rights to cultural self-determination are crucial given the historical pattern of forced assimilation shared by so many Indigenous peoples around the globe.

"Religious" rights may seem rather flat in contrast to the robust facets of Indigenous cultures that integrate with medicine, food, health, education, and land tenure. Alternatively, because of a view of "religion" as standing in stark contrast to politics and economics, religious rights may seem too diffuse as they are applied to those putatively nonreligious aspects of Indigenous life. "Religion," as we have seen, can be said to feel like a colonizer's term; indeed, in much international law discourse it often attaches to the religions of Christianity or Islam, which for Indigenous communities have been key to the suppression of cultural self-determination.

As a consequence, the distinctly Indigenous religious concerns are absorbed into what Anaya identifies as the norm of "cultural integrity," one shaped by the Declaration but also found in Article 27 of the ICCPR, which affirms "the right to belong to ethnic, linguistic, or religious minorities" and "to enjoy their own culture, to profess and practice their own religion and to use their own language." To be sure, Anaya doesn't disregard religion in his discussion of the norm of cultural integrity, but neither does he lift up the religious as particularly salient. The cultural integrity norm calls on states for positive steps to support and foster that integrity: the promotion of Indigenous languages and accommodations for their use, safeguards for control of Indigenous knowledge, and in the case of religion, for the protection of access and integrity of sacred sites.[65]

Following Anaya's suit, as Walter Echo-Hawk turns to implementation of Declaration norms in US law and policy, he enumerates cultural rights in terms of rights to Indigenous languages, rights to culturally appropriate education, intellectual property rights, rights to transmit culture, right to Indigenous habitat, and "protection of religious places." Protection of religious places actually appears first in Echo-Hawk's series, and he gets specific as to how the application of international law norms would, for example, prompt courts to dispense with *Lyng* and other sacred land decisions. Not only do Articles 12 and 25 of the Declaration specifically name access to and integrity of sacred places as constitutive of Indigenous religious practice and cultural integrity, international law also generally "places a duty upon the United States to protect Native American religion 'that goes beyond not coercing or penalizing Native American religious practitioners.' "[66] But Echo-Hawk, like Anaya, has placed the religious under the aegis of cultural rights.

While nearly all of my religious studies colleagues would agree there is no *essential* distinction between religion and other aspects of culture—no *essence* to religion—many would agree there can be analytical value in making some clear but provisional distinctions. And in any case, there is no dispute that there is enough of a rhetorical, not to mention legal, distinction in the United States that we should think twice before divesting "religion" of any of its special rhetorical or legal import.

The emphasis on norms of cultural integrity of Indigenous peoples makes particular sense in terms of remediation for the wholesale violation of those rights in the policies of assimilation. But as recent trends in anthropology have made abundantly clear, "culture" brings forth its own indeterminacies. In a discussion titled "Culture and the Judiciary: An Unstable Concept as a Source of Rights," anthropologist Ronald Niezen cautions about an Indigenous rights discourse that reifies culture even as the discipline has critically exploded the concept.[67] Karen Engle expresses concern about the possible essentialism that can accompany Indigenous peoples' claims to collective cultural rights as a matter or strategy but that can lock them into "traditional" culture in ways that forego their fuller self-determination.[68]

To be sure, international law institutions have clarified the culture concept in ways that make cultural protections better apply to living cultures. In a 2009 formal comment on the ICESCR's affirmation of "the right of everyone to take part in cultural life," ECOSOC enumerated a broad approach to the culture concept, including tangible and intangible dimensions, natural environments, and religion:

> Culture ... encompasses, inter alia, ways of life, language, oral and written literature, music and song, non-verbal communication, religion or belief systems, rites and ceremonies, sport and games, methods of production or technology, natural and man-made environments, food, clothing, and shelter and the arts, customs and traditions through which individuals, groups of individuals, and communities express their humanity and the meaning they give to their existence, and build their worldview representing their encounter with the external forces affecting their lives.[69]

EMRIP followed those contours in its own nonexclusive definition of culture. While EMRIP's definition includes such religious facets as spiritual values, rituals, ceremonies, and "cosmovisions" there is no salient *religiousness* that sets these elements of culture off from others, or that even taxonomically brings them together:

> Indigenous peoples' cultures include tangible and intangible manifestations of their ways of life, achievements and creativity, and are an expression of their self-determination and of their spiritual and physical relationships with their lands, territories and resources. Indigenous culture is a holistic concept based on common material and spiritual values and includes distinctive manifestations in language, spirituality, membership, arts, literature, traditional knowledge, customs, rituals, ceremonies, methods of production, festive events, music, sports and traditional games, behaviour, habits, tools, shelter, clothing, economic activities, morals, value systems, cosmovisions, laws, and activities such as hunting, fishing, trapping and gathering.[70]

The long lists of elements that count as culture seems to underserve their purpose in bringing clarity to certain elements that require special consideration as states are held to account for implementing Indigenous cultural rights.

The same reluctance to focus declarative statements characterizes the three paragraphs clarifying rights to "Indigenous spirituality." Consider the first sentence:

> The concept of Indigenous spirituality is the application of respect for Creation into everyday living and relationships.

And then the list:

> The important elements of Indigenous spirituality include maintaining connections with ancestors and spirits or deities, social relations, respect for nature and the relationship with their lands, territories and resources. Indigenous spirituality is inclusive and may be practised by holding rituals, ceremonies, applying positive and respectful values, and by ensuring spirituality is transferred through generations. It is closely linked to Indigenous culture and nature. In particular, land is a source of spirituality. There is a strong belief that belongingness to land is also socio-economical, emotional and political.[71]

The last two observations about land do help identify the distinctive features of Indigenous spiritualities from other religions. The next paragraph is helpful for the way it makes more explicit that rights to Indigenous spirituality are often in tension with incursions of what EMRIP calls "mainstream religions" (and distinguishes as *religion*). Although it is not made clear here or elsewhere, rights to Indigenous "spirituality" may very well require some measure of regulation of missionary activity, and this might not comport with religious freedom rights as conventionally understood.

> Mainstream religions can be a threat to Indigenous peoples' cultural development, particularly if governments adopt policies to promote a particular religion or prohibit Indigenous spiritual practices or if States' laws and policies and courts do not recognize Indigenous peoples' spirituality and spiritual associations, including to land, territories and resources, as equal to other forms of spirituality. Some argue that to lose one's language means one can no longer practise spirituality as originally given.[72]

But again, none of this is made clear in any finer-grained treatment than that allotted it in EMRIP's document. There has yet to be any implementation study by EMRIP or the Permanent Forum or any other body that focuses in any sustained way on religion or on the spiritual elements of culture. But my brief analysis suggests that the way forward to protect spiritual or religious facets of Indigenous cultural integrity could benefit from more sustained treatment by the bodies helping implement the Declaration. In 2013, the Office of the High Commissioner for Human Rights published an implementation manual for UNDRIP broadly, with no explicit discussion of implementing UNDRIP for the protection of Indigenous *religions* as an element of Indigenous cultures pertinent to self-determination.[73]

Rethinking the Articulation of Indigenous
Rights in Light of US Religious Freedom

To implement UNDRIP's norms of cultural integrity in the United States, construing religion as culture and enumerating the religious on long lists of cultural elements risks missing an opportunity to align such norms with the legal force of US religious freedom law. Granted, US courts have often failed to deliver religious freedom protections to Native communities, but it is no less true that religion is a power word in US law by virtue of its place in the Constitution. Culture, by contrast, appears nowhere.

To more fully implement UNDRIP in the United States, it may help to invert international law's regard for religion as a subset of culture, to seize opportunities to implement UNDRIP and advance cultural rights under the rubric of religious freedom. Instead of positioning religion as a part of cultural rights, what about incorporating wider elements of cultural integrity and self-determination within the discourse of religion, at least as a rhetorical strategy?

On the part of international bodies like EMRIP, it would helpful at the very least to render the norms of UNDRIP more legibly for the United States, where religion is not only a power word but where religious freedom discourse seems to grow in stature with a rightward shift on the Supreme Court. In this context, one may ask how accessible is the term "cosmovision," in EMRIP's clarifications of cultural rights in UNDRIP. Or one may revisit the wisdom of characterizing Indigenous religious traditions as spiritual traditions, in light of the unintended consequences that "spirituality" can entail. Whatever the intellectual difficulties of the term *religion*, to replace spiritual and cosmovision with terms more legibly religious in the United States would offer a clearer road map for implementation, and leverage the force of protections for religious freedom.

Rethinking Religious Freedom Law in Light of Indigenous Rights

But what of rethinking domestic religious freedom law as it applies to Native peoples? How can and should the Declaration and its insistence that existing human rights norms to religious belief and practice be applied collectively as well as individually to Indigenous peoples in the United States?

There is not an explicit discussion of religious freedom as a collective right in UNDRIP or as yet in its clarifying or implementation materials, but it is clearly understood from the Declaration's overall insistence that recognized human rights must be considered as collective rights if they are to work for Indigenous peoples. And if EMRIP, the Special Rapporteur, or the Permanent Forum would turn more attention to it, elements of Indigenous collective rights to religious freedom might come into better focus. James Anaya and Walter Echo-Hawk have identified the low-hanging fruit of revisiting religious freedom jurisprudence as it applies to *Lyng* and other sacred lands cases.[74] In his Special Rapporteur country report on the United States, Anaya showed how international human rights law, especially as clarified in UNDRIP, calls into question minimal analyses of "substantial burden" in religious freedom cases on sacred lands like that on the San Francisco Peaks. "States cannot content themselves with merely guarding against coercion to act against one's religious beliefs," Anaya writes. "This reigning view of substantial burden in U.S. law fails to protect religious exercise of Indigenous peoples." Then turning to "the plain language" of ICCPR's Article 18, Special Rapporteur Anaya observes that *any* clearly observable limitation that makes for a meaningful restriction on the exercise of religion should be subject to strict scrutiny. He concludes that "the limitation on Indigenous religion at the mountain was neither for public safety, order, health, or morals—or the human rights of others."[75]

Beyond applying international law norms for Indigenous rights directly into religious freedom law, what of embedding arguments for other urgent matters of Indigenous rights in the language of religion? As we have seen, the legislative accomplishments of AIRFA and NAGPRA relied on such a strategy. Think of Indigenous habitats, for example. In the last chapter, we found there has yet to be a recognized right to healthy Indigenous habitats via explicit treaty protected hunting and fishing rights, but perhaps it could be argued more explicitly that healthy landscapes are necessary, in Indigenous cases, to the exercise of practices that arguably fit within the constellation of constitutionally protected religious freedom. Little Traverse Odawa leader Frank Ettawageshik put it well when he remarked that Odawa treaties with the United States protect rights to have a relationship with the fish in Lake Michigan, not narrowly to a property right in 50 percent of the lake's fish harvest. If pollution renders the fish inedible, for example, the property right may be fulfilled but the right to relationship would not.[76]

Another opportunity presents itself in seizing on the insistence in Indigenous rights discourse about spiritual relationships with land. As we have seen, *spirituality* is not a constitutional term—religion is—and distinctions between religion and spirituality, made often for the right reasons, do not amount to stronger legal protections. One way to speak about the religiousness of spiritual relationships to land is to stress duties and obligations to ancestors in land. Perhaps as Bryan Neihart suggests following the concurring opinion in *Awas Tingni*, "collective ownership rights for many Indigenous peoples should also be grounded in the right to religious freedom."[77] The three judges in their concurrence reasoned that sacred places associated with burials and ancestors introduce an "intertemporal" element to the Indigenous collective claims in the case that compel recognition of Indigenous collective land ownership rights despite no such rights in Nicaragua's domestic law. Neihart argues that religious freedom jurisprudence, more firmly established than collective property law, offers tests that could resolve the difficult issue of deciding which groups count for group rights to property.

Although the argument was aimed not to the United States, where collective rights to tribal lands are already acknowledged firmly under treaties, there may be value in more substantively connecting claims to traditional off-reservation sacred lands, or to sacred site claims by tribes that are not federally recognized, or to special accommodations that would survive equal protection challenges, by heeding the legal implications of claims asserted in the religious idiom of ancestral well-being or of religious duties to ancestors.[78] This distinctive facet of Indigenous religion can help more brightly distinguish a given group as Indigenous under international Indigenous rights norms for the linkage between religion and land use.

But US courts are unlikely to turn on a dime, so perhaps there is good reason to revisit the effort to make new law by bringing a legal cause of action for Native American sacred places. The logic would follow the effort to legally protect rights to sacramental Peyote in the wake of its criminalization by the Supreme Court in *Smith*: not by amending religious freedom law to include Native Americans but by adding legal teeth to the American Indian Religious Freedom Act, and in effect safeguarding the collective religious freedom rights of Native peoples and their members to sacred places. The political viability of such a proposal at the time of this writing may not be great, but it may be the surest way to implement norms of the Declaration as they pertain to sacred lands. In the meantime, proposals could be heard for setting the consultation processes under NHPA and environmental laws on the firmer foundation of free, prior, and informed consent, to which we now turn.

From Consultation to Free, Prior, and Informed Consent

Perhaps the most effective nearer term way to implement UNDRIP to bolster Native American religious freedom in domestic US law and policy turns neither on the indeterminate category of *culture* nor *religion*, but instead operationalizes the self-determination principle of "free, prior, and informed consent" (FPIC). UNDRIP requires free, prior, and informed consent for any government legislation or administrative actions that affect Indigenous peoples (Art. 19) or development activities that affect their territories, lands, and livelihoods (Art. 32). The Declaration elaborates on free, prior, and informed consent in another four articles (10, 11, 28, and 29), and UNDRIP implementation efforts have focused on promoting FPIC.

The Declaration's insistence on free, prior, and informed consent offers perhaps the most forceful way that religion as peoplehood can become tangible for Native American peoples, especially as it can raise to international law standards the current US policy of government-to-government consultation. Here, Indigenous communities need not make a showing for the religiousness of what's important to them or to why associated threats constitute a substantial burden on religion; they need merely to assert what's important to them in an established formal process that ensures their concerns are taken seriously and that their consent is freely given or withheld.

Crucial to religious freedom as peoplehood for Native American nations is the obligation for the United States to consult with federally recognized tribes on federal actions that will affect them as part of the government-to-government relationship. In the 1970s the trust relationship was clarified in such documents as AIRFA "to protect and preserve" the languages, cultures, and religions of the communities. President Clinton issued Executive Order 13175, "Consultation and Coordination with Indian Tribal Governments" and President Obama signed a memorandum raising the ante.[79] And the US government consultations have, at times, been subject to judicial review.[80]

UNDRIP's free, prior, and informed consent establishes far more substantive standards than the mere obligation to consult. As we have seen in the case of Standing Rock's opposition to the Dakota Access Pipeline's Missouri River crossing, consultation can be perfunctory or even cynically deployed to the disadvantage of the Indigenous nation. But the human rights basis of UNDRIP matters. As EMRIP's 2018 study on free, prior, and informed consent put it, such "exploitations of the ambiguities of the consultation process don't start from the human rights basis of UNDRIP's FPIC regime":

> The need for effective mechanisms for the operationalization of free, prior and informed consent are becoming urgent. The absence of rights-based regulatory mechanisms defining how to carry out a consultation encourages contradictory interpretations of which measures and projects need to be preceded by consultation processes and which require consent.[81]

The Declaration's Article 32 addresses Indigenous peoples' right to determine and develop priorities and strategies for the development or use of their lands or territories and other resources, and specifies that "good faith" consultation with tribal governments or representative institutions will be "in order to obtain their free and informed consent prior to the approval of any project affecting their lands or territories and other resources. States shall provide effective mechanisms for just and fair redress for any such activities, and appropriate measures shall be taken to mitigate adverse environmental, economic, social, cultural or spiritual impact."

The edges of the consent standard come into relief in one of the stipulated reservations with which the United States adopted the Declaration in 2010. The United States said it "recognizes the significance of the Declaration's provisions on free, prior and informed consent, which the United States understands to call for a process of meaningful consultation with tribal leaders, but not necessarily the agreement of those leaders, before the actions addressed in those consultations are taken."[82] The government in this statement is not simply taking the FPI and changing the C from consent to consultation: the government states it "recognizes the significance of the Declaration's provisions on free, prior, and informed consent." But the United States is making clear that its understanding of the provisions it adopts "call[s] for a process of meaningful consultation with tribal leaders," a process that the government acknowledges requires discipline, resources, and commitment beyond good faith.

UN guidelines explain how fears that FPIC provides Indigenous peoples a veto power over all government actions or development are overinflated. Implementation materials elaborate that UNDRIP requires a "general obligation to have consent as the objective of consultation."[83] The Declaration explicitly requires consent of Indigenous peoples in cases of government relocation from their lands or territories (Art. 10) or storage or disposal of hazardous materials on Indigenous peoples' lands or territories (Art. 29). In other provisions (Art. 19, Art. 32(2)) UNDRIP calls on states to "cooperate and consult in good faith ... in order to obtain their free, prior, and informed consent."

In its 2018 study of best practices for operationalizing FPIC, EMRIP observes that while full consent is always the goal of consultations under UNDRIP, consent is required "if a measure or project is likely to have a significant, direct impact on Indigenous peoples' lives or land, territories or resources." Such a "sliding scale approach" carries the support of the UN Human Rights Committee and ECOSOC.[84] Surely consent can be considered necessary in the many cases where significant impacts affect Native American sacred places beyond reservation boundaries.

I find helpful Carla Fredericks's consideration of a continuum from consultation to consent. On this continuum, "meaningful consultation," the standard referenced in the Obama administration's endorsement of UNDRIP, is not the aspiration; it is the starting point. Fredericks acknowledges the gains of President Clinton's executive order and President Obama's memorandum, but she argues that "to fully realize this commitment, the United States should embrace a policy shift away from the currently articulated meaningful consultation standard:

> U.S. law and policy should move toward viewing Indigenous consultation as involving a spectrum of requirements—with good-faith, meaningful consultation as a minimum and with consent required in certain contexts, including large-scale extractive industries.[85]

Indigenous nations need not wait for state implementation.[86] They can exercise self-determination by asserting their own FPIC protocols to ensure consultation proceeds in accordance with the Declaration's norms and their own cultural protocols for decision-making.

Fredericks notes that this would enable Native nations themselves to determine who is informed and consulted and whose consent is required. Consultation is keyed to elected representatives of tribal governments, their environmental officers or tribal historic preservation officers, and only with recognized tribes. If there are other people, or internal decision-making processes and timeliness necessary for free, prior, and informed consent, Fredericks says, Native nations can generate it.

Imagined on a continuum from consultation to consent, FPIC is not a veto power on all development; it provides a realizable standard that builds Native peoples' capacity for religious and cultural self-determination, to negotiate religious and cultural interests as they see fit, and to be able to shape events before they snowball, as at Standing Rock, into insurmountable standoffs with high legal bars.

But FPIC is also an appropriately high standard for redress in the wake of its absence. Indigenous people whose lands or territories have been taken without their free, prior, and informed consent are entitled under UNDRIP to replacement of lands of equal value or just compensation, and those whose cultural, intellectual, religious, and spiritual property have been taken without their consent are likewise entitled to redress.[87]

Conclusion: A Window of Opportunity

The developments of international law considered in this chapter are in many respects liberative. Rights to "religion" are not artificially set off but are reintegrated into the complex wholes that Indigenous cultures strive to maintain and renew, and which need no parsing into Western categories like "religion". By turns, Indigenous land tenure, government, medicine, agriculture, and law need not devolve into purely secular matters. This would have particular significance in parts of the world where religious freedom is anything but an orienting discourse and perhaps even received as a colonizing imposition on other ways of navigating religious difference. Given the profoundly collective nature of Indigenous religious traditions, the elision of religious rights into the rights of peoplehood and self-determination is a compelling way forward. And yet, the translation of Indigenous religious claims into the broader language of culture or peoplehood entails limitations as well as possibilities.

Translating religion into secular discourses (culture, development, resource, heritage, land rights, collective self-determination, cultural property) or enumerating the spiritual as among the distinct facets of those discourses worthy of enumeration in articles on, say, cultural or resource rights, reinscribes and maybe even extends the reductive logic of the Enlightenment even as it aspires to move beyond the religious/secular divide. To dissolve arguably religious claims to those of culture, or to render religion as the adjective modifier *spiritual*, can dull the edges of certain Indigenous concerns that are, for lack of a better term, irreducibly sacred, sacrosanct, urgent, or ultimate, and in the doing lower the barrier to violation of those rights as merely cultural, and as capable of being suspended under a variety of prevailing concerns of national security or interest defined by states.

As the norms, monitoring processes, and structures for fuller Indigenous presence in international bodies are elaborated in time, there are fruitful possibilities for accentuating the religious freedom implications of UNDRIP, of envisioning what collective rights to religious freedom might look like in light of the Declaration. Again, this is a strategic point, not a substantive one. I have no particular point to make about some essential nature of religion that distinguishes itself sui generis from other aspects of culture. It has been the argument of this book that Native American traditions are not particularly well served analytically by the category of religion, but neither are they likely, at least in the United States, to be adequately served by the category of culture, which lacks a constitutional basis in US law. To claim that desecration of

San Francisco Peaks is more than a cultural injury, that it obstructs the flow of spiritual power, that it can render healing ceremonies null and void, or that it can interrupt ancestral afterlives and related natural cycles, is more than "cultural" injury; it meaningfully rises to that aspect of culture that the US Constitution aspires to protect as a bedrock principle of *religious* freedom.

In the nearer term, I would suggest, UNDRIP's norm of collectivizing existing human rights as they are to apply to Indigenous peoples can be profoundly useful in rethinking how religious freedom law is to apply to Native American nations. As we have seen, these nations are not legally distinguished by their race or their ethnicity in federal Indian law. In the language of international law, these nations are not distinguished by their population-hood—as minority groups among other minority groups—but by their peoplehood.

Although the norms of Indigenous rights in international law are yet ripening, and although full implementation in the United States might require our reading religion back into international Indigenous rights discourse, making claims to religion as peoplehood may very well be the best answer yet to the questions posed in this book, and in any event brings the other legal strategies discussed in these chapters up to a standard befitting Indigenous peoples.

9

Conclusion

THIS BOOK HAS sustained four key arguments on the problem of Native American religious freedom. First, *religion* and *religious freedom* have been discourses available to those with power to exclude as well as to include, but because they are powerful discourses, they have also been significant to Native communities in efforts to safeguard what they consider sacred. Second, if *religious freedom* claims have failed consistently in courts to protect sacred lands, Native communities have creatively appropriated discourses of religious freedom and the sacred, drawn on their rhetorical power, and extended their logic into legislative and regulatory successes beyond the First Amendment. Third, the collective shape of Native religious traditions may seem inevitably ill-suited to *religious freedom* in US law, which privileges the individualized faith and interiorized spirituality of traditions like Protestantism. But a considerable body of law and administrative policy has set out to "protect and preserve the religions and cultures" of Native peoples under the rubric of the nation-to-nation relationship between the United States and recognized Native nation governments, and the courts have recognized, if inadvertently, collective rights to Native religions, especially where treaty provisions point the way. More vociferous and all-encompassing is the affirmation of those collective rights in the UN Declaration on the Rights of Indigenous Peoples. Although many of its norms are only slowly growing legal teeth, the Declaration makes abundantly clear that if established human rights like religious freedom are to apply meaningfully to Indigenous peoples, they must apply collectively as well as individually. Fourth, this book has shown time and again how Native efforts to defend the sacred have been generative of religion, a source of renewal and a spirited sense of peoplehood.

In and through and after efforts to engage the law to protect what's important to them, Native peoples have made more than claims; they have made themselves.

I have tracked, chapter by chapter, how Native peoples have turned to different legal languages to defend the sacred, making claims to religion as religion/spirituality under religious freedom law, to religion as cultural resource under environmental and historic preservation law, to religion as collective right in statutes specific to Native American peoples under the trust responsibility, religion as peoplehood under federal Indian law's doctrine of inherent sovereignty (fragile as it may be given the colonizing moorings of federal Indian law), and finally religion as peoplehood under the fuller throated Indigenous rights under international law.

Toward Negotiated Agreements

The point all along has been to suggest what is gained and what is lost by seeking to defend the sacred in these available legal languages, not to rank them in order of presumed priority. To succeed in defending the sacred, Native nations know they must stay resourceful and agile, engaging multiple legal discourses at once with an awareness of the possibilities and trade-offs of each.

At the end of the day, most Native peoples are not looking to capture a headline with a court victory as much as they are looking to continue to practice their sacred traditions, to pass them on to younger generations, and to renew those traditions in the face of interruption, assimilation, and changed circumstances. Making claims in these multiple legal registers is often a matter of last resort after efforts to find agreement have failed. And the claim-making is often instrumental, with the goal of reaching agreements out of court and out of public view that enable these traditions to continue and flourish. If it stands to reason, it is not at all obvious in studies that take case law as their primary source material. Making the legal claims is often necessary to creating conditions favorable to such agreements, but the making of the legal claims is a means, not an end in itself.

As the Dakota Access Pipeline case has shown, negotiated agreements or out of court settlements don't just happen out of the goodness of everybody's heart—though goodwill has played a role in some of the cases in this book. The No-DAPL process took the sacrifice of thousands who camped and staged civil disobedience actions, those who fed them and clothed them and held ceremony with them. To reach favorable negotiated agreements, Native nations need law's muscle. This book has explored how Native nations have either gone and found that muscle or generated it themselves.

Bears Ears National Monument

An example of generating that muscle themselves, in the receptive context of goodwill of allies, is the creation of Bears Ears National Monument in 2017. National monuments are designated by presidents, of course, and Bears Ears is no different in this respect. But the story of Bears Ears is less the story of the Obama administration than it is the story of decades of activism and the concerted strategic efforts of a consortium of Native nations. When President Obama designated 1.35 million acres of southeast Utah lands as Bears Ears National Monument, he authorized a new experiment in cooperation, even collaboration, between the United States and Native nations in safeguarding sacred lands.[1] In what were formerly lands of the Navajo, Ute, and other nations, it was the culmination of at least fifty years of Indigenous efforts to

FIG. 9.1. Bears Ears Buttes
The Bears Ears Buttes from the south. Designated by President Obama in 2016,
Bears Ears National Monument was the brainchild of an intertribal coalition
to protect a wealth of sacred sites, traditional cultural properties,
and traditional knowledge related to the land. (USGS Photo)

protect their land. Obama's proclamation took its cue from a proposal by the Bears Ears Inter-Tribal Commission, made up of Navajo, Hopi, Ute, Ute Mountain Ute, and Zuni, each of whom regard the canyons, mesas, tables, mountains, and ancestral structures and objects as heritage necessary for continued ceremony, culture, and healing.

The second-largest national monument in the lower forty-eight when declared, Bears Ears is named for a landform of twin buttes "so distinctive that in each of the native languages of the region their name is the same: Hoon'Naqvut, Shash Jáa, Kwiyagatu Nukavachi, Ansh An Lashokdiwe, or 'Bears Ears.'"[2] The buttes are representative of the sophisticated relationships the nations have with more than 100,000 ancestral shrines, structures, and sites within the monument. Although the Navajo and others were formally dispossessed of this landscape in the nineteenth century, these are not only places of past heritage; the inter-tribal coalition's proposal identified the entire landscape in terms of enduring "Native presence," what it identified as the "beating heart" of Bears Ears. The proposal cites Joseph Suina of Cochiti Pueblo:

> We go with offerings to our sites. We knock on that wall and say our names— just like you should—you make your entry properly, and address those that reside there as grandmothers and grandfathers as they are. There is no dimension of time in the spirit world. It's good to come here to the sites, to your grandmothers' homes, you remember how it was to be there. With an offering, perhaps some corn meal, you identify yourself, you sing a song and the children dance, and we just speak our language.[3]

Indeed, part of what the monument celebrates and protects is the ongoing presence of ancestors and traditional Indigenous knowledge that is rooted in specific sites but that extends to the entire landscape around them. So the promise of Bears Ears is not only its protection of tangible historic cultural resources but also its nurture of Indigenous knowledge, medicine, healing, and continuing presence. For the Native nations, Bears Ears as is much about the future as it is about the past.

THE ANTIQUITIES ACT AND THE
DISTINCT HISTORY OF BEARS EARS

Since its passage in 1906, the American Antiquities Act has become a crucial legal vehicle for setting aside federal lands for conservation and other purposes. Congress delegated to the president the power to "proclaim historic

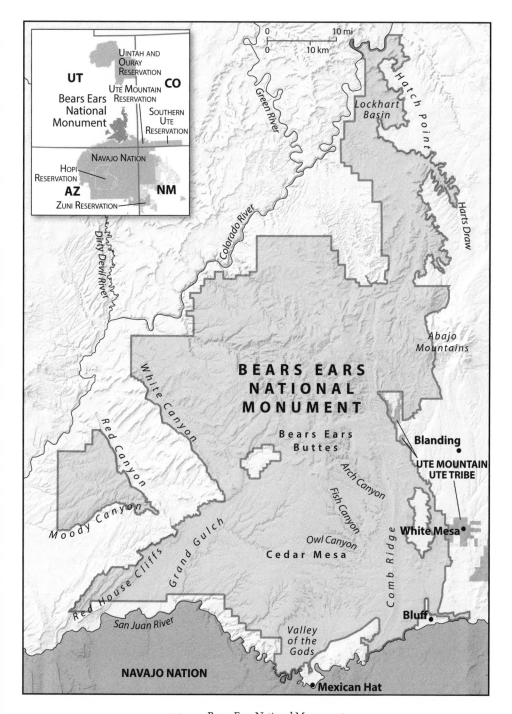

FIG. 9.2. Bears Ears National Monument

Bears Ears National Monument as it was proclaimed by President Obama, showing the surrounding
Native nations that had coalesced to propose and collaboratively manage the monument.
One year later, a proclamation by President Trump un-designated 85 percent of the monument,
opening the door to mining and oil and gas development. Legal challenges are
playing out in the courts. (Adapted from National Park Service)

landmarks, historic and prehistoric structures, and other objects of historic or scientific interest" as national monuments and to reserve lands subject to few statutory limits save that reserved parcels "shall be confined to the smallest area compatible with the proper care and management of the objects to be protected."[4] Because congressional action can be unwieldy and difficult to secure, national monument proclamations have become useful for their agile protection of Native sacred places, even if made under the rubric of conservation, recreation and scientific value. Advocates of the act's passage were deeply concerned with threats to the integrity of archeological sites, which were deemed American Antiquities even though they were associated of course with living Native nations. The first national monument was declared in 1906 by President Roosevelt, proclaiming Mato Tipila "Devil's Tower National Monument." As with national parks such as Yellowstone and the Grand Canyon, though, Native peoples were largely excluded from traditional uses, including ceremonial uses, of their lands.

The recent history of the Bears Ears region involved efforts by Native peoples, especially the Navajo, to protect ancestral lands and places of significance from a variety of threats. Utah Senator Robert F. Bennett had begun a Public Lands Initiative (PLI) to integrate competing voices in management of the existing set aside federal lands in the area, incorporating Native input. A Navajo nonprofit organization, Utah Diné Bikeyah (UDB) formed to conduct a cultural mapping project and, according to Charles Wilkinson, to ensure a strong Native voice in the initiative.[5] But when Bennett was ousted in a primary, his initiative was transformed by Utah congressmen Robert Bishop and Jason Chaffetz, who "conducted the process," according to Wilkinson, "in ways that marginalized conservationist and tribal voices." Instead, they located the development of the PLI proposal and public comment at the local level of the Commission of San Juan County, which through gerrymandering had all but ensured two of the three elected commissioners would be responsive to non-Navajo interests even though more than half the county's population is Navajo.[6] UDB felt largely shut out of the process, and public comments were largely ignored. "Nonetheless, the tribal leaders were willing to enter into negotiations with the delegation, although they withdrew when it was apparent no reasonable compromise could be made."[7]

Outside these shut doors, the Bears Ears Inter-Tribal Coalition formed, and drawing on the work of UDB, made its 2015 proposal to President Obama to proclaim a national monument. With Congress failing to pass the PLI the following fall, President Obama proclaimed Bears Ears National Monument in late December. His proclamation did not endorse every aspect of the coalition's proposal, but it was enough to earn a reputation as what Charles Wilkinson calls the "first Native national monument."[8]

Because of the distinctive history behind the creation of Bears Ears National Monument, Sarah Krakoff acknowledges its potential to go beyond the "dark side" of the history of conservation lands.[9]

COLLABORATIVE MANAGEMENT OF SACRED PLACES

In its proposal, the inter-tribal coalition stated, "the effort to preserve Bears Ears has always been premised on collaborative management between the tribes and the federal government. Only then will we Native people have real influence on how this sacred land is managed."[10] While President Obama did not enact the coalition's proposal that a body representing the Native nations collaborate as equals in the management with federal officials, his proclamation created an advisory Bears Ears Commission, made up of representatives chosen by the five Native governments, and directed the Interior and Agriculture Secretaries to "meaningfully engage the Commission ... in the development of the management plan and to inform subsequent management of the monument."[11]

Bolstering what the commission would bring to the table beyond mere advice, Obama's proclamation further directed federal officials "to carefully and fully consider integrating the traditional and historical knowledge and special expertise of the Commission." Although federal officials were the managers ultimately, President Obama structured federal accountability to the commission into the deal. If officials "decide not to incorporate specific recommendations submitted to them in writing by the Commission or comparable entity," the proclamation continued, "they will provide the Commission or comparable entity with a written explanation of their reasoning."

Wilkinson concluded based on knowledge of the negotiations that "in the end, the tribes and agency officials reached an understanding that was reflected in the Proclamation. There would be no joint decision making as the tribes initially proposed it, but the tribes would have a truly robust role in management and decision-making that goes far beyond traditional consultation."[12]

TRUMP TAKES AIM

In December 2017, President Trump took the unprecedented, and presumably unlawful, step of citing his authority under the Antiquities Act to eviscerate and effectively reverse national monument designation for Bears Ears.[13] Trump eviscerated Bears Ears by 85 percent—1.15 million acres—and left two small management units as a remainder. Cynically, the proclamation sugar-coated the devastating blow to the monument by using the Diné term for Bears Ears, Shash Jáa, to designate one of the two units of the remaining monument. The proclamation also watered down the collaborative manage-ment by adding a San Juan County representative to the advisory commis-sion. And a Bears Ears Monument Management Plan released in July 2019 elaborated the Trump proclamation's changes to the original structure for col-laborative management.[14] The administration effectively gave the go-ahead to oil and uranium mining exploration on the uninstated lands.[15]

Earlier in 2017, Trump asked his Interior secretary to review all national monument designations made since 1996 that were greater than 100,000 acres or "where the Secretary of Interior determines that the designation or expansion was made without adequate public outreach or coordination with relevant stakeholders."[16] Secretary Zinke's review fleshed out much of the ra-tionale for reducing monuments, with Bears Ears being the most politically charged and thus most symbolic. Citing the limitations clause of the Antiqui-ties Act, Trump's proclamation began with the finding that "the area of Fed-eral land reserved in the Bears Ears National Monument established by Proc-lamation 9558 is not confined to the smallest area compatible with the proper care and management of those objects."[17]

Unsurprisingly, Trump's action is under a barrage of litigation.[18] While the only result at the time of this writing has been a federal judge's rejection of the government's effort to relocate the proceedings to Utah from courts in the DC circuit,[19] Trump's proclamation will likely be held unlawful by federal courts until presumably appealed to the Supreme Court, since Congress intended the Antiquities Act to protect, not to undo, protection of natural and cultural resources. Presidents in the past indeed have reduced the size of national monuments designated by their predecessors, but these were not challenged in the courts.[20] More recently, lower courts have faced a number of challenges to excessive use of the Antiquities Act monument proclamations but thus far have found those challenges unavailing.[21] If this makes Bears Ears advocates optimistic, their optimism is guarded by knowledge that the presently con-figured Supreme Court could well reverse the momentum of that case law.[22]

LESSONS OF BEARS EARS

Even as ongoing litigation makes Bears Ears something of a dynamic situation for premature conclusion-drawing, the open questions it raises are fitting to conclude a book that poses more questions than it answers.

Clearly for the Navajo, Ute, Hopi, Zuni, and Ute Mountain Ute nations, Bears Ears National Monument offers a way to preserve and manage a wealth of sacred places and to do so largely on their own terms. While Obama's proclamation did not enact all provisions of the Bears Ears Inter-Tribal Coalition's 2015 proposal, especially in terms of its full-throated structure for collaborative management, the proclamation did endorse the key points made by the nations: the protection of sacred places and sacred knowledge under the rubric of an ancestral landscape. Although backed up by maps of sacred sites, the proclamation or public-facing materials need not disclose these places or the knowledge around them as *religion*. Indeed, Obama's proclamation gestures toward Indigenous sovereignty and peoplehood in several regards. The proclamation incorporates the historic dispossession of the Navajo and other nations from Bears Ears land and references the continued relationships asserted in spite of that dispossession by the nations through pilgrimage, medicine gathering, and stories. What is more, following the Native coalition's proposal, Obama's proclamation imagines the protections of the 100,000 objects and sites not simply in terms of their geo-specificity but also in terms of the relationship Indigenous nations have with those places, and even the generativity—for Native nations but also for the American nation—of the preservation of those relationships:

> The traditional ecological knowledge amassed by the Native Americans whose ancestors inhabited this region, passed down from generation to generation, offers critical insight into the historic and scientific significance of the area. Such knowledge is, itself, a resource to be protected and used in understanding and managing this landscape sustainably for generations to come.[23]

The audacity and creativity of Bears Ears on these points made it vulnerable to early attack by the Trump administration. The rationale put forward in Trump's proclamation makes clear that it was not only extraction industry access to federal lands that were in the sights. Trump's proclamation bases its gutting of Bears Ears on a shrunken interpretation of the Native heritage to be preserved to lifeless "sites" and objects.

The Trump administration, it should be said, was not simply going rogue here; the policy harks back to an early twentieth-century view undergirding the preservation of Indian "antiquities" as the cultural property of the American nation at the same time as policies of assimilation were rooting out the religious and cultural practices that tied living Native nations to those places, a view that Sarah Krakoff rightly characterizes as "eliminating indigenous presence while saving the indigenous past."[24]

Trump's proclamation took pains to *objectify* the objects to be protected, to rid them of the subjectivity of ancestral presence and of ongoing intersubjective relationships and duties Native peoples have with those ancestors and associated places, much less of the living generativity of those relationships for Native peoples. Accordingly, traditional knowledge and lifeways, including ecological knowledge, failed to make the cut as "objects" to be protected. Cloaked in the language of reasonable natural and cultural resource management, such intangible heritage was severed from sites and objects. So much for the sacred.

I don't want to suggest that what has happened with Bears Ears necessarily follows any articulation of sacred claims in the discourse of cultural resource management. Following the inter-tribal coalition's proposal, Obama's proclamation set aside lands for so much more than preservation of "objects of historical and scientific interest" or tangible and intangible cultural resources. And as already observed, the collaborative management, co-management, or even formal advisory commission structure with the tribes points to ways that sacred concerns might be addressed on the terms of Indigenous sovereignty and peoplehood.

The story of Bears Ears, if unfinished, does suggest unforeseen limitations of the strategy of a national monument designation and the legal vulnerability of sacred land protections that are rooted in the discourse of cultural resource management. Indigenous challenges to Trump's proclamation are rooted in case law on the executive authority under the Antiquities Act, not on violations of their religious freedom. This is hardly surprising, given the failure of courts yet to find First Amendment or RFRA protections for Native American sacred lands. But the absence of the discourse of the sacred in the Bears Ears litigation stems more directly from the proposal's strategic articulation of sacred claims to Bears Ears landscapes in the language of environmental and cultural resource protections at an important *American* place.

By the same token, at stake for the Navajo, Hopi, Ute, Ute Mountain Ute, and Zuni nations are not simply view sheds, backpacking trails, and contemplative wilderness—interests that Native American individuals share with other Americans. What's at stake is peoplehood: the continued practice of Indigenous ways of life, ongoing engagement with traditional knowledge, and healing from historical trauma.

No One Word for Religion

I conclude with two key lessons learned from Suzan Shown Harjo in the work of the book, for both sum up its analysis well. First, if the Native maxim "we have no word for religion," is compelling for stating the problem of Native American traditions and the category of religion, it is also true that it has played into a sense of the inevitable illegibility of Native sacred claims in that legal discourse. More insidiously, perhaps, is how the expression "no word for religion" suggests a slippery slope that comes with any Native sacred claim—a deep-seated fear that because "everything is sacred," there are apparently no "limiting principles," as Kristen Carpenter puts it in an article that argues instead that Indigenous religions are all about such limiting principles. But as I indicated in the introduction, Suzan Harjo puts the matter slightly differently to great effect. It's not that Native peoples have no word for religion, she has said, it's that they "have no *one* word for religion." This is to say Indigenous peoples have religion, to be sure, but the ways they have religion are far more sophisticated and more complex than what conventional wisdom expects of the term, and certainly what conventional wisdom expects about Native spirituality. Put another way, what might be understood capaciously as "religion" informs Native lifeways in multiple registers: their economies, their polities, their law, and their ways of inhabiting lands and waters.

Second, Harjo has described religious and cultural freedoms as anything but peripheral to the political and economic concerns that often rise to the top of an Indian Country agenda. Indeed, Harjo describes religious and cultural freedoms as "atmospheric" of the rest, religious and cultural self-determination absolutely necessary to full political and economic self-determination:

> If in one hundred years, you have a situation where there's no tribal language, no tribal religion, and everyone has stopped dancing, has stopped doing anything that relates to that tribe, to that tribe's history or traditions, then how long do you think that tribe is going to be recognized for any special relationship or anything that we enjoy because of a special relationship? That'd be about a day and a half.[25]

NOTES

Introduction

1. National Historic Preservation Act, 54 U.S.C. § 300101 et seq., especially § 306108 (1966, as amended 1992).

2. Jon Eagle Sr., "Declaration of Jon Eagle, Sr. in Support of Motion for Preliminary Injunction," Standing Rock Sioux Tribe v. U.S. Army Corps of Engineers (No. 1:16-cv-1534), para. 11 (2016). Geologists conclude the spherical stones were fashioned by underground water flows.

3. J. Z. Smith, *Imagining Religion*, xi.

4. Martin, *Land Looks After Us*, x.

5. Chidester, *Savage Systems*.

6. See Joseph Epes Brown, *The Spiritual Legacy of the American Indian* (Bloomington, IN: World Wisdom, 2007), 20.

7. McNally, *Ojibwe Singers*.

8. Vine Deloria Jr., *God Is Red*, 200.

9. Suzan Shown Harjo, Remarks at Freedom Forum Roundtable on Native American Religious Freedom, Vermilion, SD, May 2008.

10. Harjo, Remarks at Freedom Forum Roundtable.

11. American Indian Religious Freedom Act 42 U.S.C. § 1996; AIRFA Peyote Amendments of 1994, 42 USC § 1996 (3); Native American Graves Protection and Repatriation Act 25 U.S.C. § 3001 et seq. (1990).

12. I make a more technical legal argument related to this book in a law review article. See McNally, "Native American Religious Freedom as a Collective Right."

13. Nabokov, *Where the Lightning Strikes*; Burton, *Worship and Wilderness*; Gulliford, *Sacred Objects and Sacred Places*; Vine Deloria Jr., *God Is Red*.

14. Michaelson, *"Is the Miner's Canary Silent"*; Vescey, *Handbook of American Indian Religious Freedom*; H. Smith, *Seat at the Table*; Weaver, *Other Words*.

15. Mihesuah, *Repatriation Reader*; Fine-Dare, *Grave Injustice*; Johnson, *Sacred Remains*; Riding In, "Repatriation: A Pawnee Perspective."

16. Wenger, *We Have a Religion*; Wenger, *Religious Freedom*; Maroukis, *Peyote Road*.

17. Johnson, *Religion in the Moment*.

18. Estes, *Our History Is the Future*; Morman, *Many Nations under Many Gods*.

19. Shrubsole, *What Has No Place Remains*.

20. Hale, *"Fugitive Religion"*; Lloyd, *"Between God and Land."*

21. *Lyng v. Northwest Cemetery Protective Association*, 485 U.S. 439 (1988) (hereafter *Lyng*). See Lloyd, "Between God and Land."

22. *Employment Division, Dept. of Human Services, State of Oregon v. Smith*, 484 U.S. 872 (1990) (hereafter *Smith*).

23. *Navajo Nation et al. v. U.S. Forest Service*, 535 F. 3d 1058 (9th Cir. 2008), cert. denied, 129 S. Ct. 2763 (2009) (hereafter Navajo Nation).

24. Navajo Nation, 535 F. 3d at 1063.

25. *Standing Rock Sioux Tribe v. United States Army Corps of Engineers*, 239 F. Supp. 3d 77 (D.D.C. 2017).

26. Wenger, *We Have a Religion*; *Native American Church* v. Navajo Tribal *Council*, 272 F. 2d 131 (1959).

27. Indian Civil Rights Act (1968), 25 U.S.C. §§ 1301–1304; *Santa Clara Pueblo v. Martinez*, 436 U.S. 48 (1978).

28. *See* Wenger, *Religious Freedom*.

29. Hamburger, *Separation of Church and State*.

30. Sehat, *Myth of American Religious Freedom*, 4–8.

31. Finbarr Curtis sees not so much a *politics* of religious freedom as an *economy* of religious freedom, seeing how religious freedom hews to the legal protection of individual ownership of privately held religious commitments. But Curtis's view of an economy of religious freedom points away from determinism to its malleability, the play of various social actors pursuing their interests and leading to a messy result. "What the study of religious freedom illustrates is the need to abandon the quest for the legal fantasy of the perfect rule, the abstract principle that governs all situations in the same way. Religious freedom cannot be abstracted from diverse contests over the distribution of social power, nor can it be divorced from the interested choices of social actors." Curtis, *Production of American Religious Freedom*, 169.

32. Asad, *Formations of the Secular*.

33. Sullivan et al., *Politics of Religious Freedom*, and related posts on "*The Immanent Frame*"; Hurd, *Beyond Religious Freedom*; Curtis, *Production of American Religious Freedom*.

34. Hurd, *Beyond Religious Freedom*, 5–6, citing Gerd Baumann, *Contesting Culture: Discourses of Identity in Multi-ethnic London* (Cambridge: Cambridge University Press, 1996), 30.

35. W. Sullivan, *Impossibility of Religious Freedom*, 1.

36. W. Sullivan, *Impossibility of Religious Freedom*, 10.

37. *Warner v. City of Boca Raton*, 64 F. Supp. 2d 1272 (S.D. Fla. 1999).

38. W. Sullivan, *Impossibility of Religious Freedom*, 10.

39. W. Sullivan, *Impossibility of Religious Freedom*, 8.

40. W. Sullivan, *Prison Religion*; W. Sullivan, *Ministry of Presence*.

41. Chidester, *Empire of Religion*; Chidester, *Savage Systems*.

42. Wenger, *Religious Freedom*, 1.

43. Civilizational assemblages are, for Wenger, "the complex interplay of ideological and institutional processes that work together to define who and what counts as civilized and thus as fully human—and by contrast, who and what does not." Wenger, *Religious Freedom*, 3.

44. Hurd, *Beyond Religious Freedom*; Sullivan et al., *Politics of Religious Freedom*; Sehat, *Myth of Religious Freedom*; Curtis, *Production of Religious Freedom*; Sullivan, *Impossibility of Religious Freedom*.

45. My position here is related to but distinct from David Decosimo. With a dialectical, philosophical, pragmatist perspective, Decosimo usefully discloses the implicit essentialism that characterized criticisms of "the very idea of religious freedom" in what he calls "the new genealogy of religious freedom." Decosimo argues that the composite critique of this "movement and mood" shares certain base assumptions with the foundationalist view of religious freedom as universal and neutral that it seeks to unmask. I agree with Decosimo that religious freedom need not be viewed as intrinsically or inherently *impossible, paradoxical,* or *incoherent* and share his dialectical, pragmatist view. But informed by how religious freedom has been used against Native peoples, I agree more with the "new genealogy" than does Decosimo. See Decosimo, "New Genealogy of Religious Freedom."

46. Wenger's second book, on religious freedom and race, sharpens my sense of the race-informed limits of religious freedom possibilities for Native peoples but lacks an appreciation of the legal/political uses of religious freedom discourses in the present and too quickly disavows religious freedom arguments. See Wenger, *Religious Freedom.*

47. Johnson, *Religion in the Moment*; Johnson and Kraft, "Standing Rock Religion(s)."

48. This was true, for example, in the cases of *Lyng* and *Navajo Nation.*

49. United Nations Declaration on the Rights of Indigenous Peoples, G.A. Res. 61/295, U.N. Doc. A/RES/61/295, Annex (September 13, 2007).

50. Sarah Krakoff, "Undoing Indian Law One Case at a Time: Judicial Minimalism and Tribal Sovereignty," *American University Law Review* 50 (2001): 1177; Richland, "Paths in the Wilderness," 239.

51. Tsosie, "Introduction: Symposium on Cultural Sovereignty," 1–2.

52. Tsosie and Coffey, "Rethinking the Tribal Sovereignty Doctrine," 196, 210.

53. Tsosie and Coffey, "Rethinking the Tribal Sovereignty Doctrine," *191.*

54. Frank Ettawageshik, "Relationships: How Our Ancestors Perceived Treaties and Property Rights," 13th *Vine Deloria Jr. Indigenous Studies Symposium*, Northwest Indian College, May 2018. www.youtube.com/watch?v=fcz7cgaLxdc, last accessed April, 2019.

55. This discussion is summarized in chapter 6, but found more fully elaborated in McNally, "Native American Religious Freedom as a Collective Right."

56. See, for example, United States v. Wilgus, 638 F. 3d 1274 (10th Cir. 2011).

57. Cairns, *Citizens Plus*; Shrubsole, *What Has No Place Remains.*

58. *Ktunaxa Nation v. British Columbia,* [2017] 2 SCR 386.

59. Congress extended US citizenship to all Native Americans only as recently as 1923.

60. *Worcester v. Georgia*, 31 U.S. 515 (1832).

61. U.S. Const. art. I. § 8, cl. 3.

62. More recent developments at the United Nations and the Organization of American States have identified this distinctive status in terms of what Native Americans share with other autochthonous (that is, springing from the land) indigenous peoples around the globe, whose nationhood falls below the level of the modern nation-state but above the level of citizens, and above or even populations made up of minority citizens.

63. U.S. v. Winans, 198 U.S. 371 (1905), 381.

64. Echo-Hawk, *In the Courts of the Conqueror*; Echo-Hawk, *In The Light of Justice*; Williams, *Like a Loaded Weapon.*

65. See Wilkinson, *American Indians, Time, and the Law.*

66. Lone Wolf v. Hitchcock, 187 U.S. 553 (1903).

67. See Deloria and Lytle, *American Indians, American Justice.*

68. See, for example, efforts by Cochiti Pueblo and Ohkeh Owingeh Pueblo (San Juan Pueblo) in the Indian Claims Commission process to reclaim lands in Bandolier National Monument and the Jemez Mountains.

69. See Thomas Cowger, *National Congress of American Indians: The Founding Years* (Lincoln: University of Nebraska Press, 2001). Until the 1960s, tribes had to have their legal representatives approved by the BIA. While there were a number of advocacy organizations established to "help" the tribes, the appearance of the Native American Rights Fund in 1970 helped advance a coordinated legal agenda.

70. See, for example, *Seminole Nation v. United States,* 316 U.S. 286 (1942).

71. Wilkins and Lomawaima, *Uneven Ground,* 64–98, 256.

72. See Pyramid Lake Paiute v. Morton, 499 F. 2d 1095 (1974).

73. *"Cobell v. Salazar Class Action Settlement Agreement,"* No. 1:96CV01285-JR Document 3660–2 *(December 7, 2009).*

74. See, for example, Gibson v. Babbitt, 223 F. 3d 1256 (11th Cir. 2000); U.S. v. Antoine, 318 F. 3d 919 (9th Cir. 2003), cert. denied, 124 S. Ct. 1505 (2004); U.S. v. Wilgus, 638 F. 3d 1274 (10th Cir. 2011).

75. Regents of the University of California v. Bakke, 438 U.S. 265 (1978).

76. Morton v. Mancari, 417 U.S. 535 (1974).

77. Santa Clara Pueblo v. Martinez, 436 U.S. 49 (1978).

78. United States v. Antelope, 430 U.S. 641 (1977). "The decisions of this Court leave no doubt that federal legislation with respect to Indian tribes, although extending to Indians as such, is not based upon impermissible racial classifications. Quite the contrary, classification singling out Indian tribes as subjects of legislation are expressly provided for in the Constitution and supported by the ensuing history of the Federal Government's relations with Indians." Antelope, 430 U.S. 641 at 682. This special status has come under recent challenge in the Indian Child Welfare Act. See Adoptive Couple v. Baby Girl, 133 S. Ct. 2552 (2013); Brackeen v. Bernhardt, No. 18–11479 (5th Cir. 2019).

79. Washington v. Confederated Bands and Tribes of the Yakima Indian Nation, 439 U.S. 463 (1979); U.S. v. Hardman, 297 F. 3d 1116 (10th Cir. 2002) (rehearing, en banc), 1128.

80. See James Clifford, "Identity at Mashpee," in *Predicament of Culture* (Cambridge, MA: Harvard University Press, 1988).

81. National Environmental Policy Act, 42 U.S.C. §§ 4321–4335 (1969); National Historic Preservation Act, 54 U.S.C. §§ 300101 et seq., especially § 306108 (1966).

Chapter 1: Religion as Weapon: The Civilization Regulations, 1883–1934

1. Wenger, *We Have a Religion;* Wenger, *Religious Freedom;* Maroukis, *Peyote Road.*

2. Roy Harvey Pearce, *Savagism and Civilization* (Berkeley: University of California Press, 1988); Berkhofer, *White Man's Indian.*

3. Alexander V, "Romanus Pontifex" (1436); Alexander VI, "Inter-Caetera II" (1493).

4. Miller, *Discovering Indigenous Lands;* Williams, *American Indian in Western Legal Thought;* Newcomb, *Pagans in the Promised Land.*

5. Johnson v. M'Intosh, 21 U.S. (8 Wheat.) 543 (1823).

6. M'Intosh, 21 U.S. at 588.

7. M'Intosh, 21 U.S. at 589.

8. M'Intosh, 21 U.S. at 590.

9. The continuing legal force of the Doctrine was clear in *Tee-Hit-Ton Indians v. United States*, 348 U.S. 272 (1955). By 2005, the Supreme Court was still referencing the Doctrine of Discovery in a holding against Oneida Nation claims to incorporate traditional lands unlawfully taken from them by the state of New York (in flagrant violation of the same principles underscored in *M'Intosh*) that they had bought back on the open market. City of Sherrill v. Oneida Indian Nation of New York, 544 U.S. 197 (2005) at n. 1.

10. Wenger, *Religious Freedom*.

11. Pearce, *Savagism and Civilization*.

12. Johnson, Klassen, and Sullivan, *Ekklesia*, 6, 3.

13. Johnson, Klassen, and Sullivan, *Ekklesia*, 77.

14. Pamela Klassen, "Spiritual Jurisdictions: Treaty People and the Queen of Canada," in Johnson, Klassen, and Sullivan, *Ekklesia*, 142.

15. Chidester, *Savage Systems*.

16. Indian Appropriations Act of 1871, 25 U.S.C. § 71; agreements continued to be made between the United States and Native peoples but not treaties requiring Senate ratification.

17. Prucha, *American Indian Policy in Crisis*; Hoxie, *Final Promise*.

18. Beaver, *Church, State, and the American Indians*.

19. George E. Tinker, *Missionary Conquest: The Gospel and Native American Cultural Genocide* (Minneapolis: Fortress Press, 1993).

20. Annual Report of the Commissioner of Indian Affairs to the Secretary of the Interior, 1874 (Washington, DC: GPO 1874) (hereafter, CIA Annual Report).

21. Graber, *Gods of Indian Country*.

22. Lone Wolf v. Hitchcock, 187 U.S. 553 (1903); Graber, *Gods of Indian Country*, 151–200.

23. Deloria and Lytle, *American Indians, American Justice*.

24. See Michelle Meyer, *The White Earth Tragedy: Ethnicity and Dispossession at a Minnesota Anishinaabe Reservation, 1889–1920* (Lincoln: University of Nebraska Press, 1994). Some reservations, like that of the Red Lake Nation in Minnesota, managed to evade allotment.

25. See K. Tsianina Lomawaima, *They Called It Prairie Light* (Lincoln: University of Nebraska Press, 1995); Brenda Child, *Boarding School Seasons* (Lincoln: University of Nebraska Press, 1998).

26. Richard Henry Pratt, *Battlefield and Classroom: Four Decades with the American Indian*, ed. Robert M. Utley (Norman: University of Oklahoma Press, 2003).

27. Data compiled from CIA Annual Reports. Calculation of 2018 dollars based on Economic History Association, https://eh.net/howmuchisthat/, accessed September 2018.

28. Bishop William Hare, Annual Report to Indian Agent, September 11, 1877, CIA Annual Report 1883, p. xi.

29. Religious studies scholars have been keen to point out that religious polemics against idolatry, heresy, infidelity, and the like wind up affirming the religious power of their adversary's purportedly empty or "fake" signs and practices. See David Chidester, *Authentic Fakes* (Berkeley: University of California Press, 2005); David Morgan, *Sacred Gaze* (Berkeley: University of California Press, 2005).

30. Secretary of the Interior Henry Teller to Commissioner of Indian Affairs Hiram Price (December 2, 1882), CIA Annual Report 1883 (hereafter Teller to Price).

31. Teller to Price.

32. On the same dynamic in Canada, see Pamela Klassen, "Spiritual Jurisdictions: Treaty People and the Queen of Canada," in Johnson, Klassen, and Sullivan, *Ekklesia*, 140–43.

33. Klassen, "Spiritual Jurisdictions," 140–43.

34. Klassen, "Spiritual Jurisdictions," 140–43.

35. Klassen, "Spiritual Jurisdictions," 140–43.

36. The 1892 Regulations were published in the CIA Annual Report 1892, 28–31. Regulations of the Indian Office Effective April 1, 1904, § 584, 1–9.

37. The precise origin of speaking of the Code of Indian Offenses as the Religious Crimes Code is uncertain, though it may very well have been popularized by John Collier at the time of his rejection of the code. A 1949 book by Collier references the regulations thus. John Collier, *Rites and Ceremonies of the Indians of the Southwest* (New York: E. P. Dutton, 1949), 30.

38. Teller to Price.

39. On the Sun Dance, see, for example, Ella Deloria, *Waterlily* (Lincoln: University of Nebraska Press, 2009); Joseph G. Jorgensen, *The Sun Dance Religion: Power for the Powerless* (Chicago: University of Chicago. Press, 1972).

40. J. M. Woodburn Jr. to Maj. L. F. Spencer, CIA Annual Report 1889, 162.

41. J. M. Woodburn Jr. to Maj. L. F. Spencer, CIA Annual Report 1889, 162.

42. CIA Annual Report 1888, 48.

43. CIA Annual Report 1892.

44. U.S. v. Kagama, 118 U.S. 375 (1886); Lone Wolf v. Hitchcock, 182 U.S. 553 (1903).

45. Kevin Gover, remarks in the Library of Congress Symposium, "Indian Religious Freedom: To Litigate or Legislate" (November 28, 2007), www.loc.gov/today/cyberlc/feature_wdesc.php?rec=4245, last accessed March 2018.

46. See, for example, CIA Annual Report 1886, xxvii; CIA Annual Report 1888, xxx.

47. U.S. v. Clapox, 35 Fed. 573 (1888).

48. *Clapox*, 35 Fed. at 577.

49. Treaty of June 9, 1855, 12 Stat. 948, art. 8; Clapox, 35 Fed. at 576.

50. *Clapox*, 35 Fed. at 576, citing U.S. v. Kagama, 118 U.S. 375 (1886).

51. Wilkins, *American Indian Sovereignty and the U.S. Supreme Court*, 8, 11–12. Noonan, *Persons and Masks of the Law*, 20.

52. Matthew L. M. Fletcher, "Failed Protectors: The Indian Trust and Killers of the Flower Moon," *Michigan Law Review* 117 (2019): 1253.

53. CIA Annual Report 1889, 154.

54. CIA Annual Report 1886, xxvii.

55. CIA Annual Report 1889, 26.

56. CIA Annual Reports 1884–1993.

57. CIA Annual Report 1890, 40.

58. CIA Annual Report 1890, 40–41.

59. "Old Chief Passes Away," *Sioux County Pioneer Arrow*, Fort Yates, North Dakota, December 23, 1932.

60. Thomas W. Foley, *Father Francis M. Craft: Missionary to the Sioux* (Lincoln: University of Nebraska Press, 2007), 40.

61. Report of Brigadier-General Ruger, September 1, 1889, in *Report of the Secretary of War Communicated to the Two Houses of Congress*, 51st Congress (Washington, DC: GPO, 1889), vol. 1, 160.

62. "A Medicine Man in Irons," *Frank Leslie's Illustrated Newspaper*, December 1, 1888, 256.

63. "Old Chief Passes Away," *Sioux County Pioneer Arrow*, Fort Yates, North Dakota, December 23, 1932. Among those receiving names were notable non-Natives like Ernest Thompson Seton, a founder of the Boy Scouts.

64. Literature on the Ghost Dance includes James Mooney, *The Ghost Dance Religion and the Sioux Outbreak of 1890* (Lincoln: University of Nebraska Press, 1991 [1896]); Michael Hittman, *Wovoka and the Ghost Dance*, exp. ed. (Lincoln: University of Nebraska Press 1997); Louis S. Warren, *God's Red Son: The Ghost Dance and the Making of Modern America* (New York: Basic Books, 2017); Hale, "Fugitive Religion."

65. McLaughlin to T. J. Morgan, October 17, 1890, CIA Annual Report 1891, 125 (hereafter McLaughlin to Morgan).

66. McLaughlin to Morgan, 125.

67. McLaughlin to Morgan, 126.

68. McLaughlin to Morgan, 126.

69. McLaughlin to Morgan, 129.

70. McLaughlin to Morgan, 124.

71. Wenger, *Religious Freedom*, 110, citing William S. E. Coleman, *Voices of Wounded Knee* (Lincoln: University of Nebraska Press), 57.

72. Wenger, *Religious Freedom*, 111; Mooney, *Ghost Dance Religion*. See Robert Ruby and John Brown, *Dreamer-Prophets of the Columbian Plateau: Smohalla and Skolaskin* (Norman: University of Oklahoma Press, 1989).

73. Wenger, *Religious Freedom*, 112, citing Raymond DeMallie, introduction to Mooney, *Ghost Dance Religion*, xix.

74. See Barbara Myerhoff, *The Peyote Hunt: The Sacred Journey of the Huichol Indians* (Ithaca, NY: Cornell University Press, 1974).

75. These histories have been told well, though interpretations have moved too quickly to regard Peyotism merely as a function of addressing deprivation. Maroukis, *Peyote Road*; H. Smith, *Seat at the Table*; Weston LaBarre, *The Peyote Cult* (Norman: University of Oklahoma Press, 2012 [1938]); Omer Stewart, *Peyote Religion: A History* (Norman: University of Oklahoma Press, 1987).

76. Maroukis, *Peyote Road*, 32.

77. Maroukis, *Peyote Road*, 32.

78. Maroukis, *Peyote Road* 32.

79. Maroukis, *Peyote Road*, 39.

80. Maroukis, *Peyote Road*, 39.

81. William T. Hagan, *Quanah Parker: Comanche Chief* (Norman: University of Oklahoma Press), 115–20, cited in Maroukis, *Peyote Road*, 33.

82. Maroukis, *Peyote Road*, 51.

83. Maroukis, *Peyote Road*, 40.

84. Maroukis, *Peyote Road*, 44.

85. F. H. Abbott, Assistant Commissioner of Indian Affairs to Leech, March 8, 1912. Yankton Superintendent's Annual Narrative 193, roll 72, cited in Maroukis, *Peyote Road*, 45.

86. Maroukis, *Peyote Road*, 45.

87. Maroukis, *Peyote Road*, 38–39.

88. Maroukis, *Peyote Road*, 39–40.

89. Indian Appropriations Act of August 24, 1913, 37 Stat. L. 519, chap. 388; CIA Annual Report 1913, 14.

90. CIA Annual Report 1909, 14; Maroukis, *Peyote Road*, 49.

91. U.S. Cong., House, HR 2614, 65th Cong. (1918).

92. Mooney earned the ire of Indian Bureau officials for his work, including prominent Native leaders like Gertrude Bonnin and Charles Eastman. He died before he could complete the in-depth study on the Peyote religion.

93. Maroukis, *Peyote Road*, 56–57.

94. Maroukis, *Peyote Road*, 107.

95. Commissioner of Indian Affairs, Circular 1665 *Indian Dancing*.

96. Commissioner of Indian Affairs, Circular 1665 *Indian Dancing*.

97. Wenger, *We Have A Religion*.

98. Wenger, *We Have a Religion*, 47–49.

99. Wenger, *We Have a Religion*, 52.

100. Wenger, *We Have a Religion*, 103

101. Wenger, *We Have a Religion*, 183

102. Wenger, *We Have a Religion*. Wenger's important point here, in my view, becomes obscured in her subsequent book. See Wenger, *Religious Freedom*.

103. Maroukis, *Peyote Road*, 113.

104. Maroukis, *Peyote Road*, 112.

105. "Problem of Indian Administration," Institute for Government Research Studies in Administration (Baltimore, MD: Johns Hopkins University Press, 1928), 22.

106. "Problem of Indian Administration," 631.

107. "Problem of Indian Administration," 845.

108. Kelly, *Assault on Assimilation*.

109. Circular 2970—Indian Religious Freedom and Indian Culture, Department of the Interior, Office of Indian Affairs, Washington, January 3, 1934.

110. Wenger, *Religious Freedom*, 105.

111. Circular 2970.

112. Wenger, *Religious Freedom*, 109.

113. Wenger, *Religious Freedom*, 142.

114. Wenger, *Religious Freedom*.

115. Martin, *Land Looks After Us*.

116. McNally, *Ojibwe Singers*; Joel Martin and Mark Nicholas, *Native Americans, Christianity, and the Reshaping of the American Religious Landscape* (Chapel Hill: University of North Carolina Press, 2010).

117. LaBarre, *Peyote Cult*; Anthony F. C. Wallace, *Death and Rebirth of the Seneca* (New York: Random House, 1969).

118. Philip Deloria, *Playing Indian*.

119. Hale, "Fugitive Religion."

120. Walter Echo-Hawk and Jack Trope, "The Native American Graves Protection and Repatriation Act: Background and Legislative History," in Miheusah, *Repatriation Reader*, 125.

121. Sullivan, *Ministry of Presence*.

122. Suzan Harjo, Remarks, Library of Congress Symposium, "Indian Religious Freedom: To Litigate or Legislate," November 28, 2007, www.loc.gov/today/cyberlc/feature_wdesc.php ?rec=4245, accessed October 2018.

Chapter 2: Religion as Spirituality: Native Religion in Prisons

1. Religious studies scholar Lee Irwin, for example, chooses the term "spirituality" over "religion" because the latter problematically rests on a distinction between sacred and profane that doesn't obtain in Native communities. Lee Irwin, "Introduction: Themes in Native American Spirituality," *American Indian Quarterly* 20, no. 3 (Summer 1996): 311.

2. *Inmate Religious Beliefs and Practices*, US Department of Justice, Federal Bureau of Prisons Technical Reference No. T5360.01 (March, 27, 2002).

3. Sullivan, *Ministry of Presence*, 13.

4. Sullivan, *Ministry of Presence*, 17.

5. Winnifred Fallers Sullivan, "Religion Naturalized," in Bender and Klassen, *After Pluralism*, 82–97.

6. Sullivan, *Ministry of Presence*, 17.

7. Sullivan, *Ministry of Presence*, 11.

8. Sullivan, "Religion Naturalized," 94.

9. Sullivan, "Religion Naturalized," 95.

10. Sullivan, *Ministry of Presence*, 14.

11. "Joint Submission to the U.N. Committee on the Elimination of Racial Discrimination Concerning Religious Freedoms of Indigenous Persons Deprived of Their Liberty in the United States of America," July 25, 2014. Huy is a Pacific Northwest advocacy organization that offers Native inmates educational, rehabilitative, and religious support.

12. For an empirical study of cases within the Tenth Circuit, see Goodrich and Busick, "Sex, Drugs, and Eagle Feathers."

13. Lawrence A. Greenfeld and Steven K. Smith, "American Indians and Crime," US Department of Justice, 1999.

14. Todd Minton, "Jails in Indian Country," US Department of Justice, September 2011.

15. "Joint Submission to the U.N. Committee on the Elimination of Racial Discrimination Concerning Religious Freedoms of Indigenous Persons Deprived of Their Liberty in the United States of America," July 25, 2014; US Census 2010.

16. Walter Echo-Hawk, "Native Worship in American Prisons," *Cultural Survival Quarterly* 19, no. 4 (1995).

17. Clyde Bellecourt with Jon Lurie, *Thunder before the Storm: The Autobiography of Clyde Bellecourt* (Saint Paul: Minnesota Historical Society Press, 2018).

18. Bob Reha, "Spiritual Freedom in Prisons," Minnesota Public Radio, April 2001. http://news.minnesota.publicradio.org/projects/2001/04/brokentrust/rehab_spiritual-m/index .shtml, last accessed April 2019.

19. A higher number reported spending most of their time "serving as an administrator helping to organize religious programs" than directly leading services, religious instruction, or counseling. Pew Forum on Religion and American Public Life, "Religion in Prisons: A 50 State Survey of Prison Chaplains," March 2012, 39.

20. AAR Correctional Chaplaincy Partnership.

21. This point was made by Larry Cloud Morgan, my late Ojibwe teacher and mentor, who spent four years in federal prison related to a civil disobedience action.

22. Religious Land Use and Institutionalized Persons Act (2000), 42 U.S.C. § 2000cc et seq.

23. *Inmate Religious Beliefs and Practices* (pages hereafter cited are from Native American Spirituality section).

24. *Inmate Religious Beliefs and Practices*, 11, 14.

25. *Inmate Religious Beliefs and Practices*, 15–16.

26. *Inmate Religious Beliefs and Practices*, ii.

27. This is consistent with the manual's discussion of Jewish membership: Although the Bureau of Prisons allows inmates to simply designate a religious preference, Jewish law, *halacha*, does not recognize this determination. That is, while an inmate may express a religious preference for Judaism, that does not make the inmate Jewish. While incarcerated, the inmate has the opportunity to worship and study. *Inmate Religious Beliefs and Practices*, "Judaism," 14.

28. *Inmate Religious Beliefs and Practices*, "Native American Spirituality," 16.

29. New York Department of Corrections and Community Service, Directive 4202, *Religious Programs and Practices* (2015), 9. "Native American designations can only be approved after appropriate verification of the inmate's ancestry by the Director of MFVS [Ministerial, Family, and Volunteer Services] in consultation with the DOCCS Native American Chaplains," 6.

30. Mitchell v. Angelone, 82 F. Supp. 2d 485 (E.D. Va. 1999).

31. Brown v. Schuetzle, 368 F. Supp. 2d 1009 (N.D. 2005).

32. There is a need to survey states on this issue. The 2014 joint submission on such matters to the UN Committee on the Elimination of All Forms of Racism calls on that committee to request the US Attorney General survey the state of religious liberty of Native prisoners, a study that has yet to transpire.

33. Morrison v. Garraghty, 239 F. 2d 648 (4th Cir. 2001). Substantiation could include tribal enrollment, BIA card, or a blood relative who is an American Indian.

34. *Morrison*, 239 F. 2d at 653, 656.

35. *Morrison*, 239 F. 2d at 648.

36. Mitchell v. Angelone; Brown v. Schuetzle; Fowler v. Crawford, 534 F. 3d 831 (8th Cir. 2008); Combs v. Correction Corp. of America, 877 F. Supp. 799 (W.D. La., 1997).

37. American Academy of Religion Government Relations Initiative: Consultations between State Officials of American Corrections Chaplains Association and Scholars of Native American Religions, November 2007; November 2016.

38. Longoria v. Dretke, 507 F. 3d 889 (5th Cir. 2007).

39. The Supreme Court incorporated the First Amendment's Free Exercise Clause into the Fourteenth Amendment in *Cantwell v. Connecticut*, 310 U.S. 296 (1940); the Establishment Clause was incorporated seven years later in *Everson v. Board of Education*, 330 U.S. 1 (1947). A notable exception is the famous case of Mormon polygamy, *Reynolds v. U.S.*, 98 U.S. 145 (1879). See Gordon, *Mormon Question*.

40. Sherbert v. Verner, 374 U.S. 398 (1963).

41. U.S. v. Seeger, 380 U.S. 163 (1965); Wisconsin v. Yoder, 406 U.S. 205 (1972).

42. *Yoder*, 406 U.S. at 215.

43. *Yoder*, 406 U.S. at 216.

44. This was apparently in answer to J. O'Connor's concurred in the judgment against Smith but found the majority opinion far too aggressive in reversing the sweep of the Free Exercise Clause cases theretofore.

45. Kristin Carpenter argues Native American religious freedom claims, at least those by federally recognized tribes or by members of those tribes, are indeed to be construed as hybrid matters of bundled rights of the sort J. Scalia speaks in the *Smith* ruling. See Carpenter, "Limiting Principles," 417–18.

46. See Sullivan, *Paying the Words Extra*; Greenawalt, "Religion as a Concept in Constitutional Law."

47. U.S. v. Seeger, 380 U.S. 163 (1965).

48. *Seeger*, 380 U.S. at 180.

49. See, for example, New Rider v. Board of Education, 480 F. 2d 693 (10th Cir. 1973), cert. denied, 414 U.S. 1097, reh. denied, 415 U.S. 939.

50. Teterud v. Gilman, 385 F. Supp. 153 (S.D. Iowa, 1974).

51. *Teterud*, 385 F. Supp. at 156.

52. Weaver v. Jago, 571 F. 2d 585 (6th Cir. 1978); Gallahan v. Hollyfield, 670 F. 2d 1345 (4th Cir. 1982).

53. O'Lone v. Shabbazz, 482 U.S. 342 (1987).

54. See Long, *Religious Freedom and Indian Rights*.

55. People v. Woody, 61 Cal. 2d 716 (Cal. Supr. Crt. 1964).

56. *Smith*, 494 U.S. at 891 (O'Connor, concurring).

57. *Smith*, 494 U.S. at 872.

58. The Rehnquist Court did strike down a Florida municipality's zoning law that had been deemed to overtly discriminate against the animal sacrifice rituals of Santería, a Cuban religious tradition. Church of Lukumi Babalu Aye v. City of Hialeah, 508 U.S. 520 (1993).

59. *Smith*, 494 U.S. at 888.

60. *Smith*, 494 U.S. at 917 (J. Blackmun, dissenting). A prominent criticism is Carter, *Culture of Disbelief*.

61. *Smith*, 494 U.S. at 887, citing United States v. Lee, 455 U.S. 252, 263 n. 2 (Stevens, J., concurring).

62. In *Bowen v. Roy*, the Court was unconvinced that a Native individual's daughter had a First Amendment right to an exemption from being assigned a Social Security number for fear of harming her spirit. Bowen v. Roy, 476 U.S. 693 (1986).

63. Kevin Washburn, class lecture, American Indian Law, University of Minnesota Law School, April 2007.

64. Religious Freedom Restoration Act (1993), 42 U.S.C. § 2000bb.

65. Boerne v. Flores, 521 U.S. 507 (1997).

66. Religious Land Use and Institutionalized Persons Act (2000), 42 U.S.C.§ 2000cc–1.

67. Cutter v. Wilkinson, 544 U.S. 723 (2005).

68. Holt v. Hobbs, 135 S. Ct. 853, 574 U.S. ___ (2015).

69. *Holt*, 135 S. Ct. at 862, citing O'Lone v. Estate of Shabazz, 482 U.S. 342, 351–52 (1987) and Turner v. Safley, 482 U.S. 78, 90 (1987).

70. *Holt*, 135 S. Ct. at 862.

71. Clinton Oxford, "Failing Native American Prisoners: RLUIPA and the Dilution of Strict Scrutiny," *Georgetown Journal of Law and Modern Critical Race Perspectives* 9 (2017): 203.

72. Sullivan, *Ministry of Presence*, 13.

73. Warsoldier v. Woodford, no. 04–55879 (9th Cir. 2005).

74. An oft-cited precedent was set in *Teterud*.

75. Oxford, "Failing Native American Prisoners."

76. Knight v. Thompson, 723 F. 3d 1275 (11th Cir. 2013).

77. Schlemm v. Wall, No. 11 CV 272 (W.D. Wisc., 2015).

78. Schlemm v. Wall, 784 F. 3d 362 (7th Cir. 2015).

79. Schlemm v. Wall, 165 F. Supp. 3d 751 (W.D. Wisc., 2016).

80. Schlemm v. Wall, 165 F. Supp. 3d 751, citing Dkt. #161–5.

81. DAI Policy 309.61.03, "Religious Diets." "Effective January 1, 2016, DOC continues to provide inmates attending an annual, celebratory religious meal with the regular meal tray served to the entire institution that day. Under the new policy, however, inmates may also request "individual accommodation to purchase an individual portion of a shelf-stable ceremonial food item for personal consumption" in conjunction with a religious group's feast.

82. "Use of Tobacco for American Indian Ceremonies," Minnesota Department of Corrections Division Directive 302.310 (2015).

83. Native American Council of Tribes v. Weber, 897 F. Supp. 2d 828 (D.S.D. 2012).

84. Native American Council of Tribes v. Weber, 750 F. 3d 742 (8th Cir. 2014).

85. Native American Council of Tribes v. Weber, 750 F. 3d 742 (8th Cir. 2014).

86. Louis M. Holscher, "Sweat Lodges and Headbands: An Introduction to the Rights of Native American Prisoners," *New England Journal on Criminal a Civil Confinement* 18 (1992): 33.

87. Yellowbear v. Lampert, 741 F. 3d 48 (10th Cir. 2014).

88. *Yellowbear*, 741 F. 3d at 53.

89. Abdulhaseeb v. Calbone, 600 F. 3d 1301, at 1315 (10th Cir. 2010).

90. *Yellowbear*, 741 F. 3d at 56.

91. *Yellowbear*, 741 F. 3d at 60.

92. *Yellowbear*, 741 F. 3d at 48.

93. Brault, "Sweating in the Joint."

94. Haight v. Thompson, 763 F. 3d 554 (6th Cir. 2014).

95. http://kool.corrections.ky.gov/, last accessed April 2019.

96. *Haight*, 763 F. 3d at 562.

97. Cubero v. Burton, 96 F. 3d 1450, 1450 (7th Cir. 1996) (unpublished) (Wisconsin); Allen v. Toombs, 827 F. 3d 563, 565 n. 5 (9th Cir. 1987) (Oregon); Brown v. Schuetzle, 368 F. Supp. 2d. 1009, 1011–12 (D.N.D. 2005) (North Dakota); Youngbear v. Thalacker, 174 F. Supp. 2d 902, 912 (N.D. Iowa 2001) (Iowa); Indian Inmates v. Gunter, 660 F. Supp. 394, 398 (D. Neb. 1987) (Nebraska); Mathes v. Carlson, 534 F. Supp. 226, 228 (W.D. Mo. 1982) (Missouri).

98. The Sixth Circuit distinguished a 2008 Eighth Circuit holding that upheld a Missouri maximum security prison's prohibitions on a sweat lodge against an inmate's RLUIPA challenge. In *Fowler v. Crawford*, 534 F. 3d 931, 942 (8th Cir. 2008), the *Haight* court said, a prison context of frequent violence and the inflexibility of the inmate's request for antlers, shovels, and a minimum of seventeen ceremonies per year made the case different from *Haight*, where

the prisoners had been dutifully flexible in working with the prison leadership. *Haight*, 763 F. 3d at 563. See also Pounders v. Kempker, 79 F. App'x 941, 942–43 (8th Cir. 2003) (per curiam).

99. Yellowbear v. Hargett, No. 15-CV-213-J (D. Wyo. 2016).

100. Haight v. Thompson, No. 5:11-CV-00118-GNS (W.D. KY, 2015).

101. Federal Bureau of Prisons, Program Statement, Religious Beliefs and Practices, § 548.10 (c) 12/31/2004.

Chapter 3: Religion as Spirituality: Sacred Lands

1. Important studies of Native claims and relations to sacred places include Vine Deloria Jr., *God Is Red*; Nabokov, *Where the Lightning Strikes*; Basso, *Wisdom Sits in Places*; Burton, *Worship and Wilderness*; King, *Places That Count*, Morman, *Many Nations under Many Gods*; Shrubsole, *What Has No Place Remains*.

2. Navajo Nation et al. v. U.S. Forest Service, 535 F. 3d 1058 (9th Cir. 2008), cert. denied, 129 S. Ct. 2763 (2009) (hereafter *Navajo Nation*). The three judge panel ruling is Navajo Nation et al. v. U.S. Forest Service, 479 F. 3d 1024 (9th Cir. 2007) rev'd en banc, 535 F. 3d 1058 (9th Cir. 2008). The en banc judgment was an 8–3 decision.

3. Wilson v. Block, 708 F. 2d 735 (D.C. Cir. 1983), cert. denied, 464 U.S. 956 (1983).

4. 42 U.S.C. §§ 2000bb et seq. (1993).

5. *Navajo Nation*, 535 F. 3d at 1063.

6. *Navajo Nation*, 535 F. 3d at 1063.

7. Navajo Nation et al. v. U.S. Forest Service, 129 S. Ct. 2763 (2009).

8. Burwell v. Hobby Lobby Stores, Inc., 573 U.S. 682 (2014).

9. One important gloss on this case suggests how it involves a narrow modern Western view of property in terms of wealth and rights of exclusion and alienability rather than in distinctively Indigenous terms of relationship. Carpenter, Katyal, and Riley, "In Defense of Property."

10. Peter Zwick, "2009 Note of the Year: A Redeemable Loss; *Lyng*, Lower Courts, and American Indian Free Exercise on Public Lands," *Case Western Reserve Law Review* 60 (2009): 241; Seth Schermerhorn, "Secularization by the 'Sacred'? Discourses of Religion and the San Francisco Peaks," *Eras* 11 (November 2009).

11. *Navajo Nation*, 535 F. 3d at 1096 (J. Fletcher, dissenting); Thomas King, "Commentary: What Burdens Religion?" *Great Plains Natural Resources Journal* 1 (2010): 1–3; John Copeland Nagle, "The Idea of Pollution," *U.C. Davis Law Review* 43 (2009): 75. For an excellent treatment of the case as engaged by the Hopi, see Richland, "Paths in the Wilderness."

12. Zackeree S. Kelin and Kimberly Younce Schooley, "Dramatically Narrowing RFRA's Definition of 'Substantial Burden' in the Ninth Circuit," *South Dakota Law Review* 55 (2010): 426, 455–58.

13. *Navajo Nation*, 535 F. 3d at 1063.

14. Testimony about Native practices and beliefs from the district court trial are summarized in Judge Fletcher's dissent, *Navajo Nation*, 535 F. 3d at 1100–1101.

15. The Apache have a cognate ceremonial tradition. See Talamantez, "Presence of Isanaklesh."

16. Charlotte J. Frisbie and David P. McAllester, eds., *Navajo Blessingway Singer: The Autobiography of Frank Mitchell, 1881–1967* (Tucson: University of Arizona Press, 1978).

17. *Navajo Nation*, 535 F. 3d at 1101.

18. For a rich treatment of Hopi practices and views of the Peaks, see Richland, "Paths in the Wilderness," 224–25.

19. *Navajo Nation*, 535 F. 3d at 1101–2 (J. Fletcher, dissenting).

20. *Navajo Nation*, 535 F. 3d at 1098 (J. Fletcher, dissenting), citing trial transcript 722–23. Indeed, Judge Fletcher, in his dissent, drew on this distinction in the trial transcripts between sacred and holy in a manner roughly congruent with the pairing of spirituality and religion.

21. The Supreme Court has yet to settle differences among various federal appellate courts in terms of what constitutes a "substantial burden" on religious exercise under RFRA. The Eighth Circuit followed the Tenth Circuit's approach in *Werner v. McCotter*, which considers government conduct to substantially burden a person's religious exercise when it "significantly inhibit[s] or constrain[s] religious conduct or expression. . . . meaningfully curtail[s] his ability to express adherence to his or her faith; or den[ies] him reasonable opportunities to engage in those activities that are fundamental to his religion." Werner v. McCotter, 49 F. 3d 1476, 1480 (10th Cir. 1995). See also In re Young, 82 F. 3d 1407, 1418 (8th Cir. 1996). More recently, in *Comanche Nation v. U.S.*, 393 F. Supp. 2d 1196 (W.D. Okla. 2008), an Oklahoma district court applied this Tenth Circuit approach and expressly rejected the government's request to invoke the Ninth Circuit interpretation of substantial burden in *Navajo Nation*. It found an RFRA substantial burden because the development of a building at Fort Sill would obstruct a traditional view of Medicine Bluffs, a sacred site to the Comanche, and would significantly inhibit the "spiritual experience" of tribal members. Other circuits took middle positions. See Civil Liberties for Urban Believers v. City of Chicago, 342 F. 3d 752, 761 (7th Cir. 2003), cert. denied, 541 U.S. 1096 (2004); Adkins v. Kaspar, 393 F. 3d 559, 568 (Fifth Cir. 2004), cert. denied, 545 U.S. 1104 (2005); Washington v. Klem, 497 F. 3d at 280, n. 7 (3rd Cir. 2007); Midrash Sephardi, Inc. v. Town of Surfside, 366 F. 3d 1214, 1227 (11th Circ. 2004), cert. denied, 543 U.S. 1146 (2005).

22. Skibine, "Toward a Balanced Approach for the Protection of Native American Sacred Sites," 277–78.

23. *Navajo Nation*, 535 F. 3d at 1074 (J. Fletcher dissenting).

24. *Navajo Nation*, 535 F. 3d at 1074–78.

25. *Navajo Nation*, 535 F. 3d at 1091 (J. Fletcher, dissenting), citing Bryant v. Gomez, 46 F. 3d 948 (9th Cir. 1995).

26. *Navajo Nation*, 535 F. 3d at 1074.

27. Sherbert v. Verner, 374 U.S. 398 (1963); Wisconsin v. Yoder, 406 U.S. 205 (1972).

28. *Navajo Nation*, 535 F. 3d at 1075, citing dissent at 1086–87.

29. See Michael Dorf, "Individual Burdens on Fundamental Rights," *Harvard Law Review* 109 (1996): 1175.

30. *Navajo Nation*, 535 F. 3d at 1063.

31. See, for example, Ira Lupu, "Where Rights Begin: The Problem of Burdens on the Free Exercise of Religion," *Harvard Law Review* 102 (1989): 933; Alan Ray, "Comment, *Lyng v. Northwest Indian Cemetery Protective Association*: Government Property Rights and the Free Exercise Clause," *Hastings Constitutional Law Quarterly* 16 (1989): 483; Howard Vogel, "The Clash of Stories at Chimney Rock: A Narrative Approach to Cultural Conflict over Native American Sacred Sites on Public Land," *Santa Clara Law Review* 41 (2001): 757; Kristen Carpenter, "A Property Rights Approach to Sacred Sites Cases," *UCLA Law Review* 52, no. 4 (2006).

32. Skibine, "Toward a Balanced Approach," 279–80.

33. 42 U.S.C. 2000bb-2.

34. The *Hobby Lobby* majority did find, with what the dissent identified as weak support, "the one pre *Smith* case involving the free exercise rights of a for-profit corporation suggests if anything that for profit corporations possess such rights." *Hobby Lobby*, 573 U.S. at 714–15, citing Gallagher v. Crown Kosher Super Market, 66 U.S. 617 (1961).

35. *Hobby Lobby*, 573 U.S. at 713.

36. *Hobby Lobby*, 573 U.S. at 684, 714.

37. *Hobby Lobby*, 573 U.S. at 714.

38. *Hobby Lobby*, 573 U.S. at 714.

39. *Hobby Lobby*, 573 U.S. at 740 (J. Ginsburg, dissenting).

40. McNally, "Native American Religious Freedom as a Collective Right."

41. Lupu, "Where Rights Begin," 948.

42. Carpenter, "Limiting Principles and Empowering Practices."

43. Leigh Eric Schmidt, *Restless Souls: The Making of American Spirituality from Emerson to Oprah* (Berkeley: University of California Press, 2012); Courtney Bender, *The New Metaphysicals: Spirituality and the American Religious Imagination* (Chicago: University of Chicago Press, 2010); Nancy Ammerman, *Sacred Stories, Spiritual Tribes: Finding Religion in Everyday Life* (New York: Oxford University Press, 2014).

44. Robert C. Fuller, *Spiritual, but Not Religious* (New York: Oxford University Press, 2001); C. John Sommerville, *Religion in the National Agenda: What We Mean by Religious, Spiritual, Secular* (Waco, TX: Baylor University Press, 2008); Brian Zinnbauer and Kenneth Pargement, "Religion and Spirituality: Unfuzzying the Fuzzy," *Journal for the Scientific Study of Religion* 36 (December 1997): 549–561; John Lardas Modern, *Secularism in Antebellum America* (Chicago: University of Chicago Press, 2011).

45. Robert Wuthnow, *After Heaven: Spirituality in America since 1950* (Berkeley: University of California Press, 1997), 3–4.

46. Wuthnow, *After Heaven*, 4–5.

47. Wuthnow, *After Heaven*, 5, citing Max Lerner, *Wrestling with the Angel* (New York: Norton, 1990).

48. Wade Clark Roof, *The Spiritual Marketplace: Baby Boomers and the Remaking of American Religion* (Princeton, NJ: Princeton University Press, 1999), 82.

49. Roof, *Spiritual Marketplace*, 82.

50. Robert Ellwood, *The Fifties Spiritual Marketplace: American Religion in a Decade of Conflict* (New Brunswick, NJ: Rutgers University Press, 1997); Roger Finke and Rodney Stark, *The Churching of America, 1776–1990* (New Brunswick, NJ: Rutgers University Press, 1992); Roger Finke and Laurence R. Iannaccone, "Supply Side Explanations for Religious Change," *Annals of the American Academy of Political and Social Science* 527 (May 1993): 27–39.

51. Wuthnow, *After Heaven*, 7–8.

52. Cinnamon Moon, *A Medicine Woman Speaks* (Franklin Lakes, NJ: New Page Books, 2001).

53. Laura Donaldson, "On Medicine Women and White Shame-Ans: New Age Native Americanism and Commodity Fetishism as Pop Culture Feminism," *Signs* 24, no. 3 (1999): 677–96; Lisa Aldred, "Plastic Shamans and Astroturf Sun Dances: New Age Commercialization of Native American Spirituality," *American Indian Quarterly* 24 (Summer 2000): 329–52;

Philip Jenkins, *Dream Catchers: How Mainstream America Discovered Native Spirituality* (New York: Oxford University Press, 2004); Andrea Smith, "For Those Who Were Indian in a Past Life," in *Ecofeminism and the Sacred*, ed. C. Adams (New York: Continuum, 1994), 168–71; Owen, *Appropriation of Native American Spirituality*.

54. Philip Deloria, *Playing Indian.*

55. See Cathy Albanese, *Nature Religion in America: From the Algonkian Indians to the New Age* (Chicago: University of Chicago Press, 1990).

56. See King, *Places That Count*, 9.

57. *Navajo Nation*, 535 F. 3d at 1096 (J. Fletcher, dissenting).

58. See, for example, Tomoko Masuzawa, *The Invention of World Religions: How European Universalism Was Preserved in the Language of Pluralism* (Chicago: University of Chicago Press, 2005); Talal Asad, *Genealogies of Religion* (Baltimore, MD: Johns Hopkins University Press, 1993); Saba Mahmood, *The Politics of Piety: The Islamic Revival and the Feminist Subject* (Princeton, NJ: Princeton University Press, 2005). For an overview of such definitional questions as they pertain to questions of cultural resources, see McNally, "Religious Belief and Practice."

59. Conversely, efforts to scrupulously avoid the language of religion for Native American traditions appear unavailing. In *Jock et al. v. Ransom et al.*, 05-CV-1108 (N. Dist. N.Y, 2007), aff'd 07-CV-3162 (2nd Cir. 2009), a federal judge held against an equal protection claim raised by parents of Mohawk schoolchildren in a predominantly Native public school. They had challenged a school board prohibition on beginning the school day with the Mohawk "Thanksgiving Address." The school board decision was driven by a non-Indian parent who viewed the address as a "prayer," and the expert testimony on behalf of the Mohawk plaintiffs turned on demonstrating that the address was not a prayer, and that the prohibition on the Thanksgiving Address was discriminatory. The district court held that its ruling turned only on finding no discriminatory intent in the school board decision and thus required no judgment as to whether or not the Thanksgiving Address was prayer, and the Second Circuit affirmed.

60. *Navajo Nation*, 535 F. 3d at 1104–5 (J. Fletcher, dissenting), citing Leigh Kuwanwisiwma.

61. *Navajo Nation*, 535 F. 3d at 1104–5, citing Emory Sekaquaptewa 408 F. Supp. 2d at 895.

62. *Navajo Nation*, 535 F. 3d at 1102.

63. On the "structure" of substantial burden analyses in religious freedom law, Lupu, "Where Rights Begin," 947.

64. *Navajo Nation*, 535 F. 3d at 1063, emphasis added.

65. *Navajo Nation*, 535 F. 3d at 1063.

66. *Navajo Nation*, 535 F. 3d at 1070.

67. *Navajo Nation*, 535 F. 3d at 1063, citing Lyng v. Northwest Indian Cemetery Protective Association, 485 U.S. 439 (1988), 449.

68. *Navajo Nation*, 535 F. 3d at 1064.

69. Skibine, "Toward a Balanced Approach," 269.

70. For a further treatment of the difficulties of the collective nature of Native American religions, see Carpenter, "Limiting Principles," 396–97.

71. *Navajo Nation*, 535 F. 3d at 1070n12.

72. *Navajo Nation*, 535 F. 3d at 1070n12.

73. Navajo Nation Code, Title I, §205 (b), § 205 (d).

74. Referring to these foundational obligations, the Navajo Nation Human Rights Commission resolved to make a formal complaint to the Inter-American Commission on Human Rights: "the Navajos have a responsibility to remain on and care for the land where the Holy People placed the Navajo people." "Resolution of the Navajo Nation Human Rights Commission NNHRCMAR-27–13 Approving and Recommending that the Navajo Nation Register a Complaint of Navajo Human Rights Violation with the Organization of American States Inter-American Commission on Human Rights," March 2013.

75. U.S. v. Corrow, 941 F. Supp. 1560 (D.N.M., 1996).

76. *Corrow*, 941 F. Supp. at 1560.

77. *Corrow*, 941 F. Supp. at 1561.

78. Attakai v. U. S., 746 Fed. Supp. 1395 (D. Ariz, 1990).

79. *Attakai*, 746 Fed. Supp.at 1404.

80. *Attakai*, 746 Fed. Supp.at 1400.

81. *Attakai*, 746 Fed. Supp. at 1400–1401.

82. *Attakai*, 746 Fed. Supp.at 1402.

83. Carpenter, "Limiting Principles," 437–39.

84. Ronald R. Garet, "Communality and Existence: The Rights of Groups," *Southern California Law Review* 56 (1983): 1001. See also Douglas Laycock, "Towards a General Theory of the Religion Clauses: The Case of Church Labor Relations and the Right to Church Autonomy," *Columbia Law Review* 81 (1981): 1373; Frederick Gedicks, "Toward a Constitutional Jurisprudence of Religious Group Rights," *Wisconsin Law Review* 1 (1989): 99; Richard W. Garnett, "Religion and Group Rights: Are Churches (Just) Like the Boy Scouts?" *St. John's Journal of Legal Comment* 22 (2007): 515; Paul Horwitz, *First Amendment Institutions* (Cambridge, MA: Harvard University Press, 2013).

85. Carpenter, "Limiting Principles," 440.

86. *Lyng*, 485 U.S. at 449.

87. Bowen v. Roy, 476 U.S. 693 (1986). Justice Brennan himself joined the majority in *Bowen v. Roy*, giving perhaps more heft to the distinction he asserted in dissent on *Lyng*.

88. *Lyng*, 485 U.S. at 448, citing Bowen v. Roy, 476 U.S. at 696.

89. Bowen v. Roy, 476 U.S. at 699.

90. Bowen v. Roy, 485 U.S. at 698.

91. *Lyng*, 485 U.S. at 449 (J. Brennan dissenting). J. Brennan argued in dissent that the majority had fundamentally misunderstood Native religions. He doubted that the Native people would "derive any solace from the knowledge that although the practice of their religion will become 'more difficult' as a result of the Government's actions, they remain free to maintain their religious beliefs." "Given today's ruling," Brennan penned, "that freedom amounts to nothing more than the right to believe that their religion will be destroyed."

92. *Lyng*, 485 U.S. at 452.

93. *Lyng*, 485 U.S. at 447.

94. Although J. Brennan in dissent strongly disagreed that an "internal" governmental practice at issue in *Roy* was comparable to land use decisions, with "substantial external effects," he stopped short of differentiating *Bowen v. Roy* in these starker terms. *Lyng*, 485 U.S. at 469–70.

95. *Lyng*, 485 U.S. at 476. One scholar contends that the *Lyng* decision not only unfairly burdens Native religious traditions, it also establishes a jurisprudence that "discriminates against American Indian religious practitioners." Scott Hardt, "Comment: The Sacred Public Lands; Improper Line Drawing in the Supreme Court's Free Exercise Analysis," *University of Colorado Law Review* 60 (1989): 601, 657.

96. *Navajo Nation*, 535 F. 3d at 1065, citing Wilson v. Block, 708 F. 2d at 741–2.

97. *Navajo Nation*, 535 F. 3d at 1065. The result in *Wilson* guided the processes of environmental and historic preservation review that may have foreclosed more robust consultations with the tribes at earlier stages in the process.

98. *Navajo Nation*, 535 F. 3d at 1063–64.

99. *Navajo Nation*, 535 F. 3d at 1066.

100. Comanche Nation v. United States, 393 F. Supp. 2d 1196 (W.D. Okla. 2008).

101. Navajo Nation v. U.S. Forest Service, 129 S. Ct. 2763; 174 L. Ed. 2d 270 (2009).

102. *Navajo Nation*, 535 F. 3d at 1070.

103. Sullivan, *Impossibility of Religious Freedom*.

104. Hopi Tribe v. City of Flagstaff, 2013 Ariz. App. no. CV-13-0180-PR (Supreme Court of Arizona, 2014).

105. Suzanne Adams-Ockrassa, "Snowbowl Seeking 20 Year Contract with Flagstaff," *Arizona Daily Sun*, July 24, 2014.

106. *Hobby Lobby*, 573 U.S. at 714–15.

107. *Navajo Nation*, 535 F. 3d at 1088–90 (J. Fletcher, dissenting).

108. The January 24, 2017, memorandum directed the Army Corps "to take all actions necessary and appropriate to … review and approve in an expedited manner … requests for approvals to construct and operate the DAPL, including easements or right-of-way" and to "consider to the extent permitted by law and as warranted, whether to rescind or modify" the Army Corps Dec. 2017, decision to" pursue an Environmental Impact Statement process."

109. Standing Rock Sioux Tribe v. U.S. Army Corps of Engineers, 239 F. Supp. 3d 77 (D.D.C. 2017) (hereafter *Standing Rock II*), 82.

110. *Standing Rock II*, 239 F. Supp. 3d at 6–7 (citing Winter v. Natural Resources Defense Council, Inc., 555 U.S. 7, 22, 20 (2008)).

111. *Standing Rock II*, 239 F. Supp. 3d at 83.

112. *Standing Rock II*, 239 F. Supp. 3d at 100.

113. Cheyenne River Sioux Tribe, "Memorandum in Support of Ex Parte Application for Temporary Restraining Order and Application for Preliminary Injunction" (February 9, 2017) (henceforth CRST Motion); *Standing Rock II*, Doc. 9934.

114. CRST Motion, 33.

115. *Standing Rock II*, 239 F. Supp. 3d at 93. Note the slippage between the DC Court's discussion of a "tribe's" religious practice and the cited rendering of the burden in *Lyng* as a matter of interference "with private persons' ability to pursue spiritual fulfillment." *Standing Rock II*, 239 F. Supp. 3d at 92, citing *Lyng*, 485 U.S. at 449.

116. *Standing Rock II*, 239 F. Supp. 3d at 93, 98–99.

117. Ironically, the key Supreme Court case clarifying tribal water rights, *Winters v. United States*, 207 U.S. 564 (1908), involved reservation rights to Missouri River water in the Dakotas. *Standing Rock II*, 239 F. Supp. 3d at 99.

118. *Standing Rock II*, 239 F. Supp. 3d at 98–100. See Sioux Nation v. U.S., 448 U.S. 371 (1980); Lower Brule Sioux Tribe v. State of South Dakota, 711 F. 2d 809 (8th Cir. 1983); South Dakota v. Bourland, 508 U.S. 679 (1993).

119. In *Standing Rock II*, the judge cited *Lyng* as a pre-*Smith* case and concluded, based on RFRA legislative history references to *Lyng*, that pre-*Smith* substantial burden standards should still apply in judicial interpretations of RFRA. The judge approved of deference to *Lyng* in other appellate level RFRA and RLUIPA cases. *Standing Rock II*, 239 F. Supp. 3d at 93, citing S. Rep. No 103–1111 at 8–9 (1993) and 139 Cong. Rec. S14461, S14470 (Statement of Sen Orrin Hatch, October 27, 1993).

120. *Standing Rock II*, 239 F. Supp. 3d at 96, citing Hobby Lobby, 134 S. Ct. at 2762.

121. CRST Motion, 35, citing Holt v. Hobbs, 134 S. Ct. at 862 (2015).

122. *Standing Rock II*, 239 F. Supp. 3d at 33.

123. CRST Motion, 35, citing *Navajo Nation*, 1070.

124. CRST Motion, 35–36, citing *Navajo Nation*, 1070; *Hobby Lobby*, 134 S. Ct. 2778.

125. CRST Motion, 37.

126. Comanche Nation v. United States, 393 F. Supp. 2d 1196 (W.D. Okla. 2008).

127. See, for example, Timothy Wiseman, "Why the Religious Freedom Restoration Act Cannot Protect Sacred Sites," *American Indian Law Journal* 54 (2017): 140.

Chapter 4: Religion as Cultural Resource

1. King, *Cultural Resource Laws*, 29–30.

2. Antiquities Act (1906), Archeological Resource Protection Act (1979), Native American Graves Protection and Repatriation Act (1990), and executive orders like Executive Order 12898 on Environmental Justice.

3. Clifford, *Returns*; Niezen, *Rediscovered Self*; Brown, *Who Owns Native Culture?*

4. Niezen, *Rediscovered Self*, 67.

5. U.S. v. Gettysburg Electric Railway, 16 U.S. 668 (1896).

6. Edward Tabor Linenthal, *Sacred Ground: Americans and Their Battlefields*, 2nd ed. (Urbana: University of Illinois Press, 1993).

7. Sequoyah v. Tennessee Valley Authority, 620 F. 2d 1159, 1160 (6th Cir. 1980).

8. *Sequoyah*, 620 F. 2d at 1160.

9. T.V.A v. Hill, 437 U.S. 153, 156–59 (1978).

10. *Sequoyah*, 1161, 620 F. 2d at 1164–65.

11. King argues that Section 106 review, because it is understood to require detailed historical analysis, nonetheless gets performed often after the NEPA process has gone deep enough for an alternative to have been chosen, or after a "Finding of No Significant Impact" has been issued.

12. 40 CFR 1508.14. See King, *Cultural Resource Laws*, 55.

13. King, *Cultural Resource Laws*, 24. An example of their relationship occurs in the kinds of effects NEPA regulations flag for review. In determinations of intensity of effects under NEPA, agencies are to consider "the degree to which the action may adversely affect sites … eligible for listing in the National Register of Historic Places, or may cause loss or destruction of significant scientific, cultural, or historical resources." This folds the Section 106 review into the NEPA review, but also extends NEPA review beyond the historic properties of Section 106.

14. According to the Environmental Protection Agency, there are something of the order of five hundred EISs filed each year, and there are, according to Thomas King, about fifty thousand Environmental Assessments.

15. 40 CFR 1508 27 (b). See King, *Cultural Resource Laws*, 66.

16. Natural Resources Defense Council v. Morton, 458 F. 2d 827, 838 (D.C. Cir. 1972).

17. Metropolitan Edison Co. v. People against Nuclear Energy, 460 U.S. 766 (1983).

18. "Mitigated Finding of No Significant Impact: Environmental Assessment Dakota Access Pipeline Project, Williams, Morton, and Emmons Counties, North Dakota," signed July 25, 2016, by John W. Henderson, District Commander. The mitigation involved several conditions placed on Dakota Access to demonstrate preparedness for leaks. https://cdm16021.contentdm .oclc.org/digital/collection/p16021coll7/id/2801, last accessed April 2019 (Mitigated Finding of No Significant Impact).

19. 54 USC § 306108.

20. Pueblo of Sandia v. United States, 50 F. 3d 856 (10th Cir. 1995); Comanche Nation v. United States, 393 F. Supp. 2d 1196 (W.D. Okla. 2008).

21. 36 CFR 60.4.

22. 36 CFR 60.4.

23. 36 CFR 60.4.

24. King, *Cultural Resources Laws*, 146–47.

25. 36 CFR 800.5(a)(1).

26. 36 CFR 800.1(a), as cited in King, *Cultural Resource Laws*, 113.

27. "Guidelines for Evaluating and Documenting Traditional Cultural Properties," *National Register Bulletin 38*, by Patricia L. Parker and Thomas F. King, 1990; revised 1992, 1998 (hereafter *Bulletin 38*).

28. *Bulletin 38*, 1.

29. King, *Places That Count*, 28–31.

30. *Bulletin 38*, 3.

31. *Bulletin 38*, 12.

32. *Bulletin 38*, 13.

33. Thomas F. King, "In the Light of the Megis: The Chequamegon Bay Area as a Traditional Cultural Property: A Report to the Bad River and Red Cliff Bands of Lake Superior Tribe of Chippewa" (1998).

34. *Bulletin 38*, 15.

35. *Bulletin 38*, 16, 17.

36. Native Americans for Enola v. U.S. Forest Service, 832 F. Supp. 297 (D. Or. 1993).

37. King, *Places That Count*, 115–16.

38. King, *Places That Count*, 35–36.

39. 54 USC § 302706.

40. Advisory Council on Historic Preservation, "Consulting with Indian Tribes in the Section 106 Review Process," www.achp.gov/regs-tribes.html, last accessed June 2018. Executive Order 13007 will be discussed in the next chapter.

41. Mitigated Finding of No Significant Impact, Environmental Assessment, Dakota Access Pipeline Project, Williams, Morton, and Emmons Counties, North Dakota (July 2016).

42. *Pueblo of Sandia*; Exec. Ord. 13175, Consultation and Coordination with Indian Tribal Governments.

43. King, *Places That Count*, 8–9.

44. *Pueblo of Sandia*, 50 F. 3d 856.

45. King, *Cultural Resource Laws*, 9.

46. King, *Cultural Resource Laws*, 8.

47. Anna Willow, "Where Nature and Culture Meet: Culturally Significant Natural Resources," in *A Companion to Cultural Resource Management*, ed. Thomas F. King (Malden, MA: Wiley-Blackwell, 2011), 114–27.

48. Access Fund v. U.S. Department of Agriculture, No. 05–15585 (9th Cir. 2007). The Access Fund also unsuccessfully challenged the policy as "arbitrary and capricious" under the Administrative Procedures Act.

49. *Access Fund*, citing Cholla Ready Mix, Inc. v. Civish, 382 F. 3d at 977 (9th Cir. 2004).

50. See Michael D. McNally, "Religious Belief and Practice," in King, *Companion to Cultural Resource Management*.

51. King, *Places That Count*, 6–8.

52. Judy A. Martin, "Significant Traditional Cultural Properties of the Navajo People," Historic Preservation Department, Navajo Nation. www.hpd.navajo-nsn.gov/index.php?option=com_content&view=article&id=85&Itemid=490, last accessed June 2018.

53. *Pueblo of Sandia*, 50 F. 3d 856.

54. King, *Places That Count*; Quechan Tribe v. U.S. Dept. of Interior, 755 F. Supp. 2d 1104 (S.D. Cal. 2010).

55. See President Clinton's Executive Order 12898, "Federal Actions to Address Environmental Justice in Minority Populations and Low-Income Populations," 59 Fed. Reg. 7629 (February 11, 1994); Council on Environmental Quality, "Environmental Justice: Guidelines under the National Environmental Policy Act" (December 1997), www.epa.gov/environmentaljustice/ceq-environmental-justice-guidance-under-national-environmental-policy-act, last accessed April 2019.

56. Allison M. Dussias, "Protecting Pocahontas's World: The Mattaponi Tribe's Struggle against Virginia's King William Reservoir Project," *American Indian Law Review* 36 (2011): 1.

57. Dussias, "Protecting Pocahontas's World," 66; King, *Places That Count*, 266–67.

58. Dussias, "Protecting Pocahontas's World," 1.

59. Mattaponi Indian Tribe v. Va. Dep't of Envtl. Quality ex rel. State Water Control Bd., 541 S.E. 2d 920, 922 (Va. 2001).

60. Dussias, "Protecting Pocahontas's World," 101.

61. Alliance to Save the Mattaponi, v. U.S. Army Corps of Engineers, 606 F. Supp. 2d 121 (D.D.C., 2009).

62. Larry Nesper, "Law and Ojibwe Indian 'Traditional Cultural Property' in the Organized Resistance to the Crandon Mine in Wisconsin," *Law and Social Inquiry* 36 (Winter 2011): 151–69; Zoltan Grossman, *Unlikely Alliances: Native Nations and White Communities Join to Defend Rural Lands* (Seattle: University of Washington Press, 2017); Michael O'Brien, *Exxon and the Crandon Mine Controversy* (Madison, WI: Badger Books, 2008).

63. Clean Water Act, 33 U.S.C. § 1251–1387 (2012); Wisconsin v. Environmental Protection Agency, 266 F. 3d 741 (7th Cir. 2001).

64. Larry Nesper, Anna Willow, and Thomas F. King, *The Mushgigagamongsebe District: A Traditional Cultural Landscape of the Sokaogon Ojibwe Community*, report submitted to the Army Corps of Engineers, Saint Paul District by the Mole Lake Sokaogon Community of Great Lakes Chippewa Indians, 2002.

65. King, *Cultural Resource Laws*, 126–27.

66. Nesper, "Law and Ojibwe Indian Traditional Cultural Property," 156.

67. Amanda Marincic, "The National Historic Preservation Act: An Inadequate Attempt to Protect the Cultural and Religious Sites of Native Nations," *Iowa Law Review* 103 (2018): 1777–809.

68. San Carlos Apache Tribe v. United States, 412 F. 3d. 1091, 1092–93 (9th Cir. 2005). Courts in the Eighth Circuit have agreed in another case involving tribal challenges under NHPA to a pipeline: Sisseton Wahpeton Oyate v. U.S. Department of State, 659 F. Supp. 2d 1071 (D.S.D. 2009). Earlier decisions in two other circuits have concluded from a NHPA provision awarding attorney fees that the statute does have an implied cause of action, but these have not held sway. Boarhead Corporation v. Erickson, 923 F. 2d 1011, 1017 (3rd Cir. 1991); Vieux Carre Property Owners v. Brown, 875 F. 2d 453, 458 (5th Cir. 1989), cert. denied, 493 U.S. 1020 (1990).

69. Administrative Procedures Act, 5 USC § 702 et seq.

70. Administrative Procedures Act, 5 USC § 706(2)(a)(d).

71. Chevron U.S.A., Inc. v. Natural Resources Defense Council, Inc., 468 U.S. 837 (1984).

72. Pyramid Lake Paiute Tribe v. Morton, 354 F. Supp. 252 (D.D.C. 1972).

73. *Cohen's Handbook of Federal Indian Law*, 5.05(3)c.

74. Standing Rock Sioux Tribe v. U.S. Army Corps of Engineers, 1:16-cv-01534-JEB, Intervenor-Plaintiff Cheyenne River Sioux Tribe's First Amended Complaint for Declaratory and Injunctive Relief, Document 37 (09/08/167).

75. Standing Rock Sioux Tribe v. U.S. Army Corps of Engineers, 1:16-cv-01534-JEB, Motion for Preliminary Injunction Request for Expedited Hearing, Document 5 at 12 (08/04/16).

76. Standing Rock Sioux Tribe v. U.S. Army Corps of Engineers, 205 F. Supp. 3d. 4 (D.D.C. 2016) (hereafter *Standing Rock I*).

77. Standing Rock Sioux Tribe v. U.S. Army Corps of Engineers, 255 F. Supp. 3d 101 (D.D.C. 2017) (hereafter *Standing Rock III*).

78. Standing Rock Sioux Tribe v. U.S. Army Corps of Engineers, 282 F. Supp. 3d 91 (D.D.C. 2017) (hereafter *Standing Rock IV*).

79. *Standing Rock III*, 255 F. Supp. 3d at 112, 127–28. (citing 40 CFR § 1508.27(b)(4)).

80. *Standing Rock IV*, 8, citing Town of Cave Creek v. FAA, 325 F. 3d 320, 331 (D.C. Cir. 2003).

81. Carla Fredericks observes that the query in *Standing Rock III* concerns potentially violated treaty rights to fish and game in the Missouri River waters, begging bigger questions about why more thoroughgoing claims related to the Fort Laramie Treaties of 1851 and 1868, and the pipeline's crossing of territories designated as unceded in those treaties, failed to be engaged in the pleadings. See Carla Fredericks, "Standing Rock, the Sioux Treaties, and the Limits of the Supremacy Clause," *Colorado Law Review* 89 (2018): 477.

82. *Standing Rock IV*. On the treaty rights, the court decided: "On remand, the Corps must simply connect the dots. This, then, is not a case in which the agency 'must redo its analysis

from the ground up.' … The agency already has the data it needs to determine the impact of a spill on fish and game—indeed, it has already concluded that 'under no spill scenario would the acute toxicity threshold for aquatic organisms be exceeded.'" *Standing Rock IV* at 100.

83. *Standing Rock IV* at 98.

84. *Standing Rock IV* at 102–3.

85. "Memorandum in Support of Standing Rock Sioux Tribe's Motion for Summary Judgment on Remand," Standing Rock Sioux Tribe v. U.S. Army Corps of Engineers, 1:16-cv-01534-JEB Document 433–2 (August 16, 2019).

86. Clean Water Act, 33 U.S.C. § 1344.

87. *Pueblo of Sandia*, 50 F. 3d 856.

88. See Wyoming v. U.S. Department of the Interior, Case 2:15-CV-00041 (D. Wyo. 2016); Quechan Tribe v. U.S. Dept. of Interior, 755 F. Supp. 2d 1104 (S.D. Cal. 2010).

89. "Complaint for Declaratory and Injunctive Relief," Case 1:16-cv-01534 Doc. 1 (July 27, 2016), at paras. 23–29.

90. *Standing Rock I* at 7.

91. *Standing Rock I* at 13.

92. *Standing Rock I* at 14.

93. *Standing Rock I* at 14.

94. *Standing Rock I* at 15.

95. Richland, "Paths in the Wilderness," 233–38.

96. *Standing Rock I* at 22, citing Chiefly Decl., 29.

97. *Standing Rock I* at 20–21.

98. *Standing Rock I* at 21.

99. *Standing Rock I* at 23.

100. *Standing Rock I* at 25.

101. *Standing Rock I* at 26.

102. *Standing Rock I* at 32.

103. *Standing Rock I* at 23–24.

104. Mitigated Finding of No Significant Impact.

105. 40 CFR 1408.25; King, *Places That Count*, 134.

106. King, *Places That Count*, 136.

107. "Complaint for Declaratory and Injunctive Relief," Case 1:16-cv-01534 Doc. 1 (July 27, 2016), at paras. 81–82.

108. Courts in other circumstance have upheld expansive areas of potential effect. See Wyoming Sawmills, Inc. v. U.S. Forest Service, 383 F. 3d. 1241 (10th Cir. 2004), cert. denied, 126 S. Ct. 300 (2005).

109. 40 CFR 1508.7.

110. Council on Environmental Quality, *Considering Cumulative Effects under the National Environmental Policy Act*, 8. https://ceq.doe.gov/publications/cumulative_effects.html, last accessed July 2018.

111. Anna Willow, "Cultural Cumulative Effects: Communicating Industrial Extraction's True Costs," *Anthropology Today* 33 (2017): 21–26.

112. *Standing Rock I*, at 23.

113. *Bulletin 38*, 1.

114. King, *Thinking about Cultural Resource Management*, 5.

115. Chip Colwell-Chanthaphonh, and T. J. Ferguson, eds., *Collaboration in Archaeological Practice: Engaging Descendant Communities* (Lanham, MD: AltaMira Press, 2008).

116. 40 CFR 1502.24.

117. 36 CFR 61; www.nps.gov/history/local-law/arch_stnds_9.htm, accessed July 2018.

118. King, *Our Unprotected Heritage*, 33–45.

119. King, *Our Unprotected Heritage*, 33–34.

120. King, *Our Unprotected Heritage*, 34.

121. ACRA: www.acra-crm.org/code-of-ethics, accessed July 2018; NAEP: www.naep.org/code-of-ethics, accessed July 2018. One expectation in the ACRA Code of Ethics in terms of collegial responsibility is that members "not knowingly attempt to injure the professional reputation of a colleague."

122. Standing Rock Sioux Tribe, Complaint for Declarative and Injunctive Relief, Standing Rock Sioux Tribe v. U.S. Army Corps of Engineers, Doc. 1, para 86 (July 2016).

123. Chip Colwell, "How the Archaeological Review behind the Dakota Access Pipeline Went Wrong," *The Conversation*, http://theconversation.com/how-the-archaeological-review-behind-the-dakota-access-pipeline-went-wrong-67815, accessed July 2018.

124. Declaration of William S. Scherman, Standing Rock Sioux Tribe v. U.S. Army Corps of Engineers, Doc. 66–3 (12/05/16), 27.

125. www.acra-crm.org/current-sponsors, accessed June 2018.

126. www.alpinearchaeology.com/, accessed June 2018.

127. www.merjent.com/what-we-do/, accessed July 2018.

128. Troy Eid, "Beyond the Dakota Access Pipeline: Working Effectively with Indian Tribes on Energy Projects," *American Bar Association TRENDS* 49 (March/April 2018): 4.

129. First Peoples Investment Engagement Program, "Social Cost and Material Loss: The Dakota Access Pipeline," (November 2018), available at www.colorado.edu/program/fpw/.

Chapter 5: Religion as Collective Right

1. See Suzan Shown Harjo, "American Indian Religious Freedom Act after Twenty-Five Years: An Introduction," *Wicazo Sa Review* 19 (2004): 129–36.

2. Suzan Shown Harjo, Interview Tape 1a (2009).

3. Harjo, "It Began with a Vision," 28.

4. Harjo, "It Began with a Vision," 36.

5. Harjo, Interview Tape 1.

6. Harjo, "It Began with a Vision," 36.

7. For a classic discussion of Cheyenne law, see Llewellyn, *Cheyenne Way*.

8. Harjo, Interview Tape 1a.

9. Harjo, "It Began with a Vision," 30.

10. Harjo, "It Began with a Vision."

11. Gulliford, *Sacred Objects and Sacred Places*.

12. *Lyng*, 485 U.S. 439 (1988); Badoni v. Higginson, 638 F. 2d 172 (10th Cir. 1980); Sequoyah v. Tennessee Valley Authority, 620 F. 2d 1159 (6th Cir. 1980); Crow v. Gullet, 706 F. 2d 856 (8th Cir. 1983).

13. Nabokov, *Where the Lightning Strikes*, xv.

14. "Courts of the Conqueror" is an expression from *Johnson v. M'Intosh*, 21 U.S. 543 (1823). Echo-Hawk, *In the Courts of the Conqueror*.

15. Smith, *A Seat at the Table*; Smith and Snake, *One Nation under God*.

16. Michaelson, "Is the Miner's Canary Silent?"

17. Getches, Wilkinson, and Williams, *Cases and Materials on Federal Indian Law*.

18. 42 U.S.C. § 2000bb et seq.

19. 42 U.S.C. § 2000cc et seq.

20. Navajo Nation v. U.S. Forest Service, 535 F. 3d 1058 (2008), cert. denied, 556 U.S. 1281 (2009).

21. See, for example, Seminole Nation v. United States, 316 U.S. 286 (1942).

22. See Pyramid Lake Paiute v. Morton, 499 F. 2d 1095 (1974).

23. See, for example, U.S. v. Hardman (rehearing, en banc) 297 F. 3d 1116.

24. Morton v. Mancari, 417 U.S. 535 (1974); United States v. Antelope, 430 U.S. 641 (1977); Santa Clara Pueblo v. Martinez, 436 U.S. 49 (1978); Washington v. Confederate Bands and Tribes of the Yakima Indian Nation, 439 U.S. 463 (1979).

25. Washington v. Confederated Bands and Tribes of the Yakima Indian Nation, 439 U.S. 463 (1979).

26. Indian Self-Determination and Educational Assistance Act (1975), 25 U.S.C. § 450; Indian Child Welfare Act (1978), 25 U.S.C. § 1901.

27. Remarks at Signing of Bill Restoring the Blue Lake Lands in New Mexico to the Taos Pueblo Indians, December 15, 1970.

28. Executive Order 11670, "Providing for the Return of Certain Lands to the Yakima Indian Reservation," President Richard Nixon, May 20, 1972.

29. Harjo, Interview Tape 2.

30. *Final Report of the American Indian Policy Review Commission* (Washington, DC: GPO, 1977), 551.

31. *Final Report of the American Indian Policy Review Commission*, 44.

32. Harjo, Interview Tape 2.

33. 42 U.S.C. 1996 § 1.

34. 42 U.S.C. 1996 § 2.

35. And later by way of the 1994 amendment (42 U.S.C. 1996a), a clause protecting Peyote use specifically.

36. *Badoni v. Higginson*; *Sequoyah v. T.V.A.*; *Crow v. Gullet*; U.S. v. Thirty Eight Golden Eagles, 649 F. Supp. 269 (D. Nev. 1986), aff'd, 829 F. 2d 41 (9th Cir. 1987); Bowen v. Roy, 476 U.S. 693 (1986). For a fuller list of litigation on the basis of AIRFA in its first decade, see Sharon O'Brien, "A Legal Analysis of the American Indian Religious Freedom Act," in Vecsey, *Handbook of American Indian Religious Freedom*, 27–43.

37. *Lyng*, 485 U.S. at 455. Representative Udall's remarks are cited at 124 Cong. Rec. 21444; 21444–455 (1978). In the dissenting opinion, Justice Brennan agreed AIRFA does not create any judicially enforceable rights, but this "in no way undermines the statute's significance as an express congressional determination that federal land management decisions are not 'internal' Government 'procedures,' but are instead governmental actions that can and indeed are likely to burden Native American religious practices." *Lyng*, 485 U.S. at 471 (J. Brennan, dissenting).

38. Gulliford, *Sacred Objects and Sacred Places*, 101–2. A better reading of AIRFA on this score is found in Burton, *Worship and Wilderness*.

39. Harjo, Interview Tape 2.

40. Harjo, "American Indian Religious Freedom Act," 133.

41. Harjo, "American Indian Religious Freedom Act," 133.

42. Harjo, Interview Tape 2.

43. Native American Rights Fund, *Announcements* (Winter 1979).

44. President Clinton's Executive Order 13007, "Indian Sacred Sites," 61 Fed. Reg. 26771 (May 24, 1996).

45. Morman, *One Nation under Many Gods.*

46. 16 U.S.C. 470 cc(c).

47. 16 U.S.C. 470 a(d)(6)a, b.

48. President Clinton's Executive Order 13175, "Consultation and Coordination with Indian Tribal Governments," 65 Fed. Reg. 67249 (November 9, 2000).

49. Agency actions prompted by AIRFA's policy review process resulted in, among other things, Secretary of Interior Cecil Andrus's purchase of more than one hundred acres of land for the Cheyenne and Arapaho and other communities who required ceremonial access to Bear Butte. Harjo, "It Began with a Vision," 32.

50. Harjo, "American Indian Religious Freedom Act at 25," 129.

51. Federal Agencies Task Force, American Indian Religious Freedom Act Report P. L. 95–341 (Chairman, Cecil Andrus, Secretary of the Interior), August 1979 (henceforth AIRFA Report).

52. AIRFA Report, 82.

53. AIRFA Report, 82.

54. AIRFA Report, 52.

55. AIRFA Report, 76.

56. AIRFA Report, 76.

57. AIRFA Report, 98. John Borrows is a vocal advocate of the comparative law issues at stake in many legal proceedings involving Canadian First Nations' cultural and religious traditions. See Borrows, *Canada's Indigenous Constitution.*

58. See for example, People v. Woody, 61 Cal. 2d 716 (1964).

59. James Botsford and Walter Echo-Hawk, Remarks at "Roundtable on Native American Religious Freedom," Vermillion, South Dakota (May 2009). See also Weaver, *Other Words*, 175–225.

60. Harjo, Interview Tape 5.

61. Judiciary Committee, U.S. House of Representatives, 103 Cong., House Report 103–88, "Religious Freedom Restoration Act," 1993.

62. Native American Free Exercise of Religion Act, S. 1021, 103rd Cong. (1993) (NAFERA).

63. The following year, Senator Inouye introduced an only slightly modified version, the Native American Cultural Protection and Free Exercise of Religion Act, S. 2260, 103rd Cong. (1994).

64. NAFERA; Harjo, Interview Tape 5.

65. Harjo, Interview Tape 5.

66. Botsford and Echo-Hawk, Remarks.

67. 42 U.S.C. 1996a. "The (1) the term 'Indian' means a member of an Indian tribe; (2) the term "Indian tribe" means any tribe, band, nation, pueblo, or other organized group or community of Indians, including any Alaska Native village (as defined in, or established pursuant to, the Alaska Native Claims Settlement Act (43 U.S.C. 1601 et seq.)), which is recognized as eligible for the special programs and services provided by the United States to Indians because of their status as Indians."

68. 42 U.S.C. 1996a.

69. Peyote Way Church of God v. Thornburgh, 922 F. 2d 1210 (5th Cir. 1991); Gonzales v. O Centro Espirita Beneficente Uniao do Vegetal, 546 U.S. 418 (2006); Oklevueha Native American Church of Hawaii v. Lynch, 828 F. 3d 1012 (9th Cir. 2016); Olsen v. Drug Enforcement Admin., 878 F. 2d 1458 (D.C. Cir. 1989).

70. Harjo, "The American Indian Religious Freedom Act," 135.

71. Native American Language Act, P. L. 101–477 (1990), 25 U.S.C. 31.

72. Esther Martinez Native American Language Preservation Act, P. L. 109–394 (2006).

73. Every Student Succeeds Act, P. L. 114–95 (2015), Title VI.

74. See, for example, Leanne Hinton, *How to Keep Your Language Alive* (Berkeley, CA: Heydey Press, 2002); Bernard Perley, *Defying Maliseet Language Death* (Lincoln: University of Nebraska Press, 2011).

75. Indian Arts and Crafts Act, P. L. 101–644 (1990); Indian Arts and Crafts Act of 1935, P. L. 74–355.

76. 25 U.S.C. 305 et seq.; 18 U.S.C. 1151.

77. Botsford and Echo-Hawk, Remarks.

78. This conclusion is in league with a developing body of recent scholarship among Indian law scholars who, perhaps as a result of the coalition work described above and toward NAGPRA, have returned to think more deeply about the "cultural" and "religious" bases of sovereignty. See Tsosie and Coffey, "Rethinking the Tribal Sovereignty Doctrine"; Carpenter, "Limiting Principles"; Carpenter, "Real Property and Peoplehood"; Skibine, "Towards a Balanced Approach"; Echo-Hawk, *In the Courts of the Conqueror*, 453–57.

Chapter 6: Religion as Collective Right: Repatriation and Access to Eagle Feathers

1. A majority of states now have some form of statute protecting unmarked graves, and some have even drawn on NAGPRA. See Catherine Bergin Yalung and Laurel L. Wala, "Statutory Survey: A Survey of State Repatriation and Burial Protection Statutes," *Arizona State Law Journal* 24 (1992): 419–33.

2. See Berkhofer, *White Man's Indian*.

3. See Curtis M Hinsley Jr., "Digging for Identity: Reflections on the Cultural Practice of Collecting," in Mihesuah, *Repatriation Reader*, 37–59.

4. Harjo, "It Began with a Vision," 43–44.

5. Harjo, Interview Tape 1.

6. Harvard's Peabody Museum returned the Sacred Pole to the Omaha Nation in 1990, completing a process that had begun long before NAGPRA's passage that year. The item had

been placed under the care of the museum by its keeper. See Ridington and Hastings, *Blessing for a Long Time*.

7. S. 187 Hearings before the Senate Select Committee on Indian Affairs, 100th Congress Hearing 100–90 (February 1987). Johnson, *Sacred Claims*, 48. See also Jack Trope, "The Case for NAGPRA," in Chari and Lavallee, *Accomplishing NAGPRA*, 19–54.

8. Johnson, *Sacred Claims*, 46–64.

9. Harjo, "It Began with a Vision," 40–55.

10. Harjo, Interview Tape 5.

11. Joint Hearing before the House Committee on Interior and Insular Affairs, House Committee on House Administration, Subcommittee on Libraries and Memorials, and the House Committee on Public Works and Transportation, Subcommittee on Public Works and Grounds, on H.R. 2668, 101st Cong., 1st Sess. (July 20, 1989), 225. As cited in Trope, "The Case for NAGPRA," 25.

12. Harjo interview with author, January 12, 2018.

13. William Merrill, Edmund Ladd, and T. J. Ferguson, "The Return of the Ahayu: da: Lessons for Repatriation from Zuni Pueblo and the Smithsonian Institution," *Current Anthropology* 34 (2003): 523–67.

14. Harjo interview 2018.

15. Harjo, interview 2018.

16. Harjo, interview 2018.

17. 25 U.S.C. 3001 (1990).

18. 25 U.S.C. 3005 (a).

19. 25 U.S.C. 3005 (a)5.

20. Johnson, *Sacred Claims*, 67.

21. "Statement of Suzan Shown Harjo on Implementation of the Native American Graves Protection and Repatriation Act before the U.S. Senate Committee on Indian Affairs" (July 25, 2000).

22. The transcripts of more than fifty NAGPRA Review Committee meetings, made public on the website of the National Park Service NAGPRA Office, reveal the full reach of the challenges of the law for Indigenous peoples.

23. Fine-Dare, *Grave Injustice*, 7. Johnson, *Sacred Claims*; Colwell, *Plundered Skulls*; Chari and Lavallee, *Accomplishing NAGPRA*.

24. Johnson, *Sacred Claims*; Johnson, "Apache Revelation."

25. Johnson, *Sacred Claims*, 157.

26. 25 U.S.C. 3006 (c)5.

27. 43 CFR 10.11, Disposition of Culturally Unidentifiable Human Remains.

28. Johnson, *Sacred Claims*, 157. Johnson goes on to interpret the range of reactions to religious speech as a "result of a disjuncture between expectations regarding tradition as a concept—usually imagined in rigid ways—and the realities of tradition in action."

29. This is an important facet for evidence in indigenous cases. See, for example, the Canadian Supreme Court's holding in *Delgamuukw v. British Columbia* [1997] 3 SCR 1010.

30. See Gulliford, *Sacred Objects and Sacred Places*, 22; Ridington and Hastings, *Blessing for a Long Time*; Tweedie, *Drawing Back Culture*.

31. For more, see Alice Cunningham Fletcher and Francis La Flesche, *The Omaha Tribe*, 2 vols., 27th Annual Report of the Bureau of American Ethnology (Washington, DC: Smithsonian Institution, reprinted 1992 by University of Nebraska Press).

32. Native American Public Broadcasting Consortium, *Return of the Sacred Pole*, available at http://netnebraska.org/interactive-multimedia/television/return-sacred-pole, last accessed February 2018.

33. Native American Public Broadcasting Consortium, *Return of the Sacred Pole*, at 22:30.

34. Johnson, *Sacred Claims*, 22.

35. Na Iwi O Na Kupuna O Mokapu v. Dalton, 894 F. Supp. 1397 (D. Haw. 1995); U.S. v. Corrow, 941 F. Supp. 1553 (D.N.M. 1996); San Carlos Apache Tribe v. U.S., 272 F. Supp. 2d 860 (9th Cir. 2003); Yankton Sioux Tribe v. U.S. Army Corps of Engineers, 497 F. Supp. 2d 985 (8th Cir. 2007). Na Lei Alii Kawananakoa v. Hui Malama I Na Kupuna O Hawai'i Nei 158 Fed. Appx. 53 (9th Cir. 2005).

36. The tribes were the Confederated Tribes and Bands of the Yakama Indian Nation, the Nez Perce Tribe of Idaho, the Confederated Tribes of the Umatilla Indian Reservation, the Confederated Tribes of the Colville Reservation, as well as the unrecognized Wanapam Band. *Bonnichsen et al. v. United States*, 217 F. Supp. 2d, 116 (2002), aff'd *Bonnichsen et al. v. United States*, 357 F. 3d 962 (9th Cir. 2004), amended 367 F. 3d 864 (9th Cir. 2004).

37. *Bonnichsen v. U.S., Dept. of Army*, 969 F. Supp. 628 (1997).

38. Bruce Babbitt, Secretary of the Interior to Louis Caldera, Secretary of the Army, September 21, 2000.

39. *Bonnichsen v. United States*, 217 F. Supp. 2d 1116 (2002).

40. 25 U.S.C. 3001 (9). An effort to amend NAGPRA to fix this seemingly needless ambiguity from "is indigenous to the United States" to "is *or was* indigenous to the United States" aroused opposition from the scientific community and failed to secure sufficient support. Native American Technical Corrections Act, S. 2843, 108th Congress (2004).

41. *Bonnichsen et al. v. United States*, 357 F. 3d 962 (9th Cir. 2004), amended 367 F. 3d 864 (9th Cir. 2004).

42. Burke Museum, "Statement on the Repatriation of the Ancient One" (February 20, 2017). www.burkemuseum.org/blog/kennewick-man-ancient-one, accessed February. 2018.

43. Douglas Owsley and Richard Jantz, eds., *Kennewick Man: The Scientific Investigation of an Ancient American Skeleton* (College Station: Texas A&M University Press, 2014).

44. Douglas Preston, "The Kennewick Man Finally Freed to Share His Secrets," *Smithsonian Magazine,* September 2014.

45. Preston, "Kennewick Man Finally Freed to Share His Secrets."

46. Eske Willerslev et al., "The Ancestry and Affiliation of Kennewick Man," *Nature* 523 (July 23, 2015): 455–58.

47. A provision was added to the Water Infrastructure Improvements Act for the Nation, P. L. 114–322 (December 2016) 33 U.S.C. 2201.

48. Sara Green, "A Wrong Had Finally Been Righted': Tribes Bury Remains of Ancient Ancestor Known as Kennewick Man," *Seattle Times*, February 19, 2017.

49. Thomas, *Skull Wars*, xli.

50. See, for example, Ian Barbour, *When Science Meets Religion* (San Francisco: Harper, 2000).

51. http://edsitement.neh.gov/lesson-plan/kennewick-man-science-and-sacred-rights #sect-assessment, last accessed February 2018.

52. Steven Goldberg, "Kennewick Man and the Meaning of Life," *University of Chicago Legal Forum* 271 (2006): 275–86. See also John W. Ragsdale Jr., "Tinkering with the Past," *National Law Journal* A20 (February 11, 2002).

53. Jack Trope and Walter Echo-Hawk, "The Native American Graves Protection and Repatriation Act: Background and Legislative History," in Mihesuah, *Repatriation Reader*, 123.

54. Trope and Echo-Hawk, "Native American Graves Protection and Repatriation Act: Background and Legislative History."

55. Clayton W. Dumont Jr., describes this as a process of "masquerading the colonizer's needs as everyone's needs," in "Contesting Scientists' Narrations of NAGPRA's Legislative History: Rule 10.11 and the Recovery of 'Culturally Unidentifiable' Ancestors," *Wicazo Sa Review* 26 (Spring 2011): 5–41.

56. Testimony of the Native American Rights Fund before the Senate Select Committee on Indian Affairs, Hearing 100–09 (1987), 135, as cited in Johnson, *Sacred Claims,* 68.

57. Senate Committee on Indian Affairs, 100th Cong. S. Rep. 100–601 (1988), 7, as cited in Johnson, *Sacred Claims,* 51

58. 25 U.S.C. 3010.

59. NAGPRA, 25 U.S.C. 3001 § 2(7); NMAI, 20 U.S.C. 80q-14(7), citing 25 U.S.C. § 4506.

60. AIRFA's Peyote Amendment of 1994 defines "Indian" in terms of membership in a federally recognized tribe. 42 U.S.C. 1996(c).

61. Federal Agencies Task Force, *American Indian Religious Freedom Act Report*, P. L. 95–341 (Chairman, Cecil Andrus, Secretary of the Interior), August, 1979 (henceforth *AIRFA Report),* 92.

62. AIRFA Report, 93.

63. See Garroutte, *Real Indians.*

64. AIRFA Report, 94.

65. AIRFA Report, 96.

66. 20 U.S.C. 80q(a).

67. 25 U.S.C. 3003(b)a.

68. Courts have endorsed this momentum in NAGPRA claims raised by nonrecognized Native communities. See Romero v. Becken, 256 F. 3d 349 (5th Cir. 2001); Kickapoo Traditional Tribe of Texas v. Chacon, 46 F. Supp. 2d 644 (5th Cir. 1999); N.J. Sand Hill Band of Lenape and Cherokee Indians v. Corzine, C.V. No. 09–683 (D. N.J. 2012). The indeterminacy of Native Hawaiian Organizations under NAGPRA made for extensive contestation, as Greg Johnson has chronicled. See Johnson, *Sacred Claims.*

69. 25 U.S.C. 3001 § 2(9).

70. Jennifer Richman, "NAGPRA: Constitutionally Adequate?" in Richman and Forsyth, *Legal Perspectives on Cultural Resources,* 221. Such a view is emboldened in light of the Supreme Court's holding about the status of Native Hawaiians in *Rice v. Cayetano,* 528 U.S. 495, which concerned electoral matters, not NAGPRA.

71. Angela Neller, Ramona Peters, and Brice Obermeyer, "NAGPRA's Impact on Non-Federally Recognized Tribes," in Chari and Lavallee, *Accomplishing NAGPRA,* 163, 193. Prior to

NAGPRA, occasional repatriations to nonrecognized communities were more possible than after the codification of the privileging of federal recognition.

72. See Neller's section in "NAGPRA's Impact on Non-Federally Recognized Tribes," in Chari and Lavallee, *Accomplishing NAGPRA*, 165–74.

73. See Peters's section in "NAGPRA's Impact on Non-Federally Recognized Tribes," in Chari and Lavallee, *Accomplishing NAGPRA*, 174–87.

74. 43 CFR 10.11 (C)(2)(ii)(A).

75. Pierre Bourdieu, *Language and Symbolic Power*, ed. John Thompson, trans. Gino Raymond (Cambridge, MA: Harvard University Press, 1982); David Forgacs, ed., *Antonio Gramsci Reader: Selected Writings, 1916–1935* (New York: New York University Press, 2000).

76. The Bald Eagle Protection Act of 1940, 54 Stat. 250 (1940) was amended in 1962 as the Bald and Golden Eagle Protection Act, P. L. 87–884 (76 Stat. 1346) 2, 16 U.S.C. § 668–668(d). Other statutory protections include the Migratory Bird Treaty Act, 16 U.S.C. § 703–712, Endangered Species Act, 16 U.S.C. §§ 1531–1543.

77. U.S. v. Hardman, 297 F. 3d 1116, 1128 (10th Cir. 2002) (rehearing, en banc).

78. Bald and Golden Eagle Protection Act, P. L. 87–884 (76 Stat. 1346) (1962), 16 U.S.C. § 668–668(d). The exemption was later clarified in 1981 to mean members of federally recognized Indian tribes, though the earlier meaning was implied.

79. 50 C.F.R. 22.22 (b)(1).

80. US Fish and Wildlife Service, National Eagle Repository, Permit Application, www .fws.gov/eaglerepository/applications.php, last accessed November, 2017.

81. The highest profile of the Eagle Act cases, because decided in the Supreme Court, concerned a legal question of treaty rights and Congress' power to legally abrogate them rather than the religious accommodations per se. In *U.S. v. Dion*, the Supreme Court affirmed the conviction of a Dakota man who claimed a treaty right to hunt golden eagles on the Yankton Reservation. U.S. v. Dion, 476 U.S. 734 (1986). There have been unsuccessful First Amendment Free Exercise challenges to the permit scheme on the face of it: U.S. v. Abeyta, 632 F. Supp. 1031 (D. N.M. 1986); United States v. Thirty Eight Golden Eagles, 649 F. Supp. 269 (D. Nev., 1986) aff'd 829 F. 2d 41 (9th Cir. 1987). There has been an RFRA challenge that the wooden inefficiency of the permit system violated religious freedom: United States v. Hugs, 109 F. 3d 1375 (9th Cir. 1997). And there has been a RFRA challenge to the permit requirement that applicants disclose proposed ceremonial uses as a violation of secrecy principles: U.S. v. Gonzalez, 957 F. Supp. 1225 (D. N.M., 1997).

82. McNally, "Native American Religious Freedom as a Collective Right."

83. Rupert v. Director, U.S. Fish and Wildlife Service, 957 F. 2d 32 (1st Cir. 1992); Gibson v. Babbitt, 223 F. 3d 1256 (11th Cir. 2000); United States v. Antoine, 318 F. 3d 919 (9th Cir. 2003), cert. denied, 124 S. Ct. 1505 (2004); U.S. v. Wilgus, 638 F. 3d 1274 (10th Cir. 2011).

84. U.S. v. Hardman, 297 F. 3d at 1128.

85. Rupert had a history of similar litigiousness with regard to his access to Native American religious freedom protections for smoking marijuana. Erwin L. Rupert v. City of Portland, 605 A. 2d 63 (Maine Supreme Court 1992).

86. Rupert v. Director, 957 F. 2d 32 (1st Cir. 1992).

87. Gibson v. Babbitt, 223 F. 3d 1256 (11th Cir. 2000).

88. U.S. v. Antoine, 318 F. 3d 919 (9th Cir. 2003), cert. denied, 124 S. Ct. 1505 (2004).

89. U.S. v. Hardman, 297 F. 3d 1116 (10th Cir. 2002) (rehearing, en banc); U.S. v. Wilgus, 638 F. 3d 1274 (10th Cir. 2011).

90. U.S. v. Wilgus, 638 F. 3d at 1274.

91. *Wilgus*, 638 F. 3d at 1285.

92. *Hardman*, 297 F. 3d at 1116.

93. *Wilgus*, 638 F. 3d at 1286.

94. *Wilgus*, 638 F. 3d at 473.

95. McAllen Grace Brethren Church v. Salazar, 764 F. 3d 465 (5th Cir. 2014).

96. *McAllen*, 764 F. 3d at 474, citing S. Con. Res. 438, 81st Leg., R.S. (2009).

97. "Settlement Agreement between McAllen Grace Brethren Church v. S.M.R. Jewell." Civil Action No. 7: -7-CV-060 (S.D. Tex 06/13/16).

98. National Congress of American Indians, "Eagle Feather Working Group Update," May 2010, www.ncai.org/resources/ncai_publications/ncai-eagle-feather-working-group-update, last accessed November 2017.

99. Department of Justice Memorandum on Possession or Use of the Feathers or Other Parts of Federally Protected Birds for Tribal Cultural and Religious Purposes" (October 12, 2012), 3.

100. Department of Justice Memorandum, 4.

101. Department of Justice Memorandum, 4, citing US Fish and Wildlife Service, "Enforcement Priorities," 444 FW 1 (August 25, 2005).

Chapter 7: Religion as Peoplehood: Sovereignty and Treaties in Federal Indian Law

1. R. Sullivan, *Whale Hunt*, 252.

2. Treaty with the Makah, 1855 12 Stat., 939.

3. Bowechop (Ledford), "Contemporary Makah Whaling," 408–9.

4. R. Sullivan, *Whale Hunt*, 23.

5. After a storm uncovered a buried traditional village at Ozette in 1969, the Makah's decision to curate and study an impressive collection of artifacts renewed interest in whaling.

6. Coté, *Spirits of our Whaling Ancestors*, 8.

7. For religious connotations of this shift, see Johnson, Klassen, and Sullivan, *Ekklesia*.

8. Wilkins and Lomawaima, *Uneven Ground*, 216–48.

9. Wilkinson, *American Indians, Time, and the Law*, 55.

10. Tsosie and Coffey, "Rethinking the Tribal Sovereignty Doctrine"; Tsosie, "Land, Culture, and Community."

11. Cherokee Nation v. Georgia, 30 U.S. (5 Pet.) 1 (1831).

12. Lone Wolf v. Hitchcock, 187 U.S. 553 (1903). While the basic shape of this Plenary Power has remained intact, courts subsequently have subjected it to more than good faith. See Wilkins, *American Indian Sovereignty and the Supreme Court*.

13. Echo-Hawk, *In the Courts of the Conqueror*, 6, citing Johnson v. M'Intosh, 21 U.S. 543, 588.

14. Article 1's Commerce Clause allocates to Congress the power "to regulate Commerce with foreign Nations, and among the several States, and with the Indian Tribes." U.S. Const. art. I. sec 8 cl.3.

15. Suzan Harjo, Remarks at Library of Congress Symposium, "Indian Religious Freedom: to Litigate or Legislate," November 28, 2007.

16. In the 1868 Treaty of Bosque Redondo, for example, the displaced Navajo negotiated strongly for their return to the land between the four sacred mountains.

17. Treaty at Fort Laramie, 1868, 15 Stat. 635.

18. Act of February 28, 1877, 19 Stat. 254; Act of March 2, 1889, 25 Stat. 889.

19. United States v. Sioux Nation of Indians, 448 U.S. 371 (1980).

20. Harjo, Remarks, "Indian Religious Freedom: to Litigate or Legislate."

21. Harjo, *Nation to Nation*.

22. Pamela Klassen, "Spiritual Jurisdictions: Treaty People and the Queen of Canada," in Johnson, Klassen, and Sullivan, *Ekklesia*.

23. Ordinance of 1787, Second Continental Congress of the Confederation of the States, July 13, 1787.

24. Act of March 3, 1871, 16 Stat. 544, 566, 25 U.S.C. § 71.

25. Although its law allows the United States to unilaterally abrogate treaties, including treaties with Native nations, courts have held the United States accountable to doing so expressly and have not in all cases affirmed the abrogation of treaties by federal actions.

26. Sections 7–9, "An Act to prevent the exercise of assumed and arbitrary power, by all persons under pretext of authority from the Cherokee Indians, and their laws, and to prevent white persons from residing within that part of the chartered limits of Georgia," December 22, 1830; *Acts of the General Assembly of the State of Georgia, Annual Sess.* (Milledgeville, GA: Camak and Ragland, 1831), 114–17.

27. Worcester v. Georgia, 31 U.S. (6 Pet.) 515, 551 (1832).

28. *Worcester*, 31 U.S. at 559–60.

29. *Worcester*, 31 U.S. at 520

30. Act of March 3, 1871, 16 Stat. 544, 566, 25 U.S.C. § 71.

31. United States v. Kagama, 118 U.S. 375 (1886); Major Crimes Act of 1885, 23 Stat. 362.

32. Ex parte Crow Dog, 109 U.S. 556 (1883). A Lakota man, Crow Dog, had confessed to killing Chief Spotted Tail on the Pine Ridge Reservation and succumbed to a judgment under Lakota customary law for restitution between the two families. But he was arrested and sentenced in a territorial court to hang for the murder. In *Ex parte Crow Dog*, the Supreme Court affirmed that he was not subject to US law on the reservation, affirming that tribal law was an aspect of inherent sovereignty. Harring, *Crow Dog's Case*, 129.

33. *Kagama*, 118 U.S. at 375.

34. Lecture, "Federal Indian Law," University of Minnesota, January 31, 2007.

35. Lone Wolf v. Hitchcock, 187 U.S. 553 (1903). "Dred Scott" comment in Sioux Nation v. United States, 601 F. 2d 1157, 1173 (Ct. Cl. 1979), affirmed, 448 U.S. 371 (1980).

36. For a religious studies discussion of the case, see Graber, *Gods of Indian Country*.

37. "When, therefore, treaties were entered into between the US and a tribe of Indians it was never doubted that the *power* to abrogate existed in Congress, and in a contingency such power might be availed of from considerations of governmental policy, particularly if consistent with perfect good faith towards the Indians." Lone Wolf v. Hitchcock, 187 U.S. at 556.

38. For analysis of the slippage between multiple senses of plenary power, see Wilkins and Lomawaima, *Uneven Ground*, 98–116.

39. For cases stepping up judicial scrutiny of claimed congressional plenary power, see *Sioux Nation*, 408–9.

40. U.S. v. Dion, 476 U.S. 734 (1986).

41. Tee Hit Ton Indians v. United States, 348 U.S. 272 (1955); Oliphant v. Suquamish, 35 U.S. 191 (1978); United States v. Wheeler, 435 U.S. 313 (1978).

42. Ex parte Crow Dog, 109 U.S. 556 (1883); Talton v. Mayes, 163 U.S. 376 (1896).

43. U.S. v. Winans, 198 U.S. 371 (1905).

44. *Winans*, 198 U.S. at 381.

45. *Cohen's Handbook* was cited so often it "attained something of the weight of a Supreme Court opinion." Wilkinson, *American Indians, Time, and the Law*, 58.

46. Getches, Wilkinson, and Williams, *Cases and Materials on Federal Indian Law*, 197.

47. Felix Cohen, *Handbook of Federal Indian Law* (Washington, DC: GPO, 1942), 122–23; as cited in Getches, Wilkinson, and Williams, *Cases and Materials on Federal Indian Law*, 197.

48. Washington v. Washington State Commercial Passenger Fishing Vessel Association, 443 U.S. 658 (1979) (hereafter Vessel Association).

49. United States v. Washington, 384 F. Supp. 312 (W.D. Wash. 1974), affirmed 520 F. 2d 676 (9th Cir. 1975), cert. denied, 423 U.S. 1086 (1976) (hereafter *Boldt Decision*).

50. Tulee v. Washington, 315 U.S. 681 (1942); Puyallup Tribe, v. Department of Game, 391 U.S. 392 (1968).

51. Fay G. Cohen, *Treaties on Trial: the Continuing Controversy over Northwest Indian Fishing Rights* (Seattle: University of Washington Press, 1986).

52. *Boldt Decision*, at 330.

53. *Boldt Decision*, at 351.

54. *Boldt Decision*, at 382.

55. *Boldt Decision*, at 382.

56. *Vessel Association*, 443 U.S. at 665.

57. Treaty of Medicine Creek, 1854, *Boldt Decision*, 312. For excerpts of Stevens treaties transcripts, see Hank Adams, "The Game and Fish Were Made for Us," in Harjo, *Nation to Nation*, 181–85.

58. *Boldt Decision*, at 357.

59. McClanahan v. State Tax Commission, 411 U.S. 164, 174 (1973); Winters v. United States, 207 U.S. 564, 576–77.

60. Choctaw Nation v. Oklahoma, 397 U.S. 620, 631 (1970); Worcester v. Georgia, 582.

61. Choctaw Nation v. United States, 318 U.S. 423, 431–32 (1943).

62. *Boldt Decision*, at 343

63. *Vessel Association*, 443 U.S. at 675–76.

64. *Vessel Association*, 443 U.S. at 675–76, citing Jones v. Meehan, 175 U.S. 1 (1899).

65. *Vessel Association*, 443 U.S. at 685–86, citing Arizona v. California, 373 U.S. 546 (1963), Winters v. United States, 207 U.S. 564 (1908).

66. United States v. Washington, 759 F. 2d 1353 (9th Cir. 1985) (en banc).

67. In addition to the *United States v. Washington* line of litigation, a related line began with *United States v. Oregon*, 302 F. Supp. 899 (1974), decided in light of the Boldt Decision's 50 percent rule.

68. United States v. Washington, 759 F. 2d 1353, 1357 (9th Cir. 1985) (en banc).

69. United States v. Washington, 584 U.S. ___ (2018). Justice Kennedy recused himself for involvement in earlier versions of the case while on the Ninth Circuit. The Ninth Circuit decision, which stands, is United States v. Washington, 827 F. 3d 836 (9th Cir. 2016).

70. Ann Renker, "Whale Hunting and the Makah Tribe: A Needs Assessment" (2002), Appendix A to *Application for Waiver of the MMPA Take Moratorium to Exercise Gray Whale Hunting Rights Secured in the Treaty of Neah Bay* (2005), 6.

71. Willie Sport, in Martha Black, *Huupukwanum Tupasat, Out of the Mist: Treasures of the Nuu-chah-nulth Chiefs* (Victoria: Royal British Columbia Museum, 1990), 33, as cited in Coté, *Spirits of Our Whaling Ancestors*, 34.

72. Richard E. Umeek Atleo, *Tsawalk: A Nuu-chah-nulth Worldview* (Vancouver: University of British Columbia Press, 2004), as cited in Coté, *Spirits of Our Whaling Ancestors*, 25

73. A whaler's wife during a hunt was in such a state of power, she "could exert such a special influence over the whale that she could actually call it to the shore." Coté, *Spirits of Our Whaling Ancestors*, 26–27.

74. Treaty with the Makah, 1855. 12 Stat., 939.

75. An Act to further amend the Indian Act, 1884, S.C. 1884 (47 Vict.) C. 27.

76. Coté, *Spirits of Our Whaling Ancestors*, 63–64.

77. Renker, "Whale Hunting and the Makah Tribe: A Needs Assessment" (2002), 3.

78. Sullivan, *Whale Hunt*, 41.

79. Coté, *Spirits of Our Whaling Ancestors*, 133–34.

80. Metcalf v. Daley, No. CV-98–05289-FDB (W.D. Wash. 1998), reversed, Metcalf v. Daley, 214 F. 3d 1135 (9th Cir. 2000).

81. Bowechop (Ledford), "Contemporary Makah Whaling"; Sullivan, *Whale Hunt*.

82. Renker, "Whale Hunting and the Makah Tribe," 28. For an account of the hunt, see Bowechop (Ledford), "Contemporary Makah Whaling."

83. Bowechop (Ledford), "Contemporary Makah Whaling," 415.

84. In 1995, a gray whale that had been caught in a fishing net was approved by the United States for distribution to tribal members.

85. Coté, *Spirits of Our Whaling Ancestors*, 193.

86. Bowechop (Ledford), "Contemporary Makah Whaling," 419.

87. Renker, "Whale Hunting and the Makah Tribe," 33–34.

88. Metcalf v. Daley, 214 F. 3d 1135 (9th Cir. 2000).

89. Coté, *Spirits of Our Whaling Ancestors*, 175.

90. Anderson v. Evans, No. CV-02–00081-FDB, reversed, Anderson v. Evans, 350 F. 3d 815 (9th Cir. 2003).

91. See Zachary Tomlinson, "Note: Abrogation or Regulation? How *Anderson v. Evans* Discards the Makah's Treaty Whaling Right in the Name of Conservation Necessity," *Washington Law Review* 78 (2003): 1101.

92. Makah Indian Tribe v. Quileute Indian Tribe, 873 F. 3d 1157 (9th Cir. 2017).

93. United States v. Michigan, 471 F. Supp. 192 (W.D. Wis. 1979), aff'd in relevant part, 653 F. 2d 277 (6th Cir. 1981), cert. denied, 454 U.S. 1124 (1981).

94. Eddie Benton-Banai, *The Mishomis Book: The Voice of the Ojibway* (Minneapolis: University of Minnesota Press, 2010).

95. For an excellent overview, see Winona LaDuke, "Seeds of Our Ancestors, Seeds of Life," TedX Talk, June 2011, www.youtube.com/watch?v=pHNlel72eQc, last accessed April 2019.

96. McNally, *Honoring Elders*.

97. Wilkinson, "To Feel the Summer in the Spring," 385.

98. Treaty with the Chippewa, 1837, 7 Stat. 536., art. 5.

99. Treaty of LaPointe, 1842, 7 Stat. 591, art. 2.

100. Nesper, *Walleye War*, 49–51; Bruce White, "Criminalizing the Seasonal Round," presented at the Annual Meeting of the Ethnohistory Society, unpublished, 1998.

101. Karl Jacoby, *Crimes against Nature: Squatters, Poachers, Thieves, and the Hidden History of American Conservation* (Berkeley: University of California Press, 2003).

102. State v. Morrin, 136 Wis. 552 (1908).

103. See Chantal Norrgard, *Seasons of Change: Labor, Treaty Rights, and Ojibwe Nationhood* (Chapel Hill: University of North Carolina Press, 2014).

104. Rick Whaley with Walt Bresette, *Walleye Warriors: An Effective Alliance against Racism and for the Earth* (Philadelphia, PA: New Society, 1994), 18.

105. Wilkinson, "To Feel the Summer in the Spring."

106. Lac Courte Oreilles Band v. Voigt, 700 F. 2d 341 (7th Cir. 1983), cert denied, 464 U.S. 805 (1983) (hereafter *LCO I*), reversing United States v. Bouchard, 464 F. Supp. 1316 (W.D. Wis. 1978).

107. Nesper, *Walleye War*, 60.

108. Nesper, *Walleye War*, 4

109. *LCO I* at 352.

110. *LCO I* at 366. The court followed the Supreme Court's proclamation in the Vessel Association version of the salmon case: "a treaty is basically a contract between Sovereign equals," and applied a straightforward contract law approach to the treaty recognized title or rights rather than the aboriginal title approach that Tee Hit Ton had made relatively easy for Congress to extinguish.

111. Lac Courte Oreilles Band of Lake Superior Chippewa Indians v. Wisconsin, 760 F. 2d 177 (7th Cir. 1985) (*LCO II*); Lac Courte Oreilles Band of Lake Superior Chippewa Indians v. Wisconsin, 653 F. Supp. 1420 (W.D. Wis. 1987) (*LCO III*); Lac Courte Oreilles Band of Lake Superior Chippewa Indians v. Wisconsin, 668 F. Supp. 1233 (W.D. Wis. 1987) (*LCO IV*); Lac Courte Oreilles Band of Lake Superior Chippewa Indians v. Wisconsin, 686 F. Supp. 226 (W.D. Wis. 1987) (*LCO V*); Lac Courte Oreilles Band of Lake Superior Chippewa Indians v. Wisconsin, 707 F. Supp. 1034 (W.D. Wis. 1989) (*LCO VI*); Lac Courte Oreilles Band of Lake Superior Chippewa Indians v. Wisconsin, 740 F. Supp. 1400, 1421 (W.D. Wis. 1990) (*LCO VII*). See Wilkinson, "To Feel the Summer in the Spring."

112. Lac Courte Oreilles Band of Lake Superior Chippewa Indians v. Wisconsin, 686 F. Supp. 226 (W.D. Wis. 1987).

113. In Michigan, the Chippewa Ottawa Resource Authority serves these purposes for tribes with rights under the 1836 treaty. In Minnesota, the 1854 Treaty Authority does so.

114. Minnesota v. Mille Lacs Band of Chippewa Indians, 526 U.S. 172 (1999) (hereafter *Mille Lacs*).

115. *Mille Lacs*, 526 U.S. at 204. The dissenting opinion vigorously disagreed on this point. *Mille Lacs*, 219 (C. J. Rehnquist, dissenting), citing Ward v. Race Horse, 163 U.S. 504 (1896).

116. Treaty of Washington with the Chippewa, 1855, 10 Stat. 1165, art. 1., *Mille Lacs*, 526 U.S. at 196–97.

117. United States v. Michigan, 471 F. Supp. at 279.

118. *Cohen's Handbook* 18.04 [2]g[g].

119. *Fishing Vessel*, 443 U.S. at 678–79.

120. *Fishing Vessel*, 443 U.S. at 678–79.

121. *Boldt Decision*, at 203, 208.

122. United States. v. Washington, 759 F. 2d 1353, 1357 (9th Cir. 1985) (en banc).

123. United States v. Washington, 827 F. 3d 836, 852 (9th Cir. 2016) (hereafter *Culverts*).

124. *Culverts*, 827 F. 3d at 853.

125. *Culverts*, 827 F. 3d at 852, citing United States v. Adair, 723 F. 2d 1394 (9th Cir. 1983).

126. *Cohen's Handbook* 18.04[2]g. See Ed Goodman, "Protecting Habitat for Off-Reservation Tribal Hunting and Fishing Rights: Tribal Co-management as a Reserved Right," *Environmental Law* 30 (2000): 279; Michael C Blumm and Brent M. Swift, "The Indian Treaty Piscary Profit and Habitat Protection in the Pacific Northwest: A Property Rights Approach," *Colorado Law Review* 69 (1998): 407.

127. Frank Ettawageshik, "Relationships: How Our Ancestors Perceived Treaties and Property Rights," 13th Vine Deloria, Jr. Indigenous Studies Symposium, Northwest Indian College, May 2018. www.youtube.com/watch?v=fcz7cgaLxdc, last accessed April, 2019.

128. As this book was going to press, the Supreme Court released an important decision affirming the treaty-protected hunting rights of a member of the Crow Nation against Wyoming's position that statehood had extinguished those rights. Herrera v. Wyoming, 139 S. Ct. 1686 (2019).

129. U.S. v. Dion, 762 F. 2d 674 (8th Cir. 1985), *reversed* 476 U.S. 734 (1986).

130. See Carpenter, "Limiting Principles and Empowering Practices."

131. Wesper, *Walleye War*, 4.

132. Great Lakes Indian Fish and Wildlife Commission, "Crossing the Line: Tribble Brothers," *Ogichidaa Storytellers: Gathering the Pieces Series*, www.glifwc.org/publications/#Media, last accessed July 2018.

133. Winters v. United States, 207 U.S. 564 (1908).

134. United States v. Billie, 667 F. Supp. 1485 (S.D. Fla. 1987)

135. As quoted or paraphrased by Kevin Washburn, lecture notes, *Federal Indian Law*, University of Minnesota Law School, January 2007.

Chapter 8: Religion as Peoplehood: Indigenous Rights in International Law

1. United Nations Declaration on the Rights of Indigenous Peoples, G.A. Res. 61/295, U.N. Doc. A/RES/61/295, Annex (September 13, 2007).

2. Organization of American States, "Record of the Current Status of the Draft American Declaration on the Rights of Indigenous Peoples," OEA/Ser.K/XVI/ GT/DADIN/doc.334/ 08 rev. 7 (May 2, 2012).

3. Charters and Stavenhagen, *Making the Declaration Work*; Echo-Hawk, *In the Light of Justice*.

4. Anaya, *Indigenous Peoples in International Law*.

5. Carpenter and Riley, "Indigenous Peoples and the Jurisgenerative Moment."

6. Carpenter and Riley draw on an influential article by Robert Cover about these "paideic communities that live their commitments and absorb, process, and create law 'all the way down.'" Robert M. Cover, "The Supreme Court, 1982 Term—Foreword: Nomos and Narrative," *Harvard Law Review* 97 (1983): 4.

7. Carpenter and Riley, "Indigenous Peoples and the Jurisgenerative Moment," 200.

8. Siegfried Wiessner, "Reenchanting the World: Indigenous Peoples' Rights as Essential Parts of a Holistic Human Rights Regime," *UCLA Journal of International Law and Foreign Affairs* 15 (2010): 241.

9. Siv Ellen Kraft, "U.N. Discourses on Indigenous Religion," in Johnson and Kraft, *Handbook of Indigenous Religions*, 80.

10. Anaya, "Right of Indigenous Peoples to Self-Determination in the Post-Declaration Era," in Charters and Stavenhagen, *Making the Declaration Work*; Echo-Hawk, *In the Light of Justice*; Rebecca Tsosie, "Indigenous Human Rights and the Ethics of Remediation: Redressing the Legacy of Radioactive Contamination for Native Peoples and Native Lands," *Santa Clara Journal of International Law* 13 (2015): 203; Robert T. Coulter, "The Law of Self-Determination and the United Nations Declaration on the Rights of Indigenous Peoples," *UCLA Journal of International Law and Foreign Affairs* 15 (Spring 2010): 1–27; Carpenter and Riley, "Indigenous Peoples and the Jurisgenerative Moment." See also the International Law Association's study, "Rights of Indigenous Peoples," Sofia Conference (2012).

11. For a discussion of how the international law norms operate at the heart of federal Indian law, see *Cohen's Handbook of Federal Indian Law* 5.07(1).

12. Echo-Hawk, *In the Light of Justice*, 63.

13. Echo-Hawk, *In the Light of Justice*; see also Williams, *Like a Loaded Weapon*, 173–80.

14. See Clinton, "Redressing the Legacy of Conquest"; Williams, *Like a Loaded Weapon*, 173–80.

15. Duane Champagne, among others, has found this not only to be an irony but also potentially a contradiction. Duane Champagne, "UNDRIP: Human, Civil, and Indigenous Rights," *Wicazo Sa Review* 28, no. 1 (Spring 2013): 15.

16. Williams, *Like a Loaded Weapon*, 177, citing Jack L. Goldsmith and Eric Posner, *The Limits of International Law* (New York: Oxford University Press, 2005), and Robert Laurence, "Learning to Live with the Plenary Power of Congress over Indian Nations," *Arizona Law Review* 30 (1988): 429–30; See Carpenter and Riley, "Indigenous Peoples and the Jurisgenerative Moment," 193–95, for a fuller discussion of the broad criticisms.

17. Navajo Nation Human Rights Commission, *Assessing Race Relations between Navajos and Non-Navajos, 2008–2009* (2010).

18. Human Rights Council, *Report of the Special Rapporteur on the Rights of Indigenous Peoples, James Anaya, on the Situation of Indigenous Peoples in the U.S.*, 21st Sess., U.N. Doc. A/HRC/21/47/Add.1 (August 30, 2012), para. 44.

19. The commission also petitioned for remediation measures and a halt to any continued snowmaking. Navajo Nation Human Rights Commission, "Petition to the Inter-American Commission on Human Rights Submitted by the Navajo Nation against the U.S.A." (March 2, 2015), 4.

20. Carpenter and Riley, "Indigenous Peoples and the Jurisgenerative Moment," 222–26.

21. L. Hauptman, *Seven Generations of Iroquois Leadership: The Six Nations since 1800* (Syracuse, NY: Syracuse University Press, 2008).

22. Akwesasne Notes, ed., *Basic Call to Consciousness* (Summertown, TN: Book Publishing, 1978).

23. International Covenant on Civil and Political Rights, opened for signature December 16, 1966, 999 U.N.T.S. 171.

24. Sosa v. Alvarez-Machain, 542 U.S. 692 (2004). Non-self-executing treaties can be raised, however, in a "defensive context and, perhaps, in administrative proceedings." They can also serve in judicial interpretations of federal law. *Cohen's Handbook* 5.07 (2)(c). U.S. ratification strengthens the argument that ICCPR concerns are binding as matters of customary international law.

25. Kraft, "U.N. Discourses on Indigenous Religion," 80–91.

26. Department of Economic and Social Affairs of the United Nations Secretariat, *State of the World's Indigenous Peoples*, vol. 1 (2009). ST/ESA/328, 60.

27. Department of Economic and Social Affairs of the United Nations Secretariat, *State of the World's Indigenous Peoples*, 60.

28. UN Human Rights Committee, *General Comment 23* (August 4, 1994). CCPR/C/21/Rev. 1/Add. 5, para. 7.

29. UN Human Rights Committee, *General Comment 23*, para. 9.

30. UN Human Rights Committee, *General Comment 23*, para. 9.

31. In a 1990 case pushing the limits of the Optional Protocol's limitation of grievances to individuals, the Human Rights Committee found Canada had violated the Lubicon Cree's Art. 27 rights by leasing aboriginal Cree lands to developers and endangering Cree economic and social activities on those lands. See Ominayak, Chief of the Lubicon Lake Band, v. Canada, Communication No. 267/1984, *Report of the Human Rights Committee*, U.N. GOAR, 45th Sess., Supp. No. 40, Vol. 2, U.N. Doc. A/45/40, Annex 9 (A) (1990).

32. International Labour Organization Convention (No. 169), *Concerning Indigenous and Tribal Peoples in Independent Countries*, June 27, 1989, 1650 U.N.T.S. 383.

33. Lee Swepston, "The ILO Indigenous and Tribal Peoples Convention (No. 169): Eight Years after Adoption," in Cynthia Price, ed., *Human Rights of Indigenous Peoples* (Ardsley, NY: Transnational, 1998), 18–28.

34. Anaya, *Indigenous Peoples in International Law*, 58–61.

35. Charter of the United Nations, Art. 2.

36. UNDRIP, Art. 46 (1).

37. UNDRIP, Art. 25.

38. Asia Pacific Forum and the Office of the United Nations High Commissioner for Human Rights, *UNDRIP: A Manual for National Human Rights Institutions*, Asia Pacific Forum of National Human Rights Institutions (August 2013), 14.

39. OAS Draft American Declaration on the Rights of Indigenous Peoples, Art. XII(3) (updated upon the conclusion of the Twelfth Meeting of Negotiations, OEA/Ser.K/XVI GT/DADIN/doc.334/08 rev. 7 (May 2, 2012) (henceforth *OAS Draft Declaration*).

40. *OAS Draft Declaration*, Art. XII (3).

41. *OAS Draft Declaration*, Art. XVIII (1) (Approved on April 16, 2008—Eleventh Meeting of Negotiations in the Quest for Points of Consensus).

42. Art. XV(1) was also approved by consensus and as such is not docketed for further negotiation.

43. Manybeads v. United States, 730 F. Supp. 1515 (D. Ariz. 1989).

44. International Convention on the Elimination of All Forms of Racial Discrimination, *adopted* March 7, 1966, 660 U.N.T.S. 195 (ratified by US in 1994) (hereafter, ICERD). But ICERD was expressly declared to be non-self-executing.

45. ICERD, Art. 5(d)vii. An example of Indigenous activism is a "shadow report" submitted to the UN Committee on the Elimination of Racial Discrimination in response to the United States' periodic report. An example is the International Indian Treaty Council, "Racial Discrimination against Indigenous Peoples in the United States: Consolidated Indigenous Shadow Report" (January 6, 2008). This was in response to the United States' sixth periodic report, Cerd/C/USA/6 (October 24, 2007).

46. Sosa v. Alvarez-Machain, 542 U.S. 692 (2004).

47. Echo-Hawk, *In the Light of Justice*, 78.

48. Anaya, *Indigenous Rights in International Law*, 61.

49. Echo-Hawk, *In the Light of Justice*, 78.

50. See, for example, Committee of U.S. Citizens v. Reagan, 859 F. 2d 929, 935 (D.D.C. 1988).

51. *Cohen's Handbook of Federal Indian Law* 5.07(1), citing *Restatement (Third) of Foreign Relations Law* § 102 cmt. i.

52. Mayagna (Sumo) Awas Tingni Community v. Nicaragua, Inter-Am. Ct. H.R. (ser. C) No. 79 (2001).

53. *Awas Tingni*, 149. See Carpenter and Riley, "Indigenous Peoples and the Jurisgenerative Moment," 208.

54. Yakye Axa Indigenous Community v. Paraguay, Inter-Am. Ct. H.R. (ser. C) No. 125, ¶ 137 (June 17, 2005); Sawhoyamaxa Indigenous Cmnty. v. Paraguay, Inter-Am. Ct. H.R. (ser. C) No. 146 (March 29, 2006); Moiwana Cmnty. v. Suriname, Inter-Am. Ct. H.R. (ser. C) No. 124, 131–34 (June 15, 2005).

55. Dann v. United States, Case 11.140, Inter-American Commission on Human Rights, Report No. 75/02, OEA/Ser.L./V/II.117, doc. 5 rev. para. 5 (2002).

56. Carpenter and Riley, "Indigenous Peoples and the Jurisgenerative Moment," 211. But even rulings favorable to Indigenous peoples can involve insufficient redress.

57. Aurelio Cal v. Belize, Supreme Court of Belize (Claims No. 171 and 172 of 2007) (October 18, 2007).

58. Asia Pacific Forum, *UNDRIP: A Manual for National Human Rights Institutions* (2013) HR/PUB/13/2 (2013).

59. www.ohchr.org/en/issues/ipeoples/emrip/pages/emripindex.aspx, last accessed September 2018.

60. *Report of the Special Rapporteur on the Rights of Indigenous Peoples, James Anaya, on the Situation of Indigenous Peoples in the U.S.*, 21st Sess., U.N. Doc. A/HRC/21/47/Add.1 (August 30, 2012).

61. *Report of the Special Rapporteur on the Rights of Indigenous Peoples on Her Mission to the United States of America*, A/HRC/36/46/Add.1 (August 9, 2017).

62. Echo-Hawk, *In the Light of Justice*, 67.

63. Echo-Hawk, *In the Light of Justice*, 81

64. See Kristen Carpenter and Edyael Casaperalta, "Implementing the UN Declaration on the Rights of Indigenous Peoples in the United States: A Call to Action for Inspired Advocacy in Indian Country," Conference Report, *Colorado Law Review Forum* (forthcoming).

65. Anaya, *Indigenous Peoples in International Law*, 138–40.

66. Echo-Hawk, *In the Light of Justice*, 196–97. Echo-Hawk here quotes from Anaya's Rapporteur 2012 report on the United States, in a paragraph elaborating on the violations of international Indigenous rights norms on the San Francisco Peaks case. See Human Rights Council, *Report of the Special Rapporteur on the Rights of Indigenous Peoples, James Anaya, on the Situation of Indigenous Peoples in the U.S.*, para. 44.

67. Niezen, *Rediscovered Self*, 67.

68. Karen Engle, *Elusive Promise of Indigenous Development: Rights, Culture, Strategy* (Durham, NC: Duke University Press, 2010).

69. ECOSOC *General Comment* 21 on ICESCR, Art. 15 "The Right of Everyone to Take Part in Cultural Life" C/C.12/GC/21 (November 20, 2009), paras. 6, 13.

70. A/HRC/EMRIP/2012/3, paras. 51–52.

71. A/HRC/EMRIP/2012/3, para. 56.

72. A/HRC/EMRIP/2012/3, para. 57.

73. Asia Pacific Forum, *UNDRIP: A Manual for National Human Rights Institutions*, HR/PUB/13/2 (2013).

74. *Report of the Special Rapporteur on the Rights of Indigenous Peoples, James Anaya, on the Situation of Indigenous Peoples in the U.S.*, para. 44; Echo-Hawk, *In the Light of Justice*, 195.

75. *Report of the Special Rapporteur on the Rights of Indigenous Peoples, James Anaya, on the Situation of Indigenous Peoples in the U.S*, n. 29.

76. Frank Ettawageshik, unpublished remarks in Cultural Rights Workshop, *Implementing UNDRIP, University of Colorado Law School* (March 2019).

77. Bryan Neihart, "Case Note: *Awas Tingni v. Nicaragua* Reconsidered: Grounding Indigenous Peoples' Land Rights in Religious Freedom," *Denver Journal of International Law and Policy* 42, no. 1 (Fall 2013): 77, 79.

78. Greg Johnson pays close attention to such facets of Native Hawaiian advocacy on behalf of Mauna Kea. Johnson, *Religion in the Moment*.

79. President Clinton's Executive Order 13175, 65 Fed. Reg. 67249 (November 6, 2000); President Obama's Memorandum on Tribal Consultation, 2009 Daily Comp. Pres. Doc. 887 (November 5, 2009).

80. See Pueblo of Sandia v. United States, 50 F. 3d 856 (10th Cir. 1995).

81. EMRIP, *Free, Prior, and Informed Consent: A Human Rights-Based Approach* (2018) A/HRC/39/62, 61.

82. US Department of State, "Announcement of U.S. Support for the United Nations Declaration on the Rights of Indigenous Peoples" (December 16, 2010).

83. UN-REDD Programme, Guidelines on Free, Prior and Informed Consent (January 2013), www.uncclearn.org/sites/default/files/inventory/un-redd05.pdf.

84. EMRIP, *Free, Prior, and Informed Consent: A Human Rights-Based Approach* (2018) A/HRC/39/62, 35.

85. Carla F. Fredericks, "Operationalizing Free, Prior, and Informed Consent," *Albany Law Review* 80 (2016/17): 429, at 464–65.

86. Fredericks, "Operationalizing Free, Prior, and Informed Consent," 464–65.

87. UN-REDD Programme, Guidelines on Free, Prior and Informed Consent (January 2013).

Chapter 9: Conclusion

1. President Obama Proclamation 9558, "Establishment of Bears Ears National Monument" December 28, 2016, 82 Fed. Reg. 1139.

2. Obama Proclamation 9558, 1139.

3. Bears Ears Inter-Tribal Coalition, "Proposal to President Barack Obama for the Creation of Bears Ears National Monument" (October 15, 2015), 8 (hereafter Proposal).

4. American Antiquities Act, 16 U.S.C. §§ 431–33 (1906).

5. Charles Wilkinson, "'At Bears Ears We Can Hear the Voices of Our Ancestors in Every Canyon and on Every Mesa Top': The Creation of the First Native National Monument," *Arizona State Law Journal* 50 (2018): 317.

6. Subsequently, a federal judge ordered new districting for the commission, and in the 2018 elections, two of three of the commissioners are Navajo. Navajo Nation v. San Juan County, 266 F. Supp. 3d 1341 (D. Utah, 2017).

7. Wilkinson, "At Bears Ears," 328.

8. Wilkinson, "At Bears Ears."

9. Sarah Krakoff, "Public Lands, Conservation, and the Possibility of Justice," *Harvard Civil Rights–Civil Liberties Law Review* 53 (Winter 2018): 213.

10. Proposal.

11. Obama Proclamation 9558, 1144.

12. Wilkinson, "At Bears Ears," 331.

13. President Trump Proclamation 9681 (December 4, 2017), 82 Fed. Reg. 58081.

14. Bureau of Land Management, "Bears Ears National Monument: Proposed Monument Management Plans and Final Environmental Impact Statement, Shash Jáa and Indian Creek Units" (July 2019). Notably, the five Native nations of the Bears Ears Inter-Tribal Coalition elected not to participate in consultation, since they are challenging the lawfulness of the Trump proclamation that sets the terms for the environmental review and management plan.

15. Based on thousands of released Department of the Interior emails, the *New York Times* reported that energy interests drove Secretary Zinke's review and in some instances drafted the maps of the shrunken monument. Erik Lipton and Lisa Friedman, "Oil Was Central in Decision to Shrink Bears Ears, Emails Show," *New York Times*, March 2, 2018.

16. President Trump's Executive Order 13792, 82 Fed. Reg. 20429 (April 26, 2017).

17. Trump Proclamation 9681.

18. The litigation includes Hopi Tribe et al. v. Trump, Case 1: 17-cv-02590 (D.D.C., 2017–); Utah Dine Bikeyah et al. v. Trump et al.; NRDC et al. v. Trump; and two additional lawsuits related to the reduction of neighboring Grand Staircase/Escalante National Monument.

19. Hopi et al. v. Trump, 1: 17-cv-02590-TSC, "Order Denying Transfer Motion," Document 48 (D.D.C. 09/24/18). The judge subsequently rejected the US's motion to dismiss on

account of the plaintiffs' alleged lack of legal standing. 1:17-cv-02590-TSSC, Document 141 (D.D.C. 09/30/19). The tribes amended their complaint to encompass the harms from commenced mining operations and oil and gas exploration.

20. Mark Squillace, "The Monumental Legacy of the Antiquities Act of 1906," *Georgia Law Review* 37 (2003): 473.

21. Mountain States Legal Foundation v. Bush, 306 F. 3d 1132 (D.C. Cir. 2002); Tulare County v. Bush, 306 F 3d 1138 (D.C. Cir. 2002).

22. John Murdock, "Monumental Power: Can Past Proclamations under the Antiquities Act Be Trumped," *Texas Review of Law and Policy* 22 (2018): 357.

23. Obama Proclamation 9558, 58081.

24. Krakoff, "Public Lands, Conservation, and the Possibility of Justice," 220.

25. Harjo, Interview Tape 2.

BIBLIOGRAPHY

Anaya, S. James. *Indigenous Peoples in International Law*. 2nd ed. New York: Oxford University Press, 2004.

Asad, Talal. *Formations of the Secular: Christianity, Islam, Modernity*. Stanford, CA: Stanford University Press, 2003.

———. *Genealogies of Religion: Discipline and Reasons of Power in Christianity and Islam*. Baltimore: Johns Hopkins University Press, 1993.

Basso, Keith. *Wisdom Sits in Places*. Albuquerque: University of New Mexico Press, 1996.

Beaver, R. Pierce. *Church, State, and the American Indians*. Saint Louis, MO: Concordia, 1966.

Bell, Catherine, and Robert K. Paterson, eds. *Protection of First Nations Cultural Heritage: Laws, Policy, and Reform*. Vancouver: University of British Columbia Press, 2009.

Bender, Courtney, and Pamela Klassen, *After Pluralism: Reimagining Religious Engagement*. New York: Columbia University Press, 2010.

Beran, Stephanie. "Native Americans in Prison: The Struggle for Religious Freedom." *Nebraska Anthropologist* 2 (2005): 46–55.

Berger, Benjamin. *Law's Religion: Religious Difference and the Claims of Constitutionalism*. Toronto: University of Toronto Press, 2015.

Berkhofer, Robert. *The White Man's Indian: Images of the American Indian from Columbus to the Present*. New York: Vintage Books, 1978.

Borrows, John, *Canada's Indigenous Constitution*. Toronto: University of Toronto Press, 2010.

———. *Drawing Out Law: A Spirit's Guide*. Toronto: University of Toronto Press, 2010.

———. *Freedom and Indigenous Constitutionalism*. Toronto: University of Toronto Press, 2016.

Bowechop (Ledford), Janine. "Contemporary Makah Whaling." In *Coming to Shore: Northwest Coast Ethnology, Traditions, and Visions*, edited by Marie Mauzé, Michael Eugene Harkin, and Sergei Kan, 407–19. Lincoln: University of Nebraska Press, 2004.

Brault, Emily. "Sweating in the Joint: Personal and Cultural Renewal and Healing through Sweat Lodge Practice by Native Americans in Prison." PhD diss., Vanderbilt University, 2005.

Brown, Michael F. *Who Owns Native Culture?* Cambridge, MA: Harvard University Press, 2003.

Burton, Lloyd. *Worship and Wilderness: Culture, Religion, and Law in Public Lands Management*. Madison: University of Wisconsin Press, 2002.

Cairns, Alan C. *Citizens Plus: Aboriginal Peoples and the Canadian State*. Vancouver: University of British Columbia Press, 2001.

Carmean, Kelli. *Spider Woman Walks This Land: TCPs and the Navajo Nation*. Walnut Creek, CA: AltaMira Press, 2002.

Carpenter, Kristen. "Limiting Principles and Empowering Practices in American Indian Religious Freedoms." *Connecticut Law Review* 45, no. 2 (2012): 387.

———. "Real Property and Peoplehood." *Stanford Environmental Law Journal* 27 (2008): 313–40.

Carpenter Kristen, and Angela Riley. "Indigenous Peoples and the Jurisgenerative Moment in Human Rights." *California Law Review* 102 (2014): 173.

———. "Owning Red: A Theory of Indian (Cultural) Appropriation." *Texas Law Review* 94, no. 5 (2016): 859.

Carpenter, Kristen, Sonia Katyal, and Angela Riley. "In Defense of Property." *Yale Law Journal* 118, no. 6 (2009): 1022.

Carter, Stephen L. *The Culture of Disbelief: How American Law and Politics Trivialize Religious Devotion*. New York: Penguin, 1994.

Champagne, Duane. "UNDRIP: Human, Civil, and Indigenous Rights." *Wicazo Sa Review* 28 (Spring 2013): 9–22.

Chari, Sangita, and Jaime M. N. Lavallee, eds. *Accomplishing NAGPRA: Perspectives on the Intent, Impact, and Future of the Native American Graves Protection and Repatriation Act*. Corvallis: Oregon State University Press, 2013.

Charters, C., and R. Stavenhagen, eds. *Making the Declaration Work: The United Nations Declaration on the Rights of Indigenous Peoples*. Copenhagen: International Working Group for Indigenous Affairs, 2009.

Chidester, David. *Empire of Religion: Imperialism and Comparative Religion*. Chicago: University of Chicago Press, 2014.

———. *Savage Systems: Colonialism and Comparative Religion in Southern Africa*. Charlottesville: University of Virginia Press, 1996.

Clifford, James. *Returns: Becoming Indigenous in the Twenty-First Century*. Cambridge, MA: Harvard University Press, 2013.

Clinton, Robert N. "Redressing the Legacy of Conquest: A Vision Quest for a Decolonized Federal Indian Law." *Arkansas Law Review* 46 (1993): 77.

Cohen's Handbook of Federal Indian Law, 2005 Edition. Edited by Nell Jessup Newton et al. Albuquerque, NM: American Indian Law Center and LexisNexis, 2005.

Colwell, Chip. *Plundered Skulls and Stolen Spirits: Inside the Fight to Reclaim Native America's Culture*. Chicago: University of Chicago Press, 2017.

Coombe, Rosemary. *The Cultural Life of Intellectual Properties: Authorship, Appropriation, and the Law*. Durham, NC: Duke University Press, 1998.

Coté, Charlotte. *Spirits of Our Whaling Ancestors: Revitalizing Makah and Nuu-chah-nulth Traditions*. Seattle: University of Washington Press, 2010.

Curtis, Finbarr. *The Production of American Religious Freedom*. New York: New York University Press, 2016.

Decosimo, David. "The New Genealogy of Religious Freedom." *Journal of Law and Religion* 33, no. 1 (April 2018): 3–41.

DeGirolami, Marc O. *The Tragedy of Religious Freedom*. Cambridge, MA: Harvard University Press, 2013.

Deloria, Philip. *Playing Indian*. New Haven, CT: Yale University Press, 1998.

Deloria, Vine, Jr. *God Is Red: A Native View of Religion*. Lincoln: University of Nebraska Press, 2007.

———. "Secularism, Civil Religion, and the Religious Freedom of American Indians." In *Repatriation Reader*, edited by Devon Mihesuah, 169–79. Lincoln: University of Nebraska Press, 2000.

———. "Trouble in High Places: Erosion of American Indian Rights to Religious Freedom in the United States." In *The State of Native America*, edited by M. Annette Jaimes, 267–90. Boston: South End Press, 1992.

Deloria, Vine, Jr., and Clifford Lytle. *American Indians, American Justice*. Austin: University of Texas Press, 1983.

Dussias, Allison. "Ghost Dance and Holy Ghost: The Echoes of Nineteenth-Century Christianization Policy in Twentieth-Century Native American Free Exercise Cases." *Stanford Law Review* 49, no. 4 (1997): 773.

Echo-Hawk, Walter R. *In the Courts of the Conqueror: The 10 Worst Indian Law Cases Ever Decided*. Golden, CO: Fulcrum, 2010.

———. *In the Light of Justice: The Rise of Human Rights in Native America and the U.N. Declaration on the Rights of Indigenous Peoples*. Golden, CO: Fulcrum, 2013.

Echo-Hawk, Walter R., Lenny Foster, Alan Parker, and Wallace Coffey. "Issues in the Implementation of the American Indian Religious Freedom Act: Panel Discussion. *Wicazo Sa Review* 19 (Fall 2004): 153–67.

Epps, Garrett. *Peyote vs. the State: Religious Freedom on Trial*. Norman: University of Oklahoma Press, 2009.

———. *To an Unknown God: Religious Freedom on Trial*. New York: St. Martin's Press, 2001.

Estes, Nick. *Our History Is the Future: Standing Rock versus the Dakota Access Pipeline, and the Long Tradition of Indigenous Resistance*. New York: Verso, 2019.

Estes, Nick, and Jaskiran Dhillon, eds. *Standing with Standing Rock: Voices from the #NoDAPL Movement*. Minneapolis: University of Minnesota Press, 2019.

Fine-Dare, Kathleen. *Grave Injustice: The American Indian Repatriation Movement and NAGPRA*. Lincoln: University of Nebraska Press, 2002.

Fisher, Louis. "Indian Religious Freedom: To Litigate or Legislate?" *American Indian Law Review* 26, no. 1 (2001/2002): 1–39.

Galloway, Colin. *Pen and Ink Witchcraft: Treaties and Treaty Making in American Indian History*. New York: Oxford University Press, 2013.

Garroutte, Eva Marie. *Real Indians: Identity and Survival of Native America*. Berkeley: University of California Press, 2003.

Getches, David, Charles F. Wilkinson, and Robert A. Williams Jr. *Cases and Materials on Federal Indian Law*. 5th ed. Saint Paul, MN: Thomson West, 2005.

Goodrich, Luke, and Rachel Busick. "Sex, Drugs, and Eagle Feathers: An Empirical Study of Federal Religious Freedom Cases." *Seton Hall Law Review* 48 (2018): 353.

Gordon, Sarah Berringer. *The Mormon Question: Polygamy and Constitutional Conflict in Nineteenth-Century America*. Chapel Hill: University of North Carolina Press, 2002.

———. *The Spirit of the Law: Religious Voices and the Constitution in Modern America*. Cambridge, MA: Harvard University Press, 2010.

Gover, Kevin and Patsy Phillips, eds. *A Promise Kept: The Inspiring Life and Works of Suzan Shown Harjo*. Washington, DC: Smithsonian, 2020.

Graber Jennifer. *The Gods of Indian Country*. New York: Oxford University Press, 2018.

Greenawalt, Kenneth. "Religion as a Concept in Constitutional Law." *California Law Review* 72 (1984): 753.

Gulliford, Andrew. *Sacred Objects and Sacred Places: Preserving Tribal Traditions*. Boulder: University Press of Colorado, 2000.

Hale, Tiffany. "Fugitive Religion: The Ghost Dance and the Racial State." PhD diss., Yale University, 2018.

Hamburger, Philip. *The Separation of Church and State*. Cambridge, MA: Harvard University Press, 2002.

Harjo, Suzan Shown. Interviews with author, 2009. National Museum of the American Indian.

———. "It Began with a Vision in a Sacred Place." In *Past, Present, and Future: Challenges of the National Museum of the American Indian*, edited by NMAI, 25–52. Washington, DC: Smithsonian Institution, 2011.

Harjo, Suzan Shown, ed. *Nation to Nation: Treaties between the United States and American Indian Nations*. Washington, DC: Smithsonian Institution, 2014.

Harjo, Suzan, Kevin Gover, and Dean Suagee. Remarks in "Indian Religious Freedom: To Litigate or Legislate." Library of Congress, November 28, 2007. www.loc.gov/today/cyberlc/feature_wdesc.php?rec=4245, last accessed October 2017.

Harring, Sidney L. *Crow Dog's Case: American Indian Sovereignty, Tribal Law, and United States Law in the Nineteenth Century*. New York: Cambridge University Press, 1994.

Hoxie, Frederick E. *A Final Promise: The Campaign to Assimilate the Indians, 1880–1920*. Lincoln: University of Nebraska Press, 1984.

Hurd, Elizabeth Shakman. *Beyond Religious Freedom: The New Global Politics of Religion*. Princeton, NJ: Princeton University Press, 2015.

Irwin, Lee, ed. *Native American Spirituality: A Critical Reader*. Lincoln: University of Nebraska Press, 2000.

Johnson, Greg. "Apache Revelation: Making Religion in the Legal Sphere." In *Secularism and Religion-Making*, edited by Markus Dressler and Arvind-Pal S. Mandair, 170–86. Oxford: Oxford University Press, 2011.

———. "Courting Culture: Unexpected Relationships between Religion and Law in Contemporary Hawai'i." In *After Secular Law*, edited by Winnifred Sullivan, Mateo Taussig, and Robert Yelle, 282–301. Palo Alto, CA: Stanford University Press, 2011.

———. "Incarcerated Tradition: Native Hawaiian Identities and Religious Practice In Prison Contexts." In *Historicizing Tradition in the Study of Religion*, edited by Steven Engler and Gregory Grieve, 195–210. Berlin: Walter de Gruyter, 2009.

———. *Religion in the Moment: Tradition, Performance, and Law in Contemporary Hawai'i*. Chapel Hill: University of North Carolina Press, forthcoming.

———. *Sacred Claims: Repatriation and Living Tradition*. Charlottesville: University of Virginia Press, 2007.

———. "Social Lives of the Dead: Contestations and Continuities in Native Hawaiian Repatriation Contexts." In *Culture and Belonging: Symbolic Landscapes and Contesting Identity in*

Divided Societies, edited by Marc Ross, 41–61. Philadelphia: University of Pennsylvania Press 2009.

Johnson, Greg, and Siv Ellen Kraft, *Handbook of Indigenous Religion(s)*. Leiden: Brill, 2017.

———. "Standing Rock Religion(s): Ceremonies, Social Media, and Music Videos." *Numen* 65 (2018): 1–32.

Johnson, Paul Christopher, Pamela Klassen, and Winnifred Fallers Sullivan. *Ekklesia: Three Inquiries in Church and State*. Chicago: University of Chicago Press, 2018.

Keller, Robert. *American Protestants and Grant's Indian Peace Policy*. Lincoln: University of Nebraska Press, 1983.

Kelly, Klara, and Harris Francis. *Navajo Sacred Places*. Bloomington: Indiana University Press, 1994.

Kelly, Lawrence. *Assault on Assimilation: John Collier and the Origins of Indian Policy Reform*. Albuquerque: University of New Mexico Press, 1983.

King, Thomas F. *Cultural Resource Laws and Practice*. 3rd ed. Walnut Creek, CA: AltaMira Press, 2008.

———. *Our Unprotected Heritage: Whitewashing the Destruction of Our Cultural and Natural Environment*. Walnut Creek, CA: Left Coast Press, 2009.

———. *Places That Count: Traditional Cultural Properties in Cultural Resource Management*. Lanham, MD: AltaMira Press, 2003.

King, Thomas F., ed. *A Companion to Cultural Resource Management*. Chichester, West Sussex: Wiley-Blackwell, 2011.

King, Thomas F., and Claudia Nissley. *Consultation and Cultural Heritage: Let Us Reason Together*. Walnut Creek, CA: Left Coast Press, 2014.

Kymlicka, Will. *Liberalism, Community, and Culture*. New York: Oxford University Press, 1989.

———. *Multicultural Citizenship: A Liberal Theory of Minority Rights*. New York: Oxford University Press, 1995.

Lawson, Michael L. *Dammed Indians Revisited: The Continuing History of the Pick-Sloan Plan and the Missouri River Sioux*. Pierre: South Dakota Historical Society Press, 2009.

Llewellyn, Karl. *The Cheyenne Way: Conflict and Case Law in Primitive Jurisprudence*. Norman: University of Oklahoma Press, 1941.

Lloyd, Dana. "Between God and Land: On Sovereignty, Indigeneity, and Religious Freedom." PhD diss., Syracuse University 2018.

Long, Carolyn. *Religious Freedom and Indian Rights: The Case of* Oregon v. Smith. Lawrence: University Press of Kansas, 2001.

Makley, Matthew, and Michael Makley. *Cave Rock: Climbers, Courts, and a Washoe Indian Sacred Place*. Reno: University of Nevada Press, 2010.

Marincic, Amanda M. "The National Historic Preservation Act: An Inadequate Attempt to Protect the Cultural and Religious Sites of Native Nations." *Iowa Law Review* 103 (2018): 1777.

Maroukis, Thomas. *The Peyote Road: Religious Freedom and the Native American Church*. Norman: University of Oklahoma Press, 2012.

Martin, Joel. *The Land Looks After Us: A History of Native American Religion*. New York: Oxford University Press, 2001.

McKeown, C. Timothy. *In the Smaller Scope of Conscience: The Struggle for National Repatriation Legislation, 1986–1990.* Tucson: University of Arizona Press, 2013.

McNally, Michael D. "From Substantial Burden on Religion to Diminished Spiritual Fulfillment: The San Francisco Peaks Case and the Misunderstanding of Native American Religion." *Journal of Law and Religion* 30, no. 1 (2015): 36–64.

———. *Honoring Elders: Aging, Authority, and Ojibwe Religion.* New York: Columbia University Press, 2009.

———. "Native American Religious Freedom as a Collective Right." *BYU Law Review* 2019 (Fall 2019): 205.

———. "Native American Religious Freedom beyond the First Amendment." In *After Pluralism*, edited by Courtney Bender and Pamela Klassen. New York: Columbia University Press, 2009.

———. "No One Word for Religion: The Struggle for Native Religious and Cultural Rights." In *A Promise Kept*, edited by Kevin Gover and Patsy Phillips. Washington, DC: Smithsonian, 2020.

———. *Ojibwe Singers: Hymns, Grief, and a Native Culture in Motion.* New York: Oxford University Press, 2000.

———. "Religious Belief and Practice." In *Companion to Cultural Resource Management*, edited by Thomas F. King. New York: Wiley-Blackwell, 2011.

———. "Religion as Peoplehood: Native American Religious Freedom and the Discourse of Indigenous Rights in International Law." In *Brill Handbook of Indigenous Religions*, edited by Greg Johnson and Siv Ellen Kraft. Leiden: Brill, 2017.

Michaelson, Robert. "Is the Miner's Canary Silent." *Journal of Law and Religion* 6 (1988): 97.

Mihesuah, Devon, ed. *Repatriation Reader: Who Owns American Indian Remains?* Lincoln: University of Nebraska Press, 2000.

Miller, Robert J., et al. *Discovering Indigenous Lands: The Doctrine of Discovery in the English Colonies.* New York: Oxford University Press, 2012.

Morman, Todd. *Many Nations under Many Gods: Public Land Management and American Indian Sacred Sites.* Norman: University of Oklahoma Press, 2018.

Nabokov, Peter. *Where the Lightning Strikes: The Lives of American Indian Sacred Places.* New York: Penguin, 2007.

Nesper, Larry. "Law and Ojibwe Indian Traditional Cultural Property in the Organized Resistance to the Crandon Mine in Wisconsin." *Law and Social Inquiry* 36 (Winter 2011): 151–69.

———. *The Walleye War: The Struggle for Ojibwe Spearfishing and Treaty Rights.* Lincoln: University of Nebraska Press, 2002.

Newcomb, Steve. *Pagans in the Promised Land: Decoding the Doctrine of Christian Discovery.* Golden, CO: Fulcrum, 2009.

Newman, Dwight, ed. *Religious Freedom and Communities.* Toronto: LexisNexis Canada, 2016.

Niezen, Ronald. *The Origins of Indigenism: Human Rights and the Politics of Identity.* Berkeley: University of California Press, 2003.

———. *The Rediscovered Self: Indigenous Identity and Cultural Justice.* Montreal: McGill University Press, 2009.

Noonan, John T., Jr. *Persons and Masks of the Law.* New York: Farrar, Straus, and Giroux, 1976.

Owen, Suzanne. *The Appropriation of Native American Spirituality*. London: Bloomsbury, 2008.

Parker, Alan R. *Pathways to Indigenous Nation Sovereignty: A Chronicle of Federal Policy Developments*. East Lansing: Michigan State University Press, 2018.

Pommersheim, Frank. *Broken Landscape: Indians, Indian Tribes, and the Constitution*. New York: Oxford University Press, 2009.

Prucha, Francis Paul. *American Indian Policy in Crisis: Christian Reformers and the Indians, 1865–1900*. Norman: University of Oklahoma Press, 1976.

———. *The Great Father: The United States Government and the American Indian*. 2 vols. Lincoln: University of Nebraska Press, 1984.

Richland, Justin B. *Arguing with Tradition: The Language of Law in Hopi Tribal Court*. Chicago: University of Chicago Press, 2008.

———. "Jurisdictions of Significance: Narrating Time-Space in a Hopi-US Tribal Consultation. *American Ethnologist* 45 (May 2018): 1–29.

———. "Paths in the Wilderness?: The Politics and Practices of Hopi Religious Freedom in Hopitutskwa." *Maryland Journal of International Law* 31, no. 1 (2017): 217.

Richland, Justin B., Maria Glowacka, and Dorothy Washburn. "Nuvantukya'ovi, San Francisco Peaks: Balancing Western Economies with Native American Spiritualities." *Current Anthropology* 50 (2009): 547–61.

Richman, Jennifer, and Marion Forsyth, eds. *Legal Perspectives on Cultural Resources*. Walnut Creek, CA: AltaMira Press, 2004.

Riding In, James. "Repatriation: A Pawnee's Perspective." *American Indian Quarterly* 20 (Spring 1996): 238–50.

Ridington, Robin, and Dennis Hastings. *Blessing for a Long Time: The Sacred Pole of the Omaha Tribe*. Lincoln: University of Nebraska Press, 1997.

Ross, Michael Lee. *First Nations Sacred Sites in Canada's Courts*. Vancouver: University of British Columbia Press, 2005.

Sehat, David. *The Myth of American Religious Freedom*. New York: Oxford University Press, 2010.

Shrubsole, Nicholas. *What Has No Place Remains: The Challenges for Indigenous Religious Freedom in Canada Today*. Toronto: University of Toronto Press, 2019.

Skibine, Alex Tallchief. "Towards a Balanced Approach for the Protection of Native American Sacred Sites." *Michigan Journal of Race and Law* 17 (2012): 269.

Smith, Huston (in conversation with Native Americans on Religious Freedom). *A Seat at the Table*, edited by Phil Cousineau. Berkeley: University of California Press, 2004.

Smith, Huston, and Reuben Snake, eds. *One Nation under God: The Triumph of the Native American Church*. Santa Fe, NM: Clear Light, 1996.

Smith, Jonathan Z. *Imagining Religion from Babylon to Jonestown*. Chicago: University of Chicago Press, 1988.

Stoffle, Richard W., and Michael J Evans. "Holistic Conservation and Cultural Triage: American Indian Perspectives on Cultural Resources." *Human Organization* 49 (1990): 95.

Su, Anna. *Exporting Freedom: Religious Liberty and American Power*. Cambridge, MA: Harvard University Press, 2016.

Sullivan, Robert. *A Whale Hunt*. New York: Simon and Schuster, 2000.

Sullivan, Winnifred Fallers. *The Impossibility of Religious Freedom*. Princeton, NJ: Princeton University Press, 2007.

———. *A Ministry of Presence: Chaplaincy, Spiritual Care, and the Law*. Chicago: University of Chicago Press, 2014.

———. *Paying the Words Extra: Religious Discourse in the Supreme Court of the United States*. Cambridge, MA: Harvard University Press, 1995.

———. *Prison Religion: Faith-Based Reform and the Constitution*. Princeton, NJ: Princeton: University Press 2009.

Sullivan, Winnifred, Elizabeth Shakman Hurd, Saba Mahmood, and Peter Danchin, eds. *The Politics of Religious Freedom*. Chicago: University of Chicago Press, 2015.

Sullivan, Winnifred, Mateo Taussig, and Robert Yelle, eds. *After Secular Law*. Stanford, CA: Stanford University Press, 2011.

Talamantez, Inés. "The Presence of Isanaklesh: The Apache Female Deity and the Path of Pollen." In *Unspoken Worlds: Women's Religious Lives*, edited by Nancy Auer Falk and Rita Gross. Belmont, CA: Wadsworth Press, 2000.

Thomas, David Hurst. *Skull Wars: Kennewick Man, Archeology, and the Battle for Native American Identity*. New York: Basic Books, 2000.

Tsosie, Rebecca. "Introduction: Symposium on Cultural Sovereignty." *Arizona State Law Journal* 34 (2002): 1.

———. "Land, Culture, and Community: Reflections on Native Sovereignty and Property in America." *Indiana Law Review* 34, no. 4 (2001).

Tsosie, Rebecca, and Wallace Coffey. "Rethinking the Tribal Sovereignty Doctrine: Cultural Sovereignty and the Collective Future of Indian Nations." *Stanford Law and Policy Review* 12 (2001): 191–222.

Tully, James. *Strange Multiplicity: Constitutionalism in an Age of Diversity*. Cambridge: Cambridge University Press, 1995.

Tweedie, Ann. *Drawing Back Culture: The Makah Struggle for Repatriation*. Seattle: University of Washington Press, 2002.

Vecsey, Christopher, ed. *Handbook of American Indian Religious Freedom*. New York: Crossroad, 1991.

Weaver, Jace. *Other Words: American Indian Literature, Law, and Culture*. Norman: University of Oklahoma Press, 2001.

Wenger, Tisa. *Religious Freedom: The Contested History of an American Ideal*. Chapel Hill: University of North Carolina Press, 2017.

———. *We Have a Religion: The 1920s Pueblo Indian Dance Controversy and American Religious Freedom*. Chapel Hill: University of North Carolina Press, 2009.

Wilkins, David E. *American Indian Sovereignty and the U.S. Supreme Court: The Masking of Justice*. Austin: University of Texas Press, 1997.

Wilkins, David E., and K. Tsianina Lomawaima. *Uneven Ground: American Indian Sovereignty and Federal Law*. Norman: University of Oklahoma Press, 2001.

Wilkinson, Charles F. *American Indians, Time, and the Law*. New Haven, CT: Yale University Press, 1987.

———. "To Feel the Summer in the Spring: The Treaty Fishing Rights of the Wisconsin Chippewa." *Wisconsin Law Review*, no. 3 (1991): 375–414.

Wilkinson, Charles F., and Hank Adams. *Messages from Frank's Landing*. Seattle: University of Washington Press, 2000.

Williams, Robert A., Jr. *The American Indian in Western Legal Thought: The Discourses of Conquest*. New York: Oxford University Press, 1990.

———. *Like a Loaded Weapon: The Rehnquist Court, Indian Rights, and the Legal History of Racism in America*. Minneapolis: University of Minnesota Press, 2005.

Wunder, John R. *"Retained by the People": A History of American Indians and the Bill of Rights*. New York: Oxford University Press, 1994.

Wunder, John R., ed. *Native American Cultural and Religious Freedoms*. New York: Garland, 1999.

Yablon, Marcia. "Note: Property Rights and Sacred Sites; Federal Regulatory Responses to American Indian Religious Claims on Public Land." *Yale Law Journal* 113 (2004): 1623.

Yelle, Robert. *Sovereignty and the Sacred: Secularism and the Political Economy of the Sacred*. Chicago: University of Chicago Press, 2018.

INDEX

Page numbers in *italics* refer to illustrations.

whales, whaling, 8; Boldt Decision and, 236–37, 256; commercial vs. ceremonial and subsistence, 224–25, 243, 246, 255–56; cultural and spiritual functions of, 29, 224, 226, 228, 241–42, 254; by the Makah, 224–28, 241–46, 257; regulation of, 225, 243–44, 245–46; treaty rights to, 19, 31, 223, 226–27, 231, 242–43, 255, 258

Where the Lightning Strikes (Nabokov), 176–77

White, Bruce, 248

White Earth Ojibwe, 39

White Mountain Apache, 96, 100, 114, 119, 120

Wicca, 78, 107

Wiessner, Siegfried, 261

wild rice, 9; environmental review and, 129, 145; off-reservation gathering of, 231, 248, 252; religious and cultural significance of, 6, 19, 247, 254

Wilkins, David, 27, 47

Wilkinson, Charles, 236, 247–48, 300, 301

Willerslev, Eske, 209

Williams, Robert, Jr., 22, 229, 262, 264

Willow, Anna, 150

Wilson, Gregory, 91

Wilson v. Block (1983), 101, 118

Winnebago (Ho-Chunk), 56

Wisconsin, 31, 150, 246–49, 251, 257

Wisconsin v. Yoder (1972), 80–81, 82, 101–2, 117

wolves, 129, 145

Woodburn, J. M., 44

Worcester, Samuel, 232

Worcester v. Georgia (1832), 24–25, 232–33, 236, 258, 263

Work, Herbert, 61

World Conference on Indigenous Peoples (2014), 279

World Council on Indigenous Peoples, 263

Wounded Knee Massacre (1890), 48, 51–53

Wovoka, 51

Wuthnow, Robert, 105–6, 107

Yakama, 141, 175, 180, 235, 237, 238

Yankton Reservation, 55, 56, 255

Yavapai Apache, 96, 120

Yellowbear, Andrew, 90–91, 92

Yellowbear v. Lampert (2014), 90–91, 92, 122

Yellow Smoke, 206

Yellowstone National Park, 145, 300

Yurok, 11, 102

Zinke, Ryan, 302

zoning, 86

Zuni Pueblo, 167, 175, 201, 298, 303, 304